WILLIAM BLAKE

After the painting by Thomas Phillips, R.A.

THE POETICAL WORKS OF
WILLIAM BLAKE

Including the unpublished
FRENCH REVOLUTION
together with the
MINOR PROPHETIC BOOKS
and Selections from
THE FOUR ZOAS, MILTON
AND JERUSALEM

EDITED WITH AN
INTRODUCTION AND
TEXTUAL NOTES BY
JOHN SAMPSON
HON. D.LITT. OXON.

Geoffrey Cumberlege
OXFORD UNIVERSITY PRESS
London   New York   Toronto

WILLIAM BLAKE

Born, 28 Broad Street, Golden Square, London . .
. . 28 November 1757
Died, 3 Fountain Court, Strand . . 12 August 1827

This edition of the Poetical Works of William Blake was first published in 1913, and reprinted in 1914, 1925, 1928, 1934, 1938, 1941, 1943, 1948, 1949 and 1952.

PRINTED IN GREAT BRITAIN

O.S.A.

TABLE OF CONTENTS

	PAGE
BIBLIOGRAPHICAL INTRODUCTION	xv
CHRONOLOGICAL TABLE	liii

POETICAL SKETCHES

To Spring	3
To Summer	3
To Autumn	4
To Winter	5
To the Evening Star	5
To Morning	6
Fair Elenor	6
Song: How sweet I roam'd from field to field	8
Song: My silks and fine array	9
Song: Love and harmony combine	10
Song: I love the jocund dance	10
Song: Memory, hither come	11
Mad Song	12
Song: Fresh from the dewy hill, the merry year	13
Song: When early morn walks forth in sober grey	13
To the Muses	14
Gwin, King of Norway	15
An Imitation of Spenser	18
Blind Man's Buff	20
King Edward the Third	23
Prologue, intended for a Dramatic Piece of King Edward the Fourth	42
Prologue to King John	43
A War Song to Englishmen	44
The Couch of Death	45
Contemplation	46
Samson	47

Appendix

Song by a Shepherd	52
Song by an Old Shepherd	52

Table of Contents

                                                                                     PAGE

SONGS FROM AN ISLAND IN THE MOON

Little Phoebus came strutting in	55
Honour and Genius is all I ask	55
When Old Corruption first begun	56
Hear then the pride and knowledge of a sailor!	57
The Song of Phoebe and Jellicoe	57
Lo! the Bat with leathern wing	58
Want Matches?	58
As I walk'd forth one May morning	59
Hail Matrimony, made of Love!	59
To be or not to be	60
This city and this country has brought forth many mayors	61
O, I say, you Joe	62
Leave, O leave me to my sorrows	62
There's Doctor Clash	63

SONGS OF INNOCENCE AND OF EXPERIENCE

SONGS OF INNOCENCE

Introduction	65
The Echoing Green	66
The Lamb	67
The Shepherd	67
Infant Joy	68
The Little Black Boy	68
Laughing Song	69
Spring	70
A Cradle Song	71
Nurse's Song	72
Holy Thursday	72
The Blossom	73
The Chimney Sweeper	74
The Divine Image	75
Night	75
A Dream	77
On Another's Sorrow	78
The Little Boy Lost	79
The Little Boy Found	79

SONGS OF EXPERIENCE

Introduction	81
Earth's Answer	82
Nurse's Song	83
The Fly	84
The Tiger	85

Table of Contents

	PAGE
The Little Girl Lost	88
The Little Girl Found	90
The Clod and the Pebble	92
The Little Vagabond	92
Holy Thursday	93
A Poison Tree	94
The Angel	94
The Sick Rose	95
To Tirzah	95
The Voice of the Ancient Bard	96
My Pretty Rose-Tree	97
Ah! Sun-Flower	97
The Lily	98
The Garden of Love	98
A Little Boy Lost	99
Infant Sorrow	100
The Schoolboy	100
London	102
A Little Girl Lost	103
The Chimney-sweeper	104
The Human Abstract	105

Appendix

A Divine Image	106

POEMS FROM 'THE ROSSETTI MANUSCRIPT'

I. EARLIER POEMS

Never seek to tell thy Love	109
I laid me down upon a Bank	110
I saw a Chapel all of Gold	110
I askèd a Thief	111
I heard an Angel singing	111
A Cradle Song	113
Silent, silent Night	114
I fear'd the fury of my wind	114
Infant Sorrow	115
Why should I care for the men of Thames	117
Thou hast a lap full of seed	118
In a Myrtle Shade	118
To my Myrtle	119
To Nobodaddy	120
Are not the joys of morning sweeter	120

Table of Contents

	PAGE
The Wild Flower's Song	121
Day	121
The Fairy	122
Motto to the Songs of Innocence and of Experience	123
Lafayette	123

Appendix to I
    A Fairy leapt upon my knee 127

II. LATER POEMS
My Spectre around me night and day	128
When Klopstock England defied	132
Mock on, mock on, Voltaire, Rousseau	133
I saw a Monk of Charlemaine	134
Morning	137
The Birds	138
You don't believe — I won't attempt to make ye	138
If it is true what the Prophets write	139
I will tell you what Joseph of Arimathea	139
Why was Cupid a boy	140
Now Art has lost its mental charms	141
I rose up at the dawn of day	142
The Caverns of the Grave I've seen	144

Addendum to II
    To the Queen 145

III. THE EVERLASTING GOSPEL 146

THE PICKERING MANUSCRIPT
The Smile	161
The Golden Net	161
The Mental Traveller	162
The Land of Dreams	166
Mary	166
The Crystal Cabinet	168
The Grey Monk	169
Auguries of Innocence	171
Long John Brown and Little Mary Bell	178
William Bond	179

POEMS FROM LETTERS
| To my Dearest Friend, John Flaxman, these lines | 183 |
| To my dear Friend, Mrs. Anna Flaxman | 184 |

Table of Contents

	PAGE
To Thomas Butts : To my friend Butts I write	184
To Mrs. Butts	187
To Thomas Butts : With Happiness stretch'd across the hills	187
To Thomas Butts : O! why was I born with a different face?	190

GNOMIC VERSES, EPIGRAMS, AND SHORT SATIRICAL PIECES

GNOMIC VERSES

Great things are done when men and mountains meet	193
To God	193
They said this mystery never shall cease	193
An Answer to the Parson	193
Lacedaemonian Instruction	193
Nail his neck to the cross : nail it with a nail	193
Love to faults is always blind	194
There souls of men are bought and sold	194
Soft Snow	195
Abstinence sows sand all over	195
Merlin's Prophecy	195
If you trap the moment before it's ripe	195
An Old Maid early ere I knew	195
The sword sung on the barren heath	196
O lapwing! thou fliest around the heath	196
Terror in the house does roar	196
Several Questions Answered	196
Eternity	196
The look of love alarms	196
Soft deceit and idleness	197
What is it men in women do require	197
An ancient Proverb	197
If I e'er grow to man's estate	197
Since all the riches of this world	197
Riches	198
The Angel that presided o'er my birth	198
Grown old in love from seven till seven times seven	198
Do what you will this life's a fiction	198

ON ART AND ARTISTS

Advice of the Popes who succeeded the Age of Raphael	198
On the great encouragement given by English nobility and gentry to Correggio, Rubens, Reynolds, Gainsborough, Catalani, Du Crow, and Dilbury Doodle	199
I askèd my dear friend Orator Prig	199

Table of Contents

	PAGE
O dear Mother Outline! of wisdom most sage	200
On the Foundation of the Royal Academy	200
These are the idiots' chiefest arts	200
The cripple every step drudges and labours	201
You say their pictures well painted be	201
When you look at a picture, you always can see	201
The Washerwoman's Song	202
English Encouragement of Art: Cromek's opinions put into rhyme	202
When I see a Rubens, Rembrandt, Correggio	202
Give pensions to the learned pig	203
On Sir Joshua Reynolds' disappointment at his first impressions of Raphael	203
Sir Joshua praisèd Rubens with a smile	203
Sir Joshua praises Michael Angelo	203
Can there be anything more mean	204
To the Royal Academy	204
Florentine Ingratitude	204
No real style of colouring ever appears	205
When Sir Joshua Reynolds died	205
A Pitiful Case	206
On Sir Joshua Reynolds	206
I, Rubens, am a statesman and a saint	206
On the school of Rubens	206
To English Connoisseurs	206
A Pretty Epigram for the encouragement of those who have paid great sums in the Venetian and Flemish ooze	207
Raphael, sublime, majestic, graceful, wise	207
On the Venetian Painter	207
A pair of stays to mend the shape	207
Venetian! all thy colouring is no more	208
To Venetian Artists	208
All pictures that's painted with sense and with thought	208
Call that the public voice which is their error!	209

On Friends and Foes

I am no Homer's hero you all know	209
Anger and wrath my bosom rends	209
If you play a game of chance, know, before you begin	209
Of Hayley's birth: Of H—— 's birth this was the happy lot	210
On Hayley: To forgive enemies H—— does pretend	210
To Hayley: Thy friendship oft has made my heart to ache	210

Table of Contents

	PAGE
On Hayley's Friendship : When H——y finds out what you cannot do	210
On Hayley the Pickthank : I write the rascal thanks, till he and I	210
My title as a genius thus is prov'd	211
To Flaxman : You call me mad, 'tis folly to do so	211
To Flaxman : I mock thee not, though I by thee am mockèd	211
To Nancy Flaxman : How can I help thy husband's copying me?	211
To Flaxman and Stothard : I found them blind : I taught them how to see	211
To Stothard : You all your youth observ'd the golden rule	212
Cromek speaks : I always take my judgement from a fool	212
On Stothard : You say reserve and modesty he has	212
On Stothard : S——, in childhood, on the nursery floor	212
Mr. Stothard to Mr. Cromek : For Fortune's favours you your riches bring	213
Mr. Cromek to Mr. Stothard : Fortune favours the brave, old proverbs say	213
On Cromek : Cr—— loves artists as he loves his meat	213
On Cromek : A petty sneaking knave I knew	213
On P —— : P—— lovèd me not as he lov'd his friends	213
On William Haines : The Sussex men are noted fools	214
On Fuseli : The only man that e'er I knew	214
To Hunt : 'Madman' I have been call'd	214
To Hunt : You think Fuseli is not a great painter	214
On certain Mystics : Cosway, Frazer, and Baldwin of Egypt's lake	214
And his legs carried it like a long fork	215
For this is being a friend just in the nick	217
Was I angry with Hayley who us'd me so ill	217
Having given great offence by writing in prose	218

MISCELLANEOUS EPIGRAMS

His whole life is an epigram, smart, smooth, and neatly penn'd	219
He has observ'd the golden rule	219
And in melodious accents I	219
Some people admire the work of a fool	220
He's a blockhead who wants a proof of what he can't perceive	220
Great men and fools do often me inspire	220
Some men, created for destruction, come	220
An Epitaph : Come knock your heads against this stone	220
Another : I was buried near this dyke	220

Table of Contents

	PAGE
Another: Here lies John Trot, the friend of all mankind	221
When France got free, Europe, 'twixt fools and knaves	221
On the virginity of the Virgin Mary and Johanna Southcott	221
Imitation of Pope: a compliment to the Ladies	221
When a man has married a wife, he finds out whether	221
To Chloe's breast young Cupid slyly stole	221

TIRIEL 225

THE BOOK OF THEL 241

THE MARRIAGE OF HEAVEN AND HELL 247

THE FRENCH REVOLUTION 263

A SONG OF LIBERTY 283

VISIONS OF THE DAUGHTERS OF ALBION . . . 285

AMERICA: A PROPHECY 293

EUROPE: A PROPHECY 303

THE [FIRST] BOOK OF URIZEN 313

THE SONG OF LOS 331

THE BOOK OF LOS 335

THE BOOK OF AHANIA 341

SELECTIONS FROM 'THE FOUR ZOAS'

Introduction to Night the First	349
The Wanderer	350
A Vision of Eternity	350
The Song sung at the Feast of Los and Enitharmon	350
The Song of Enitharmon over Los	351
The Wail of Enion	352
Winter	354
The Woes of Urizen in the Dens of Urthona	354
Los in his Wrath	356
The War-Song of Orc	357
Vala's Going Forth	357
Urizen's Words of Wisdom	358
The Shade of Enitharmon	359
The Serpent Orc	359

Table of Contents

	PAGE
The Last Judgement	360
The Lament of Albion	362
Accuser and Accused	363
The Tillage of Urizen	363
Song of the Sinless Soul	364
Vala in Lower Paradise	366

SELECTIONS FROM 'MILTON'

Preface	369
The Invocation	370
The Mills of Satan	371
The Sin of Leutha	371
Milton's Journey to Eternal Death	371
The Nature of Infinity	372
The Sea of Time and Space	373
The Mundane Shell	373
A River in Eden	374
Los	374
Swedenborg	374
Whitefield and Wesley	375
The Forge of Los	375
The Wine-Press of Los	376
The Building of Time	378
The Heavens and the Earth	378
The Birds and the Flowers	379
Love and Jealousy	380
Reason and Imagination	381
The Song of the Shadowy Female	382

SELECTIONS FROM 'JERUSALEM'

To the Public	385
Introduction	386
The Reasoning Power	387
The Words of Los	387
The Builders of Golgonooza	387
A Vision of Albion	388
Punishment and Forgiveness	388
The Lament of Albion	388
Jerusalem	389
To the Jews	389
A Female Will	**393**

xi

Table of Contents

	PAGE
The Universal Family	394
Man's Spectre	394
Pretences	394
Fourfold and Twofold Vision	395
The Remembrance of Sin	395
To the Deists	395
Albion's Spectre	398
The Holiness of Minute Particulars	398
A Vision of Joseph and Mary	399
Tirzah	401
The Warrior and the Daughter of Albion	402
Men and States	403
To the Christians	403
A Vision of Jerusalem	406
The Worship of God	407
The Cry of Los	408
Albion upon the Rock	409
The Wrath of God	409
The Divine Image	410
The End of the Song of Jerusalem	410

VERSES FROM 'THE GATES OF PARADISE'

Prologue	413
The Keys of the Gates	414
Epilogue. To the Accuser who is The God of this World	417

THE GHOST OF ABEL 421

APPENDIX TO THE PROPHETIC BOOKS

There is No Natural Religion	425
All Religions are One	427
From Blake's Engraving of the Laocoon	428
On Homer's Poetry	430
On Virgil	431

FROM BLAKE'S 'DESCRIPTIVE CATALOGUE'

Sir Geffrey Chaucer and the Nine and twenty Pilgrims on their journey to Canterbury 432

INDEX OF FIRST LINES 445

LIST OF ILLUSTRATIONS

Portrait of Blake: from the portrait by Thomas Phillips, R.A.	*Frontispiece*
Title-page of *Songs of Innocence and of Experience*	*To face p.* 64
Title-page of *Songs of Innocence*	,, 64
Title-page of *Songs of Experience*	,, 80
Title-page of *The Book of Thel* (reduced)	,, 240
Title-page of *The Marriage of Heaven and Hell* (reduced)	,, 246
Title-page of *The Visions of the Daughters of Albion* (reduced)	,, 284
Title-page of *America: a Prophecy* (reduced)	,, 292
Title-page of *Europe: a Prophecy* (reduced)	, 302
Title-page of *The [First] Book of Urizen* (reduced)	,, 312
Title-page of *The Song of Los* (reduced)	,, 330
Title-page of *The Book of Los* (reduced)	,, 334
Title-page of *The Book of Ahania* (reduced)	,, 340
Title-page of *The Four Zoas* (reduced)	,, 348
Title-page of *Milton* (reduced)	,, 368
Title-page of *Jerusalem* (reduced)	,, 384

BIBLIOGRAPHICAL INTRODUCTION

THE aim of this new edition of Blake is to present within the compass of a single volume the main body of his poetry, comprehending under this term not only the purely lyrical poems but also those written in irregular unrimed verse or rhythmed prose. Explicitly, the book contains, in addition to the lyrics brought together in my previous edition, the earlier blank verse poems *Tiriel*, *Thel*, and the hitherto unprinted *French Revolution*, the whole of the minor Prophetic Books (including for the sake of completeness the prose *Marriage of Heaven and Hell*, the so-called 'Sibylline Leaves', and the tractates on Natural and Supersensual Religion), together with selections from the three longer Prophecies, *The Four Zoas*, *Milton*, and *Jerusalem*. I add also, that the Reader may not be obliged to seek it elsewhere, the notable passage from the *Descriptive Catalogue* containing Blake's account of the Canterbury Pilgrims—in Charles Lamb's view the finest criticism ever written of Chaucer's poem.

The text of the lyrical poems is in the main identical with that of the Clarendon Press edition of 1905 and smaller unannotated edition of 1906 : one or two trifling errors have been discovered and corrected ; in a few cases, where the pieces have been left in rough draft and subjected to many successive changes in the MS., I have not, as before, invariably adhered to the later version when the earlier one seemed preferable ; a deleted stanza has sometimes been restored, printed within square brackets, where it seemed necessary to the integrity of the poem, while in a single instance ('My Spectre around me') I have ventured to insert three unplaced stanzas in the position demanded by the sense. I have also, in the case of the Epigrams and Gnomic Verses, substituted a more convenient classified arrangement of these pieces in place of the strictly paginal sequence of the earlier edition. The additional matter constitutes a new text prepared by me for the present edition from the engraved, letterpress, or MS. originals.

Bibliographical Introduction

Blake's spelling, including that of proper names, has been modernized throughout, but with the necessary retention of his use of -d and -ed (here printed -'d and -èd) to distinguish between the elision or accentuation of the final syllable of the preterite, not always obvious on metrical grounds alone. No absolutely consistent practice has been followed with regard to capitalization, though majuscule initials have generally been retained or inserted in the case of symbolic terms, and occasionally, but to a lesser extent, in words or phrases in the lyrics for the sake of emphasis or artistic colour.

Blake's punctuation, always erratic and sometimes omitted altogether, is not the least of his editor's difficulties. Though taken into account in dealing with doubtful passages, the pointing of the original—whether his own as in the MS. and engraved books, or that of the typographer, as in *The Poetical Sketches* and *French Revolution*—has here been abandoned in favour of a more uniform and intelligible system.

The footnotes in the present edition are restricted to Blake's own earlier, variant, or cancelled readings, all of which are recorded in full; and, where necessary, to such short explanations of the changes found in the original MS. as may render clear the reasons which have guided me in adopting the version given in the text. I omit here altogether variorum readings—at best a painful necessity in my earlier book—while exegetical notes, even in the form of interpretative passages selected from Blake's own writings, fall outside the scope of this edition.

Before entering upon a detailed description of Blake's writings, it may be pertinent to call attention to the poet's attitude towards publication, since to this cause must be largely attributed his lack of influence upon his own and even the succeeding generation. There is ample evidence that the rare and extraordinary quality of Blake's poetry, or at least the lyrical part of it, met with due and immediate recognition from those of his contemporaries who had an opportunity of making acquaintance with his poems. That these readers and admirers were so few, and that Blake remained

Bibliographical Introduction

'hid', seems to have been his own choice ; and the assumption of Gilchrist, repeated by derivative biographers, that Blake at first sought and failed to obtain a publisher for his works, and was merely restrained by poverty from printing them at his own expense, is unsupported by fact and contrary to anything we know of his aims and ideas. Artist as well as poet, imbued with a contempt for purely mechanical processes, Blake, like Morris, seems from the first to have striven after some more ideal mode of book-production than that afforded by the typography of his day. Of the two volumes of his poems which appeared in ordinary type, one, the *Poetical Sketches*, was printed at the desire of his friend Flaxman, and seems to have been treated with scant regard by Blake himself, since he omits it from the list of his works offered for sale in 1793, and so far as our knowledge extends made no attempt to place the copies in circulation. The other, *The French Revolution*, though it bears Johnson's imprint, did not as I show elsewhere pass the proof stage, and presumably was withdrawn by the author before any copies were printed off.

By far the greater number of Blake's works were produced by a process of his own discovery, which he terms 'Illuminated Printing', a name suggestive of the manner in which, as in a mediaeval MS., text and design are interwoven into a single artistic harmony. 'The Author', says Blake, 'has invented a method of Printing both Letterpress and Engraving in a style more ornamental, uniform and grand than any before discovered, while it produces works at less than one-fourth of the expense. If a method of Printing which combines the Painter and the Poet is a phenomenon worthy of public attention, provided that it exceeds in elegance all former methods, the Author is sure of his reward.' In this process the text and surrounding pictorial embellishments were executed in reverse in some species of varnish upon copper plates, which were afterwards etched in a bath of acid until the whole design stood in relief as on a stereotype. From these plates impressions were printed in various schemes of monochrome, and afterwards delicately tinted by the artist in washes of water-colour, each copy thus possessing an individuality of its own. We are told by

Bibliographical Introduction

Blake's biographer, J. T. Smith, that the secret of this new mode of printing was revealed to the artist in a vision by the spirit of his favourite brother Robert. It is clear, however, from a passage in the early MS. known as *An Island in the Moon*,[1] that, at least five years before his first essay in relief-engraving in 1788, Blake had contemplated some form of artistic printing. Beautiful as the result proved in his hands, the new process must have been an extremely slow and laborious one, as indeed we gather from his last letter to Cumberland, dated 1827.[2] To this fact may perhaps be attributed the interval, sometimes as in the longer Prophecies of several years, that elapsed between the actual completion of the work and the first engraving of the dated title-page, with which it was Blake's somewhat misleading practice to begin his task. Another drawback consequent upon the use of this mode of relief-engraving is that no subsequent alterations were possible, except such deletions as could be made by chipping out part of the lettering, or by re-engraving and substituting an entirely new plate. Naturally under these circumstances few copies were issued, nor was there an actual edition in the ordinary sense of the term of any of the engraved works; impressions, as in the case of the early fifteenth century block-books, being struck off as required. Of the most widely known of Blake's publications, the *Songs of Innocence and of Experience*, hardly more than twenty copies (chiefly produced during his last years) are known to exist; of others like *Jerusalem* Blake himself perfected but a single example; of *The Book of Ahania* a solitary copy survives; while another engraved Prophecy, *Outhoun*, would seem to have entirely disappeared.

Many of Blake's poems, among them some of his most striking

[1] This passage begins, imperfectly, at the head of the recto of the ninth leaf: '. . . . "Illuminating the Manuscript "—"Ay," said she, "that would | be excellent." "then," said he, "I would have all the writing Engraved | instead of Printed, & at every other leaf a high finish'd | print, all in three Volumes folio. & sell them a hundred pounds | a piece. they would Print off two thousand." "then," said she, " whoever | will not have them, will be ignorant fools & will not deserve to live."'

[2] *Letters*, ed. A. G. B. Russell, p. 222.

Bibliographical Introduction

and beautiful lyrics, were left in MS., while others, including 'epic poems as long as Homer and tragedies as long as *Macbeth*', were only 'published in Eternity', and hence fall outside the province of the mere mundane bibliographer. It was Blake's belief, as he tells us in *Jerusalem*, and as we learn from letters to Butts and conversations with Crabb Robinson, that long passages, or even whole poems, were merely transcribed by him from the dictation of spirits. The evidence of extant MSS., however, shows that he himself saw nothing final or absolute in this verbal inspiration, but submitted these writings like any others to such successive changes as at length satisfied his artistic conscience. All Blake's holographs, indeed, indicate how little basis there is for the common belief that he was one of those who never blotted a line, almost the sole exception being the fairly written Pickering MS., where the poems are obviously transcripts. Blake's meticulous care in composition is everywhere apparent in the poems preserved in rough draft—perhaps the most informing illustrations of a poet's method of writing which have come down to us. There we find the first crude version, or single stanza around which his idea was to take shape, followed by alteration on alteration, re-arrangement after re-arrangement, deletions, additions and inversions, until at last the poem as in the case of 'The Tiger' attains its perfect form, or as in 'My Spectre' is practically completed, or, on the other hand, like the lines on Lafayette abandoned for the time unachieved. A phrase or even a line, thus hardly won, has a tendency to become converted into a symbol of a mood or idea, and to be repeated when occasion offers. If we compare Blake's use of the pen and the graver, we see that whereas in his pictorial art there is a constant development from the dry, severe manner and 'hard wiry outline' of his old master Basire, to the fully emancipated 'drawing on copper' of the *Book of Job*, his use of words as tools tended increasingly to harden into what he himself calls 'vast petrific forms', harsh, opaque and unbeautiful. In the Prophetic Books, whether engraved or in MS., this habit of mind and the repeated changes consequent upon the growth of Blake's

Bibliographical Introduction

symbolism account to some extent, especially in the later works, for the lack of unity and coherence which has been urged against them. Thus in the MS. of *The Four Zoas* whole sections have been painfully erased and rewritten, while long passages have been excerpted and transferred bodily to the pages of *Milton* and *Jerusalem*. In the two latter books plates have been cancelled and, after the lapse of several years, re-engraved in a new form and interpolated in the work without great regard for continuity. Sometimes, as in *Milton*, they embody a form of the myth not found in the Prophecy itself. The few copies we possess of the rarer engraved writings vary in content as well as in arrangement, and it is often difficult from the subject-matter alone to determine whether or not a poem has reached us in its complete form. We find the same process of disintegration and re-arrangement even in the lyrics of the *Rossetti MS.*, where poems like the untitled 'Monk of Charlemaine' have 'fallen into division', the Spectral half being engraved as part of *Jerusalem*, and the Emanative counterpart conserved in 'The Grey Monk' of the *Pickering MS.*

Before turning from the MSS. it may be observed that part of the contents of Blake's note-books are in the nature of rough jottings, sometimes mere doggerel set down from whim or to relieve a mood, and never probably, any more than our own most casual utterances, intended to see the light in cold print. Such without doubt is the fragment known as *An Island in the Moon*, and such too are most of the epigrams in the *Rossetti MS.*

Blake's earliest poems, written between his twelfth and twentieth year but not printed until 1783, are contained in the rare little volume called *Poetical Sketches*, a slender demy octavo of 38 leaves, privately issued without publisher's or printer's name. The title-page reads: POETICAL | SKETCHES. | By W. B. | London: | Printed in the Year MDCCLXXXIII. The first quire of two leaves comprises the title and 'advertisement', followed by nine quires in fours, signed B—K (K⁴ blank) and paginated [1]-70. The book is without an index or table of the contents, which are

Bibliographical Introduction

here given in full in the original order. The *Poetical Sketches* was produced in ordinary typography, obviously from the poet's own MS., the punctuation being apparently supplied or corrected by the printer, and the stanza-lines indented to indicate the rime instead of being alined in Blake's usual fashion. A few serious misprints such as 'cares' for 'ears' in '*An Imitation of Spenser*', and 'her' for 'his' in the fourth stanza of the song 'Love and Harmony combine', suggest that Blake either had no opportunity of correcting the proofs, or failed to avail himself of it

These poems, as we learn from Blake's biographers J. T. Smith and Allan Cunningham, were printed at the suggestion of Flaxman, who shared the expense with his early patron the Rev. Henry Mathew, handing the unbound sheets to the author 'to dispose of for his own advantage'. The preface to the *Poetical Sketches*, on the recto of the second leaf, was the composition of Mathew,[1] who, as Smith tells us, 'not only acquiesced' in the 'truly kind offer of defraying the expense of printing them . . . . but, with his usual urbanity, wrote the . . . **advertisement**, which precedes the poems'. Reading between the lines of this composition in the light of Smith's reference to the artist's 'unbending deportment, or what his adherents are pleased to call his manly firmness of opinion', it seems evident that Mathew must have advised, and Blake refused to make any correction of the 'irregularities and defects to be found in almost every page'—a kind office undertaken later, when the author was not there to be dealt with, by other worthies who shared this critic's view. The edition was probably a very small one, and of it Blake seems to have been content with presenting a few copies to his more intimate friends, making no attempt to dispose of the remainder either privately or through the medium of a bookseller.

On the fly-leaves of one of these presentation copies, with the inscription '[present *del.*] from Mrs. Flaxman May 15 1784', are three poems, undoubtedly by Blake though not in his auto-

---

[1] As also, it may be conjectured, the conventional heading 'Miscellaneous Poems', which seems intended to cover the shorter pieces preceding *King Edward the Third* (pp. 3-22 of this ed.).

Bibliographical Introduction

graph, with the heading Songs by Mr. Blake'. The first and third of these, entitled respectively 'Song 1st by a Shepherd' and 'Song 3d by an Old Shepherd', are here printed as an Appendix to the *Poetical Sketches*. The intermediate poem, 'Song 2d by a Young Shepherd,' is an early form of the 'Laughing Song' afterwards engraved as one of the *Songs of Innocence*, in my text of which this variant version of the first and second stanzas is quoted in a foot-note.

To the same period, or perhaps a little later than the pieces in rhythmed prose at the end of the *Poetical Sketches*, should be assigned the early holograph which I call the *Seven-Page MS*. The MS, which is incomplete, consists of four leaves of crown 8vo paper, $7\frac{1}{2} \times 5$ inches, the verso of the last leaf being blank. There is no dated watermark. These leaves are now mounted upon rather larger paper, on the outer cover of which is inscribed '7 (seven) Pages MS.: The handwriting of William Blake'. This book contains two pieces written straightforwardly as if prose, though actually irregular unrimed verse, the first and longer of which begins: (p. [1]): 'then She bore Pale desire, father of Curiosity, | a Virgin ever young. And after Leaden Sloth, | from whom came Ignorance, who brought forth | wonder. These are the Gods which came from | fear —[*interpolated* for Gods like these nor male nor female are, | but Single Pregnate; or, if they list, together ming|ling bring forth mighty powers]—She knew them not; yet they all war with | Shame, and Strengthen her weak arm.'; ending (p. [5]): 'Go! see the City— | friends Join'd Hand in Hand: Go! see the Natu|ral tie of flesh & blood: Go! see, more strong, | the ties of marriage love; thou Scarce Shalt | find but Self love Stands Between.'

The second piece begins (p. [6]): ' "Woe," cried the muse, tears started at the Sound, Grief perch'd | upon my brow, and thought Embrac'd Her. "What does this | mean", I cried, "when all around Summer hath spred her | Plumes, and tunes her Notes? When Buxom Joy | doth fan his wings, & Golden Pleasures Beam around my | head, why, Grief, dost thou accost me?"' and ends (p. [6], l. 22): ' "O'er yonder lake | the winds their Sad Com-

xxii

Bibliographical Introduction

plainings bear for Comrade lost, | untimely lost, thy Comrade once, When living, thee I | lov'd even unto Death ; now Dead, I'll guard thee from | approaching ill. farewell, my time is gone." it Said | no more, but vanished ever from my Sight.'

The first fragment has been printed by Mr. W. M. Rossetti,[1] who divides the poem into metrical lines, and entitles it 'The Passions'. These imperfect and immature compositions, which, in such frigid personifications as 'pale Desire', 'leaden Sloth', and 'Hate, meagre hag', show Blake less happy in the idiom of his own century than in the earlier Elizabethan imitations, are not included in the present edition.

Next in order of Blake's extant writings is the short satirical sketch commonly called *An Island in the Moon*, which must have been written after the publication of the *Poetical Sketches* in 1783, though probably not much later than the end of 1784. This fragment, which can hardly have been intended for publication, was unknown to Blake's earlier biographers and critics. The original holograph is now in the Fitzwilliam Museum, to which it was recently presented by its late owner Mr. Fairfax Murray. In format the MS. is a thin foolscap folio of 16 leaves, lacking two, or perhaps four, leaves through the loss of one or two sheets from the centre of the single quire of which it is composed. The MS. is in Blake's early hand, and begins at the head of the first page :

'In the Moon is a certain Island, near by a mighty continent, which small | island seems to have some affinity to England, & what is more extraordinary the | people are so much alike, & their language so much the same, that you would | think you was among your friends. in this Island dwells three Philosophers, | Suction the Epicurean, Quid the Cynic, and Sipsop the Pythagorean. I call them | by the names of those sects ; tho' the sects are not ever mention'd there, as being | quite out of date. however the things still remain, and the vanities are the | same. the three Philosophers sat together thinking of nothing. in comes | Ftruscan Column, the Antiquarian, & after an abundance of Enquiries to |

[1] *Monthly Review*, August 1903, vol. xii, pp. 120-9.

Bibliographical Introduction

no purpose sat himself down & described something that nobody listen'd to. | so they were employ'd when Mrs. Gimblet came in.' It ends abruptly, or rather is left unfinished by the author, on line 19 of the recto of the leaf following the lacuna in the text, the remaining pages being blank. There is no internal evidence as to the origin or occasion of this brochure, but whatever the uncouth circle against which its satire was directed, it can assuredly not have been, as some have assumed, the salon of the 'accomplished Mrs. Mathew'. The chief interest of *An Island in the Moon*, apart from the passage foreshadowing the invention of Blake's Illuminated Printing (quoted elsewhere), lies in the songs placed in the mouths of the several characters, which include in rough draft three of the simple idylls of the *Songs of Innocence* as well as, in another but equally characteristic vein, the strange and savage lines on 'Surgery'. A few allusions throw light upon Blake's literary interests at this time. In Chapters V and VII he refers to the Chatterton controversy,[1] which reached its height in 1782, while in Chapter VIII Steelyard the Lawyer quotes 'My crop of corn is but a field of tares', a line of Chidiock Tichborne's, which Blake may have met with in the *Reliquiae Wottonianae*.

In 1788 Blake, as he tells us in the colophon to the *Ghost of Abel*, engraved his 'original stereotype', and it has been commonly supposed that the plate to which he here refers was one of those forming part of the *Songs of Innocence*, the first of the series of works in Illuminated Printing advertised in his Prospectus of Oct. 10, 1793. But as I attempt to show later, there seems reason to believe that the undated tracts entitled *There is No Natural Religion* and *All Religions are One* and not the *Songs of Innocence* were Blake's first experiments in this new art. The *Songs*, moreover, are dated 1789, presumably the year in which the engraving of the plates was begun, unless we suppose that in this instance Blake had not yet

---

[1] Blake's poem 'Good English Hospitality' may have been suggested by Chatterton's essay on the 'Antiquity of Christmas Games', which contains the phrase 'Old English hospitality is long since deceased'. Compare also the first verse of Quid's song on 'Surgery' (Chap. VI) with the opening line of the chorus in *Goddwyn: A Tragedie* 'Whan Freedom, dreste yn blodde-steyned veste'.

Bibliographical Introduction

adopted his subsequent practice of commencing with the title-page. In its earliest form the *Songs of Innocence* contained 31 plates, printed upon both sides of the leaf, including 5 ('The Little Girl Lost' (2 plates), 'The Little Girl Found', 'The Voice of the Ancient Bard', and 'The Schoolboy') afterwards generally transferred to the *Songs of Experience*, though the two last were occasionally placed among the *Songs of Innocence*. Some four or five years later, towards the end of 1793, the engraving of the companion volume, the *Songs of Experience*, written in the interval, was completed by Blake, who advertised the two books in his Prospectus at the price of 5*s*. apiece. Each is described as containing 25 designs, a collation which would seem to leave out of account the two frontispieces and title-pages, while including one additional plate, perhaps the suppressed song 'A Divine Image'. There are two slightly varying forms of the title-page to the *Songs of Experience*, one being without year, and the other bearing the date 1794. Later, Blake added an undated general title-page to both series,[1] which thenceforward were issued by him as a single work, the plates being printed on one side of the leaf only, and numbered consecutively by hand 1–54. The book has no table of contents, and my collation of 22 copies described in the 1905 edition shows that the order in which the songs are arranged varies in almost every instance. The sequence here observed is taken from a MS. index in Blake's autograph, headed 'The Order in which the *Songs of Innocence and of Experience* ought to be paged and placed', which coincides with that of the Monckton Milnes copy (printed not earlier than 1818) sold at the Crewe sale in 1903. It should be recognized, however, that Blake himself did not adhere to this scheme. Later issues exhibit an entirely different order, five copies, foliated by the artist, placing the plates in identical sequence, and others approximating closely to the same standard. This later arrangement of the *Songs* is as follows:

1. General Title. 2. Frontispiece. 3. Title-page to Songs of Innocence. 4. Introduction. 5. The Shepherd. 6, 7. The

[1] See the facsimiles of all three title-pages facing pp. 64 and 80.

Bibliographical Introduction

Echoing Green. 8. The Lamb. 9, 10. The Little Black Boy. 11. The Blossom. 12. The Chimney Sweeper. 13. The Little Boy Lost. 14. The Little Boy Found. 15. Laughing Song. 16, 17. Cradle Song. 18. The Divine Image. 19. Holy Thursday. 20, 21. Night. 22, 23. Spring. 24. Nurse's Song. 25. Infant Joy. 26. A Dream. 27. On Another's Sorrow. [End of Songs of Innocence.] 28. Frontispiece. 29. Title-page to Songs of Experience. 30. Introduction. 31. Earth's Answer. 32. The Clod and Pebble. 33. Holy Thursday. 34-6. The Little Girl Lost. The Little Girl Found. 37. The Chimney Sweeper. 38. Nurse's Song. 39. The Sick Rose. 40. The Fly. 41. The Angel. 42. The Tiger. 43. My pretty Rose Tree. 44. The Garden of Love. 45. The Little Vagabond. 46. London. 47. The Human Abstract. 48. Infant Sorrow. 49. A Poison Tree. 50. A Little Boy Lost. 51. A Little Girl Lost. 52. To Tirzah. 53. The School Boy. 54. The Voice of the Ancient Bard. [End of Songs of Experience.]

In my foot-note to 'Tirzah' I draw attention to the recent discovery that this poem, despite its occurrence (with a single exception) in every copy of the *Songs of Experience*—even in the first issue printed upon both sides of the leaf—is a later substitution for an original illustrated plate without text. From this it would appear that, since the clear and definite symbolism of 'Tirzah' (identical with that of the revised form of *The Four Zoas, Milton,* and *Jerusalem*) could hardly have been written before the year 1800, every known issue of the *Songs of Innocence and of Experience*, with the unique exception noted above, must have been produced at least six years later than the date on the title-page, many of them being indeed, as we know from the watermarks, the work of his last years.

Dealing now with the two early dogmatic tractates which have as their theme the contrast between natural and supersensual religion, I have to emend and supplement the bibliographical description given in my previous book (pp. 342-3), when the additional leaves in the possession of Mr. William Muir were unknown to me. Both booklets are engraved in relief upon tiny

Bibliographical Introduction

plates measuring about 2 × 1½ inches, and constitute the smallest examples we possess of Blake's Illuminated Printing. As these plates were printed upon loose sheets, they were consequently liable to loss and disarrangement, so that the contents of each book are to some extent conjectural, and only to be determined by a study of the subject-matter and minute differences of style and technique in the engraving. The extant impressions known to me are:[1] (1) a series in the Print Room of the British Museum containing eleven plates mounted in an album (perhaps by the previous owner, F. T. Palgrave), where the order is as follows: The Argument (*italic script*) 'Man has no notion' etc.; I (*large type*) 'Man's Perceptions are not bounded' etc.; II–VI (*small type*), as in my text of Part I; followed by I (*small type*) 'Man cannot naturally perceive' etc.; II (*large type*) 'Reason, or the Ratio' etc.; the inference (*large italic script*) 'Therefore God becomes as we are' etc.; and the colophon, or *quaere* frontispiece, in reversed characters 'The Author & Printer W. Blake'.

(2) An imperfect set of plates in the possession of Mr. Muir, reproduced in his facsimile of 1886. These, besides the title-page: THERE | IS NO | NATURAL | RELIGION, consist of four additional propositions numbered IV–VII (*large type*); two plates containing respectively the 'Conclusion' and the 'Application'; the title-page: ALL | RELIGIONS | ARE | ONE; and a plate without text representing an upright clothed, and a semi-recumbent nude figure with Gothic background.

(3) A collection of ten plates in the possession of the Linnell family. These impressions, which are printed in monotint upon large quarto paper, consist of the title-page 'There is No Natural Religion'; the frontispiece 'The Voice of one crying in the Wilderness'; The Argument; and Principles 1–7 as in my text of the second tractate.

It will be observed that in the British Museum album a title-page is lacking, and that the collection contains two different versions

---

[1] Some six or seven other copies of the first tractate, as I learn from Mr. G. Keynes, all imperfect and all arbitrarily arranged, are in existence in various public and private Libraries.

Bibliographical Introduction

of the first and second propositions, which (unless we assume that one was intended to replace the other) appear to belong to separate series. I agree with Mr. Muir in regarding the new propositions IV–VII as the continuation of the large type I and II in the Print Room copy, both of which are distinguished from the other series by their bolder lettering and simpler ornamentation. I have also followed him in his general reconstruction of the text of *There is No Natural Religion* from the two sources specified above, treating the little work as a tractate in two parts, the first dealing with the perceptions derived from organic senses only, and the second with those received through imagination or inspiration.

The remaining series of plates, in the possession of the Linnell Trustees, evidently form a separate work. These impressions, as the large paper and absence of colouring would seem to indicate, may have been printed after Blake's death, perhaps by Tatham, so that, as the theme also suggests, there is some warrant for believing that the wrong title has been prefixed to the plates containing the motto, Argument, and Seven Principles. I have, therefore, restored to this group what must have undoubtedly been its true title-page, *All Religions are One*, a plate occurring in the collection of Mr. Muir, though by him interpolated somewhat awkwardly between Parts I and II of the first tractate.

Neither booklet bears a date. In my earlier edition of Blake's *Poems* I had conjecturally assigned the two tractates to 1790 *circa*, guided chiefly by their similarity in doctrine and argument to parts of the *Marriage of Heaven and Hell*. I have since, however, come to the conclusion that the tract *There is No Natural Religion* must have been Blake's first essay in relief engraving, and consequently should be dated 1788,[1] the companion work *All Religions are One* being perhaps a little later. Presumptive evidence of this may be found in the minute size of the plates and general roughness of execution, which seem to point to an early experimental stage, coupled with the fact that the imprint

---

[1] Since writing the above I am pleased to find that I have been anticipated in this suggestion by Mr. A. G. B. Russell in his authoritative work on *The Engravings of William Blake*, p. 205 *ft.-note*.

Bibliographical Introduction

on the frontispiece of the first tract 'The Author & Printer W. Blake' appears in reversed characters, indicating a want of familiarity in the use of the new process.

Intermediately between the *Songs of Innocence* and the *Songs of Experience* Blake began the series of mythological writings, which were to culminate in *Jerusalem*. The earlier group, dimly foreshadowed by 'The Passions', consists of three works, *Tiriel*, *Thel*, and the *Marriage of Heaven and Hell*, which, though characterized by little or no symbolism, may be regarded as the precursors of the Prophetic Books proper. The first of these is *Tiriel*, a poem without date but written *circa* 1788-9, which remained in MS. until printed by Mr. W. M. Rossetti in 1874. The holograph consists of eight leaves of foolscap quarto, the last page being blank. There is no title-page or heading, but the original blue-grey paper cover bears the inscription in Blake's autograph 'TIRIEL | MS. by Mr. Blake', obviously a reminder of authorship and ownership intended for some person to whom the MS. had been lent or submitted. It is not improbable that this reader may have been Blake's friend, the publisher J. Johnson, who two years later set up in type the first book of *The French Revolution*, and that both poems may have been brought before his notice at the same time, presumably at his own request.

Following *Tiriel*, and closely connected with it, came a beautiful example of Blake's Illuminated Printing, with the title THE | BOOK | OF | THEL | The Author & Printer Willm Blake 1789. The poem, which was advertised in the Prospectus at 3s., is a small quarto containing 'Thel's Motto', title-page, and six plates of text about 6 × 4½ inches. That *Thel* was a later work than *Tiriel*, instead of, as some have thought, immediately preceding it, is apparent from the lines of the 'Motto':

> Can Wisdom be put in a silver rod,
> Or Love in a golden bowl?

which are borrowed from the MS. poem. Another proof is found in the opening line:

The daughters of Mne Seraphim led round their sunny flocks

Bibliographical Introduction

where it is plain that Blake had at first intended to write 'The daughters of Mnetha', one of the personages in *Tiriel*, and afterwards mentally changed this to 'The daughters of the Seraphim', while neglecting to erase the meaningless 'Mne' from the plate.

To 1788, or at latest 1789, must be attributed Blake's marginalia to his copy of Lavater's *Aphorisms on Man* and of Swedenborg's *Wisdom of Angels*, published in the earlier year. Both series of annotations anticipate in thought and expression the extraordinary work of a year or two later, where Blake's wit and wisdom run riot in the domain of Emanuel Swedenborg. This book, with the simple title THE | MARRIAGE | OF | HEAVEN | AND HELL, is without imprint or date, but the opening sentence, 'As a new heaven is begun, and it is now thir|ty-three years since its advent, the Eternal Hell | revives,' can only refer to the new era of the dispensation of the Spirit, predicted by the Swedish mystic for 1757, synchronous, it will be noted, with the year of Blake's birth. The work, which is one of the noblest achievements of his press, is advertised in the Prospectus as a 'Quarto, with 14 designs, price 7s. 6d.,' a description which ignores the unillustrated plates of text. In all, the book contains 25 plates, 6 × 4 inches, the title-page and the 'Argument' occupying one plate each, followed by 22 plates of text. Appended to the *Marriage* in at least one copy, apparently as issued by the author, we find the 3 plates containing *A Song of Liberty*, which, however, is certainly a separate and later Prophecy, nearer in style and symbolism to *America*.

The text ends: 'Note! This Angel, who is now become a Devil, is | my particular friend: we often read the Bible to-|gether in its infernal or diabolical sense, which | the world shall have if they behave well. | I have also The Bible of Hell, which the world | shall have whether they will or no. | ' That Blake actually planned, and perhaps even executed such a work, we know from a draft of a title-page sketched at the back of one of his uncoloured designs, reading 'THE BIBLE OF HELL, IN NOCTURNAL VISIONS COLLECTED. Vol. I. Lambeth.' W. M. Rossetti dates this design '*circa* 1791 (?)', but the title on the verso cannot, of course, be

Bibliographical Introduction

earlier than 1793, the year of Blake's removal to Lambeth. No MS. or engraved copy exists of the *Bible of Hell*, which may possibly have formed part of Tatham's holocaust.

In 1791 the bookseller Johnson set up in type with a view to publication Blake's *French Revolution*, Book I, a work known to us from a single copy only, and here reprinted for the first time. This copy, since lost sight of for half a century, would appear to have been seen by Gilchrist, Swinburne, and the Rossettis, who quote the title-page though no part of the contents. A transcript, partial or complete, made by Palmer about the same time for the Gilchrists, also disappeared; while, as stated in my previous edition, the late Mr. John Linnell, who had been credited with the possession of the original, disclaimed any knowledge of the book. This, however, would seem to have been an oversight, as after the death of Mr. Linnell this work was rediscovered in the family collection, and with great generosity placed at my service by Mr. Herbert Linnell. The book is a demy quarto of 18 pages, $11\frac{1}{4} \times 8\frac{3}{4}$ inches, printed in ordinary typography. The first quire of two leaves contains the title-page and the 'Advertisement' (both with verso blank), followed by two quires, B and C, in fours, paginated at head 1–16 within square brackets. The title-page runs: THE | FRENCH REVOLUTION | A Poem, | in Seven Books. | Book the First. | London: | Printed for J. Johnson, No. 72, St. Paul's Church-yard. | MDCCXCI. | [Price One Shilling.] At the left-hand top corner, in pale black ink, is the inscription, not reproduced in our facsimile, 'John Linnell. Red Hill, 1860,' the ascription 'By Wm. Blake' between the third and fourth lines of the title being also in the autograph of the original owner. The poem begins on p. [1] with the dropped heading THE | FRENCH REVOLUTION. | [line] BOOK THE FIRST [line], and concludes on p. 16, the *explicit* reading 'END OF THE FIRST BOOK'.

There are strong reasons for concluding that though prepared for the press this book was never actually printed off or published. In the first place it is demonstrable that this, the only known copy, was not one of a number issued in any edition, however small,

xxxi

Bibliographical Introduction

but was merely a page-proof of a work which never saw the light of day, preserved perhaps by Blake in lieu of the original MS. This proof, though 'perfected,' i.e. printed on both sides, reveals a defective register, showing that the formes were not made finally ready for printing. Further evidence of this being a proof only is found in the 'excessive impression' or heavy pull of the press almost cutting through the thin paper, in the tell-tale thumb-mark of the printer, the grey and uneven colouring and blurriness at ends of lines, the fact that the final line 'End of the First Book' is out of centre, and other typographical details. The text, though set with fair accuracy and punctuated to the best of the printer's ability, has more than one misprint which could hardly have escaped the eye of the proof-reader: e.g. 'Eeternally' at the beginning of line 15 of p. 3, 'were away' for 'wear away' on p. 5 l. 5, and an inverted 8 in the page number, etc. Lastly, the sheets are not stitched through the centre of the quires as in an ordinary pamphlet, but are fastened to the pale-blue paper which forms the cover in Blake's usual rude mode of binding by a fine cord laced through three punctured holes.

An advertisement on the recto of A2 states that 'The remaining Books are finished, and will be published in their order', and if this statement is to be accepted literally these books would seem to be irretrievably lost. The period dealt with in the First Book, treated of course imaginatively rather than historically, describes the Convocation of the Notables before the summoning of the States General and the fall of the Bastille. Probably this First Book was written in the same year 1789, and, as I have elsewhere conjectured, submitted to the publisher together with *Tiriel*. The fact that the compositors' labours occupied a year or two is in accordance with Johnson's reputation as a slow and dilatory printer.[1]

---

[1] Cp. Cowper's letter to Newton, Oct. 30, 1784: 'My bookseller I suppose will be as tardy as before. I do not expect to be born into the world till the month of March, when I and the crocuses shall peep together'; also to William Unwin, April 30, 1785: 'The man, Johnson, is like unto some vicious horses that I have known. They would not budge till they were spurred, and when they were spurred they would kick.' *Letters*, ed. J. G. Frazer, vol. i, pp. 320, 353.

Bibliographical Introduction

We have no knowledge of the reason which interfered with the regular publication of this work; but it can scarcely have been a rupture with his friend the bookseller, for whom Blake continued to engrave during several years, and who acted as his co-publisher in *For Children: The Gates of Paradise*, in 1793. Possibly Johnson, who, in spite of his revolutionary sympathies, had in 1791 declined to publish Paine's *Rights of Man*, might have thought it prudent not to proceed further with Blake's work, or the latter, feeling that the book would be out of date before it appeared, may himself have withdrawn it prior to publication.

We have no work of Blake's specifically dated 1792, though in all probability to this year should be assigned *A Song of Liberty*, being, as the symbolism shows, later than *The French Revolution* and earlier than *America*. This poem, which, as mentioned above, is sometimes bound up with the *Marriage of Heaven and Hell*, consists of 3 plates of Illuminated Printing without separate title-page, imprint, or illustrations.

Before the end of the same year Blake must also have written several of the *Songs of Experience* and other lyrics transcribed from earlier rough drafts into the *Rossetti MS*. This precious volume, otherwise known as the *MS. Book*, now in the possession of Mr. W. A. White of Brooklyn, New York, was acquired by D. G. Rossetti twenty years after Blake's death, under circumstances noted in a pencilled memorandum on the verso of the fly-leaf, over his earlier signature D. G. C. R.: 'I purchased this original MS. of Palmer, an attendant in the Antique Gallery at the British Museum, on the 30th April '47.' The holograph is a foolscap quarto volume of 58 leaves, composed of one quire of 10 leaves, and four of 16 and 8 leaves alternately. Bound in at the end is a folded sheet of different and smaller paper forming two leaves, upon which are written part of 'The Everlasting Gospel', and part of the first draft of Blake's description of his 'Canterbury Pilgrims'; as well as 28 additional leaves containing Rossetti's own transcript of a portion of the contents headed 'Verse and Prose by William Blake (Natus 1757: obiit 1827). All that is of any value in the foregoing pages has here been copied out. D. G. C. R.'

Bibliographical Introduction

The *Rossetti MS.* covers a period of at least twenty years of Blake's life, being first used as a sketch-book, and when it had served this purpose converted into a note-book for poetry, and still later for prose. Since the sketches include designs afterwards engraved for the *Marriage of Heaven and Hell* (1790), the *Gates of Paradise*, the *Visions of the Daughters of Albion*, the *Songs of Experience*, *Urizen*, and *America* (1793-4), but none for Blake's earlier works, the *Songs of Innocence* and the *Book of Thel*, we may conclude that his use of the Sketch-book began not earlier than 1789-90. About 1793, when most of the leaves were partially filled with sketches, Blake commenced to use the book for the transcription of the poems already referred to, reversing the volume and beginning to write on the three blank pages at the end. These poems, which form the first section of the book, must all have been written before the end of the year 1793.

During the next seven years, while Blake was occupied in the production of the Lambeth Prophecies, he laid aside the Sketch-book altogether, resuming his use of it as a note-book during his stay at Felpham, the poems and prose in this later section (*circa* 1800-11) being written not as before from the reversed end, but from the original beginning of the volume. The interval of seven years between the writings in the first and in the second sections is emphasized by a clearly marked difference of matter and manner. While the lyrics in the former are either rough drafts or transcripts of the *Songs of Experience* or contemporaneous poems of the same order, those in the latter, with a few exceptions, embody the symbolism of the greater Prophetic Books. Here (*circa* 1807-10) we meet with the epigrams and satirical pieces on friends and foes, and art and artists, the latter an overflow from Blake's marginalia to his copy of Reynolds' *Discourses*, written in 1808. Still later are the rough drafts of the *Advertisements to Blake's Canterbury Pilgrims from Chaucer, containing anecdotes of Artists* (Rossetti's 'Public Address'), and *For the year 1810: Additions to Blake's Catalogue of Pictures, &c.* (sometimes called 'A Vision of the Last Judgement'). Last of all (*circa* 1810), in a category of its own, stands all that survives of that

Bibliographical Introduction

astounding poem 'The Everlasting Gospel'. The earliest dated entry in the *MS. Book* is the note on p. 10, 'I say I shan't live five years. And if I live one it will be a Wonder. June 1793,' the latest being an extract 'From *Bell's Weekly Messenger*, Aug. 4th, 1811'.[1]

In 1793, the year that saw the earliest entries in the *Rossetti MS.*, Blake published under his own name coupled with that of Johnson a little work entitled *For Children: The Gates of Paradise*, described in his Prospectus as 'a small book of Engravings', priced at 3s. In this first form, as a picture-book for children, it consisted of 18 plates of emblematic designs, which some fifteen or twenty years afterwards were converted by the artist into an exposition of his maturer symbolism by the alteration of *For Children* to *For the Sexes*, the addition of a Prologue on the title-page, and of three supplementary plates containing the explanatory verses entitled 'The Keys of the Gates', and the lines 'To the Accuser', with other minor changes. There is evidence of Blake's intention to bring out the first issue 'For Children' in its contrary state in a design for a title-page reading *For Children: The Gates of Hell*, described by Mr. W. M. Rossetti in his 'Annotated Lists of Blake's Paintings, Drawings and Engravings' (Gil. *Life*, ii. 269, no. 135).

Here, too, should perhaps be noticed, for any whom it may concern, a companion volume advertised in the same Prospectus, entitled '*The History of England*, a small book of Engravings. Price 3s.' No copy of this book is known, but the subjects depicted may be conjectured from an entry in the *Rossetti MS.* to which I have previously drawn attention. This very Blakean list of contents runs as follows, marginal additions being indicated by square brackets: '1. Giants ancient inhabitants of England. 2. The Landing of Brutus. 3. Corineus throws Gogmagog the Giant into the sea. 4. King Lear. 5. The Ancient Britons according to Caesar. 6. The Druids. 7. The Landing of Julius Caesar. 8. Boadicea inspiring the Britons against the Romans. [The Britons' distress & depopulation. Women fleeing

---

[1] For a complete paginal list of contents of the *Rossetti MS.* see my previous edition, pp. 141-50.

Bibliographical Introduction

from War. Women in a Siege.] 9. Alfred in the countryman's house. 10. Edwin & Morcar stirring up the Londoners to resist W. the Conq[r]. 11. W. the Con[q] crown'd. 12. King John & Mag. Charta. [A Famine occasioned by the Popish interdict.] 13. Edward at Calais. 14. Edward the Black Prince brings his Captives to his father. 15. The Penance of Jane Shore. 16. The Cruelties used by Kings & Priests. 17. The Reformation by H. VIII. 18. Ch. I beheaded. 19. The Plague. 20. The fire of London. 21. A prospect of Liberty. 22. A Cloud.

With the *Visions of the Daughters of Albion* begin the Prophetic Books proper, unless indeed there existed a still earlier work *Outhoun*, which has disappeared. Our sole information regarding this book is contained in a letter from Blake's widow to an artist named James Ferguson,[1] offering for sale certain works, among them 'Outhoun 12 plates, 6 inches more or less, Price £2 2s o'. It has been conjectured that this may have been a mistitled reference to the *Visions of the Daughters of Albion*, where 'Oothoon' is a principal figure; but it is difficult to suppose that Mrs. Blake, who had been for so many years the artist's coadjutrix in printing, and even, as we are told, in colouring the various books, should have erred in such exact matters as the title and number of plates. Moreover, 'Outhoun' for 'Oothoon' (invariably found in the *Visions* and the later books) does seem to point to an earlier and separate work written before Blake had permanently adopted his final spelling of the name.[2] If, as would appear, the copy of *Outhoun* remained unsold, it presumably passed into the possession of Tatham after Mrs. Blake's death, and may perhaps in view of subject or treatment, Oothoon symbolizing feminine revolt against conventional sex-morality, have commended itself to the Irvingite mind as a fit heresy for the stake. On the other hand,

---

[1] This letter is unfortunately not given in full in W. M. Rossetti's Annotated Lists of Blake's Paintings, Drawings, and Engravings from which I quote (Gilchrist's *Life*, ii, p. 284).

[2] Cp. the similar changes of 'Tiriel' to 'Thiriel' in the *Book of Urizen*, and 'Entuthon Benithon' of *The Four Zoas* to 'Entuthon Benython' in *Milton* and *Jerusalem*.

Bibliographical Introduction

as against the existence of such a work, it may be noted that it is not included in the Prospectus of 1793, nor in the lists of works offered for sale in letters to Dawson Turner in 1818, and George Cumberland in 1827.

The earlier Prophetic Books are seven in number, all produced in Illuminated Printing and all bearing the Lambeth imprint, with the exception of the *Visions of the Daughters of Albion*, which may have been engraved before Blake's removal from Poland Street to Hercules Buildings. These seven Prophecies, commonly called the Lambeth Books, are as follows:

VISIONS | OF | THE DAUGHTERS OF | ALBION | The Eye sees more than the Heart knows | Printed by Willm Blake: 1793. Collation: title-page and 'The Argument' 1 plate each, 'Visions' 8 plates, a full-page design of Bromion's cave, sometimes placed last and sometimes as frontispiece, 1 plate; in all 11 plates, about $6\frac{3}{4} \times 4\frac{5}{8}$ inches. The book is advertised in the Prospectus as 'Folio with 8 designs, price 7s. 6d.'

AMERICA | A | PROPHECY | Lambeth | Printed by William Blake in the year 1793. Collation: frontispiece and title-page 1 plate each, 'Preludium' 2 plates, 'A Prophecy' 14 plates; in all 18 plates, about $9\frac{1}{4} \times 6\frac{5}{8}$ inches. Advertised in the Prospectus as a 'Folio with 18 designs, price 10s. 6d.'

EUROPE | A | PROPHECY | Lambeth | Printed by Willm Blake 1794. Collation: frontispiece, the 'Ancient of Days' and title-page 1 plate each, 'Preludium' 2 plates, 'A Prophecy' 11 plates, two full-page illustrations without text representing Plague and Fire, variously arranged in different copies, 2 plates; in all 17 plates, about $9\frac{1}{4} \times 6\frac{5}{8}$ inches.

THE | [FIRST] BOOK | OF | URIZEN | Lambeth Printed by Wm Blake 1794, with the colophon: 'The End of the | first book of Urizen.' Collation: title-page and 'Preludium' 1 plate each, Chap. I–IX [or rather X] 16 plates, ten full-page illustrations without text, variously arranged in different copies, 10 plates; in all 28 plates, about 6×4 inches. The book really contains ten chapters not nine, two consecutive sections being each numbered Chap. IV, instead of IV and V, by an oversight in the engraved

Bibliographical Introduction

original. The British Museum Reading Room copy lacks the plate beginning Chap II, stanza 3, l. 2 'Muster around the bleak deserts', and ending Chap. III, stanza 2, l. 4 'And enormous forms of energy'. This plate, which contains some of the finest stanzas in *Urizen*, has never, so far as I am aware, been previously printed. The word 'First' in the title-page, wanting in most copies, must have been purposely erased by Blake from the stereotype, though inadvertently suffered to remain in the colophon. As Swinburne has conjectured, *The Book of Ahania* may have been originally intended to form the second Book of Urizen.

THE | SONG OF | LOS | Lambeth Printed by W. Blake 1795, with the colophon: 'The Song of Los is Ended | Urizen Wept.' Collation: title-page 1 plate, 'Africa' 2 plates, 'Asia' 2 plates, three full-page illustrations variously arranged in different copies, 3 plates; in all 8 plates about $9 \times 6\frac{7}{8}$ inches.

THE | BOOK OF | LOS | Lambeth | Printed by W. Blake 1795, with the colophon: 'The End of the | Book of Los.' Collation: frontispiece and title-page 1 plate each, 'Los' 3 plates; in all 5 plates.

THE | BOOK OF | AHANIA | Lambeth | Printed by W. Blake 1795. Collation: frontispiece and title-page 1 plate each, 'Ahania' 4 plates; in all 6 plates about $5\frac{3}{8} \times 3\frac{7}{8}$ inches.

Blake's next work, *The Four Zoas*, the longest as well as one of the most significant of his writings, forms a valuable link between the earlier and the later Prophetic Books, indicating as it does in his successive revisions and additions the beginning of a new set of mystical ideas and symbols which we find fully developed in *Milton* and *Jerusalem*. This MS., illustrated by several pencil full-page and smaller designs, is for the most part carefully written in a formal engraver's or neat cursive script, and the date on the title-page, 1797, doubtless denotes the year in which Blake began his fair transcript of a poem probably composed a twelvemonth earlier. This work was rehandled at Felpham, and in that period of new spiritual illumination (*circa* 1800–3) was subjected to many changes, long passages being erased with the knife and laboriously rewritten, while the whole of Night VII was entirely recast in the light of his later tenets.

Bibliographical Introduction

The MS. of *The Four Zoas* consists of 70 separate leaves, 16¼ by 12¾ inches, together with 4 smaller fragments. These 70 loose sheets are made up as follows: drawing paper with watermark 'J. Whatman 1794' 21 sheets, working-proofs of Blake's illustrations to Young's *Night Thoughts* (published 1797) 47 sheets, an old engraving by Blake cut into two and written upon the back only, 2 sheets. Of these 68 sheets, 61 have the text written upon both sides of the paper, that upon the illustrations to *Night Thoughts* occupying the blank rectangular space in the middle of each sheet reserved for the text of Young's poem. *The Four Zoas* is written in ink throughout, the pages, with the exception of the first 14, being unnumbered, though the beginning and end of each 'Night' are indicated by Blake. The title in its first form, as written in ink, reads: 'VALA | OR | THE DEATH and | JUDGEMENT | OF THE | ANCIENT MAN | A Dream | of Nine Nights | by William Blake 1797.' This was afterwards altered in pencil to: 'THE FOUR ZOAS | THE TORMENTS OF LOVE & JEALOUSY IN | THE DEATH AND | JUDGEMENT | OF ALBION THE | ANCIENT MAN | by William Blake 1797.' At the head of the second sheet, the page upon which the poem begins, is a motto from the Greek Testament, Ephes. vi. 12, followed in bold script capitals by the heading 'Vala', which is not here, as on the title-page, erased in favour of *The Four Zoas*. There is no evidence that Blake at any time contemplated engraving and publishing this work in the same manner as the other prophetic writings. Indeed, the extreme care and finish with which the greater part of the book is written point rather to an intention to produce a single perfect copy only in MS. form. This conjecture is supported by the fact that Blake afterwards excerpted long passages from the poem and engraved them as part of *Milton* and *Jerusalem*.

Before dealing with the two later Prophetic Books reference should be made to the lyrical poems written during Blake's stay at the Sussex cottage (1800-3). The earliest of these, in letters to Butts and the Flaxmans, reflect his newly recovered power of joy and vision under the mild influence of 'lovely Felpham'. To

Bibliographical Introduction

the same period belong the earlier lyrics in the second section of the *Rossetti MS.* previously mentioned, as well as those found in the separate smaller autograph collection, which I term the *Pickering MS.* This holograph was known to D. G. Rossetti, who made use of it in preparing his selection of 'Poems hitherto unpublished' for the second volume of Gilchrist's *Life*. Three years later the MS. was purchased by Basil Montagu Pickering, the publisher, who first printed its contents in their entirety, together with the *Songs of Innocence and of Experience*, in R. H. Shepherd's edition of 1866, reprinted 1868 and 1874. After the death of Pickering in 1878 the MS. passed out of the ken of students of Blake, the version printed by Shepherd becoming the standard text. In June 1905, after the lapse of nearly a generation, this unique transcript reappeared in America, having during the interval lain hidden in the Rowfant Library. It now forms part of the collection of Mr. W. A. White. *The Pickering MS.* is a foolscap quarto of 11 leaves of letter-paper, without watermark, paginated 1–22, a modern binding by Bedford now replacing Blake's original paper covers. The contents, here given in full, are evidently fair copies of poems already written in approved form, all the pieces having titles, which with Blake were generally afterthoughts. There is not a single alteration in the first seventeen pages, the few corrections found elsewhere being chiefly capitals added for emphasis. As in the *Rossetti MS.* there is little or no punctuation. The book has no title-page, ascription, or other indication of the circumstances under which, or the person for whom, this special collection was made. The pages are without illustration and contain no prose matter. None of the poems are dated, though there is internal evidence that they must have been composed not later than 1803, though possibly a year or two earlier. 'Mary' was certainly written before August 16 of that year, when Blake in one of his letters to Butts introduces two of its lines in a slightly altered form, and in a different sense. The original drafts of 'The Golden Net' and 'The Grey Monk', which appear in a perfected form in this MS., are found on two leaves of the second section of the *Rossetti MS.* written probably in 1803,

Bibliographical Introduction

while several of the lyrics contain symbolic terms repeated in *Milton* and *Jerusalem*, the engraving of which books was begun in the following year.

Turning next to these two epics, the greatest of the Prophetic Books, as well as the longest of the works produced by Illuminated Printing, we may first note a passage in a letter to Butts written from Felpham, April 25, 1803:

'But none can know the spiritual acts of my three years' slumber on the banks of ocean, unless he has seen them in the spirit, or unless he should read my long poem descriptive of those acts; for I have in these years composed an immense number of verses on one grand theme, similar to Homer's *Iliad* or Milton's *Paradise Lost*, the persons and machinery entirely new to the inhabitants of earth (some of the persons excepted). I have written this poem from immediate dictation, twelve or sometimes twenty or thirty lines at a time, without premeditation, and even against my will. The time it has taken in writing was thus rendered non-existent, and an immense poem exists which seems to be the labour of a long life, all produced without labour or study. I mention this to show you what I think the grand reason of my being brought down here.'

Again, in another letter to the same friend dated July 6, 1803, Blake writes:

'Thus I hope that all our three years' trouble ends in good luck at last, and shall be forgot by my affections, and only remembered by my understanding; to be a memento in time to come, and to speak to future generations by a sublime allegory, which is now perfectly completed into a grand poem. I may praise it, since I dare not pretend to be any other than the secretary; the authors are in eternity. I consider it as the grandest poem that this world contains. Allegory addressed to the intellectual powers, while it is altogether hidden from the corporeal understanding, is my definition of the most sublime poetry. It is also somewhat in the same manner defined by Plato. This poem shall, by Divine assistance, be progressively printed and ornamented with prints, and given to the Public. But of this work I take care to say little to Mr. Hayley, since he is as much averse to my poetry as he is to a chapter in the Bible. He knows that I have writ it, for I have shown it to him

Bibliographical Introduction

and he has read part by his own desire, and has looked with sufficient contempt to enhance my opinion of it.'

There is no general agreement as to whether these passages refer to *Milton* or to *Jerusalem*. If exclusively to either, it would seem more probable that the latter was intended, for though it is true that *Milton* deals more directly with Blake's actual life at Felpham, yet it is clear that it cannot by any stretch of language be called an 'immense poem', while the close resemblance of the first-quoted passage with the opening words of the address 'To the Public' in *Jerusalem*, would seem rather to identify the work here described with the latter. There is room however for a third hypothesis which reconciles both theories, namely, that Blake in the words quoted refers to the whole body of visionary verse composed at Felpham as a single great poem; that this original MS. was used, like *The Four Zoas*, as a common quarrying-ground for the two books; and that *Milton* and *Jerusalem*, as we know them, are merely selected portions of a more complete gospel.

In no case can there be any doubt that *Milton* is the earlier of the two Prophecies, or that it recounts in all their freshness Blake's first spiritual experiences at Felpham. The poem is indeed—a thing rare in Blake—redolent of the country-side and its new images, the plough and harrow, insect life, the scent of flowers, the song of birds, and the aspects of the sky, conceived in the same spirit of exaltation which characterizes the letters to Butts and Flaxman. *Milton*, like *Jerusalem*, is dated 1804, the title-page reading 'MIL|TON a Poem | in 2 Books | The Author | & Printer W. Blake | 1804 | To Justify the Ways of God to Men'. A misreading of the words 'in 2 Books' as 'in 12 Books' has given rise to the view expressed by some writers that *Milton* was at first intended as a much longer work. In its complete form the book consisted (as we learn from Blake's letter to Dawson Turner dated June 9, 1818) of 50 plates about $6\frac{1}{4} \times 4\frac{1}{4}$ inches, which consequently must have contained the title-page and 'Preface' 1 plate each, 'Book the First' 26 plates (numbered ff. 3–28), 'Book the Second' 17 plates (numbered ff. 29–45) together with the 5 extra leaves (numbered 3* 5* 8* 17* 32*).

Bibliographical Introduction

In *Jerusalem* even more than in *Milton*, we meet with the complete statement of Blake's fully developed system of mythology, and although both poems form part of the great Felpham inspiration, the later origin of the former is readily demonstrable on grounds of symbolism alone. The title-page of this book reads: 'JERUSALEM | THE | EMANATION OF | THE GIANT | ALBION | 1804 | Printed by W. Blake Sth Molton St.' *Jerusalem* consists of 100 plates, about $9 \times 6\frac{1}{2}$ inches, the collation being as follows: frontispiece, title-page, 'To the Public' 1 plate each (ff. 1–3); 'Chap. 1' 22 plates (ff. 4–25); frontispiece to Chap. 2 (f. 26), 'To the Jews' (f. 27); 'Chap. 2' 23 plates (ff. 28–50); frontispiece to Chap. 3 (f. 51), 'To the Deists' (f. 52); 'Chap. 3' 23 plates (ff. 53–75); frontispiece to Chap. 4 (f. 76), 'To the Christians' (f. 77); 'Chap. 4' 22 plates (ff. 78–99); full-page end-piece (f. 100).

Blake, as we have seen, began the engraving of both works shortly after his return to London, but when either was finished or published is a matter of inference or conjecture. Probably the engraving of the earlier work *Milton* was first undertaken and completed in intervals of leisure, instead of both books being proceeded with simultaneously. This would account for the difference between the two poems, since during these years Blake doubtless, according to his usual habit, made many alterations in the manuscript or only partially engraved *Jerusalem*.

Between the years 1805 and 1810 we find more than one allusion in Blake's letters and writings to the forthcoming publication of a work descriptive of his experiences at Felpham, but, as before, it is anything but clear whether these passages refer to the same book, and if so whether *Milton* or *Jerusalem* is intended. In a letter to Hayley dated December 11, 1805, Blake says: 'It will not be long before I shall be able to present the full history of my spiritual sufferings to the dwellers upon earth, and of the spiritual victories obtained for me by my friends.' In 1809, in the account of his picture of 'The Ancient Britons' (*Descriptive Catalogue*, pp. 41–2) he tells us 'The Strong Man represents the human sublime; the Beautiful Man represents the human pathetic, which was in the wars of Eden divided into male and female;

Bibliographical Introduction

the Ugly Man represents the human reason. They were originally one man, who was fourfold; he was self-divided, and his real humanity slain on the stems of generation, and the form of the fourth was like the Son of God. How he became divided is a subject of great sublimity and pathos. The Artist has written it under inspiration, and will, if God please, publish it; it is voluminous, and contains the ancient history of Britain, and the world of Satan and of Adam.' This is the very theme of *Jerusalem* and certainly can only refer to that work. We may conclude, therefore, that the engraving of the earlier epic had been finished before May 1809, and since the three known copies all bear the watermark 1808, and cannot have been produced earlier, it is evident that *Milton* was completed either in that year or in the following spring, the extra leaves (ff. 3* 5* 8* 17* 32*) which occur in the Beckford copy now in the Lenox Library being a subsequent addition. It is not, however, until some ten years later that we meet with a definite reference to *Milton* in the letter to Dawson Turner dated June 9, 1818, where it forms the last of a list of works offered by Blake for sale, being priced at 10 guineas.

The publication of *Jerusalem* to which Blake hopefully looked forward in 1809 was delayed or postponed for over a decade. Clearly it was still in the author's hands when in 1810 in the 'Public Address' or *Advertisements to Blake's Canterbury Pilgrims* (*Rossetti MS.*, p. 52) he writes: 'The manner in which my character has been blasted these thirty years, both as an artist and a man, may be seen particularly in a Sunday paper called the *Examiner*, published in Beaufort's Buildings; and the manner in which I have rooted out the nest of villains will be seen in a poem concerning my three years' Herculean labours at Felpham, which I shall soon publish.' Indeed from Blake himself we hear nothing further of *Jerusalem* until the year of his death, when in a letter to Cumberland dated April 12, 1827, he says: 'The last work I produced is a poem entitled *Jerusalem, the Emanation of the Giant Albion*, but find that to print it will cost my time the amount of twenty guineas. One I have finished, but it is not likely I shall find a customer for it.' By 'finishing',

Bibliographical Introduction

Blake here undoubtedly means the final process of his Illuminated Printing—i.e. the tinting of the illustrations in water-colour—while his reference to the cost of printing another copy seems to establish the fact that he himself had produced only one complete set of impressions from the plates.[1] This must have been the coloured copy described by 'Janus Weathercock' [T. G. Wainwright], which afterwards was acquired or appropriated by Tatham, and now, bound up with the latter's *Life* of Blake, is in a private library. In Wainwright's article contributed to the *London Magazine* (Sept. 1820) he writes:

'Talking of articles, my learned friend Dr. Tobias Ruddicombe, M.D., is, at my earnest entreaty, casting a tremendous piece of ordnance, an *eighty-eight pounder*! which he proposeth to fire off in your next. It is an account of an ancient, newly discovered, illuminated manuscript, which has to name "Jerusalem, the Emanation of the Giant Albion". It contains a good deal anent one "*Los*", who, it appears, is now and hath been from the Creation, the sole and four-fold dominator of the celebrated city of *Golgonooza*! The doctor assures me that the redemption of mankind hangs on the universal diffusion of the doctrines broached in this MS.'

We may safely assume that this copy was not in existence in June 1818, or the author would have included it in the list supplied to Dawson Turner. It is clear therefore that *Jerusalem* must have been published (if publication it can be called) between that date and September 1820, and since the watermark bears the latter date, it seems practically certain that it was in this year Blake's great epic first saw the light.[2]

With *Milton* and *Jerusalem* Blake's prophetic scriptures draw to a close, though one or two short leaflets of the same character still remain to be noticed. The little book of emblems, *For the Sexes:*

[1] Tatham probably produced others. See his Memoir of Blake reprinted in Russell's edition of the *Letters*, p. 44: 'The author of this is now in possession of . . . a very great number of copperplates, of whom impressions may be obtained.'

[2] This view is further confirmed by the same watermark 1820 of a coloured full-page illustration (f. 51) in the possession of the Linnell Trustees (Russell's *Catalogue of Loan Exhibition of Works by William Blake*, 1913, no. 101).

Bibliographical Introduction

The Gates of Paradise, written *circa* 1810, I have already dealt with, the others being the three pieces to which Gilchrist gave the name 'Sibylline Leaves'. The first of these consists of a series of aphorisms on the identity of art and religion, surrounding a line-engraving of the 'Laocoon', $10\frac{1}{4} \times 8\frac{1}{2}$ inches, with the imprint 'Drawn & Engraved by William Blake'. On Oct. 1, 1815, Blake had engraved for Rees' *Cyclopaedia* a plate in stipple of the same group, and this mystical version, therefore, may be dated a year or two later. We have next a small tract in relief-engraving on a single plate, measuring $4\frac{1}{2} \times 3\frac{7}{8}$ inches, containing two manifestoes '*On Homer's Poetry*' and '*On Virgil*', which perhaps, as a development of the same theme, may also be assigned to 1817 *circa*. Latest of these leaflets, addressed or dedicated 'to Lord Byron in the Wilderness' and doubtless suggested by the recent appearance of *Cain : a Mystery*,[1] is the short but noble dramatic poem where, as in the stage direction, 'the curtain falls' on Blake's writings, and the long series of Visions and Prophecies comes to an end not without befitting majesty and solemn beauty. The title of this little work, which is engraved upon two plates about $4\frac{7}{8} \times 6\frac{9}{16}$ inches, runs : 'THE GHOST OF ABEL | A Revelation In the Visions of Jehovah | Seen by William Blake.' The colophon is dated 1822, and the artist's note that 'W. Blake's Original Stereotype was 1788' seems intended to record the *hic jacet* of his Illuminated Printing.

Turning back to the few remaining works written between the inception and completion of *Jerusalem*, in addition to those previously described in my account of the second section of the *Rossetti MS.*, we come first to one of Blake's most characteristic writings, the catalogue of his pictures in the exhibition of 1809. This rare book is a duodecimo of vi+66 pages, measuring $7\frac{1}{8} \times 4\frac{1}{4}$ inches, with title-page reading : 'A | DESCRIPTIVE CATALOGUE | OF | PICTURES, | POETICAL AND HISTORICAL IN-VENTIONS, | Painted by | William Blake, | in | Water Colours, | Being the Ancient Method of | Fresco Painting Restored : |

[1] Blake some five years earlier had made this the subject of one of his engravings. See W. M. R.'s 'Annotated Lists' (Gil. *Life,* ii, p. 280).

xlvi

Bibliographical Introduction

and | Drawings, | For Public Inspection, | and for | Sale by Private Contract. | London : | Printed by D. N. Shury, 7, Berwick-Street, Soho, | for J. Blake, 28, Broad-Street, Golden-Square | 1809. | '
Here, among fierce outbursts against certain repugnant schools of art, we meet, in Rossetti's phrase, with many 'sudden great things, greatly said', as well as with the keen critical insight exemplified in Blake's account of his 'Canterbury Pilgrims', a piece three years later reprinted in pamphlet form by the publisher Harris with the title: *The Prologue and Characters of Chaucer's Pilgrims*, 12mo 1812.

The Catalogue is, without doubt, the work referred to by Blake in a letter to Cumberland dated December 19, 1808. He there writes : 'I have, however, the satisfaction to inform you that I have myself begun to print an account of my various inventions in Art, for which I have procured a publisher, and am determined to pursue the plan of publishing, that I may get printed without disarranging my time, which in future must alone be designing and painting. When I have got my work printed I will send it you first of anybody.'[1] That this passage can only allude to the *Descriptive Catalogue* is further shown in Blake's printed Prospectus of his intended engraving of the Canterbury Pilgrims, dated May 15, 1809, where, speaking of fresco-painting, he says : 'The art has been lost : I have recovered it. How this was done, will be told, together with the whole process, in a work on Art, now in the press.'

Besides the *Descriptive Catalogue* Blake wrote two additional and somewhat similar addresses on art which deserve further mention. The earlier of these is the piece commonly known as the 'Public Address', which may well be that other 'work on Painting' mentioned two years earlier in the account of his 'Spiritual Form of Pitt guiding Behemoth'.[2] This was evidently intended

---

[1] *Letters*, p. 206, ed. Russell, who however differs from me in regarding this as a reference to some work which was never published.

[2] *Descriptive Catalogue*, No II : 'Let the works of modern Artists since Rubens' time witness the villainy of some one at that time, who first brought Oil Painting into general opinion and practice : since which we have never had a Picture painted, that could show itself by the side of an earlier produc-

Bibliographical Introduction

to accompany Blake's engraving of his picture of the 'Canterbury Pilgrims', completed on October 8, 1810. It is not clear that it was ever printed in leaflet form, but that Blake had at least contemplated doing so is seen from the entry on p. 56 of the *Rossetti MS.*: 'This day is Publish'd Advertisements to Blake's Canterbury Pilgrims from Chaucer, containing anecdotes of Artists.' The other piece called by Gilchrist, or rather by D. G. Rossetti, '*A Vision of the Last Judgement*,' for which the author's own title reads *For the year 1810: Additions to Blake's Catalogue of Pictures, &c.*, was similarly designed to expound the symbolism of Blake's great painting of this subject. As the picture does not seem to have been publicly exhibited, we may assume that the description itself was never published. Both this and the preceding work are known to us only in the rough draft scattered through the last pages of the *Rossetti MS.*

To the same MS. source we owe our sole knowledge of two pieces —*Barry: a Poem* and the *Book of Moonlight*—both of which would appear to have been satires upon the English encouragement of art, written *circa* 1808-9. The incomplete lines on patronage in the *MS. Book* beginning 'I asked my dear friend Orator Prig' are followed by Blake's note 'to come in *Barry: a Poem*'; and it may have been his intention to unite under this title the various fragments on the same theme and in the same rough measure jotted down in the later section of the *Rossetti MS.* Allusions to Barry, who died in 1806, occur in Blake's marginalia to Reynolds' *Discourses*[1] and in the *Advertisements* or 'Public Address',[2] where the same views are expressed in prose. Of the *Book of Moonlight* nothing is known beyond the entry on p. 46 of the *MS. Book*:

tion. Whether Rubens or Vandyke, or both, were guilty of this villainy, is to be enquired in *another work on Painting*, and who first forged the silly story and known falsehood about John of Bruges inventing oil-colours: in the meantime let it be observed, that before Vandyke's time and in his time all the genuine Pictures are on Plaster or Whiting grounds, and none since.'

[1] Vol. i, p. 120.
[2] *Rossetti MS.*, pp. 23 and 53.

Bibliographical Introduction

> 'Delicate Hands & Heads will never appear
> While Titian &c——

as in the Book of Moonlight, p. 5.' This poem, therefore, which doubtless presented in a versified form Blake's contempt for the Venetian school, must, as the '&c' shows, have been transcribed elsewhere, perhaps from lack of space in the *Rossetti MS.*

There only remains to be dismissed a work said to be in Blake's handwriting, though not perhaps of his composition. On these points I can speak with no certainty, not having been afforded an opportunity of seeing the MS., which is the property of Mr. Buxton Forman. The title of this piece, some description of which has been given by Mr. Arthur Symons in his *William Blake* (pp. 140–143), reads: GENESIS | THE SEVEN DAYS | OF THE CREATED WORLD. | The poem begins:

> Thou Sire of Heaven & of the Eternal Sire
> Eternal Son & Offspring Increate
> Of the unchangeful Mind the only birth'

and ends (according to Symons) somewhere about the line 200:

> Since whatsoe'er benificence supreme
> Has [*May* del.] fill'd, his heavenly praise may also fill
> Adorn the whole & with its radiance gild
> Thro' all its midmost & extremest parts.'

The hand (for which Mr. Symons seems to vouch) may indeed be the hand of Esau, but the voice is that of some Augustan Jacob, and it is hard to believe that these lines could have been composed by Blake even under the malign influence of Hayley. Nor, on the other hand, can they be readily identified with the 'Vision of Genesis' written 'in a style resembling the Bible', which the poet read to Crabb Robinson in the year preceding his death.[1]

---

[1] See Crabb Robinson, *Diary*, Feb. 18, 1826: 'He showed me his Vision (for so it may be called) of Genesis—"as understood by a Christian Visionary," in which, in a style resembling the Bible, the spirit is given. He read a passage at random. It was striking. He will not print any more.' Also *Reminiscences*, Feb. 19, 1826: 'He showed me his Version of Genesis,'

Bibliographical Introduction

In this, as in my former book, I desire to record my great indebtedness to those owners of manuscripts and original editions who have courteously placed them at my service. To Mr. Herbert Linnell, the grandson of Blake's friend and patron, my gratitude is due not only for his constant interest and friendly assistance in this, and another projected work, but also for the loan of some of the chief treasures in the family collection, and the generous desire of himself and his co-trustee to withhold nothing that would render this edition more accurate and complete. In November 1908 Mr. Linnell hastened to inform me of his rediscovery of the unique copy of Blake's *French Revolution*, and with a fine liberality lent me the original, and allowed me to print it here for the first time. I owe also to Mr. Linnell's kindness the loan of the MS. of *The Four Zoas*, and of the rare tractate here printed with the title *All Religions are One*. I have to thank him, moreover, for the text of the proem to *Europe*, found only in the Linnell copy, for photographs of the title-pages of some of the engraved books here reproduced, as well as for much helpful information in his frequent letters to me.

To Mr. W. A. White of Brooklyn, New York, to whose exact and careful transcripts of the poems in the *Rossetti MS.* my former edition owed a great part of any value it possessed, I am again under a further obligation for a photograph of the title-page of his unique copy of *The Book of Ahania*.

To Mr. J. P. R. Wallis, himself a learned Blake scholar, and now, in collaboration with Mr. D. J. Sloss, engaged upon an annotated edition of the Prophetic Books and a complete concordance of Blake's symbolism, I owe the photograph of a page of *The Book of Urizen* lacking in the British Museum copy, and omitted in all existing texts.

I am indebted to my friend Mr. A. G. B. Russell, author of the descriptive catalogue of Blake's Engravings and editor of Blake's Letters, for an important emendation in the 'Lines to Mrs. Anna

for so it may be called, as understood by a Christian Visionary. He read a wild passage in a sort of Bible style. "I shall print no more" he said.' (Symons' *William Blake*, pp. 267 and 302).

Bibliographical Introduction

Flaxman' (l. 10)—the original of which I had before been unable to trace—and for the correction of two misreadings in 'The Everlasting Gospel' (γ, l. 43) and 'The Keys of the Gates' (l. 13). Mr. Thomas Wright of Olney has likewise drawn my attention to a mistake, here corrected, in the lines beginning: 'I will tell you what Joseph of Arimathea.' I have to thank Mr. Geoffrey Keynes for a note respecting the Flaxman copy of the *Poetical Sketches*, containing valuable information afterwards embodied in his paper contributed to *Notes and Queries* (11 S. II, Sept. 24, 1910); for the loan of his collations of copies of *There is No Natural Religion*; and for a transcript of three early cancelled leaves of *America*, which unfortunately reached me too late for incorporation in the present book.

Mr. Forman, while holding the view that any external attempt to pronounce an opinion as to the authenticity of the MS. entitled *Genesis* would be premature, has permitted me to quote his transcript of the opening and closing lines of this fragment.

I very gladly welcome this opportunity of correcting the error made by me in my previous book in assuming that the emendations of Blake's editors extended in one instance to the interpolation of a line intended to link together two separate epigrams (*Rossetti MS.*, nos. XCV and XCVI, ed. 1905). This mistake, which did Mr. W. M. Rossetti a grave injustice, was pointed out by him in a most friendly letter, and on a further scrutiny by Mr. White the line in question was found, written obscurely in pencil and upside down among some prose matter, to which unless closely examined it seemed to belong. I hope I make *amende* by restoring these seven lines to the form in which they were given by Mr. Rossetti in the Aldine Edition.

Readers of this Introduction who may have been impressed by the weight of typographical technicality in my description of the unique copy of *The French Revolution*, upon p. xxxii, should accredit the greater part of the detailed evidence there adduced to the expert knowledge of Mr. Horace Hart, to whom Mr. R. W. Chapman kindly submitted my conjecture that the example in question was merely a proof, and not part of an edition.

Bibliographical Introduction

In conclusion it is a pleasure to acknowledge the help of Mr. J. S. Munday, Junior Assistant in the University Library, in reading the proofs of the Lyrical Poems, and that of Mr. Wallis in checking my text of the Prophetic Books.

J. S.

UNIVERSITY OF LIVERPOOL.
October 1913.

CHRONOLOGICAL TABLE

1757   William Blake, third child of James and Catherine Blake, born at 28 Broad Street, Carnaby Market, Golden Square, November 28.

1760   Birth of his brother John, 'the evil one', March 20.

1762   Birth of his brother Robert, July 11.

1764   Birth of his sister Catherine Elizabeth, January 7.

1765   Childish visions.

1767   Begins the study of art at Pars' Drawing School in the Strand.

1768 or –69   Earliest of the *Poetical Sketches* written.

1771   Apprenticed to Basire, engraver to the Society of Antiquaries.

1773   Employed in sketching monuments in Westminster Abbey. Engraves his plate of 'Joseph of Arimathea among the rocks of Albion'.

1776 or –77   Latest of the *Poetical Sketches* written.

1777 *circa*   Seven-Page MS. containing the poem called 'The Passions' and another piece.

1778   Termination of apprenticeship.

Studies for a short time under Moser in the Antique School of the newly-founded Royal Academy.

Begins water-colour painting with his 'Penance of Jane Shore'.

1779   Employed as engraver by J. Johnson and other booksellers.

1780   Makes the acquaintance of Stothard and by him introduced to Flaxman.

Meets Fuseli, his neighbour in Broad Street.

Exhibits for the first time at the Royal Academy.

1781   Falls in love with 'a lively little girl' named Polly Wood, who rejects him.

Recuperates from illness at Kew, in the house of a market-gardener named Boucher, and is consoled by his daughter Catherine.

1782   Marries Catherine Boucher (or Butcher) at St. Mary's, Battersea, August 18.

Commences housekeeping in lodgings at 23 Green Street, Leicester Fields.

Introduced by Flaxman to Mrs. Mathew, and becomes for a while a frequenter of her salon at 27 Rathbone Place.

1783   *Poetical Sketches* printed at the expense of Flaxman and the Rev. Henry Mathew.

Chronological Table

1784 Death of Blake's father, July.
Aided by Mrs. Mathew, opens a print-seller's shop at 27 Broad Street in partnership with Parker, a former fellow apprentice. Takes his younger brother Robert as pupil.

1784 *circa* Writes *An Island in the Moon*, containing earliest of *Songs of Innocence*, and foreshadowing a scheme of 'Illuminated Printing'.

1787 Death of Robert, February.
Gives up print-shop, dissolving partnership with Parker, and removing to 28 Poland Street.

1788 'W. Blake's original stereotype,' i.e. first use of new process of relief-engraving employed in his 'Illuminated Printing'.
Quaere, engraves the two tractates entitled *There is No Natural Religion* and *All Religions are One*.

1788-9 *circa* Marginalia to Lavater's *Aphorisms*, published 1788.
Marginalia to Swedenborg's *Wisdom of Angels*, published 1788.
Writes *Tiriel*.

1789 *Songs of Innocence*.
Book of Thel.

1790 *circa* Begins to use the Sketch-Book (*Rossetti MS.*) for illustrations.

1790 *Marriage of Heaven and Hell*.

1791 *The French Revolution*, Book the First, set up in type by Johnson with a view to publication.

1792 Death of Blake's mother, aet. 70, September.
Warns Thomas Paine of impending arrest.

1792 *circa* *A Song of Liberty*.
Quaere, engraves *Outhoun*.

1793 Begins to use Sketch-Book as a note-book for poetry.
Visions of the Daughters of Albion.
Removes to 13 Hercules Buildings, Lambeth (now 23 Hercules Road).
Note in *Rossetti MS.*: 'I say I shan't live five years. And if I live one it will be a Wonder,' June.
Publishes two small books of engravings: *The History of England* and *For Children: The Gates of Paradise*.
Sketches title-pages for the *Bible of Hell*, and *For Children: The Gates of Hell*.
America: a Prophecy.
Prospectus 'To the Public' giving a list of 'Works now published and on sale at Mr. Blake's', October 10.

1793 *circa* Makes the acquaintance of future patron, Thomas Butts.

1794 *Songs of Experience*.
Europe: a Prophecy.
The [First] Book of Urizen.

1795 *The Song of Los*.

Chronological Table

1795 *The Book of Los.*
The Book of Ahania.

1796 Designs for Bürger's *Leonora.*
Engaged on designs and engravings to Young's *Night Thoughts* (published 1797).

1797 Begins to transcribe and illustrate his fair copy of *The Four Zoas.*

1797-9 Suffers from lack of employment as engraver. Turns to designs in water-colour. Commissions from Butts.

1800 Introduced by Flaxman to Hayley.
Leaves Lambeth and settles at Felpham, September.
Resumes use of Sketch-Book as a note-book for poetry.

1800-3 Works for Hayley.
Letters to Flaxman and Butts.
Revises *The Four Zoas.*
Begins the composition of *Milton* and *Jerusalem.*

1801-3 *circa* Writes poems in *Pickering MS.*

1803 Strained relations with Hayley; determines to leave Felpham, April.
Affray with dragoon; warrant issued for his arrest on charge of sedition, August.
Returns to London, to rooms at 17 South Molton Street, September.

1804 Tried at Chichester Quarter Sessions and acquitted, January 11.
Begins engraving *Milton* and *Jerusalem.*

1804-5 Letters to Hayley.

1805 Designs for Blair's *Grave*, purchased by Cromek, who, in violation of his agreement, gives the engraving to Schiavonetti.

1806 Malkin's account of Blake in *A Father's Memoirs of his Child*, January 4.
Writes epigram 'Grown old in love from seven till seven times seven'.

1806 *circa* Cromek sees Blake's design 'The Canterbury Pilgrims' and commissions Stothard to paint a picture on the same subject.

1807 Note in *Rossetti MS.*: 'Tuesday Jany 20, 1807, between Two & seven in the Evening, Despair.'
Stothard's 'Canterbury Pilgrimage' exhibited. Final rupture with Cromek, May.

1807-8 Designs in illustration of *Paradise Lost.*

1807-10 Epigrams in *Rossetti MS.*

1808 Completes water-colour painting of 'The Last Judgement' for Countess of Egremont, February 18.
Publication of Blake's Illustrations to Blair's *Grave*, Summer.
Review of same in Hunt's *Examiner*, August 7.
Marginalia to Reynolds' *Discourses.*

1808-9 *Quaere*, writes *Barry: a Poem* and *Book of Moonlight.*
Completes engraving of *Milton.*

Chronological Table

1809   Exhibition of pictures at 28 Broad Street, May to September.
Prospectus of engraving of 'Canterbury Pilgrims,' May 15.
Descriptive Catalogue.
Critique of Exhibition in *Examiner*, September 17.

1810   Note in *Rossetti MS.* : 'Found the Word Golden,' May 23.
Drafts in *Rossetti MS.* 'Advertisements to Blake's Canterbury Pilgrims from Chaucer containing anecdotes of Artists' (*Public Address*).
Publication of his engraving of the 'Canterbury Pilgrims', October 8.
Drafts in *Rossetti MS.* a description of his painting of 'The Last Judgement' entitled *For the year 1810 · Additions to Blake's Catalogue of Pictures &c.*

1810 *circa*   'The Everlasting Gospel.'
Re-issues *Gates of Paradise* (For the Sexes), with Prologue, Epilogue, and Keys of the Gates.

1811–17   Years of obscurity.

1812   Reprints *The Prologue and Characters of Chaucer's Pilgrims.*

1817 *circa*   Engraves leaflets *Laocoon*, and *On Homer's Poetry* [and] *On Virgil.*

1818   Introduced by Cumberland to Linnell, June.

1819   Introduced by Linnell to Varley.
Executes the 'Visionary Heads'.

1820   Begins large 'fresco' of 'The Last Judgement'.
Designs and executes woodcuts for Thornton's *Pastorals of Virgil.*
Completes engraving of *Jerusalem.*

1821   Removes to 3 Fountain Court, Strand.

1821 *circa*   Executes water-colour designs illustrating the *Book of Job* for Butts.

1822   Receives a donation of £25 from the Royal Academy.
The Ghost of Abel.

1823   Commissioned by Linnell to paint and engrave replicas of the designs for *Job*, March 25.

1825   Completion of engravings for *Job*, March (published March, 1826).
First meeting with Crabb Robinson, December 10.

1825 *circa*   Meets Tatham.

1825–6   Executes designs in illustration of Dante for Linnell.

1826   Attacks of illness, February and May.

1827   Dies, August 12.

1831   Death of Catherine Blake, October 18.

POETICAL

SKETCHES.

By W. B.

LONDON:

Printed in the Year M DCC LXXXIII.

MISCELLANEOUS POEMS

To Spring

O thou with dewy locks, who lookest down
Thro' the clear windows of the morning, turn
Thine angel eyes upon our western isle,
Which in full choir hails thy approach, O Spring!

The hills tell each other, and the list'ning
Valleys hear; all our longing eyes are turnèd
Up to thy bright pavilions: issue forth,
And let thy holy feet visit our clime.

Come o'er the eastern hills, and let our winds
Kiss thy perfumèd garments; let us taste
Thy morn and evening breath; scatter thy pearls
Upon our love-sick land that mourns for thee.

O deck her forth with thy fair fingers; pour
Thy soft kisses on her bosom; and put
Thy golden crown upon her languish'd head,
Whose modest tresses were bound up for thee.

To Summer

O thou who passest thro' our valleys in
Thy strength, curb thy fierce steeds, allay the heat
That flames from their large nostrils! thou, O Summer,
Oft pitched'st here thy golden tent, and oft
Beneath our oaks hast slept, while we beheld
With joy thy ruddy limbs and flourishing hair.

Poetical Sketches

Beneath our thickest shades we oft have heard
Thy voice, when noon upon his fervid car
Rode o'er the deep of heaven; beside our springs
Sit down, and in our mossy valleys, on   10
Some bank beside a river clear, throw thy
Silk draperies off, and rush into the stream:
Our valleys love the Summer in his pride.

Our bards are fam'd who strike the silver wire:
Our youth are bolder than the southern swains: 15
Our maidens fairer in the sprightly dance:
We lack not songs, nor instruments of joy,
Nor echoes sweet, nor waters clear as heaven,
Nor laurel wreaths against the sultry heat.

To Autumn

O Autumn, laden with fruit, and stainèd
With the blood of the grape, pass not, but sit
Beneath my shady roof; there thou may'st rest,
And tune thy jolly voice to my fresh pipe,
And all the daughters of the year shall dance!   5
Sing now the lusty song of fruits and flowers.

'The narrow bud opens her beauties to
The sun, and love runs in her thrilling veins;
Blossoms hang round the brows of Morning, and
Flourish down the bright cheek of modest Eve,   10
Till clust'ring Summer breaks forth into singing,
And feather'd clouds strew flowers round her head.

'The spirits of the air live on the smells
Of fruit; and Joy, with pinions light, roves round
The gardens or sits singing in the trees.'   15
Thus sang the jolly Autumn as he sat;
Then rose, girded himself, and o'er the bleak
Hills fled from our sight; but left his golden load.

To the Evening Star

To Winter

'O Winter! bar thine adamantine doors:
The north is thine; there hast thou built thy dark
Deep-founded habitation. Shake not thy roofs,
Nor bend thy pillars with thine iron car.'

He hears me not, but o'er the yawning deep   5
Rides heavy; his storms are unchain'd, sheathèd
In ribbèd steel; I dare not lift mine eyes,
For he hath rear'd his sceptre o'er the world.

Lo! now the direful monster, whose skin clings
To his strong bones, strides o'er the groaning rocks: 10
He withers all in silence, and in his hand
Unclothes the earth, and freezes up frail life.

He takes his seat upon the cliffs,—the mariner
Cries in vain. Poor little wretch, that deal'st
With storms!—till heaven smiles, and the monster   15
Is driv'n yelling to his caves beneath mount Hecla.

To the Evening Star

Thou fair-hair'd angel of the evening,
Now, whilst the sun rests on the mountains, light
Thy bright torch of love; thy radiant crown
Put on, and smile upon our evening bed!
Smile on our loves, and while thou drawest the   5
Blue curtains of the sky, scatter thy silver dew
On every flower that shuts its sweet eyes
In timely sleep. Let thy west wind sleep on
The lake; speak silence with thy glimmering eyes,
And wash the dusk with silver. Soon, full soon,   10
Dost thou withdraw; then the wolf rages wide,
And the lion glares thro' the dun forest:
The fleeces of our flocks are cover'd with
Thy sacred dew: protect them with thine influence.

Poetical Sketches

To Morning

    O holy virgin! clad in purest white,
    Unlock heav'n's golden gates, and issue forth;
    Awake the dawn that sleeps in heaven; let light
    Rise from the chambers of the east, and bring
    The honey'd dew that cometh on waking day.   5
    O radiant morning, salute the sun
    Rous'd like a huntsman to the chase, and with
    Thy buskin'd feet appear upon our hills.

Fair Elenor

    The bell struck one, and shook the silent tower;
    The graves give up their dead: fair Elenor
    Walk'd by the castle gate, and lookèd in.
    A hollow groan ran thro' the dreary vaults.

    She shriek'd aloud, and sunk upon the steps,   5
    On the cold stone her pale cheeks.   Sickly smells
    Of death issue as from a sepulchre,
    And all is silent but the sighing vaults.

    Chill Death withdraws his hand, and she revives;
    Amaz'd, she finds herself upon her feet,   10
    And, like a ghost, thro' narrow passages
    Walking, feeling the cold walls with her hands.

    Fancy returns, and now she thinks of bones
    And grinning skulls, and corruptible death
    Wrapp'd in his shroud; and now fancies she hears   15
    Deep sighs, and sees pale sickly ghosts gliding.

    At length, no fancy but reality
    Distracts her.   A rushing sound, and the feet
    Of one that fled, approaches.—Ellen stood
    Like a dumb statue, froze to stone with fear.   20

Fair Elenor

The wretch approaches, crying: 'The deed is done;
Take this, and send it by whom thou wilt send;
It is my life—send it to Elenor:—
He's dead, and howling after me for blood!

'Take this,' he cried; and thrust into her arms   25
A wet napkin, wrapp'd about; then rush'd
Past, howling: she receiv'd into her arms
Pale death, and follow'd on the wings of fear.

They pass'd swift thro' the outer gate; the wretch,
Howling, leap'd o'er the wall into the moat,   30
Stifling in mud. Fair Ellen pass'd the bridge,
And heard a gloomy voice cry 'Is it done?'

As the deer wounded, Ellen flew over
The pathless plain; as the arrows that fly
By night, destruction flies, and strikes in darkness.   35
She fled from fear, till at her house arriv'd.

Her maids await her; on her bed she falls,
That bed of joy, where erst her lord hath press'd:
'Ah, woman's fear!' she cried; 'ah, cursèd duke!
Ah, my dear lord! ah, wretched Elenor!   40

'My lord was like a flower upon the brows
Of lusty May! Ah, life as frail as flower!
O ghastly death! withdraw thy cruel hand,
Seek'st thou that flow'r to deck thy horrid temples?

'My lord was like a star in highest heav'n   45
Drawn down to earth by spells and wickedness;
My lord was like the opening eyes of day
When western winds creep softly o'er the flowers;

'But he is darken'd; like the summer's noon
Clouded; fall'n like the stately tree, cut down;   50
The breath of heaven dwelt among his leaves.
O Elenor, weak woman, fill'd with woe!'

Poetical Sketches

Thus having spoke, she raisèd up her head,
And saw the bloody napkin by her side,
Which in her arms she brought; and now, tenfold
More terrifièd, saw it unfold itself.

Her eyes were fix'd; the bloody cloth unfolds,
Disclosing to her sight the murder'd head
Of her dear lord, all ghastly pale, clotted
With gory blood; it groan'd, and thus it spake:

'O Elenor, I am thy husband's head,
Who, sleeping on the stones of yonder tower,
Was 'reft of life by the accursèd duke!
A hirèd villain turn'd my sleep to death!

'O Elenor, beware the cursèd duke;
O give not him thy hand, now I am dead;
He seeks thy love; who, coward, in the night,
Hirèd a villain to bereave my life.'

She sat with dead cold limbs, stiffen'd to stone;
She took the gory head up in her arms;
She kiss'd the pale lips; she had no tears to shed;
She hugg'd it to her breast, and groan'd her last.

Song

How sweet I roam'd from field to field
And tasted all the summer's pride,
Till I the Prince of Love beheld
Who in the sunny beams did glide!

He show'd me lilies for my hair,
And blushing roses for my brow;
He led me through his gardens fair
Where all his golden pleasures grow.

How sweet, &c.] According to Malkin (*Father's Memoirs*, 1806, this poem was written by Blake before the age of fourteen.

Song

With sweet May dews my wings were wet,
And Phoebus fir'd my vocal rage;
He caught me in his silken net,
And shut me in his golden cage.

He loves to sit and hear me sing,
Then, laughing, sports and plays with me;
Then stretches out my golden wing,
And mocks my loss of liberty.

Song

My silks and fine array,
My smiles and languish'd air,
By love are driv'n away;
And mournful lean Despair
Brings me yew to deck my grave;
Such end true lovers have.

His face is fair as heav'n
When springing buds unfold;
O why to him was't giv'n
Whose heart is wintry cold?
His breast is love's all-worshipp'd tomb,
Where all love's pilgrims come.

Bring me an axe and spade,
Bring me a winding-sheet;
When I my grave have made
Let winds and tempests beat:
Then down I'll lie as cold as clay.
True love doth pass away!

Poetical Sketches

Song

Love and harmony combine,
And around our souls entwine
While thy branches mix with mine,
And our roots together join.

Joys upon our branches sit,
Chirping loud and singing sweet;
Like gentle streams beneath our feet
Innocence and virtue meet.

Thou the golden fruit dost bear,
I am clad in flowers fair;
Thy sweet boughs perfume the air,
And the turtle buildeth there.

There she sits and feeds her young,
Sweet I hear her mournful song;
And thy lovely leaves among,
There is love, I hear his tongue.

There his charming nest doth lay,
There he sleeps the night away;
There he sports along the day,
And doth among our branches play.

Song

I love the jocund dance,
The softly breathing song,
Where innocent eyes do glance,
And where lisps the maiden's tongue.

1 love the laughing vale,
I love the echoing hill,
Where mirth does never fail,
And the jolly swain laughs his fill.

16 his] **her;** an obvious misprint, in the original.

Song

I love the pleasant cot,
I love the innocent bow'r,
Where white and brown is our lot,
Or fruit in the mid-day hour.

I love the oaken seat,
Beneath the oaken tree,
Where all the old villagers meet,
And laugh our sports to see.

I love our neighbours all,
But, Kitty, I better love thee;
And love them I ever shall;
But thou art all to me.

Song

Memory, hither come
And tune your merry notes:
And, while upon the wind
Your music floats,
I'll pore upon the stream
Where sighing lovers dream,
And fish for fancies as they pass
Within the watery glass.

I'll drink of the clear stream,
And hear the linnet's song;
And there I'll lie and dream
The day along:
And when night comes, I'll go
To places fit for woe,
Walking along the darken'd valley
With silent Melancholy.

Poetical Sketches

Mad Song

    The wild winds weep,
    And the night is a-cold;
    Come hither, Sleep,
    And my griefs unfold:
    But lo! the morning peeps 5
    Over the eastern steeps,
    And the rustling beds of dawn
    The earth do scorn.

    Lo! to the vault
    Of pavèd heaven, 10
    With sorrow fraught
    My notes are driven:
    They strike the ear of night,
    Make weep the eyes of day;
    They make mad the roaring winds, 15
    And with tempests play.

    Like a fiend in a cloud,
    With howling woe
    After night I do crowd,
    And with night will go; 20
    I turn my back to the east
    From whence comforts have increas'd;
    For light doth seize my brain
    With frantic pain.

17 Cp. 'Infant Sorrow' in the *Songs of Experience*:

    Helpless, naked, piping loud,
    Like a fiend hid in a cloud.

Song

Song

Fresh from the dewy hill, the merry year
Smiles on my head and mounts his flaming car;
Round my young brows the laurel wreathes a shade,
And rising glories beam around my head.

My feet are wing'd, while o'er the dewy lawn, 5
I meet my maiden risen like the morn:
O bless those holy feet, like angels' feet;
O bless those limbs, beaming with heav'nly light.

Like as an angel glitt'ring in the sky
In times of innocence and holy joy; 10
The joyful shepherd stops his grateful song
To hear the music of an angel's tongue.

So when she speaks, the voice of Heaven I hear;
So when we walk, nothing impure comes near;
Each field seems Eden, and each calm retreat; 15
Each village seems the haunt of holy feet.

But that sweet village where my black-eyed maid
Closes her eyes in sleep beneath night's shade,
Whene'er I enter, more than mortal fire
Burns in my soul, and does my song inspire. 20

Song

When early morn walks forth in sober grey,
Then to my black-eyed maid I haste away;
When evening sits beneath her dusky bow'r,
And gently sighs away the silent hour,
The village bell alarms, away I go, 5
And the vale darkens at my pensive woe.

To that sweet village, where my black-eyed maid
Doth drop a tear beneath the silent shade,
I turn my eyes; and pensive as I go
Curse my black stars and bless my pleasing woe. 10

Poetical Sketches

Oft when the summer sleeps among the trees,
Whisp'ring faint murmurs to the scanty breeze,
I walk the village round; if at her side
A youth doth walk in stolen joy and pride,
I curse my stars in bitter grief and woe,   15
That made my love so high and me so low.

O should she e'er prove false, his limbs I'd tear
And throw all pity on the burning air;
I'd curse bright fortune for my mixèd lot,
And then I'd die in peace and be forgot.   20

To the Muses

Whether on Ida's shady brow,
Or in the chambers of the East,
The chambers of the sun, that now
From ancient melody have ceas'd;

Whether in Heaven ye wander fair,   5
Or the green corners of the earth,
Or the blue regions of the air
Where the melodious winds have birth;

Whether on crystal rocks ye rove,
Beneath the bosom of the sea   10
Wand'ring in many a coral grove,
Fair Nine, forsaking Poetry!

How have you left the ancient love
That bards of old enjoy'd in you!
The languid strings do scarcely move!   15
The sound is forc'd, the notes are few.

Gwin, King of Norway

Gwin King of Norway

Come, kings, and listen to my song:
When Gwin, the son of Nore,
Over the nations of the North
His cruel sceptre bore;

The nobles of the land did feed
Upon the hungry poor;
They tear the poor man's lamb, and drive
The needy from their door.

'The land is desolate; our wives
And children cry for bread;
Arise, and pull the tyrant down!
Let Gwin be humblèd!'

Gordred the giant rous'd himself
From sleeping in his cave;
He shook the hills, and in the clouds
The troubl'd banners wave.

Beneath them roll'd, like tempests black,
The num'rous sons of blood;
Like lions' whelps, roaring abroad,
Seeking their nightly food.

Down Bleron's hills they dreadful rush,
Their cry ascends the clouds;
The trampling horse and clanging arms
Like rushing mighty floods!

Their wives and children, weeping loud,
Follow in wild array,
Howling like ghosts, furious as wolves
In the bleak wintry day.

'Pull down the tyrant to the dust,
Let Gwin be humblèd,'
They cry, 'and let ten thousand lives
Pay for the tyrant's head.'

Poetical Sketches

From tow'r to tow'r the watchmen cry,
'O Gwin, the son of Nore,
Arouse thyself! the nations, black
Like clouds, come rolling o'er!

Gwin rear'd his shield, his palace shakes,
His chiefs come rushing round;
Each, like an awful thunder cloud,
With voice of solemn sound:

Like rearèd stones around a grave
They stand around the King;
Then suddenly each seiz'd his spear,
And clashing steel does ring.

The husbandman does leave his plough
To wade thro' fields of gore;
The merchant binds his brows in steel,
And leaves the trading shore;

The shepherd leaves his mellow pipe,
And sounds the trumpet shrill;
The workman throws his hammer down
To heave the bloody bill.

Like the tall ghost of Barraton
Who sports in stormy sky,
Gwin leads his host, as black as night
When pestilence does fly,

With horses and with chariots—
And all his spearmen bold
March to the sound of mournful song,
Like clouds around him roll'd.

Gwin lifts his hand—the nations halt;
'Prepare for war!' he cries—
Gordred appears!—his frowning brow
Troubles our northern skies.

Gwin, King of Norway

The armies stand, like balances
Held in th' Almighty's hand;—
'Gwin, thou hast fill'd thy measure up:
Thou'rt swept from out the land.'

And now the raging armies rush'd
Like warring mighty seas;
The heav'ns are shook with roaring war,
The dust ascends the skies!

Earth smokes with blood, and groans and shakes
To drink her children's gore,
A sea of blood; nor can the eye
See to the trembling shore!

And on the verge of this wild sea
Famine and death doth cry;
The cries of women and of babes
Over the field doth fly.

The King is seen raging afar,
With all his men of might;
Like blazing comets scattering death
Thro' the red fev'rous night.

Beneath his arm like sheep they die,
And groan upon the plain;
The battle faints, and bloody men
Fight upon hills of slain.

Now death is sick, and riven men
Labour and toil for life;
Steed rolls on steed, and shield on shield,
Sunk in this sea of strife!

The god of war is drunk with blood;
The earth doth faint and fail;
The stench of blood makes sick the heav'ns;
Ghosts glut the throat of hell!

O what have kings to answer for
Before that awful throne;
When thousand deaths for vengeance cry,
And ghosts accusing groan!   100

Like blazing comets in the sky
That shake the stars of light,
Which drop like fruit unto the earth
Thro' the fierce burning night;

Like these did Gwin and Gordred meet,   105
And the first blow decides;
Down from the brow unto the breast
Gordred his head divides!

Gwin fell: the sons of Norway fled,
All that remain'd alive;   110
The rest did fill the vale of death,
For them the eagles strive.

The river Dorman roll'd their blood
Into the northern sea;
Who mourn'd his sons, and overwhelm'd 115
The pleasant south country.

An Imitation of Spenser

Golden Apollo, that thro' heaven wide
Scatter'st the rays of light, and truth's beams,
In lucent words my darkling verses dight,
And wash my earthy mind in thy clear streams,
That wisdom may descend in fairy dreams,   5
All while the jocund hours in thy train
Scatter their fancies at thy poet's feet;
And when thou yields to night thy wide domain,
Let rays of truth enlight his sleeping brain.

An Imitation of Spenser

For brutish Pan in vain might thee assay
With tinkling sounds to dash thy nervous verse,
Sound without sense; yet in his rude affray,
(For ignorance is Folly's leasing nurse
And love of Folly needs none other's curse)
Midas the praise hath gain'd of lengthen'd ears,
For which himself might deem him ne'er the worse
To sit in council with his modern peers,
And judge of tinkling rimes and elegances terse.

And thou, Mercurius, that with wingèd brow
Dost mount aloft into the yielding sky,
And thro' Heav'n's halls thy airy flight dost throw,
Entering with holy feet to where on high
Jove weighs the counsel of futurity;
Then, laden with eternal fate, dost go
Down, like a falling star, from autumn sky,
And o'er the surface of the silent deep dost fly:

If thou arrivest at the sandy shore
Where nought but envious hissing adders dwell,
Thy golden rod, thrown on the dusty floor,
Can charm to harmony with potent spell.
Such is sweet Eloquence, that does dispel
Envy and Hate that thirst for human gore;
And cause in sweet society to dwell
Vile savage minds that lurk in lonely cell.

O Mercury, assist my lab'ring sense
That round the circle of the world would fly,
As the wing'd eagle scorns the tow'ry fence
Of Alpine hills round his high aëry,
And searches thro' the corners of the sky,

15 ears] misprinted 'cares' in the original.

Poetical Sketches

    Sports in the clouds to hear the thunder's sound,   40
    And see the wingèd lightnings as they fly;
    Then, bosom'd in an amber cloud, around
    Plumes his wide wings, and seeks Sol's palace high.

    And thou, O warrior maid invincible,
    Arm'd with the terrors of Almighty Jove,   45
    Pallas, Minerva, maiden terrible,
    Lov'st thou to walk the peaceful solemn grove,
    In solemn gloom of branches interwove?
    Or bear'st thy Ægis o'er the burning field,
    Where, like the sea, the waves of battle move?   50
    Or have thy soft piteous eyes beheld
    The weary wanderer thro' the desert rove?
    Or does th' afflicted man thy heav'nly bosom move?

Blind Man's Buff

    When silver snow decks Susan's clothes,
    And jewel hangs at th' shepherd's nose,
    The blushing bank is all my care,
    With hearth so red, and walls so fair;
    'Heap the sea-coal, come, heap it higher,   5
    The oaken log lay on the fire.'
    The well-wash'd stools, a circling row,
    With lad and lass, how fair the show!
    The merry can of nut-brown ale,
    The laughing jest, the love-sick tale,   10
    Till, tir'd of chat, the game begins.
    The lasses prick the lads with pins;
    Roger from Dolly twitch'd the stool,
    She, falling, kiss'd the ground, poor fool!

    1, 2] Blake repeats these lines in the 'Song by an old Shepherd', with change of 'Susan's' to 'Sylvia's', and 'th' shepherd's' (possibly a printer's emendation) to 'shepherd's'.

Blind Man's Buff

She blush'd so red, with side-long glance
At hob-nail Dick, who griev'd the chance.
But now for Blind man's Buff they call;
Of each encumbrance clear the hall—
Jenny her silken 'kerchief folds,
And blear-eyed Will the black lot holds.
Now laughing stops, with 'Silence! hush!'
And Peggy Pout gives Sam a push.
The Blind man's arms, extended wide,
Sam slips between:—'O woe betide
Thee, clumsy Will!'—but titt'ring Kate
Is penn'd up in the corner straight!
And now Will's eyes beheld the play;
He thought his face was t'other way.
'Now, Kitty, now! what chance hast thou,
Roger so near thee!—Trips, I vow!'
She catches him—then Roger ties
His own head up—but not his eyes;
For thro' the slender cloth he sees,
And runs at Sam, who slips with ease
His clumsy hold; and, dodging round,
Sukey is tumbled on the ground!—
'See what it is to play unfair!
Where cheating is, there's mischief there.'
But Roger still pursues the chase,—
'He sees! he sees!' cries, softly, Grace;
'O Roger, thou, unskill'd in art,
Must, surer bound, go thro' thy part!
Now Kitty, pert, repeats the rimes,
And Roger turns him round three times,
Then pauses ere he starts—but Dick
Was mischief bent upon a trick;
Down on his hands and knees he lay
Directly in the Blind man's way,
Then cries out 'Hem!' Hodge heard, and ran
With hood-wink'd chance—sure of his man;

Poetical Sketches

But down he came.—Alas, how frail
Our best of hopes, how soon they fail!
With crimson drops he stains the ground;
Confusion startles all around.
Poor piteous Dick supports his head,   55
And fain would cure the hurt he made;
But Kitty hasted with a key,
And down his back they straight convey
The cold relief; the blood is stay'd,
And Hodge again holds up his head.   60
Such are the fortunes of the game,
And those who play should stop the same
By wholesome laws; such as all those
Who on the blinded man impose
Stand in his stead; as, long a-gone,   65
When men were first a nation grown,
Lawless they liv'd, till wantonness
And liberty began t' increase,
And one man lay in another's way;
Then laws were made to keep fair play.   70

KING EDWARD THE THIRD

PERSONS.

King Edward.
The Black Prince.
Queen Philippa.
Duke of Clarence.
Sir John Chandos.
Sir Thomas Dagworth.
Sir Walter Manny.
Lord Audley.
Lord Percy.
Bishop.
William, Dagworth's Man.
Peter Blunt, a common Soldier.

SCENE.

The Coast of France. King Edward and Nobles before it. The Army.

King. O thou, to whose fury the nations are
But as dust, maintain thy servant's right!
Without thine aid, the twisted mail, and spear,
And forgèd helm, and shield of seven-times beaten brass,
Are idle trophies of the vanquisher. 5
When confusion rages, when the field is in a flame,
When the cries of blood tear horror from heav'n,
And yelling Death runs up and down the ranks,
Let Liberty, the charter'd right of Englishmen,
Won by our fathers in many a glorious field, 10
Enerve my soldiers; let Liberty
Blaze in each countenance, and fire the battle.
The enemy fight in chains, invisible chains, but heavy;
Their minds are fetter'd, then how can they be free?
While, like the mounting flame, 15
We spring to battle o'er the floods of death!
And these fair youths, the flow'r of England,

Poetical Sketches

Venturing their lives in my most righteous cause,
O sheathe their hearts with triple steel, that they
May emulate their fathers' virtues. 20
And thou, my son, be strong; thou fightest for a crown
That death can never ravish from thy brow,
A crown of glory—but from thy very dust
Shall beam a radiance, to fire the breasts
Of youth unborn! Our names are written equal 25
In fame's wide-trophied hall; 'tis ours to gild
The letters, and to make them shine with gold
That never tarnishes: whether Third Edward,
Or the Prince of Wales, or Montacute, or Mortimer,
Or ev'n the least by birth, shall gain the brightest fame, 30
Is in His hand to whom all men are equal.
The world of men are like the num'rous stars
That beam and twinkle in the depth of night,
Each clad in glory according to his sphere;
But we, that wander from our native seats 35
And beam forth lustre on a darkling world,
Grow larger as we advance: and some, perhaps
The most obscure at home, that scarce were seen
To twinkle in their sphere, may so advance
That the astonish'd world, with upturn'd eyes, 40
Regardless of the moon, and those that once were bright,
Stand only for to gaze upon their splendour.
  [*He here knights the Prince, and other young Nobles.*
Now let us take a just revenge for those
Brave Lords, who fell beneath the bloody axe
At Paris. Thanks, noble Harcourt, for 'twas 45
By your advice we landed here in Brittany,
A country not yet sown with destruction,
And where the fiery whirlwind of swift war
Has not yet swept its desolating wing.—
Into three parties we divide by day, 50
And separate march, but join again at night;
Each knows his rank, and Heav'n marshal all.   [*Exeunt.*

King Edward the Third

SCENE. *English Court. Lionel, Duke of Clarence, Queen Philippa; Lords; Bishop, &c.*

Clarence. My Lords, I have by the advice of her
Whom I am doubly bound to obey, my Parent
And my Sovereign, call'd you together.
My task is great, my burden heavier than
My unfledg'd years;
Yet, with your kind assistance, Lords, I hope
England shall dwell in peace; that, while my father
Toils in his wars, and turns his eyes on this
His native shore, and sees commerce fly round
With his white wings, and sees his golden London
And her silver Thames, throng'd with shining spires
And corded ships, her merchants buzzing round
Like summer bees, and all the golden cities
In his land overflowing with honey,
Glory may not be dimm'd with clouds of care.
Say, Lords, should not our thoughts be first to commerce?
My Lord Bishop, you would recommend us agriculture?

Bishop. Sweet Prince, the arts of peace are great,
And no less glorious than those of war,
Perhaps more glorious in the philosophic mind.
When I sit at my home, a private man,
My thoughts are on my gardens and my fields,
How to employ the hand that lacketh bread.
If Industry is in my diocese,
Religion will flourish; each man's heart
Is cultivated and will bring forth fruit:
This is my private duty and my pleasure.
But, as I sit in council with my Prince,
My thoughts take in the gen'ral good of the whole,
And England is the land favour'd by Commerce;
For Commerce, tho' the child of Agriculture,
Fosters his parent, who else must sweat and toil,
And gain but scanty fare. Then, my dear Lord,

Poetical Sketches

Be England's trade our care; and we, as tradesmen,
Looking to the gain of this our native land. 35

   Clar. O my good Lord, true wisdom drops like honey
From your tongue, as from a worshipp'd oak.
Forgive, my Lords, my talkative youth, that speaks
Not merely what my narrow observation has
Pick'd up, but what I have concluded from your lessons. 40
Now, by the Queen's advice, I ask your leave
To dine to-morrow with the Mayor of London:
If I obtain your leave, I have another boon
To ask, which is the favour of your company.
I fear Lord Percy will not give me leave. 45

   Percy. Dear Sir, a prince should always keep his state,
And grant his favours with a sparing hand,
Or they are never rightly valuèd.
These are my thoughts; yet it were best to go
But keep a proper dignity, for now 50
You represent the sacred person of
Your father; 'tis with princes as 'tis with the sun;
If not sometimes o'er-clouded, we grow weary
Of his officious glory.

   Clar. Then you will give me leave to shine sometimes, 55
My Lord?

   Lord. Thou hast a gallant spirit, which I fear
Will be imposèd on by the closer sort. [*Aside.*

   Clar. Well, I'll endeavour to take
Lord Percy's advice; I have been usèd so much 60
To dignity that I'm sick on't.

   Queen Phil. Fie, fie, Lord Clarence! you proceed not to business,
But speak of your own pleasures.
I hope their Lordships will excuse your giddiness.

   Clar. My Lords, the French have fitted out many 65
Small ships of war, that, like to ravening wolves,
Infest our English seas, devouring all
Our burden'd vessels, spoiling our naval flocks.

King Edward the Third

The merchants do complain and beg our aid
  Percy. The merchants are rich enough; 70
Can they not help themselves?
  Bish. They can, and may; but how to gain their will
Requires our countenance and help.
  Percy. When that they find they must, my Lord, they will:
Let them but suffer awhile, and you shall see 75
They will bestir themselves.
  Bish. Lord Percy cannot mean that we should suffer
This disgrace: if so, we are not sovereigns
Of the sea—our right, that Heaven gave
To England, when at the birth of nature 80
She was seated in the deep; the Ocean ceas'd
His mighty roar, and fawning play'd around
Her snowy feet, and own'd his awful Queen.
Lord Percy, if the heart is sick, the head
Must be aggriev'd; if but one member suffer, 85
The heart doth fail. You say, my Lord, the merchants
Can, if they will, defend themselves against
These rovers: this is a noble scheme,
Worthy the brave Lord Percy, and as worthy
His generous aid to put it into practice. 90
  Percy. Lord Bishop, what was rash in me is wise
In you; I dare not own the plan. 'Tis not
Mine. Yet will I, if you please,
Quickly to the Lord Mayor, and work him onward
To this most glorious voyage; on which cast 95
I'll set my whole estate,
But we will bring these Gallic rovers under.
  Queen Phil. Thanks, brave Lord Percy; you have the thanks
Of England's Queen, and will, ere long, of England. [*Exeunt*

Poetical Sketches

SCENE. *At Cressy. Sir Thomas Dagworth and Lord Audley meeting.*

Audley. Good morrow, brave Sir Thomas; the bright morn
Smiles on our army, and the gallant sun
Springs from the hills like a young hero
Into the battle, shaking his golden locks
Exultingly: this is a promising day.

Dagworth Why, my Lord Audley, I don't know.
Give me your hand, and now I'll tell you what
I think you do not know. Edward's afraid of Philip.

Audley. Ha! Ha! Sir Thomas! you but joke;
Did you e'er see him fear? At Blanchetaque,
When almost singly he drove six thousand
French from the ford, did he fear then?

Dagw. Yes, fear—that made him fight so.

Aud. By the same reason I might say tis fear
That makes you fight.

Dagw. Mayhap you may: look upon Edward's face,
No one can say he fears; but when he turns
His back, then I will say it to his face;
He is afraid: he makes us all afraid.
I cannot bear the enemy at my back.
Now here we are at Cressy; where to-morrow,
To-morrow we shall know. I say, Lord Audley,
That Edward runs away from Philip.

Aud. Perhaps you think the Prince too is afraid?

Dagw. No; God forbid! I'm sure he is not.
He is a young lion. O! I have seen him fight
And give command, and lightning has flashed
From his eyes across the field: I have seen him
Shake hands with death, and strike a bargain for
The enemy; he has danc'd in the field
Of battle, like the youth at morris-play.
I'm sure he's not afraid, nor Warwick, nor none—

King Edward the Third

None of us but me, and I am very much afraid.
    Aud. Are you afraid too, Sir Thomas?
I believe that as much as I believe 35
The King's afraid: but what are you afraid of?
    Dagw. Of having my back laid open; we turn
Our backs to the fire, till we shall burn our skirts.
    Aud. And this, Sir Thomas, you call fear? Your fear
Is of a different kind then from the King's; 40
He fears to turn his face, and you to turn your back.
I do not think, Sir Thomas, you know what fear is.

Enter Sir John Chandos.

    Chand. Good morrow, Generals; I give you joy:
Welcome to the fields of Cressy. Here we stop,
And wait for Philip. 45
    Dagw. I hope so.
    Aud. There, Sir Thomas, do you call that fear?
    Dagw. I don't know; perhaps he takes it by fits.
Why, noble Chandos, look you here—
One rotten sheep spoils the whole flock; 50
And if the bell-wether is tainted, I wish
The Prince may not catch the distemper too.
    Chand. Distemper, Sir Thomas! what distemper?
I have not heard.
    Dagw. Why, Chandos, you are a wise man, 55
I know you understand me; a distemper
The King caught here in France of running away.
    Aud. Sir Thomas, you say you have caught it too.
    Dagw. And so will the whole army; 'tis very catching,
For, when the coward runs, the brave man totters. 60
Perhaps the air of the country is the cause.
I feel it coming upon me, so I strive against it;
You yet are whole; but, after a few more
Retreats, we all shall know how to retreat
Better than fight.—To be plain, I think retreating 65
Too often takes away a soldier's courage.

Poetical Sketches

Chand. Here comes the King himself: tell him your thoughts
Plainly, Sir Thomas.
Dagw. I've told him before, but his disorder
Makes him deaf. 70

Enter King Edward and Black Prince.

King. Good morrow, Generals; when English courage fails,
Down goes our right to France.
But we are conquerors everywhere; nothing
Can stand our soldiers; each man is worthy
Of a triumph. Such an army of heroes 75
Ne'er shouted to the Heav'ns, nor shook the field.
Edward, my son, thou art
Most happy, having such command: the man
Were base who were not fir'd to deeds
Above heroic, having such examples. 80

Prince. Sire, with respect and deference I look
Upon such noble souls, and wish myself
Worthy the high command that Heaven and you
Have given me. When I have seen the field glow,
And in each countenance the soul of war 85
Curb'd by the manliest reason, I have been wing'd
With certain victory; and 'tis my boast,
And shall be still my glory, I was inspir'd
By these brave troops.

Dagw. Your Grace had better make 90
Them all generals.

King. Sir Thomas Dagworth, you must have your joke,
And shall, while you can fight as you did at
The Ford.

Dagw. I have a small petition to your Majesty. 95

King. What can Sir Thomas Dagworth ask that Edward
Can refuse?

Dagw. I hope your Majesty cannot refuse so great
A trifle; I've gilt your cause with my best blood,
And would again, were I not forbid 100

King Edward the Third

By him whom I am bound to obey: my hands
Are tièd up, my courage shrunk and wither'd,
My sinews slacken'd, and my voice scarce heard;
Therefore I beg I may return to England.

   King. I know not what you could have ask'd, Sir Thomas,   105
That I would not have sooner parted with
Than such a soldier as you have been, and such a friend:
Nay, I will know the most remote particulars
Of this your strange petition: that, if I can,
I still may keep you here.   110

   Dagw. Here on the fields of Cressy we are settled
Till Philip springs the tim'rous covey again.
The wolf is hunted down by causeless fear;
The lion flees, and fear usurps his heart,
Startled, astonish'd at the clam'rous cock;   115
The eagle, that doth gaze upon the sun,
Fears the small fire that plays about the fen.
If, at this moment of their idle fear,
The dog doth seize the wolf, the forester the lion,
The negro in the crevice of the rock   120
Doth seize the soaring eagle; undone by flight,
They tame submit: such the effect flight has
On noble souls. Now hear its opposite:
The tim'rous stag starts from the thicket wild,
The fearful crane springs from the splashy fen,   125
The shining snake glides o'er the bending grass;
The stag turns head and bays the crying hounds,
The crane o'ertaken fighteth with the hawk,
The snake doth turn, and bite the padding foot.
And if your Majesty 's afraid of Philip,   130
You are more like a lion than a crane:
Therefore I beg I may return to England.

   King. Sir Thomas, now I understand your mirth,
Which often plays with Wisdom for its pastime,
And brings good counsel from the breast of laughter.   135
I hope you'll stay, and see us fight this battle,

31

Poetical Sketches

And reap rich harvest in the fields of Cressy;
Then go to England, tell them how we fight,
And set all hearts on fire to be with us.
Philip is plum'd, and thinks we flee from him, 140
Else he would never dare to attack us. Now,
Now the quarry's set! and Death doth sport
In the bright sunshine of this fatal day.

Dagw. Now my heart dances, and I am as light
As the young bridegroom going to be marrièd. 145
Now must I to my soldiers, get them ready,
Furbish our armours bright, new-plume our helms;
And we will sing like the young housewives busièd
In the dairy: my feet are wing'd, but not
For flight, an please your grace. 150

King. If all my soldiers are as pleas'd as you,
'Twill be a gallant thing to fight or die;
Then I can never be afraid of Philip.

Dagw. A raw-bon'd fellow t'other day pass'd by me;
I told him to put off his hungry looks— 155
He answer'd me, 'I hunger for another battle.'
I saw a little Welshman with a fiery face;
I told him he look'd like a candle half
Burn'd out; he answer'd, he was 'pig enough
To light another pattle.' Last night, beneath 160
The moon I walk'd abroad, when all had pitch'd
Their tents, and all were still;
I heard a blooming youth singing a song
He had compos'd, and at each pause he wip'd
His dropping eyes. The ditty was 'If he 165
Return'd victorious, he should wed a maiden
Fairer than snow, and rich as midsummer.'
Another wept, and wish'd health to his father.
I chid them both, but gave them noble hopes
These are the minds that glory in the battle, 170
And leap and dance to hear the trumpet sound.

King. Sir Thomas Dagworth, be thou near our person;

King Edward the Third

Thy heart is richer than the vales of France:
I will not part with such a man as thee.
If Philip came arm'd in the ribs of death,
And shook his mortal dart against my head,
Thou'dst laugh his fury into nerveless shame!
Go now, for thou art suited to the work,
Throughout the camp; inflame the timorous,
Blow up the sluggish into ardour, and
Confirm the strong with strength, the weak inspire,
And wing their brows with hope and expectation:
Then to our tent return, and meet to council. [*Exit Dagworth.*

Chand. That man's a hero in his closet, and more
A hero to the servants of his house
Than to the gaping world; he carries windows
In that enlargèd breast of his, that all
May see what's done within.

Prince. He is a genuine Englishman, my Chandos,
And hath the spirit of Liberty within him.
Forgive my prejudice, Sir John; I think
My Englishmen the bravest people on
The face of the earth.

Chand. Courage, my Lord, proceeds from self-dependence.
Teach man to think he's a free agent,
Give but a slave his liberty, he'll shake
Off sloth, and build himself a hut, and hedge
A spot of ground; this he'll defend; 'tis his
By right of Nature: thus set in action,
He will still move onward to plan conveniences,
Till glory fires his breast to enlarge his castle;
While the poor slave drudges all day, in hope
To rest at night.

King. O Liberty, how glorious art thou!
I see thee hov'ring o'er my army, with
Thy wide-stretch'd plumes; I see thee
Lead them on to battle;
I see thee blow thy golden trumpet, while

Poetical Sketches

Thy sons shout the strong shout of victory!
O noble Chandos, think thyself a gardener,   210
My son a vine, which I commit unto
Thy care: prune all extravagant shoots, and guide
Th' ambitious tendrils in the paths of wisdom;
Water him with thy advice; and Heav'n
Rain fresh'ning dew upon his branches!   And,   215
O Edward, my dear son! learn to think lowly of
Thyself, as we may all each prefer other—
'Tis the best policy, and 'tis our duty.   [*Exit King Edward.*
   Prince.   And may our duty, Chandos, be our pleasure.
Now we are alone, Sir John, I will unburden,   220
And breathe my hopes into the burning air,
Where thousand Deaths are posting up and down.
Commission'd to this fatal field of Cressy.
Methinks I see them arm my gallant soldiers,
And gird the sword upon each thigh, and fit   225
Each shining helm, and string each stubborn bow,
And dance to the neighing of our steeds.
Methinks the shout begins, the battle burns;
Methinks I see them perch on English crests,
And roar the wild flame of fierce war upon   230
The throngèd enemy!   In truth I am too full
It is my sin to love the noise of war.
Chandos, thou seest my weakness; strong Nature
Will bend or break us: my blood, like a springtide
Does rise so high to overflow all bounds   235
Of moderation; while Reason, in her
frail bark, can see no shore or bound for vast
Ambition.   Come, take the helm, my Chandos,
That my full-blown sails overset me not
In the wild tempest: condemn my venturous youth,   240
That plays with danger, as the innocent child
Unthinking plays upon the viper's den:
I am a coward in my reason, Chandos.
   Chand.   You are a man, my Prince, and a brave man,

King Edward the Third

If I can judge of actions; but your heat
Is the effect of youth, and want of use:
Use makes the armèd field and noisy war
Pass over as a summer cloud, unregarded,
Or but expected as a thing of course.
Age is contemplative; each rolling year
Brings forth fruit to the mind's treasure-house:
While vacant youth doth crave and seek about
Within itself, and findeth discontent,
Then, tir'd of thought, impatient takes the wing,
Seizes the fruits of time, attacks experience,
Roams round vast Nature's forest, where no bounds
Are set, the swiftest may have room, the strongest
Find prey; till tired at length, sated and tired
With the changing sameness, old variety,
We sit us down, and view our former joys
With distaste and dislike.
  Prince. Then, if we must tug for experience,
Let us not fear to beat round Nature's wilds,
And rouse the strongest prey: then, if we fall,
We fall with glory. I know the wolf
Is dangerous to fight, not good for food,
Nor is the hide a comely vestment; so
We have our battle for our pains. I know
That youth has need of age to point fit prey,
And oft the stander-by shall steal the fruit
Of th' other's labour. This is philosophy;
These are the tricks of the world; but the pure soul
Shall mount on native wings, disdaining
Little sport, and cut a path into the heaven of glory,
Leaving a track of light for men to wonder at.
I'm glad my father does not hear me talk;
You can find friendly excuses for me, Chandos.
But do you not think, Sir John, that if it please
Th' Almighty to stretch out my span of life,
I shall with pleasure view a glorious action

Poetical Sketches

Which my youth master'd?
  Chand. Considerate age, my Lord, views motives,
And not acts; when neither warbling voice
Nor trilling pipe is heard, nor pleasure sits
With trembling age, the voice of Conscience then,   285
Sweeter than music in a summer's eve,
Shall warble round the snowy head, and keep
Sweet symphony to feather'd angels, sitting
As guardians round your chair; then shall the pulse
Beat slow, and taste and touch and sight and sound and smell,   290
That sing and dance round Reason's fine-wrought throne,
Shall flee away, and leave them all forlorn;
Yet not forlorn if Conscience is his friend.   [*Exeunt.*

    SCENE.   *In Sir Thomas Dagworth's Tent. Dagworth, and
              William his Man.*

  Dagw. Bring hither my armour, William.
Ambition is the growth of ev'ry clime.
  Will. Does it grow in England, sir?
  Dagw. Aye, it grows most in lands most cultivated.
  Will. Then it grows most in France; the vines here are finer than any we have in England.
  Dagw. Aye, but the oaks are not.
  Will. What is the tree you mentioned? I don't think I ever saw it.
  Dagw. Ambition.
  Will. Is it a little creeping root that grows in ditches?
  Dagw. Thou dost not understand me, William.
It is a root that grows in every breast;
Ambition is the desire or passion that one man
Has to get before another, in any pursuit after glory;
But I don't think you have any of it.
  Will. Yes, I have; I have a great ambition to know every thing, Sir.
  Dagw. But when our first ideas are wrong, what follows must

King Edward the Third

all be wrong, of course; 'tis best to know a little, and to know that little aright.

Will. Then, Sir, I should be glad to know if it was not ambition that brought over our King to France to fight for his right?

Dagw. Tho' the knowledge of that will not profit thee much, yet I will tell you that it was ambition.

Will. Then, if ambition is a sin, we are all guilty in coming with him, and in fighting for him.

Dagw. Now, William, thou dost thrust the question home; but I must tell you that, guilt being an act of the mind, none are guilty but those whose minds are prompted by that same ambition.

Will. Now, I always thought that a man might be guilty of doing wrong without knowing it was wrong.

Dagw. Thou art a natural philosopher, and knowest truth by instinct, while reason runs aground, as we have run our argument. Only remember, William, all have it in their power to know the motives of their own actions, and 'tis a sin to act without some reason.

Will. And whoever acts without reason may do a great deal of harm without knowing it.

Dagw. Thou art an endless moralist.

Will. Now there's a story come into my head, that I will tell your honour if you'll give me leave.

Dagw. No, William, save it till another time; this is no time for story-telling. But here comes one who is as entertaining as a good story!

Enter Peter Blunt.

Peter. Yonder's a musician going to play before the King; it's a new song about the French and English; and the Prince has made the minstrel a squire, and given him I don't know what, and I can't tell whether he don't mention us all one by one; and he is to write another about all us that are to die, that we may be remembered in Old England, for all our blood and bones are in France; and a great deal more that we shall all hear by and by.

Poetical Sketches

and I came to tell your honour, because you love to hear war-songs.

Dagw. And who is this minstrel, Peter, dost know?

Peter. O aye, I forgot to tell that; he has got the same name as Sir John Chandos, that the Prince is always with—the wise man that knows us all as well as your honour, only ain't so good-natured.

Dagw. I thank you, Peter, for your information; but not for your compliment, which is not true. There's as much difference between him and me as between glittering sand and fruitful mould; or shining glass and a wrought diamond, set in rich gold, and fitted to the finger of an Emperor; such is that worthy Chandos.

Peter. I know your honour does not think anything of yourself, but everybody else does.

Dagw. Go, Peter, get you gone; flattery is delicious, even from the lips of a babbler. [*Exit Peter.*

Will. I never flatter your honour.

Dagw. I don't know that.

Will. Why, you know, Sir, when we were in England, at the tournament at Windsor, and the Earl of Warwick was tumbled over, you ask'd me if he did not look well when he fell; and I said no, he look'd very foolish; and you was very angry with me for not flattering you.

Dagw. You mean that I was angry with you for not flattering the Earl of Warwick. [*Exeunt.*

SCENE. *Sir Thomas Dagworth's Tent. Sir Thomas Dagworth—to him enter Sir Walter Manny.*

Sir Walter. Sir Thomas Dagworth, I have been weeping
Over the men that are to die to-day.

Dagw. Why, brave Sir Walter, you or I may fall.

Sir Walter. I know this breathing flesh must lie and rot,
Cover'd with silence and forgetfulness.—
Death wons in cities' smoke, and in still night,   5

6 wons] i. e. 'dwells', an archaism probably borrowed from Spenser.

King Edward the Third

When men sleep in their beds, walketh about!
How many in wallèd cities lie and groan,
Turning themselves upon their beds,
Talking with Death, answering his hard demands!   10
How many walk in darkness, terrors are round
The curtains of their beds, destruction is
Ready at the door! How many sleep
In earth, cover'd with stones and deathy dust,
Resting in quietness, whose spirits walk   15
Upon the clouds of heaven, to die no more!
Yet death is terrible, tho' borne on angels' wings.
How terrible then is the field of Death,
Where he doth rend the vault of heaven,
And shake the gates of hell!   20
O Dagworth, France is sick! the very sky,
Tho' sunshine light it, seems to me as pale
As the pale fainting man on his death-bed,
Whose face is shown by light of sickly taper
It makes me sad and sick at very heart,   25
Thousands must fall to-day.

   Dagw. Thousands of souls must leave this prison-house,
To be exalted to those heavenly fields,
Where songs of triumph, palms of victory,
Where peace and joy and love and calm content   30
Sit singing in the azure clouds, and strew
Flowers of heaven's growth over the banquet-table.
Bind ardent Hope upon your feet like shoes,
Put on the robe of preparation,
The table is prepar'd in shining heaven,   35
The flowers of immortality are blown;
Let those that fight fight in good steadfastness,
And those that fall shall rise in victory.

   Sir Walter. I've often seen the burning field of war
And often heard the dismal clang of arms;   40
But never, till this fatal day of Cressy,
Has my soul fainted with these views of death.

Poetical Sketches

I seem to be in one great charnel-house,
And seem to scent the rotten carcases;
I seem to hear the dismal yells of Death, 45
While the black gore drops from his horrid jaws;
Yet I not fear the monster in his pride—
But O! the souls that are to die to-day!

   Dagw. Stop, brave Sir Walter; let me drop a tear,
Then let the clarion of war begin; 50
I'll fight and weep, 'tis in my country's cause;
I'll weep and shout for glorious liberty.
Grim War shall laugh and shout, deckèd in tears,
And blood shall flow like streams across the meadows,
That murmur down their pebbly channels, and 55
Spend their sweet lives to do their country service:
Then shall England's verdure shoot, her fields shall smile,
Her ships shall sing across the foaming sea,
Her mariners shall use the flute and viol,
And rattling guns, and black and dreary war, 60
Shall be no more.

   Sir Walter. Well, let the trumpet sound, and the drum beat;
Let war stain the blue heavens with bloody banners;
I'll draw my sword, nor ever sheathe it up
Till England blow the trump of victory, 65
Or I lay stretch'd upon the field of death.
                                                       [*Exeunt.*

SCENE. *In the Camp. Several of the Warriors meet at the King's Tent with a Minstrel, who sings the following Song:*

O sons of Trojan Brutus, cloth'd in war,
Whose voices are the thunder of the field,
Rolling dark clouds o'er France, muffling the sun
In sickly darkness like a dim eclipse,
Threatening as the red brow of storms, as fire 5
Burning up nations in your wrath and fury!

Your ancestors came from the fires of Troy,
(Like lions rous'd by light'ning from their dens,

King Edward the Third

Whose eyes do glare against the stormy fires),
Heated with war, fill'd with the blood of Greeks,   10
With helmets hewn, and shields coverèd with gore,
In navies black, broken with wind and tide:

They landed in firm array upon the rocks
Of Albion; they kiss'd the rocky shore;
'Be thou our mother and our nurse,' they said;   15
'Our children's mother, and thou shalt be our grave,
The sepulchre of ancient Troy, from whence
Shall rise cities, and thrones, and arms, and awful pow'rs.'

Our fathers swarm from the ships.   Giant voices
Are heard from the hills, the enormous sons   20
Of Ocean run from rocks and caves, wild men,
Naked and roaring like lions, hurling rocks,
And wielding knotty clubs, like oaks entangled
Thick as a forest, ready for the axe.

Our fathers move in firm array to battle;   25
The savage monsters rush like roaring fire,
Like as a forest roars with crackling flames,
When the red lightning, borne by furious storms,
Lights on some woody shore; the parchèd heavens
Rain fire into the molten raging sea.   30

The smoking trees are strewn upon the shore,
Spoil'd of their verdure.   O how oft have they
Defy'd the storm that howlèd o'er their heads!
Our fathers, sweating, lean on their spears, and view
The mighty dead: giant bodies streaming blood,   35
Dread visages frowning in silent death.

Then Brutus spoke, inspir'd; our fathers sit
Attentive on the melancholy shore:
Hear ye the voice of Brutus—'The flowing waves
Of time come rolling o'er my breast,' he said;   40
'And my heart labours with futurity:
Our sons shall rule the empire of the sea.

Poetical Sketches

Their mighty wings shall stretch from east to west.
Their nest is in the sea, but they shall roam
Like eagles for the prey ; nor shall the young 45
Crave or be heard ; for plenty shall bring forth,
Cities shall sing, and vales in rich array
Shall laugh, whose fruitful laps bend down with fulness.

'Our sons shall rise from thrones in joy,
Each one buckling on his armour ; Morning 50
Shall be prevented by their swords gleaming,
And Evening hear their song of victory :
Their towers shall be built upon the rocks,
Their daughters shall sing, surrounded with shining spears.

'Liberty shall stand upon the cliffs of Albion, 55
Casting her blue eyes over the green ocean ;
Or, tow'ring, stand upon the roaring waves,
Stretching her mighty spear o'er distant lands ;
While, with her eagle wings, she covereth
Fair Albion's shore, and all her families.' 60

Prologue, intended for a Dramatic Piece of King Edward the Fourth

O for a voice like thunder, and a tongue
To drown the throat of war ! When the senses
Are shaken, and the soul is driven to madness,
Who can stand ? When the souls of the oppressèd
Fight in the troubled air that rages, who can stand ? 5
When the whirlwind of fury comes from the
Throne of God, when the frowns of his countenance
Drive the nations together, who can stand ?
When Sin claps his broad wings over the battle,
And sails rejoicing in the flood of Death ; 10
When souls are torn to everlasting fire,
And fiends of Hell rejoice upon the slain,

Prologue to King John

O who can stand? O who hath caused this?
O who can answer at the throne of God?
The Kings and Nobles of the Land have done it! 15
Hear it not, Heaven, thy Ministers have done it!

Prologue to King John

Justice hath heaved a sword to plunge in Albion's breast; for Albion's sins are crimson dy'd, and the red scourge follows her desolate sons. Then Patriot rose; full oft did Patriot rise, when Tyranny hath stain'd fair Albion's breast with her own children's gore. Round his majestic feet deep thunders roll; each heart does tremble, and each knee grows slack. The stars of heaven tremble; the roaring voice of war, the trumpet, calls to battle. Brother in brother's blood must bathe—rivers of death. O land most hapless! O beauteous island, how forsaken! Weep from thy silver fountains, weep from thy gentle rivers! The angel of the island weeps. Thy widowed virgins weep beneath thy shades. Thy aged fathers gird themselves for war. The sucking infant lives to die in battle; the weeping mother feeds him for the slaughter. The husbandman doth leave his bending harvest. Blood cries afar! The land doth sow itself! The glittering youth of courts must gleam in arms. The aged senators their ancient swords assume. The trembling sinews of old age must work the work of death against their progeny; for Tyranny hath stretch'd his purple arm, and 'Blood!' he cries; 'the chariots and the horses, the noise of shout, and dreadful thunder of the battle heard afar!' Beware, O proud! thou shalt be humbled; thy cruel brow, thine iron heart, is smitten, though lingering Fate is slow. O yet may Albion smile again, and stretch her peaceful arms, and raise her golden head exultingly! Her citizens shall throng about her gates, her mariners shall sing upon the sea, and myriads shall to her temples crowd! Her sons shall joy as in the morning! Her daughters sing as to the rising year!

Poetical Sketches

A War Song to Englishmen

Prepare, prepare the iron helm of war,
Bring forth the lots, cast in the spacious orb;
Th' Angel of Fate turns them with mighty hands,
And casts them out upon the darken'd earth!
                Prepare, prepare! 5

Prepare your hearts for Death's cold hand! prepare
Your souls for flight, your bodies for the earth;
Prepare your arms for glorious victory;
Prepare your eyes to meet a holy God!
                Prepare, prepare! 10

Whose fatal scroll is that? Methinks 'tis mine!
Why sinks my heart, why faltereth my tongue?
Had I three lives, I'd die in such a cause,
And rise, with ghosts, over the well-fought field.
                Prepare, prepare! 15

The arrows of Almighty God are drawn!
Angels of Death stand in the louring heavens!
Thousands of souls must seek the realms of light,
And walk together on the clouds of heaven!
                Prepare, prepare! 20

Soldiers, prepare! Our cause is Heaven's cause;
Soldiers, prepare! Be worthy of our cause:
Prepare to meet our fathers in the sky:
Prepare, O troops, that are to fall to-day!
                Prepare, prepare! 25

Alfred shall smile, and make his harp rejoice;
The Norman William, and the learnèd Clerk,
And Lion Heart, and black-brow'd Edward, with
His loyal queen, shall rise, and welcome us!
                Prepare, prepare! 30

The Couch of Death

The Couch of Death

The veiled Evening walked solitary down the western hills, and Silence reposed in the valley; the birds of day were heard in their nests, rustling in brakes and thickets; and the owl and bat flew round the darkening trees: all is silent when Nature takes her repose.—In former times, on such an evening, when the cold clay breathed with life, and our ancestors, who now sleep in their graves, walked on the steadfast globe, the remains of a family of the tribes of Earth, a mother and a sister, were gathered to the sick bed of a youth. Sorrow linked them together; leaning on one another's necks alternately—like lilies dropping tears in each other's bosom—they stood by the bed like reeds bending over a lake, when the evening drops trickle down. His voice was low as the whisperings of the woods when the wind is asleep, and the visions of Heaven unfold their visitation. 'Parting is hard and death is terrible; I seem to walk through a deep valley, far from the light of day, alone and comfortless! The damps of death fall thick upon me! Horrors stare me in the face! I look behind, there is no returning; Death follows after me; I walk in regions of Death, where no tree is, without a lantern to direct my steps, without a staff to support me.' Thus he laments through the still evening, till the curtains of darkness were drawn. Like the sound of a broken pipe, the aged woman raised her voice. 'O my son, my son, I know but little of the path thou goest! But lo! there is a God, who made the world; stretch out thy hand to Him.' The youth replied, like a voice heard from a sepulchre, 'My hand is feeble, how should I stretch it out? My ways are sinful, how should I raise mine eyes? My voice hath used deceit, how should I call on Him who is Truth? My breath is loathsome, how should He not be offended? If I lay my face in the dust, the grave opens its mouth for me; if I lift up my head, sin covers me as a cloak. O my dear friends, pray ye for me! Stretch forth your hands that my Helper may come! Through the void space I walk, between the sinful world and eternity! Beneath me burns eternal fire! O for a hand to pluck me forth!' As the voice of an omen heard in the silent valley, when the few inhabitants cling trembling together; as the voice of the Angel of Death, when the thin beams of the moon give a faint light, such was this young man's voice to his friends. Like the bubbling waters of the brook in the dead of night, the aged woman raised her cry, and said, 'O Voice, that dwellest in my breast, can I not cry, and lift my eyes to Heaven? Thinking of this, my spirit is turned within me into confusion! O my child, my child, is thy breath infected? so is mine. As the deer wounded, by the brooks of water, so the arrows of sin stick in my flesh; the poison hath entered into my marrow.' Like rolling waves upon a desert shore, sighs succeeded sighs; they covered their faces and wept. The youth lay silent, his mother's arm was under his head; he was like a cloud tossed by the winds, till the sun shine, and the drops of rain glisten, the yellow harvest breathes, and the thankful eyes of the villagers are turned up in smiles. The traveller, that hath taken shelter under an oak, eyes the distant country with joy. Such smiles were seen upon the face of the youth: a visionary hand wiped away his tears, and a ray of light beamed around his head. All was still. The moon hung not out her lamp, and the stars faintly glimmered in the summer sky; the breath of night slept among the leaves of the forest; the bosom of the lofty hill drank in the silent dew, while on his majestic brow the voice of Angels is heard, and stringed sounds ride upon the wings of night. The sorrowful pair lift up their heads, hovering Angels are around them, voices of comfort are heard over the Couch of Death, and the youth breathes out his soul with joy into eternity.

Contemplation

Who is this, that with unerring step dares tempt the wilds, where only Nature's foot hath trod? 'Tis Contemplation, daughter of the grey Morning! Majestical she steppeth, and with her pure quill on every flower writeth Wisdom's name; now lowly bending, whispers in mine ear, 'O man, how great, how little, thou! O man, slave of each moment, lord of eternity! seest thou

Contemplation

where Mirth sits on the painted cheek? doth it not seem ashamed of such a place, and grow immoderate to brave it out? O what an humble garb true Joy puts on! Those who want Happiness must stoop to find it; it is a flower that grows in every vale. Vain foolish man, that roams on lofty rocks, where, 'cause his garments are swoln with wind, he fancies he is grown into a giant! Lo, then, Humility, take it, and wear it in thine heart; lord of thyself, thou then art lord of all. Clamour brawls along the streets, and destruction hovers in the city's smoke; but on these plains, and in these silent woods, true joys descend: here build thy nest; here fix thy staff; delights blossom around; numberless beauties blow; the green grass springs in joy, and the nimble air kisses the leaves; the brook stretches its arms along the velvet meadow, its silver inhabitants sport and play; the youthful sun joys like a hunter roused to the chase, he rushes up the sky, and lays hold on the immortal coursers of day; the sky glitters with the jingling trappings. Like a triumph, season follows season, while the airy music fills the world with joyful sounds.' I answered, 'Heavenly goddess! I am wrapped in mortality, my flesh is a prison, my bones the bars of death; Misery builds over our cottage roofs, and Discontent runs like a brook. Even in childhood, Sorrow slept with me in my cradle; he followed me up and down in the house when I grew up; he was my schoolfellow: thus he was in my steps and in my play, till he became to me as my brother. I walked through dreary places with him, and in church-yards; and I oft found myself sitting by Sorrow on a tomb-stone.'

Samson

Samson, the strongest of the children of men, I sing; how he was foiled by woman's arts, by a false wife brought to the gates of death! O Truth! that shinest with propitious beams, turning our earthly night to heavenly day, from presence of the Almighty Father, thou visitest our darkling world with blessed feet, bringing good news of Sin and Death destroyed! O white-robed Angel,

Poetical Sketches

guide my timorous hand to write as on a lofty rock with iron pen the words of truth, that all who pass may read.—Now Night, noon-tide of damned spirits, over the silent earth spreads her pavilion, while in dark council sat Philista's lords; and, where strength failed, black thoughts in ambush lay. Their helmed youth and aged warriors in dust together lie, and Desolation spreads his wings over the land of Palestine: from side to side the land groans, her prowess lost, and seeks to hide her bruised head under the mists of night, breeding dark plots. For Dalila's fair arts have long been tried in vain; in vain she wept in many a treacherous tear. 'Go on, fair traitress; do thy guileful work; ere once again the changing moon her circuit hath performed, thou shalt overcome, and conquer him by force unconquerable, and wrest his secret from him. Call thine alluring arts and honest-seeming brow, the holy kiss of love, and the transparent tear; put on fair linen that with the lily vies, purple and silver; neglect thy hair, to seem more lovely in thy loose attire; put on thy country's pride, deceit, and eyes of love decked in mild sorrow; and sell thy lord for gold.' For now, upon her sumptuous couch reclined in gorgeous pride, she still entreats, and still she grasps his vigorous knees with her fair arms. 'Thou lov'st me not! thou 'rt war, thou art not love! O foolish Dalila! O weak woman! it is death clothed in flesh thou lovest, and thou hast been encircled in his arms! Alas, my lord, what am I calling thee? Thou art my God! To thee I pour my tears for sacrifice morning and evening. My days are covered with sorrow, shut up, darkened! By night I am deceived! Who says that thou wast born of mortal kind? Destruction was thy father, a lioness suckled thee, thy young hands tore human limbs, and gorged human flesh. Come hither, Death; art thou not Samson's servant? 'Tis Dalila that calls, thy master's wife; no, stay, and let thy master do the deed: one blow of that strong arm would ease my pain; then should I lay at quiet and have rest. Pity forsook thee at thy birth! O Dagon furious, and all ye gods of Palestine, withdraw your hand! I am but a weak

1 pen] misprinted 'pens'. Cp. 'Everlasting Gospel', γ l. 12.

Samson

woman. Alas, I am wedded to your enemy! I will go mad, and tear my crisped hair; I'll run about, and pierce the ears o' th' gods! O Samson, hold me not; thou lovest me not! Look not upon me with those deathful eyes! Thou wouldst my death, and death approaches fast.' Thus, in false tears, she bath'd his feet, and thus she day by day oppressed his soul: he seemed a mountain, his brow among the clouds; she seemed a silver stream, his feet embracing. Dark thoughts rolled to and fro in his mind, like thunder clouds troubling the sky; his visage was troubled; his soul was distressed. 'Though I should tell her all my heart, what can I fear? Though I should tell this secret of my birth, the utmost may be warded off as well when told as now.' She saw him moved, and thus resumes her wiles. 'Samson, I'm thine; do with me what thou wilt: my friends are enemies; my life is death; I am a traitor to my nation, and despised; my joy is given into the hands of him who hates me, using deceit to the wife of his bosom. Thrice hast thou mocked me and grieved my soul. Didst thou not tell me with green withs to bind thy nervous arms; and, after that, when I had found thy falsehood, with new ropes to bind thee fast? I knew thou didst but mock me. Alas, when in thy sleep I bound thee with them to try thy truth, I cried, "The Philistines be upon thee, Samson!" Then did suspicion wake thee; how didst thou rend the feeble ties! Thou fearest nought, what shouldst thou fear? Thy power is more than mortal, none can hurt thee; thy bones are brass, thy sinews are iron. Ten thousand spears are like the summer grass; an army of mighty men are as flocks in the valleys; what canst thou fear? I drink my tears like water; I live upon sorrow! O worse than wolves and tigers, what canst thou give when such a trifle is denied me? But O! at last thou mockest me, to shame my over-fond inquiry. Thou toldest me to weave thee to the beam by thy strong hair; I did even that to try thy truth; but, when I cried "The Philistines be upon thee!" then didst thou leave me to bewail that Samson loved me not.' He sat, and inward griev'd; he saw and lov'd the beauteous suppliant, nor could conceal aught that might appease her; then, leaning on her bosom, thus he spoke: 'Hear, O Dalila! doubt no more of Samson's love; for that fair breast was made the ivory palace of my inmost heart, where it shall lie at rest: for sorrow is the lot of all of woman born: for care was I brought forth, and labour is my lot: nor matchless might, nor wisdom, nor every gift enjoyed, can from the heart of man hide sorrow. Twice was my birth foretold from heaven, and twice a sacred vow enjoined me that I should drink no wine, nor eat of any unclean thing; for holy unto Israel's God I am, a Nazarite even from my mother's womb. Twice was it told, that it might not be broken. "Grant me a son, kind Heaven," Manoa cried; but Heaven refused. Childless he mourned, but thought his God knew best. In solitude, though not obscure, in Israel he lived, till venerable age came on: his flocks increased, and plenty crowned his board, beloved, revered of man. But God hath other joys in store. Is burdened Israel his grief? The son of his old age shall set it free! The venerable sweetener of his life receives the promise first from Heaven. She saw the maidens play, and blessed their innocent mirth; she blessed each new-joined pair; but from her the long-wished deliverer shall spring. Pensive, alone she sat within the house, when busy day was fading, and calm evening, time for contemplation, rose from the forsaken east, and drew the curtains of heaven: pensive she sat, and thought on Israel's grief, and silent prayed to Israel's God; when lo! an angel from the fields of light entered the house. His form was manhood in the prime, and from his spacious brow shot terrors through the evening shade. But mild he hailed her, "Hail, highly favoured!" said he; "for lo! thou shalt conceive, and bear a son, and Israel's strength shall be upon his shoulders, and he shall be called Israel's Deliverer. Now, therefore, drink no wine, and eat not any unclean thing, for he shall be a Nazarite to God." Then, as a neighbour, when his evening tale is told, departs, his blessing leaving, so seemed he to depart: she wondered with exceeding joy, nor knew he was an angel. Manoa left his fields to sit in the house, and take his evening's rest from labour—the sweetest time that God has allotted mortal man He sat, and heard with joy, and praised God, who Israel still doth keep. The time rolled on, and Israel groaned oppressed. The sword was bright, while the ploughshare rusted, till hope grew feeble, and was ready to give place to doubting. Then prayed Manoa: "O Lord, thy flock is scattered on the hills! The wolf teareth them, Oppression stretches his rod over our land, our country is ploughed with swords, and reaped in blood. The echoes of slaughter reach from hill to hill. Instead of peaceful pipe the shepherd bears a sword, the ox-goad is turned into a spear. O when shall our Deliverer come? The Philistine riots on our flocks, our vintage is gathered by bands of enemies. Stretch forth thy hand, and save!" Thus prayed Manoa. The aged woman walked into the field, and lo! again the angel came, clad as a traveller fresh risen on his journey. She ran and called her husband, who came and talked with him. "O man of God," said he, "thou comest from far! Let us detain thee while I make ready a kid, that thou mayest sit and eat, and tell us of thy name and warfare; that, when thy sayings come to pass, we may honour thee." The Angel answered, "My name is Wonderful; inquire not after it, seeing it is a secret; but, if thou wilt, offer an offering unto the Lord."'

[END OF POETICAL SKETCHES]

APPENDIX TO POETICAL SKETCHES

Song by a Shepherd

    Welcome, stranger, to this place,
    Where joy doth sit on every bough,
    Paleness flies from every face;
    We reap not what we do not sow.

    Innocence doth like a rose   5
    Bloom on every maiden's cheek;
    Honour twines around her brows,
    The jewel health adorns her neck.

Song by an Old Shepherd

    When silver snow decks Sylvio's clothes,
    And jewel hangs at shepherd's nose,
    We can abide life's pelting storm,
    That makes our limbs quake, if our hearts be warm.

    Whilst Virtue is our walking-staff,   5
    And Truth a lantern to our path,
    We can abide life's pelting storm,
    That makes our limbs quake, if our hearts be warm.

    Blow, boisterous wind, stern winter frown,
    Innocence is a winter's gown.   10
    So clad, we'll abide life's pelting storm,
    That makes our limbs quake, if our hearts be warm.

These songs, which are written, though not in Blake's autograph, upon the fly-leaves of a presentation copy of the *Poetical Sketches*, dated May 15, 1784, were first printed by R. H. Shepherd in Pickering's reprint of 1868. Besides these, with the title 'Song 2[d] by a Young Shepherd', is an earlier version of the 'Laughing Song' in the *Songs of Innocence*.

SONGS

from

AN ISLAND IN THE MOON
(MS. *circa* 1784)

SONGS

FROM

AN ISLAND IN THE MOON

I

Little Phoebus came strutting in,
With his fat belly and his round chin.
What is it you would please to have?
Ho! Ho!
I won't let it go at only so and so!

II

Honour and Genius is all I ask,
And I ask the Gods no more!
   No more! No more! } *the three Philosophers bear chorus.*
   No more! No more!

The songs in this section are taken from the unfinished MS., without title but known as *An Island in the Moon*, where they are sung by some of the characters in that quaint satirical brochure. Among them, for the sake of completeness, I include a few pieces of intentional doggerel, omitting only three fragments which were not written by Blake, and the early versions of three of the *Songs of Innocence*, the variant readings of which are given elsewhere in the footnotes.

I and II] Sung by Quid the Cynic, MS., chap. iii.

Songs from an Island in the Moon

III

When Old Corruption first begun,
Adorn'd in yellow vest,
He committed on Flesh a whoredom—
O, what a wicked beast!

From then a callow babe did spring,
And Old Corruption smil'd
To think his race should never end,
For now he had a child.

He call'd him Surgery and fed
The babe with his own milk;
For Flesh and he could ne'er agree:
She would not let him suck.

And this he always kept in mind;
And form'd a crooked knife,
And ran about with bloody hands
To seek his mother's life.

And as he ran to seek his mother
He met with a dead woman.
He fell in love and married her—
A deed which is not common!

She soon grew pregnant, and brought forth
Scurvy and Spotted Fever,
The father grinn'd and skipt about,
And said 'I'm made for ever!

'For now I have procur'd these imps
I'll try experiments.'
With that he tied poor Scurvy down,
And stopt up all its vents.

III Sung by Quid the Cynic, MS., chap. vi.

Songs from an Island in the Moon

And when the child began to swell
He shouted out aloud—
'I've found the dropsy out, and soon
Shall do the world more good.'

He took up Fever by the neck,
And cut out all its spots;
And, thro' the holes which he had made,
He first discover'd guts.

IV

Hear then the pride and knowledge of a sailor!
His sprit sail, fore sail, main sail, and his mizen.
A poor frail man—God wot! I know none frailer,
I know no greater sinner than John Taylor.

V

The Song of Phoebe and Jellicoe

Phoebe drest like beauty's queen,
Jellicoe in faint pea-green,
Sitting all beneath a grot,
Where the little lambkins trot.

Maidens dancing, loves a-sporting,
All the country folks a-courting,
Susan, Johnny, Bob, and Joe,
Lightly tripping on a row.

Happy people, who can be
In happiness compar'd with ye?
The pilgrim with his crook and hat
Sees your happiness complete.

IV Sung by Steelyard the Lawgiver, MS., chap. viii.
V Sung by Miss Gittipin, MS., chap. viii.

Songs from an Island in the Moon

VI

Lo! the Bat with leathern wing,
Winking and blinking,
Winking and blinking,
Winking and blinking.
Like Dr. Johnson.

Quid. 'O ho!' said Dr. Johnson
To Scipio Africanus,

. . . .
. . . .

Suction. 'A ha!' to Dr. Johnson
Said Scipio Africanus,

. . . .
. . . .

And the Cellar goes down with a step. (*Grand Chorus.*)

VII

1st Vo.   Want Matches?
2nd Vo.   Yes! Yes! Yes!
1st Vo.   Want Matches?
2nd Vo.   No!

1st Vo.   Want Matches?
2nd Vo.   Yes! Yes! Yes!
1st Vo.   Want Matches?
2nd Vo.   No!

VI MS., chap. ix.
VII Song of boy match-sellers, MS., chap. ix.

Songs from an Island in the Moon

VIII

As I walk'd forth one May morning
To see the fields so pleasant and so gay,
O! there did I spy a young maiden sweet,
Among the violets that smell so sweet,
                smell so sweet,   5
                smell so sweet,
Among the violets that smell so sweet.

IX

Hail Matrimony, made of Love!
To thy wide gates how great a drove
On purpose to be yok'd do come;
Widows and Maids and Youths also,
That lightly trip on beauty's toe,   5
Or sit on beauty's bum.

Hail fingerfooted lovely Creatures!
The females of our human natures,
Formèd to suckle all Mankind.
'Tis you that come in time of need,   10
Without you we should never breed,
Or any comfort find.

For if a Damsel's blind or lame,
Or Nature's hand has crook'd her frame,
Or if she's deaf, or is wall-eyed;   15
Yet, if her heart is well inclin'd,
Some tender lover she shall find
That panteth for a Bride.

VIII Sung by Steelyard the Lawgiver, MS., chap. ix.

IX Sung by Quid the Cynic, MS., chap. ix. The subject and metre of this song were perhaps suggested by 'He that intends to take a wife' (*Pills to purge Melancholy*, iii, p. 106).

Songs from an Island in the Moon

The universal Poultice this,
To cure whatever is amiss   20
In Damsel or in Widow gay!
It makes them smile, it makes them skip;
Like birds, just curèd of the pip,
They chirp and hop away.

Then come, ye maidens! come, ye swains!   25
Come and be cur'd of all your pains
In Matrimony's Golden Cage—

X

To be or not to be
Of great capacity,
Like Sir Isaac Newton,
Or Locke, or Doctor South,
Or Sherlock upon Death—   5
I'd rather be Sutton!

For he did build a house
For agèd men and youth,
With walls of brick and stone;
He furnish'd it within   10
With whatever he could win,
And all his own.

He drew out of the Stocks
His money in a box,
And sent his servant   15
To Green the Bricklayer,
And to the Carpenter;
He was so fervent.

27 Here the song abruptly breaks off. With 'Matrimony's Golden Cage' cp. the third stanza of 'How sweet I roam'd from field to field' in the *Poetical Sketches* (p. 8).

X Sung by Obtuse Angle, MS., chap. ix.

6 Sutton] Thomas Sutton, founder of the Charterhouse (1532-1611). Perhaps Obtuse Angle was an old Carthusian.

Songs from an Island in the Moon

The chimneys were threescore,
The windows many more; 20
And, for convenience,
He sinks and gutters made,
And all the way he pav'd
To hinder pestilence.

Was not this a good man— 25
Whose life was but a span,
Whose name was Sutton—
As Locke, or Doctor South,
Or Sherlock upon Death,
Or Sir Isaac Newton? 30

XI

This city and this country has brought forth many mayors
To sit in state, and give forth laws out of their old oak chairs,
With face as brown as any nut with drinking of strong ale—
Good English hospitality, O then it did not fail!

With scarlet gowns and broad gold lace, would make a yeoman sweat; 5
With stockings roll'd above their knees and shoes as black as jet;
With eating beef and drinking beer, O they were stout and hale—
Good English hospitality, O then it did not fail!

Thus sitting at the table wide the mayor and aldermen
Were fit to give law to the city; each ate as much as ten: 10
The hungry poor enter'd the hall to eat good beef and ale—
Good English hospitality, O then it did not fail!

XI Sung by Steelyard the Lawgiver, MS., chap. ix. Cp. 'Old English hospitality is long since deceased', in Chatterton's 'Antiquity of Christmas Games', an essay reprinted in the *Miscellanies* of 1778, with which work Blake appears to have been familiar.

Songs from an Island in the Moon

XII

O, I say, you Joe,
Throw us the ball!
I've a good mind to go
And leave you all.
I never saw such a bowler   5
To bowl the ball in a tansy,
And to clean it with my hankercher
Without saying a word.

That Bill's a foolish fellow;
He has given me a black eye.   10
He does not know how to handle a bat
Any more than a dog or a cat:
He has knock'd down the wicket,
And broke the stumps,
And runs without shoes to save his pumps.   15

XIII

Leave, O leave me to my sorrows;
Here I'll sit and fade away,
Till I'm nothing but a spirit,
And I lose this form of clay.

Then if chance along this forest   5
Any walk in pathless ways,
Thro' the gloom he'll see my shadow
Hear my voice upon the breeze.

XII Sung by Tilly Lally, a schoolboy, MS., chap. xi.
XIII Sung by Miss Gittipin, MS., chap. xi.

Songs from an Island in the Moon

XIV

There's Doctor Clash,
And Signor Falalasole,
O they sweep in the cash
Into their purse hole!
Fa me la sol, La me fa sol!   5

Great A, little A,
Bouncing B!
Play away, play away,
You're out of the key!
Fa me la sol, La me fa sol!   10

Musicians should have
A pair of very good ears,
And long fingers and thumbs,
And not like clumsy bears.
Fa me la sol, La me fa sol!   15

Gentlemen! Gentlemen!
Rap! Rap! Rap!
Fiddle! Fiddle! Fiddle!
Clap! Clap! Clap!
Fa me la sol, La me fa sol!   20

XIV Sung by Mr. Scropprell, MS., chap xi.

Songs of Innocence

The Author & Printer W Blake

SONGS OF INNOCENCE
AND OF EXPERIENCE

(Engraved 1789-1794)

SONGS OF INNOCENCE

Introduction

    Piping down the valleys wild,
    Piping songs of pleasant glee,
    On a cloud I saw a child,
    And he laughing said to me:

    'Pipe a song about a Lamb!'   5
    So I piped with merry cheer.
    'Piper, pipe that song again;'
    So I piped: he wept to hear.

    'Drop thy pipe, thy happy pipe;
    Sing thy songs of happy cheer:'   10
    So I sang the same again,
    While he wept with joy to hear.

    'Piper, sit thee down and write
    In a book, that all may read.'
    So he vanish'd from my sight,   15
    And I pluck'd a hollow reed,

    And I made a rural pen,
    And I stain'd the water clear,
    And I wrote my happy songs
    Every child may joy to hear   20

Songs of Innocence

The Echoing Green

  The Sun does arise,
  And make happy the skies;
  The merry bells ring
  To welcome the Spring;
  The skylark and thrush,
  The birds of the bush,
  Sing louder around
  To the bells' cheerful sound,
  While our sports shall be seen
  On the Echoing Green.

  Old John, with white hair,
  Does laugh away care,
  Sitting under the oak,
  Among the old folk.
  They laugh at our play,
  And soon they all say:
  'Such, such were the joys
  When we all, girls and boys,
  In our youth time were seen
  On the Echoing Green.'

  Till the little ones, weary,
  No more can be merry;
  The sun does descend,
  And our sports have an end.
  Round the laps of their mothers
  Many sisters and brothers,
  Like birds in their nest,
  Are ready for rest,
  And sport no more seen
  On the darkening Green.

The Lamb

The Lamb

    Little Lamb, who made thee?
    Dost thou know who made thee?
Gave thee life, and bid thee feed,
By the stream and o'er the mead;
Gave thee clothing of delight,
Softest clothing, woolly, bright;
Gave thee such a tender voice,
Making all the vales rejoice?
    Little Lamb, who made thee?
    Dost thou know who made thee?

    Little Lamb, I'll tell thee,
    Little Lamb, I'll tell thee:
He is callèd by thy name,
For He calls Himself a Lamb.
He is meek, and He is mild;
He became a little child.
I a child, and thou a lamb,
We are callèd by His name.
    Little Lamb, God bless thee!
    Little Lamb, God bless thee!

The Shepherd

How sweet is the Shepherd's sweet lot!
From the morn to the evening he strays;
He shall follow his sheep all the day,
And his tongue shall be fillèd with praise.

For he hears the lamb's innocent call,
And he hears the ewe's tender reply;
He is watchful while they are in peace,
For they know when their Shepherd is nigh.

Songs of Innocence

Infant Joy

    'I have no name :
    I am but two days old.'
    What shall I call thee?
    'I happy am,
    Joy is my name.'
    Sweet joy befall thee!

    Pretty Joy!
    Sweet Joy, but two days old.
    Sweet Joy I call thee
    Thou dost smile,
    I sing the while,
    Sweet joy befall thee!

The Little Black Boy

    My mother bore me in the southern wild,
    And I am black, but O! my soul is white;
    White as an angel is the English child,
    But I am black, as if bereav'd of light.

    My mother taught me underneath a tree,
    And, sitting down before the heat of day,
    She took me on her lap and kissèd me,
    And, pointing to the east, began to say:

    'Look on the rising sun,—there God does live,
    And gives His light, and gives His heat away;
    And flowers and trees and beasts and men receive
    Comfort in morning, joy in the noonday.

    'And we are put on earth a little space,
    That we may learn to bear the beams of love;
    And these black bodies and this sunburnt face
    Is but a cloud, and like a shady grove.

The Little Black Boy

'For when our souls have learn'd the heat to bear,
The cloud will vanish; we shall hear His voice,
Saying: "Come out from the grove, My love and care,
And round My golden tent like lambs rejoice."' 20

Thus did my mother say, and kissèd me;
And thus I say to little English boy.
When I from black and he from white cloud free,
And round the tent of God like lambs we joy,

I'll shade him from the heat, till he can bear 25
To lean in joy upon our Father's knee;
And then I'll stand and stroke his silver hair,
And be like him, and he will then love me.

Laughing Song

When the green woods laugh with the voice of joy,
And the dimpling stream runs laughing by;
When the air does laugh with our merry wit,
And the green hill laughs with the noise of it;

When the meadows laugh with lively green, 5
And the grasshopper laughs in the merry scene,

Laughing Song] In an early MS. version of this song, written between 1783 and May 1784 (see Bibliographical Introduction), with the title 'Song 2^{d} by a Young Shepherd', the first two stanzas run as follows, the third being identical with that of the engraved version:

> When the trees do laugh with our merry wit,
> And the green hill laughs with the noise of it;
> When the meadows laugh with lively green,
> And the grasshopper laughs in the merry scene;
>
> When the greenwood laughs with the voice of joy,
> And the dimpling stream runs laughing by,
> When Edessa and Lyca and Emilie
> With their sweet round mouths sing 'Ha, Ha, He!'

The name Lyca of stanza 2 reappears ten years later in 'The Little Girl Lost' and 'The Little Girl Found' of the *Songs of Experience*.

Songs of Innocence

When Mary and Susan and Emily
With their sweet round mouths sing 'Ha, Ha, He!'

When the painted birds laugh in the shade,
Where our table with cherries and nuts is spread,   10
Come live, and be merry, and join with me,
To sing the sweet chorus of 'Ha, Ha, He!'

Spring

   Sound the flute!
   Now it's mute.
   Birds delight
   Day and night;
   Nightingale   5
   In the dale,
   Lark in sky,
   Merrily,
Merrily, merrily, to welcome in the year.

   Little boy,   10
   Full of joy;
   Little girl,
   Sweet and small;
   Cock does crow,
   So do you;   15
   Merry voice,
   Infant noise,
Merrily, merrily, to welcome in the year.

   Little lamb,
   Here I am;   20
   Come and lick
   My white neck;
   Let me pull
   Your soft wool;
   Let me kiss   25
   Your soft face:
Merrily, merrily, we welcome in the year.

A Cradle Song

A Cradle Song

Sweet dreams, form a shade
O'er my lovely infant's head;
Sweet dreams of pleasant streams
By happy, silent, moony beams.

Sweet sleep, with soft down
Weave thy brows an infant crown.
Sweet sleep, Angel mild,
Hover o'er my happy child.

Sweet smiles, in the night
Hover over my delight;
Sweet smiles, mother's smiles,
All the livelong night beguiles.

Sweet moans, dovelike sighs,
Chase not slumber from thy eyes.
Sweet moans, sweeter smiles,
All the dovelike moans beguiles.

Sleep, sleep, happy child,
All creation slept and smil'd;
Sleep, sleep, happy sleep,
While o'er thee thy mother weep.

Sweet babe, in thy face
Holy image I can trace.
Sweet babe, once like thee,
Thy Maker lay and wept for me,

Wept for me, for thee, for all,
When He was an infant small.
Thou His image ever see,
Heavenly face that smiles on thee.

Smiles on thee, on me, on all;
Who became an infant small.
Infant smiles are His own smiles;
Heaven and earth to peace beguiles.

Songs of Innocence

Nurse's Song

When the voices of children are heard on the green,
And laughing is heard on the hill,
My heart is at rest within my breast,
And everything else is still.

'Then come home, my children, the sun is gone down, 5
And the dews of night arise;
Come, come, leave off play, and let us away
Till the morning appears in the skies.'

'No, no, let us play, for it is yet day,
And we cannot go to sleep; 10
Besides, in the sky the little birds fly,
And the hills are all cover'd with sheep.'

'Well, well, go and play till the light fades away,
And then go home to bed.'
The little ones leapèd and shoutèd and laugh'd 15
And all the hills echoèd.

Holy Thursday

'Twas on a Holy Thursday, their innocent faces clean,
The children walking two and two, in red and blue and green,
Grey-headed beadles walk'd before, with wands as white as snow,
Till into the high dome of Paul's they like Thames' waters flow.

Nurse's Song] An earlier version of this song is found in the MS. known as *An Island in the Moon* (chap. xi), the first readings, most of which have been there corrected to their present form, being noted below.   1 voices] tongues *Isl. in Moon*.   2 And laughing upon the hill *Isl. in Moon 2nd rdg.* (afterwards re-corrected to its earlier and present form).   5 Then come home, children, the sun is down. *Isl. in Moon 1st rdg.*   10 And we cannot sleep till it's dark *Isl. in Moon 1st rdg.*   11 The flocks are at play and we can't go away *Isl. in Moon 1st rdg.*   12 And the meadows are cover'd with sheep *Isl. in Moon 1st rdg.*

Holy Thursday] Engraved with some corrections from the original version, which occurs in *An Island in the Moon* (chap. xi).   1 'Twas on a] Upon a *Isl. in Moon*.   2 red] grey *Isl. in Moon*.

Holy Thursday

O what a multitude they seem'd, these flowers of London town!
Seated in companies they sit with radiance all their own.
The hum of multitudes was there, but multitudes of lambs,
Thousands of little boys and girls raising their innocent hands.

Now like a mighty wind they raise to Heaven the voice of song,
Or like harmonious thunderings the seats of Heaven among. 10
Beneath them sit the agèd men, wise guardians of the poor;
Then cherish pity, lest you drive an angel from your door.

The Blossom

    Merry, merry sparrow!
    Under leaves so green,
    A happy blossom
    Sees you, swift as arrow,
    Seek your cradle narrow 5
    Near my bosom.

    Pretty, pretty robin!
    Under leaves so green,
    A happy blossom
    Hears you sobbing, sobbing, 10
    Pretty, pretty robin,
    Near my bosom.

   7 was] were *Isl. in Moon.*   8 And all in order sit waiting the chief chanter's commands *Isl. in Moon 1st rdg. del.*; Thousands of little girls and boys, etc. *ibid. 2nd rdg.*   9–12 In Blake's first draft this stood:

    Then like a mighty wind they raise to heav'n the voice of song,
    Or like harmonious thunderings the seats of heav'n among,
    When the whole multitude of innocents their voices raise
    Like angels on the throne of heav'n, raising the voice of praise.

Blake then deleted the entire stanza, and began:

    Let cherubim and seraphim now raise their voices high.

This also was cancelled, and the stanza rewritten with the slight changes noted below.   9 Now] Then *Isl. in Moon.*   11 agèd] rev'rend *Isl. in Moon.*   wise guardians] the guardians *Isl. in Moon.*

Songs of Innocence

The Chimney Sweeper

When my mother died I was very young,
And my father sold me while yet my tongue
Could scarcely cry ''weep! 'weep! 'weep! 'weep!'
So your chimneys I sweep, and in soot I sleep.

There's little Tom Dacre, who cried when his head, 5
That curl'd like a lamb's back, was shav'd: so I said
'Hush, Tom! never mind it, for when your head's bare
You know that the soot cannot spoil your white hair.'

And so he was quiet, and that very night,
As Tom was a-sleeping, he had such a sight!— 10
That thousands of sweepers, Dick, Joe, Ned, and Jack,
Were all of them lock'd up in coffins of black.

And by came an Angel who had a bright key,
And he open'd the coffins and set them all free;
Then down a green plain leaping, laughing, they run, 15
And wash in a river, and shine in the sun.

Then naked and white, all their bags left behind,
They rise upon clouds and sport in the wind;
And the Angel told Tom, if he'd be a good boy,
He'd have God for his father, and never want joy. 20

And so Tom awoke; and we rose in the dark,
And got with our bags and our brushes to work.
Tho' the morning was cold, Tom was happy and warm;
So if all do their duty they need not fear harm.

The Divine Image

The Divine Image

    To Mercy, Pity, Peace, and Love
    All pray in their distress;
    And to these virtues of delight
    Return their thankfulness.

    For Mercy, Pity, Peace, and Love
    Is God, our Father dear,
    And Mercy, Pity, Peace, and Love
    Is man, His child and care.

    For Mercy has a human heart,
    Pity a human face,
    And Love, the human form divine,
    And Peace, the human dress.

    Then every man, of every clime,
    That prays in his distress,
    Prays to the human form divine,
    Love, Mercy, Pity, Peace.

    And all must love the human form,
    In heathen, Turk, or Jew;
    Where Mercy, Love, and Pity dwell
    There God is dwelling too.

Night

    The sun descending in the west,
    The evening star does shine;
    The birds are silent in their nest,
    And I must seek for mine.
    The moon, like a flower,
    In heaven's high bower,
    With silent delight
    Sits and smiles on the night.

Songs of Innocence

Farewell, green fields and happy groves
Where flocks have took delight.
Where lambs have nibbled, silent moves
The feet of angels bright ;
Unseen they pour blessing,
And joy without ceasing,
On each bud and blossom,
And each sleeping bosom.

They look in every thoughtless nest,
Where birds are cover'd warm ;
They visit caves of every beast,
To keep them all from harm.
If they see any weeping
That should have been sleeping,
They pour sleep on their head,
And sit down by their bed.

When wolves and tigers howl for prey,
They pitying stand and weep ;
Seeking to drive their thirst away,
And keep them from the sheep.
But if they rush dreadful,
The angels, most heedful,
Receive each mild spirit,
New worlds to inherit.

And there the lion's ruddy eyes
Shall flow with tears of gold,
And pitying the tender cries,
And walking round the fold,
Saying 'Wrath, by His meekness,
And, by His health, sickness
Is driven away
From our immortal day.

Night

'And now beside thee, bleating lamb,
I can lie down and sleep;
Or think on Him who bore thy name,
Graze after thee and weep.
For, wash'd in life's river,   45
My bright mane for ever
Shall shine like the gold
As I guard o'er the fold.'

A Dream

Once a dream did weave a shade
O'er my Angel-guarded bed,
That an emmet lost its way
Where on grass methought I lay.

Troubled, 'wilder'd, and forlorn,   5
Dark, benighted, travel-worn,
Over many a tangled spray,
All heart-broke I heard her say:

'O, my children! do they cry?
Do they hear their father sigh?   10
Now they look abroad to see:
Now return and weep for me.'

Pitying, I dropp'd a tear;
But I saw a glow-worm near,
Who replied: 'What wailing wight 15
Calls the watchman of the night?

'I am set to light the ground,
While the beetle goes his round
Follow now the beetle's hum;
Little wanderer, hie thee home.'   20

Songs of Innocence

On Another's Sorrow

    Can I see another's woe,
    And not be in sorrow too?
    Can I see another's grief,
    And not seek for kind relief?

    Can I see a falling tear,
    And not feel my sorrow's share?
    Can a father see his child
    Weep, nor be with sorrow fill'd?

    Can a mother sit and hear
    An infant groan, an infant fear?
    No, no! never can it be!
    Never, never can it be!

    And can He who smiles on all
    Hear the wren with sorrows small,
    Hear the small bird's grief and care,
    Hear the woes that infants bear,

    And not sit beside the nest,
    Pouring pity in their breast;
    And not sit the cradle near,
    Weeping tear on infant's tear;

    And not sit both night and day,
    Wiping all our tears away?
    O, no! never can it be!
    Never, never can it be!

    He doth give His joy to all;
    He becomes an infant small;
    He becomes a man of woe;
    He doth feel the sorrow too.

    Think not thou canst sigh a sigh,
    And thy Maker is not by;
    Think not thou canst weep a tear,
    And thy Maker is not near.

On Another's Sorrow

O! He gives to us His joy
That our grief He may destroy;
Till our grief is fled and gone
He doth sit by us and moan.

The Little Boy Lost

'Father! father! where are you going?
O do not walk so fast.
Speak, father, speak to your little boy,
Or else I shall be lost.'

The night was dark, no father was there;
The child was wet with dew;
The mire was deep, and the child did weep,
And away the vapour flew.

The Little Boy Found

The little boy lost in the lonely fen,
Led by the wand'ring light,
Began to cry; but God, ever nigh,
Appear'd like his father, in white.

He kissèd the child, and by the hand led,
And to his mother brought,
Who in sorrow pale, thro' the lonely dale,
Her little boy weeping sought.

[END OF THE SONGS OF INNOCENCE]

The Little Boy Lost] From *An Island in the Moon* (chap. xi).   1 Father! father!] O father, father *Isl. in Moon*.   3 Speak] O speak *Isl. in Moon*. 5 The night it was dark and no father was there *Isl. in Moon*.   6 The child] And the child *Isl. in Moon*.

SONGS OF EXPERIENCE

Introduction

  Hear the voice of the Bard!
  Who present, past, and future, sees;
  Whose ears have heard
  The Holy Word
  That walk'd among the ancient trees,   5

  Calling the lapsèd soul,
  And weeping in the evening dew;
  That might control
  The starry pole,
  And fallen, fallen light renew!   10

  'O Earth, O Earth, return!
  Arise from out the dewy grass;
  Night is worn,
  And the morn
  Rises from the slumberous mass.   15

  'Turn away no more;
  Why wilt thou turn away.
  The starry floor,
  The wat'ry shore,
  Is giv'n thee till the break of day'   20

Songs of Experience

Earth's Answer

  Earth rais'd up her head
  From the darkness dread and drear.
  Her light fled,
  Stony dread!
  And her locks cover'd with grey despair.   5

  ' Prison'd on wat'ry shore,
  Starry Jealousy does keep my den:
  Cold and hoar,
  Weeping o'er,
  I hear the Father of the Ancient Men.   10

  ' Selfish Father of Men!
  Cruel, jealous, selfish Fear!
  Can delight,
  Chain'd in night,
  The virgins of youth and morning bear?   15

Earth's Answer] This and seventeen others of the *Songs of Experience* were engraved for this book from earlier drafts or transcripts in the *Rossetti MS.*, the original readings in each case being noted below.

 Title] The Earth's Answer *MS. first word del.*   3 Blake's successive changes of this line are :

> Her *eyes fled*
> *orbs dead*
>   light fled (pencil).

10 Father of the] del. in MS., and replaced by some illegible word erased.
11–15 Cancelled in MS. The original rime-arrangement abaab breaks down in this and the next stanza.   11 Selfish] Cruel *MS. 1st rdg. del.*
12 selfish] weeping *MS. 1st rdg. del.*   14 Chain'd] Clog'd *MS. 1st rdg. del.*

82

Earth's Answer

'Does spring hide its joy
When buds and blossoms grow?
Does the sower
Sow by night,
Or the ploughman in darkness plough?   20

'Break this heavy chain
That does freeze my bones around.
Selfish! vain!
Eternal bane!
That free Love with bondage bound.'   25

Nurse's Song

When the voices of children are heard on the green
And whisp'rings are in the dale,
The days of my youth rise fresh in my mind,
My face turns green and pale.

Then come home, my children, the sun is gone down,   5
And the dews of night arise;
Your spring and your day are wasted in play,
And your winter and night in disguise.

16–20 This stanza was an addition written in place of the third, which Blake cancelled but restored when engraving.   16 joy] delight *MS. 1st rdg. del.*   18, 19 Does the sower sow His seed by night *MS. 1st rdg. del.*   22 freeze] close *MS. 1st rdg. del.*   24, 25 Thou, my bane Hast my Love with bondage bound *MS. 1st rdg. del.*

Nurse's Song] 3 The *dreams* [*del. changed to* 'days'] of youth etc. *MS.*

Songs of Experience

The Fly

> Little Fly,
> Thy summer's play
> My thoughtless hand
> Has brush'd away.
>
> Am not I
> A fly like thee?
> Or art not thou
> A man like me?
>
> For I dance,
> And drink, and sing,
> Till some blind hand
> Shall brush my wing.

The Fly] In the first draft found in the *Rossetti MS.* Blake begins the song thus:

> Woe! alas! my guilty hand
> Brush'd across thy summer joy;
> All thy gilded painted pride
> Shatter'd, fled . . .

These unfinished lines were cancelled, and he then turned to the shorter metre, preserving the 'guilty hand' in the first draft of stanza i. Then follows a deleted stanza, omitted by him in the engraved version, probably because, since writing the poem, he had used its first two lines as one of his 'Proverbs of Hell' (*Marriage of Heaven and Hell*, p. 250):

> The cut worm
> Forgives the plough,
> And dies in peace,
> And so do thou.

Then come the second, third, and fifth stanzas in their present form, followed by two versions of stanza iv, which was an afterthought. Lastly, prefixed numbers were added, indicating the present order of the stanzas.

2 summer's] summer *MS.*   3 thoughtless] guilty *MS.* 1st rdg. del.

The Fly

If thought is life
And strength and breath,
And the want   15
Of thought is death;

Then am I
A happy fly,
If I live
Or if I die.   20

The Tiger

Tiger! Tiger! burning bright
In the forests of the night,
What immortal hand or eye
Could frame thy fearful symmetry?

In what distant deeps or skies   5
Burnt the fire of thine eyes?
On what wings dare he aspire?
What the hand dare seize the fire?

And what shoulder, and what art,
Could twist the sinews of thy heart?   10
And when thy heart began to beat,
What dread hand? and what dread feet?

The Fly] 13-16   Thought is life
                         And strength and breath;
                         But the want
                         Of thought is death.

MS. 1st rdg. del.

Songs of Experience

What the hammer? what the chain?
In what furnace was thy brain?
What the anvil? what dread grasp   15
Dare its deadly terrors clasp?

When the stars threw down their spears,
And water'd heaven with their tears,
Did he smile his work to see?
Did he who made the Lamb make thee?   20

Tiger! Tiger! burning bright
In the forests of the night,
What immortal hand or eye,
Dare frame thy fearful symmetry?

The original draft of 'The Tiger', written upon two opposite pages of the *Rossetti MS.*, enables us to follow every step in the composition of the poem. On the left-hand page is found the first rough cast of stanzas i, ii, iii, iv, and vi. In stanza iii the manuscript version throws light upon a verse which has proved a crux to many of Blake's readers and commentators. It will be seen from the appended transcript that Blake at first intended the line

'What dread hand and what dread feet'

as the beginning of a sentence running on into the next quatrain. Dissatisfied with the form of this unfinished stanza, he cancelled it altogether, leaving the preceding line as it stood; but subsequently, when engraving the poem for the *Songs of Experience*, converted the passage, by a change of punctuation into its present shape:

'What dread hand? & what dread feet?'

a line exactly parallel in form to

'What the hammer? what the chain?'

of the following stanza. We have yet another reading in Dr. Malkin's *Father's Memoirs of his Child* (1806), where the version of 'The Tiger', presumably supplied to the author by Blake himself, contains the variant

'What dread hand forged thy dread feet?'

On the opposite page of the *MS. Book* is the first draft of stanza v, and above it, though probably written after, a revised version of ii, which differs

The Tiger

from that finally adopted. To the right of these two stanzas follows a fair copy of i, iii, v, and vi, which, except for unimportant differences of capitalization, and the readings 'dare frame' for 'could frame' in the first, and 'hand and eye' for 'hand or eye' in the first and last stanzas, is identical with the text of the engraved *Songs*.

The following is a faithful transcript of the original draft of 'The Tiger' in the *MS.*, Blake's variant readings being indicated typographically by placing them in consecutive order, one below another, deleted words or lines being printed in italics. The manuscript is unpunctuated throughout.

THE TYGER

1   Tyger Tyger burning bright
    In the forests of the night
    What immortal hand & eye
                or
    Could frame thy fearful symmetry
    Dare

2   *In what* distant deeps or skies
    Burnt in
    Burnt the fire of thine eyes
    The cruel
    On what wings dare he aspire
    What the hand dare sieze the fire

3   And what shoulder & what art
    Could twist the sinews of thy heart
    And when thy heart began to beat
    What dread hand & what dread feet

    Could fetch it from the furnace deep
    And in thy horrid ribs dare steep
    In the well of sanguine woe
    In what clay & in what mould
    Were thy eyes of fury rolld

4   *What* the hammer   *what* the chain
    Where   *where*
    In what furnace was thy brain
    What the anvil   What *the arm*
                          arm
                          grasp
                          clasp
                     dread grasp

87

Songs of Experience

    Could its deadly terrors *clasp*
    Dare   *grasp*
                     clasp

6   Tyger Tyger burning bright
     In the forests of the night
     What immortal hand & eye
     Dare *form* thy fearful symmetry
        frame

[*On the opposite page*]

Burnt in distant deeps or skies
The cruel fire of thine eyes
Could heart descend or wings aspire
What the hand dare sieze the fire

5 *3* And *did he laugh* his work to see
       dare he *smile*
           laugh
    What the shoulder   what the knee
       ankle
   4 *Did* he who made the lamb make thee
     Dare
   1 When the stars threw down their spears
   2 And waterd heaven with their tears

The Little Girl Lost

    In futurity
    I prophetic see
    That the earth from sleep
    (Grave the sentence deep)

    Shall arise and seek   5
    For her Maker meek;
    And the desert wild
    Become a garden mild.

The Little Girl Lost] This song and its sequel, 'The Little Girl Found,' were included in the early issues of the *Songs of Innocence*, but were transferred by Blake to the *Songs of Experience*, on the completion of the latter.

The Little Girl Lost

In the southern clime,
Where the summer's prime
Never fades away,
Lovely Lyca lay.

Seven summers old
Lovely Lyca told;
She had wander'd long
Hearing wild birds' song.

'Sweet sleep, come to me
Underneath this tree.
Do father, mother, weep?
Where can Lyca sleep?

'Lost in desert wild
Is your little child.
How can Lyca sleep
If her mother weep?

'If her heart does ache
Then let Lyca wake;
If my mother sleep,
Lyca shall not weep.

'Frowning, frowning night,
O'er this desert bright,
Let thy moon arise
While I close my eyes.'

Sleeping Lyca lay
While the beasts of prey,
Come from caverns deep,
View'd the maid asleep.

The kingly lion stood,
And the virgin view'd,
Then he gamboll'd round
O'er the hallow'd ground.

Songs of Experience

Leopards, tigers, play
Round her as she lay,
While the lion old
Bow'd his mane of gold

And her bosom lick, 45
And upon her neck
From his eyes of flame
Ruby tears there came;

While the lioness
Loos'd her slender dress, 50
And naked they convey'd
To caves the sleeping maid.

The Little Girl Found

All the night in woe
Lyca's parents go
Over valleys deep,
While the deserts weep.

Tired and woe-begone, 5
Hoarse with making moan,
Arm in arm seven days
They trac'd the desert ways.

Seven nights they sleep
Among shadows deep, 10
And dream they see their child
Starv'd in desert wild.

Pale, thro' pathless ways
The fancied image strays
Famish'd, weeping, weak, 15
With hollow piteous shriek.

The Little Girl Found

Rising from unrest,
The trembling woman prest
With feet of weary woe:
She could no further go. 20

In his arms he bore
Her, arm'd with sorrow sore;
Till before their way
A couching lion lay.

Turning back was vain: 25
Soon his heavy mane
Bore them to the ground.
Then he stalk'd around,

Smelling to his prey;
But their fears allay 30
When he licks their hands,
And silent by them stands.

They look upon his eyes
Fill'd with deep surprise;
And wondering behold 35
A spirit arm'd in gold.

On his head a crown;
On his shoulders down
Flow'd his golden hair.
Gone was all their care. 40

'Follow me,' he said;
'Weep not for the maid;
In my palace deep
Lyca lies asleep.'

Then they followèd 45
Where the vision led,
And saw their sleeping child
Among tigers wild.

Songs of Experience

    To this day they dwell
    In a lonely dell;
    Nor fear the wolfish howl   50
    Nor the lions' growl.

The Clod and the Pebble

    'Love seeketh not itself to please,
    Nor for itself hath any care,
    But for another gives its ease,
    And builds a Heaven in Hell's despair.

    So sung a little Clod of Clay,
    Trodden with the cattle's feet,
    But a Pebble of the brook
    Warbled out these metres meet:

    'Love seeketh only Self to please,
    To bind another to its delight,   10
    Joys in another's loss of ease,
    And builds a Hell in Heaven's despite.'

The Little Vagabond

    Dear mother, dear mother, the Church is cold,
    But the Ale-house is healthy and pleasant and warm;
    Besides I can tell where I am used well,
    Such usage in Heaven will never do well.

    But if at the Church they would give us some ale,   5
    And a pleasant fire our souls to regale,
    We'd sing and we'd pray all the livelong day,
    Nor ever once wish from the Church to stray.

  The Clod and the Pebble] Title lacking in *MS*.   5 sung] sang *MS*.
  The Little Vagabond] The little *pretty* Vagabond [*pretty* del.] *MS*.
4 Such usage in heaven makes all go to hell *MS. 1st rdg. del*.   The poor parsons with wind like a blown bladder swell *MS. 2nd rdg*.

The Little Vagabond

Then the Parson might preach, and drink, and sing,
And we'd be as happy as birds in the spring; 10
And modest Dame Lurch, who is always at church,
Would not have bandy children, nor fasting, nor birch

And God, like a father, rejoicing to see
His children as pleasant and happy as He,
Would have no more quarrel with the Devil or the barrel, 15
But kiss him, and give him both drink and apparel.

Holy Thursday

    Is this a holy thing to see
    In a rich and fruitful land,
    Babes reduc'd to misery,
    Fed with cold and usurous hand?

    Is that trembling cry a song? 5
    Can it be a song of joy?
    And so many children poor?
    It is a land of poverty!

    And their sun does never shine,
    And their fields are bleak and bare, 10
    And their ways are fill'd with thorns:
    It is eternal winter there.

    For where'er the sun does shine,
    And where'er the rain does fall,
    Babe can never hunger there, 15
    Nor poverty the mind appal.

---

13 rejoicing to see] that joys for to see *MS. 1st rdg. del.*   16 But shake hands and kiss him and there'd be no more hell *MS. 1st rdg. del.* But kiss him and give him both *food* [*del. changed to* 'drink'] and apparel *MS. 2nd rdg*

Holy Thursday] 7 And so great a number poor *MS.*   8, 12 It is] 'Tis *MS.*   13 For] But *MS.*

Songs of Experience

A Poison Tree

I was angry with my friend:
I told my wrath, my wrath did end.
I was angry with my foe:
I told it not, my wrath did grow.

And I water'd it in fears, 5
Night and morning with my tears;
And I sunnèd it with smiles,
And with soft deceitful wiles.

And it grew both day and night,
Till it bore an apple bright; 10
And my foe beheld it shine,
And he knew that it was mine,

And into my garden stole
When the night had veil'd the pole:
In the morning glad I see 15
My foe outstretch'd beneath the tree.

The Angel

I dreamt a dream! what can it mean?
And that I was a maiden Queen,
Guarded by an Angel mild:
Witless woe was ne'er beguil'd!

And I wept both night and day, 5
And he wip'd my tears away,
And I wept both day and night,
And hid from him my heart's delight.

A Poison Tree] 'Christian Forbearance' *MS*.   4 A line drawn below this stanza in the MS. shows that Blake originally intended the poem to end at this point.   9 both] by *MS*.   11 And I gave it to my foe *MS. 1st rdg. del.*

The Angel

So he took his wings and fled;
Then the morn blush'd rosy red;
I dried my tears, and arm'd my fears
With ten thousand shields and spears.

Soon my Angel came again:
I was arm'd, he came in vain;
For the time of youth was fled,
And grey hairs were on my head.

The Sick Rose

O Rose, thou art sick!
The invisible worm,
That flies in the night,
In the howling storm,

Has found out thy bed
Of crimson joy;
And his dark secret love
Does thy life destroy.

To Tirzah

Whate'er is born of mortal birth
Must be consumèd with the earth,
To rise from generation free:
Then what have I to do with thee?

The Angel] 15, 16 The same lines with a few slight verbal changes had been used by Blake as the final couplets to two poems in the *Rossetti MS*, 'Infant Sorrow' (p. 116), and 'In a Myrtle Shade' (p. 119).   15 For] But *MS. 1st rdg. del.*

The Sick Rose] 5 Hath found etc. *MS.*   7, 8 A dark-secret love Doth life destroy *MS. 1st rdg. del.*   7 his] her *MS.*

To Tirzah] This poem, of which there is no first draft in the *MS. Book*, bears intrinsic evidence in its symbolism of having been composed at a much later date than any of the other songs, the earliest issue in which it occurs being a copy of the *Songs of Innocence and of Experience*, formerly in the possession of Mr. Butts, and now in the Rowfant Library. Further proof of this song being a late addition is found in Russell's *Engravings of William*

Songs of Experience

The sexes sprung from shame and pride, 5
Blow'd in the morn; in evening died;
But Mercy chang'd death into sleep;
The sexes rose to work and weep.

Thou, Mother of my mortal part,
With cruelty didst mould my heart, 10
And with false self-deceiving tears
Didst bind my nostrils, eyes, and ears;

Didst close my tongue in senseless clay,
And me to mortal life betray:
The death of Jesus set me free: 15
Then what have I to do with thee?

The Voice of the Ancient Bard

Youth of delight, come hither,
And see the opening morn,
Image of truth new-born.
Doubt is fled, and clouds of reason,
Dark disputes and artful teasing. 5
Folly is an endless maze,
Tangled roots perplex her ways.
How many have fallen there!
They stumble all night over bones of the dead,
And feel they know not what but care, 10
And wish to lead others, when they should be led.

Blake (no. 16, pp. 72-3), where he refers to a copy of the *Songs*, which, in place of 'To Tirzah', contains an engraving in colours representing a nude figure born aloft by winged cherubs. Perhaps, in spite of Blake's habit of repeating lines after a long interval of time, we may see some evidence of the approximate date of this poem in the fact that the final line of the first and last stanzas:

Then what have I to do with thee?

occurs also in the last poem of the *Pickering MS.* written *circa* 1801-3.

The Voice of the Ancient Bard] In all the early, as well as in most of the later issues, this was arranged as one of the *Songs of Innocence*.

My Pretty Rose-Tree

My Pretty Rose-Tree

> A flower was offer'd to me,
> Such a flower as May never bore;
> But I said 'I've a pretty Rose-tree,'
> And I passèd the sweet flower o'er.
>
> Then I went to my pretty Rose-tree,   5
> To tend her by day and by night,
> But my Rose turn'd away with jealousy,
> And her thorns were my only delight.

Ah! Sun-Flower

> Ah, Sun-flower! weary of time,
> Who countest the steps of the sun;
> Seeking after that sweet golden clime,
> Where the traveller's journey is done;
>
> Where the Youth pined away with desire,   5
> And the pale Virgin shrouded in snow,
> Arise from their graves, and aspire
> Where my Sun-flower wishes to go.

My Pretty Rose-Tree] Title wtg. in *MS*.   6 In the silence of the night *MS*. *1st rdg. del.*   her] it *MS*. *2nd rdg.*   7 turn'd away with jealousy] was turnèd from me *MS. 1st rdg. del. and replaced by* was fillèd with jealousy.   5-8 Blake's first version of this stanza may perhaps be preferred to that of the engraved *Songs*:

> Then I went to my pretty rose-tree
> In the silence of the night
> But my rose was turnèd from me,
> And her thorns were my only delight.

Songs of Experience

The Lily

The modest Rose puts forth a thorn,
The humble Sheep a threat'ning horn;
While the Lily white shall in love delight,
Nor a thorn, nor a threat, stain her beauty bright.

The Garden of Love

I went to the Garden of Love,
And saw what I never had seen:
A Chapel was built in the midst,
Where I used to play on the green.

And the gates of this Chapel were shut,
And 'Thou shalt not' writ over the door;
So I turn'd to the Garden of Love
That so many sweet flowers bore;

The Lily] In its present form this little poem might more fitly rank as a Song of Innocence than as a Song of Experience; but the first draft with its successive alterations as seen in the *Rossetti MS.*, shows that Blake originally conceived it in its 'contrary state'. Beginning by writing:

> The rose puts envious . . .

he replaced this by 'The lustful rose', finishing the line with the words 'puts forth a thorn', and concluding thus:

> The coward sheep a threat'ning horn;
> While the lily white shall in love delight,
> And the lion increase freedom and peace.

Returning to this piece, perhaps when about to engrave it as one of the *Songs,* Blake deleted the last line, substituting for it:

> The priest loves war, and the soldier peace—

but here, perceiving that his internal rime had disappeared, he cancelled this line also, and gave the poem an entirely different colour by changing the word 'lustful' to 'modest', and 'coward' to 'humble', and completing the quatrain (as in the engraved version) by a fourth line simply explanatory of the first three.

Title] Wtg. in *MS*.

The Garden of Love] Title wtg. in *MS*.   2 And saw] And saw *MS*.   7 So I] And I *MS*. 1st rdg. del.

The Garden of Love

And I saw it was fillèd with graves,
And tomb-stones where flowers should be;   10
And priests in black gowns were walking their rounds,
And binding with briars my joys and desires.

A Little Boy Lost

'Nought loves another as itself,
Nor venerates another so,
Nor is it possible to Thought
A greater than itself to know:

'And, Father, how can I love you   5
Or any of my brothers more?
I love you like the little bird
That picks up crumbs around the door.'

The Priest sat by and heard the child,
In trembling zeal he seiz'd his hair: 10
He led him by his little coat,
And all admir'd the priestly care.

And standing on the altar high,
 Lo! what a fiend is here,' said he,
'One who sets reason up for judge   15
Of our most holy Mystery.'

A Little Boy Lost] Then, Father, I cannot love you *MS. 1st rdg. del.*
6 Or] Nor *MS. 1st rdg. del.*   7 I love myself: so does the bird *MS. 1st rdg. del.*   11, 12 In the first draft:

> The mother follow'd, weeping loud,
> 'O, that I such a fiend should bear!'

which was next changed to:

> Then led him by his little coat
> To shew his zealous priestly care.

Songs of Experience

    The weeping child could not be heard,
    The weeping parents wept in vain;
    They stripp'd him to his little shirt,
    And bound him in an iron chain;   20

    And burn'd him in a holy place,
    Where many had been burn'd before:
    The weeping parents wept in vain.
    Are such things done on Albion's shore?

Infant Sorrow

    My mother groan'd, my father wept,
    Into the dangerous world I leapt;
    Helpless, naked, piping loud,
    Like a fiend hid in a cloud.

    Struggling in my father's hands,   5
    Striving against my swaddling-bands,
    Bound and weary, I thought best
    To sulk upon my mother's breast.

The Schoolboy

    I love to rise in a summer morn
    When the birds sing on every tree;
    The distant huntsman winds his horn,
    And the skylark sings with me.
    O! what sweet company.   5

19 They] And *MS. 1st. rdg. del.*

    19, 20 They bound the little ivory limbs
            In a cruel iron chain   *MS. 1st rdg. del.*

21 They burn'd him in a holy fire *MS. 1st rdg. del.*   24 Such things are done on Albion's shore *MS. 1st rdg.*

Infant Sorrow] Cp. the much fuller form of this poem in the *Rossetti MS.* (p. 115).

The Schoolboy] This song, like 'The Little Girl Lost', 'The Little Girl

The Schoolboy

But to go to school in a summer morn,
O! it drives all joy away;
Under a cruel eye outworn,
The little ones spend the day
In sighing and dismay. 10

Ah! then at times I drooping sit,
And spend many an anxious hour,
Nor in my book can I take delight,
Nor sit in learning's bower,
Worn thro' with the dreary shower. 15

How can the bird that is born for joy
Sit in a cage and sing?
How can a child, when fears annoy,
But droop his tender wing,
And forget his youthful spring? 20

O! father and mother, if buds are nipp'd
And blossoms blown away,
And if the tender plants are stripp'd
Of their joy in the springing day,
By sorrow and care's dismay, 25

How shall the summer arise in joy,
Or the summer fruits appear?
Or how shall we gather what griefs destroy,
Or bless the mellowing year,
When the blasts of winter appear? 30

Found', and 'The Voice of the Ancient Bard', originally formed one of the *Songs of Innocence*, and still appears as such in several of the later issues also.

Songs of Experience

London

    I wander thro' each charter'd street,
    Near where the charter'd Thames does flow,
    And mark in every face I meet
    Marks of weakness, marks of woe.

    In every cry of every Man,   5
    In every Infant's cry of fear,
    In every voice, in every ban,
    The mind-forg'd manacles I hear.

    How the chimney-sweeper's cry
    Every black'ning church appals;   10
    And the hapless soldier s sigh
    Runs in blood down palace walls.

    But most thro' midnight streets I hear
    How the youthful harlot's curse
    Blasts the new-born infant's tear,   15
    And blights with plagues the marriage hearse.

1, 2 charter'd] dirty *MS.*   3 And mark] And see *MS. 1st rdg. del.*
6 In every voice of every child *MS. 1st rdg. del.*   8 The german forged
links I hear *MS. 1st rdg. del.*

    9, 10 But most the chimney-sweeper's cry
           Blackens o'er the church's walls   *MS. 1st rdg. del.*

13-16 In the MS. this stanza was at first written:

    But most the midnight harlot's curse
    From every dismal street I hear,
    Weaves around the marriage hearse,
    And blasts the new-born infant's tear.

This was cancelled and followed by:

    But most from every street I hear—

A Little Girl Lost

A Little Girl Lost

> *Children of the future age,*
> *Reading this indignant page,*
> *Know that in a former time,*
> *Love, sweet Love, was thought a crime!*

In the Age of Gold,
Free from winter's cold,
Youth and maiden bright
To the holy light,
Naked in the sunny beams delight.

Once a youthful pair,
Fill'd with softest care,
Met in garden bright
Where the holy light
Had just remov'd the curtains of the night.

There, in rising day,
On the grass they play ;
Parents were afar,
Strangers came not near,
And the maiden soon forgot her fear.

Tired with kisses sweet,
They agree to meet
When the silent sleep
Waves o'er heaven's deep,
And the weary tired wanderers weep.

alt. successively to
    . . . through wintry streets I hear
and   . . . the cry of youth I hear]
How the midnight harlot's curse
Blasts the new-born infant's tear,
And *hangs* [*alt. to* smites] with plagues the marriage hearse.

103

Songs of Experience

To her father white 25
Came the maiden bright;
But his loving look,
Like the holy book,
All her tender limbs with terror shook.

'Ona! pale and weak! 30
To thy father speak:
O! the trembling fear.
O! the dismal care,
That shakes the blossoms of my hoary hair!'

The Chimney-sweeper

A little black thing among the snow,
Crying ''weep! 'weep!' in notes of woe!
'Where are thy father and mother, say?'—
'They are both gone up to the Church to pray.

'Because I was happy upon the heath, 5
And smil'd among the winter's snow,
They clothèd me in the clothes of death,
And taught me to sing the notes of woe.

'And because I am happy and dance and sing,
They think they have done me no injury, 10
And are gone to praise God and His Priest and King,
Who make up a Heaven of our misery.'

The Chimney-sweeper] The original draft of this song in the *Rossetti MS.* shows that Blake at first intended the second and third stanzas to form a poem complete in itself. The first stanza and title were an afterthought, written in pencil upon a different page. Cp. also the quatrain placed by me among *Gnomic Verses* (p. 194), 'There souls of men are bought and sold,' which may possibly have been written with the intention of its forming another stanza of this song. 3 Where are they, father and mother, say? *MS.* 4 to the church] to church *MS.* 6 winter's snow] wintry *wind* [*alt. to* snow] *MS.* 12 Who wrap themselves up in our misery *MS.* 1*st rdg. del.*

The Human Abstract

The Human Abstract

Pity would be no more
If we did not make somebody poor;
And Mercy no more could be
If all were as happy as we.

And mutual fear brings peace,
Till the selfish loves increase:
Then Cruelty knits a snare,
And spreads his baits with care.

He sits down with holy fears,
And waters the ground with tears;
Then Humility takes its root
Underneath his foot.

Soon spreads the dismal shade
Of Mystery over his head;
And the caterpillar and fly
Feed on the Mystery.

And it bears the fruit of Deceit,
Ruddy and sweet to eat;
And the raven his nest has made
In its thickest shade.

Title] 'The Earth' 1st *rdg.* cancelled, and changed to 'The Human Image'. 1 would] could *MS.* 2 If there was nobody poor *MS.* 1st *rdg. del.* 20 thickest] blackest *MS.*

Songs of Experience

> The Gods of the earth and sea
> Sought thro' Nature to find this tree;
> But their search was all in vain:
> There grows one in the Human brain.

[END OF THE SONGS OF EXPERIENCE]

APPENDIX

TO THE SONGS OF INNOCENCE AND OF EXPERIENCE

A Divine Image

> Cruelty has a human heart,
> And Jealousy a human face;
> Terror the human form divine,
> And Secrecy the human dress.
>
> The human dress is forgèd iron,   5
> The human form a fiery forge,
> The human face a furnace seal'd,
> The human heart its hungry gorge.

> 23, 24 But their search was all in vain
>   Till they sought in the human brain.
>
>   *MS. 1st rdg., last line del.*

A Divine Image] This song cannot, strictly speaking, be regarded as part of the foregoing book. A companion poem to 'The Divine Image' (p. 75), it seems to have been engraved by Blake in the same manner as the rest, with a view to its forming one of the *Songs of Experience*. It was not, however, included in any authentic copy of the *Songs* issued during the author's lifetime, and is only found in an uncoloured impression in the British Museum Reading Room copy, where the watermark of the paper, which is dated 1832, proves that it must have been printed, perhaps by Tatham, at least five years after Blake's death.

POEMS

from

'THE ROSSETTI MANUSCRIPT'

(*circa* 1793–1811)

sometimes called

'THE MANUSCRIPT BOOK'

POEMS FROM THE ROSSETTI MS.

I

Written *circa* 1793

Never seek to tell thy Love

    Never seek to tell thy love,
    Love that never told can be;
    For the gentle wind does move
    Silently, invisibly.

    I told my love, I told my love,   5
    I told her all my heart;
    Trembling, cold, in ghastly fears,
    Ah! she doth depart.

    Soon as she was gone from me,
    A traveller came by,   10
    Silently, invisibly:
    He took her with a sigh.

In this section are included all the poems in the *Rossetti MS.*, arranged in the order in which they occur, with the exception of the early versions of some of the *Songs of Experience* (the variant readings of which are given in footnotes), and the gnomic verses, epigrams, and short satirical pieces which I group together elsewhere.

Never seek, &c.] I give here the earlier and incomparably finer version of this song, which Blake subsequently altered by cancelling the first stanza (after changing 'seek' to 'pain' in l. 1), and substituting

        'O! was no deny'

for the concluding line of the poem.

Poems from the Rossetti MS.

I laid me down upon a Bank

    I laid me down upon a bank,
    Where Love lay sleeping;
    I heard among the rushes dank
    Weeping, weeping.

    Then I went to the heath and the wild,
    To the thistles and thorns of the waste;
    And they told me how they were beguil'd,
    Driven out, and compell'd to be chaste.

I saw a Chapel all of Gold

    I saw a Chapel all of gold
    That none did dare to enter in,
    And many weeping stood without,
    Weeping, mourning, worshipping.

    I saw a Serpent rise between
    The white pillars of the door,
    And he forc'd and forc'd and forc'd;
    Down the golden hinges tore,

    And along the pavement sweet,
    Set with pearls and rubies bright,
    All his shining length he drew,
    Till upon the altar white

    Vomiting his poison out
    On the Bread and on the Wine.
    So I turn'd into a sty,
    And laid me down among the swine.

I saw a Chapel, &c.] 8 Till he broke the pearly door *MS. 1st rdg. del.*

I asked a Thief

I asked a Thief

    I askèd a thief to steal me a peach:
    He turnèd up his eyes.
    I ask'd a lithe lady to lie her down:
    Holy and meek, she cries.

    As soon as I went   5
    An Angel came:
    He wink'd at the thief,
    And smil'd at the dame;

    And without one word said
    Had a peach from the tree,   10
    And still as a maid
    Enjoy'd the lady.

I heard an Angel singing

    I heard an Angel singing
    When the day was springing:
    'Mercy, Pity, Peace
    Is the world's release.'

    Thus he sang all day   5
    Over the new-mown hay,
    Till the sun went down,
    And haycocks lookèd brown.

I asked a Thief] 2 And he turnèd etc. *MS. 1st rdg. del.*   5, 6 Blake writes as a single line.   7 He] And he *MS. 1st rdg. del.*   9 said] spoke *MS. 1st rdg. del.*   11 And 'twixt earnest and joke *MS. 1st rdg. del.* 12 Enjoy'd] He enjoy'd *MS. 1st rdg. del.*

I heard an Angel singing] A variant version of 'The Human Image', engraved under the title 'The Human Abstract' in the *Songs of Experience*

Poems from the Rossetti MS.

I heard a Devil curse
Over the heath and the furze:
'Mercy could be no more
If there was nobody poor,

'And Pity no more could be,
If all were as happy as we.'
At his curse the sun went down,
And the heavens gave a frown.

[Down pour'd the heavy rain
Over the new reap'd grain;
And Misery's increase
Is Mercy, Pity, Peace.]

15 At his curse] Thus he sang and *MS. 1st rdg. del.*   16 Here, as the MS. indicates, the poem originally ended, Blake afterwards adding a fifth stanza:

> Down [at first *And down*] pour'd the heavy rain
> Over the new-reap'd grain,
> And Mercy and Pity and Peace descended;
> The Farmers were ruined and harvest was ended—

and again marking the completion of the piece by a fresh terminal line. This entire stanza was afterwards deleted, and is followed by several attempts at a new couplet, rehandling in the original metre the theme of Mercy, Pity, Peace, all of which were cancelled with the exception of the final reading:

> And Misery's increase
> Is Mercy, Pity, Peace.

These lines seem intended to form the final couplet of v, and Swinburne doubtless interprets rightly the author's intention in appending them to the first deleted couplet:

> Down pour'd the heavy rain
> Over the new-reap'd grain,

and printing this additional stanza in the form in which it appears, in square brackets, in my text.

A Cradle Song

A Cradle Song

> Sleep! sleep! beauty bright,
> Dreaming o'er the joys of night;
> Sleep! sleep! in thy sleep
> Little sorrows sit and weep.
>
> Sweet Babe, in thy face
> Soft desires I can trace,
> Secret joys and secret smiles,
> Little pretty infant wiles.
>
> As thy softest limbs I feel,
> Smiles as of the morning steal
> O'er thy cheek, and o'er thy breast
> Where thy little heart does rest.
>
> O! the cunning wiles that creep
> In thy little heart asleep.
> When thy little heart does wake
> Then the dreadful lightnings break,
>
> From thy cheek and from thy eye,
> O'er the youthful harvests nigh.
> Infant wiles and infant smiles
> Heaven and Earth of peace beguiles.

A Cradle Song] Obviously designed as the contrary of 'A Cradle Song' in the *Songs of Innocence*. As first written the poem consisted of stanzas i, iii, and iv; stanza ii was then added and the end of the song indicated by a new terminal line, while still later Blake appended a final stanza and numbered the whole in their present order.

1-4 The two couplets were originally written in reverse order. 2 Thou shalt taste the joys of night *MS. 1st rdg. del*. 4 Thou wilt every secret keep *MS. 1st rdg. del*. Canst thou any secret keep *MS. 2nd rdg. del*. 8 Such as burning youth beguiles *MS. 1st rdg. del*.

9, 10 Yet a little while the moon
        Silent— *abandoned opening of this stanza.*
9 feel] touch *MS. 1st rdg. del*.; stroke *MS. 2nd rdg. del*. 10 steal] broke *MS. 1st rdg. del*. 19 Infant ... infant] Female ... female *MS. 1st rdg. del*

Poems from the Rossetti MS.

Silent, silent Night

    Silent, silent Night,
    Quench the holy light
    Of thy torches bright;

    For possess'd of Day,
    Thousand spirits stray
    That sweet joys betray.

    Why should joys be sweet
    Usèd with deceit,
    Nor with sorrows meet?

    But an honest joy
    Does itself destroy
    For a harlot coy.

I fear'd the fury of my wind

    I fear'd the fury of my wind
    Would blight all blossoms fair and true;
    And my sun it shin'd and shin'd,
    And my wind it never blew.

    But a blossom fair or true
    Was not found on any tree;
    For all blossoms grew and grew
    Fruitless, false, tho' fair to see.

I fear'd, &c.] 1 I feared the roughness *MS. 1st rdg. del.*   4 And] But *MS. 1st rdg. del.*

Infant Sorrow

Infant Sorrow

i

My mother groan'd, my father wept;
Into the dangerous world I leapt,
Helpless, naked, piping loud,
Like a fiend hid in a cloud.

ii

Struggling in my father's hands, 5
Striving against my swaddling-bands,
Bound and weary, I thought best
To sulk upon my mother's breast.

iii

When I saw that rage was vain,
And to sulk would nothing gain, 10
Turning many a trick and wile
I began to soothe and smile.

iv

And I sooth'd day after day,
Till upon the ground I stray;
And I smil'd night after night, 15
Seeking only for delight.

v

And I saw before me shine
Clusters of the wand'ring vine;
And, beyond, a Myrtle-tree
Stretch'd its blossoms out to me. 20

Infant Sorrow] The two opening stanzas of this poem were later engraved by Blake as one of the *Songs of Experience.* Cp. also another treatment of the same theme in the first version of the 'Myrtle', which follows on the next blank leaf of the *MS. Book.*   11 I began to trick and wile *MS. 1st rdg. del.*; Seeking many an artful wile *MS. 2nd rdg. del.*   13 sooth'd] grew *MS. 1st rdg. del.*; smil'd *MS. 2nd rdg. del.*   15 smil'd] grew *MS. 1st rdg. del.*   17 From this point onwards I give in the text the earlier

Poems from the Rossetti MS.

vi

But a Priest with holy look,
In his hands a holy book,
Pronouncèd curses on his head
Who the fruits or blossoms shed.

vii

I beheld the Priest by night;
He embrac'd my Myrtle bright:
I beheld the Priest by day,
Where beneath my vines he lay.

viii

Like a serpent in the day
Underneath my vines he lay:
Like a serpent in the night
He embrac'd my Myrtle bright.

ix

So I smote him, and his gore
Stain'd the roots my Myrtle bore;
But the time of youth is fled,
And grey hairs are on my head.

---

and preferable form of the remaining stanzas. Stanza v originally began with the cancelled couplet:

> But upon the earthly ground
> No delight was to be found.

21 But a Priest] My father then *MS. 2nd rdg.*   29-32 The two couplets of this stanza were at first written in reversed order.

v–ix These last five stanzas were afterwards altered to the following form, most of the changes being dependent upon the substitution of 'many a Priest' for 'a Priest' in stanza vi:

> And I saw before me shine
> Clusters of the wand'ring vine;
> And many a lovely flower and tree
> Stretch'd their blossoms out to me.

Why should I care for the men of Thames

Why should I care for the men of Thames

    Why should I care for the men of Thames,
    Or the cheating waves of charter'd streams;
    Or shrink at the little blasts of fear
    That the hireling blows into my ear?

    Tho' born on the cheating banks of Thames,   5
    Tho' his waters bathèd my infant limbs,
    The Ohio shall wash his stains from me:
    I was born a slave, but I go to be free!

    But many a Priest with holy look,
    In their hands a holy book,
    Pronounc'd curses on my head
    And bound me in a myrtle shade.

    I beheld the Priests by night;
    They embrac'd the blossoms bright:
    I beheld the Priests by day;
    Underneath the vines they lay.

    Like to holy men by day
    Underneath the vines they lay:
    Like to serpents in the night
    They embrac'd my myrtle bright.

    So I smote them, and their gore
    Stain'd the roots my myrtle bore;
    But the time of youth is fled,
    And grey hairs are on my head.

Why should I care, &c.] 7 I spurn'd his waters away from me *MS. 1st rdg. del.*   8 I go to be free] I long to be free *MS. 1st rdg. del.*

Poems from the Rossetti MS.

Thou hast a lap full of seed

>Thou hast a lap full of seed,
>And this is a fine country.
>Why dost thou not cast thy seed,
>And live in it merrily?
>
>Shall I cast it on the sand   5
>And turn it into fruitful land?
>For on no other ground
>Can I sow my seed,
>Without tearing up
>Some stinking weed.   10

In a Myrtle Shade

>Why should I be bound to thee,
>O my lovely Myrtle-tree?
>Love, free Love, cannot be bound
>To any tree that grows on ground.
>
>O! how sick and weary I   5
>Underneath my Myrtle lie;
>Like to dung upon the ground,
>Underneath my Myrtle bound.
>
>Oft my Myrtle sigh'd in vain
>To behold my heavy chain: 10
>Oft my Father saw us sigh,
>And laugh'd at our simplicity.

Thou hast a lap full of seed] Cp. *Ahania*, chap. v, stanza 12 (p. 348 of this ed.).   5, 6 Shall I ... turn] Oft I've ... turn'd *MS. 1st rdg. del.*   7 For] But *MS. 1st rdg. del.*   9 tearing] pulling *MS. 1st rdg. del.*

In a Myrtle Shade] 5-8 This stanza, an afterthought, marked for insertion in its present position, began with the couplet afterwards deleted:

>To a lovely myrtle bound,
>Blossoms show'ring all around.

11 Oft the priest beheld us sigh *MS. 1st rdg. del.*

In a Myrtle Shade

So I smote him, and his gore
Stain'd the roots my Myrtle bore.
But the time of youth is fled,   15
And grey hairs are on my head.

To my Myrtle

To a lovely Myrtle bound,
Blossoms show'ring all around,
O how sick and weary I
Underneath my Myrtle lie!
Why should I be bound to thee,   5
O my lovely Myrtle-tree?

13-16 This stanza is identical with the final stanza of 'Infant Sorrow'.
To my Myrtle] A revised version of the preceding. Thus in the *MS. Book,* deleted lines being indicated by italics:

To my Mirtle

5 'Why should I be bound to thee   *1
6 O my lovely mirtle tree
   Love free love cannot be bound
   To any tree that grows on ground.
1 To a lovely mirtle bound   *5
2 Blossoms showring all around
   Like to dung upon the ground
   Underneath my mirtle bound
3 O how sick & weary I   *9
4 Underneath my mirtle lie.'

It will thus be seen that Blake began by transcribing, as it stood, the first stanza of the earlier version, beginning his second stanza with the couplet which he had rejected in the previous draft and adding—but in transposed order—two accepted couplets of the same stanza. He then struck out ll. *3, *4 and *7, *8, prefixing marginal numbers in his usual manner to indicate the position of the lines retained. Blake's intention is perfectly plain; yet we find all Blake's editors following Rossetti in restoring the deleted lines *3, *4, and printing the poem as two four-line stanzas.

Poems from the Rossetti MS.

To Nobodaddy

Why art thou silent and invisible,
Father of Jealousy?
Why dost thou hide thyself in clouds
From every searching eye?

Why darkness and obscurity 5
In all thy words and laws,
That none dare eat the fruit but from
The wily Serpent's jaws?
Or is it because secrecy gains females' loud applause?

Are not the joys of morning sweeter

Are not the joys of morning sweeter
Than the joys of night?
And are the vigorous joys of youth
Ashamèd of the light?

Let age and sickness silent rob 5
The vineyards in the night;
But those who burn with vigorous youth
Pluck fruits before the light.

Nobodaddy, a 'portmanteau word' for 'Nobody's Daddy', antithetical to 'Father of All', was Blake's jocular nickname for Urizen, the Father of Jealousy. The same name occurs in 'Lafayette' (p. 123) and 'When Klopstock England defied' (p. 132). 2 Father] Man *MS. 1st rdg. del.* 9 females' loud] feminine *MS. 1st rdg. del.* This line is an afterthought, added in pencil.

Are not the joys, &c.] Cp. *Visions of the Daughters of Albion*, f. 6, ll. 5-7 (p. 290 of this ed.):

> Innocence! honest, open, seeking
> The vigorous joys of morning light, open to virgin bliss,
> Who taught thee modesty, subtil modesty, child of night and sleep?

120

The Wild Flower's Song

The Wild Flower's Song

As I wander'd the forest,
The green leaves among,
I heard a Wild Flower
Singing a song.

'I slept in the earth   5
In the silent night,
I murmur'd my fears
And I felt delight.

'In the morning I went,
As rosy as morn,   10
To seek for new joy;
But I met with scorn.'

Day

The sun arises in the East,
Cloth'd in robes of blood and gold;
Swords and spears and wrath increas'd
All around his bosom roll'd,
Crown'd with warlike fires and raging desires.   5

The Wild Flower's Song] As originally written stanzas ii and iii formed the entire poem. Later, on another page, Blake added the introductory stanza, with the catchwords ('I slept in the Earth (*dark* del.) &c.') and finally the title.   3 flower] thistle *MS. 1st rdg. del.*   5 I was found in the dark *MS. 1st rdg. del.*

Day] 1 The day arises *MS. 1st rdg. del.*   4 bosom] ancles *MS. 1st rdg. del.*

Poems from the Rossetti MS.

The Fairy

'Come hither, my Sparrows,
My little arrows.
If a tear or a smile
Will a man beguile,
If an amorous delay
Clouds a sunshiny day,
If the step of a foot
Smites the heart to its root,
'Tis the marriage-ring—
Makes each fairy a king.'

So a Fairy sung.
From the leaves I sprung;
He leap'd from the spray
To flee away;
But in my hat caught,
He soon shall be taught.
Let him laugh, let him cry,
He's my Butterfly;
For I've pull'd out the sting
Of the marriage-ring.

The Fairy] Blake's first title (afterwards erased) was 'The Marriage Ring'. With these lines compare the proem to *Europe* (p. 303), and Blake's sketch of the same subject in the *MS. Book*, afterwards engraved as one of the plates of *The Gates of Paradise*. See also the poem on p. 127   7 step] tread *MS. 1st rdg. del.*   19, 20 Originally written:

> And the marriage ring
> [*a line erased.*   ]

Motto to the Songs

Motto to the Songs of Innocence and of Experience

The Good are attracted by men's perceptions,
And think not for themselves;
Till Experience teaches them to catch
And to cage the fairies and elves.

And then the Knave begins to snarl, 5
And the Hypocrite to howl;
And all his good friends show their private ends,
And the eagle is known from the owl.

[Lafayette]

i

'Let the brothels of Paris be openèd
With many an alluring dance,
To awake the physicians thro' the city!'
Said the beautiful Queen of France.

ii

The King awoke on his couch of gold, 5
As soon as he heard these tidings told:
'Arise and come, both fife and drum,
And the famine shall eat both crust and crumb.'

Motto] This motto, which was probably never engraved by Blake, is not found in any copy of the *Songs*.

Lafayette] Written upon two opposite pages of the *MS. Book*, and apparently abandoned unfinished. As it there stands, the rough draft exhibits a bewildering series of erasures, corrections, re-writings, and re-arrangements of lines into stanzas, and stanzas into various sequences, dealt with in detail in my previous edition of the *Poems*. In the present text I have attempted to give, so far as it can be ascertained, the last form and order of the stanzas as indicated by Blake's final revisions, with the earlier readings in footnotes. 3 physicians] pestilence *MS. 1st rdg. del.* 8 famine] *MS. 1st rdg. del.*; but no word substituted. ii Followed in the MS. by the two erased stanzas:

> Then old Nobodaddy aloft
> . . and belched and cough'd,

Poems from the Rossetti MS.

iii

The Queen of France just touch'd this globe,
And the pestilence darted from her robe;
But our good Queen quite grows to the ground,
And a great many suckers grow all around.

iv

Fayette beside King Lewis stood;
He saw him sign his hand;
And soon he saw the famine rage
About the fruitful land.

v

Fayette beheld the Queen to smile
And wink her lovely eye;
And soon he saw the pestilence
From street to street to fly.

> And said 'I love hanging and drawing and quartering
> Every bit as well as war and slaughtering.
> Damn praying and singing,
> Unless they will bring in
> The blood of ten thousand by fighting or swinging!'
>
> Then he swore a great and solemn oath:
> 'To kill the people I am loth;
> But if they rebel, they must go to hell:
> They shall have a priest and a passing bell.'

These were later compressed into a single stanza, afterwards cancelled:

> Then he swore a great and solemn oath:
> 'To kill the people I am loth,'
> And said 'I love hanging and drawing and quartering
> Every bit as well as war and slaughtering.'

11, 12 But the bloodthirsty people across the water
    Will not submit to the gibbet and halter.   *MS. 1st rdg. del.*

12 There is just such a tree at Java found.   *MS. 2nd rdg. del.*
iv, v These two stanzas were afterwards cancelled.

Lafayette

vi

Fayette beheld the King and Queen
In curses and iron bound;
But mute Fayette wept tear for tear,
And guarded them around.

vii

Fayette, Fayette, thou'rt bought and sold   25
And sold is thy happy morrow;
Thou gavest the tears of pity away
In exchange for the tears of sorrow.

viii

Who will exchange his own fireside
For the stone of another's door?   30
Who will exchange his wheaten loaf
For the links of a dungeon-floor?

---

22 curses] tears *MS. 1st rdg. del.*
vii Afterwards cancelled.   The stanza originally stood:

> Fayette, Fayette, thou'rt bought and sold
> For well I see thy tears
> Of Pity are exchanged for those
> Of selfish slavish fears.

Then followed the deleted beginning of an unfinished stanza:

> Fayette beside his banner stood,
> His captains false around,
> Thou'rt bought and sold—

viii, ix These two stanzas are an expansion of the earlier version:

> Will the mother exchange her new-born babe
> For the dog at the wintry door?
> Yet thou dost exchange thy pitying tears
> For the links of a dungeon-floor!

30 stone] steps *MS. 1st rdg. del.*
32 Followed in the MS. by the erased lines:

> Who will exchange his own heart's blood
> For the drops of a Harlot's eye?

Poems from the Rossetti MS.

IX

O who would smile on the wintry seas
And pity the stormy roar?
Or who will exchange his new-born child   35
For the dog at the wintry door?

36 Cp. *Urizen*, f. 23, l. 2 (p. 328, l. 448 of this ed.).

Appendix to the Earlier Poems

APPENDIX

TO THE

EARLIER POEMS IN THE ROSSETTI MS.

A Fairy leapt upon my knee
Singing and dancing merrily;
I said, 'Thou thing of patches, rings,
Pins, necklaces, and such-like things,
Disgracer of the female form, 5
Thou paltry, gilded, poisonous worm!'
Weeping, he fell upon my thigh,
And thus in tears did soft reply:
'Knowest thou not, O Fairies' lord!
How much by us contemn'd, abhorr'd, 10
Whatever hides the female form
That cannot bear the mortal storm?
Therefore in pity still we give
Our lives to make the female live;
And what would turn into disease 15
We turn to what will joy and please.'

I place here a short poem printed by Swinburne in his *Essay* (pp. 143-4, *note*), who refers to it as 'copied from a loose scrap of paper, on the back of which is a pencilled sketch of Hercules throttling the serpents, whose twisted limbs make a sort of spiral cradle around and above the child's triumphant figure: an attendant, naked, falls back in terror with sharp recoil of drawn-up limbs; Alcmene and Amphitryon watch the struggle in silence, he grasping her hand.'

I have little doubt that this 'loose scrap of paper' must have been one of those enclosed in, but not afterwards bound up with, the *MS. Book*, when it was acquired by D. G. Rossetti; the piece itself in theme and manner closely resembling 'The Fairy' in the preceding section, written *circa* 1793, and the proem to *Europe* engraved 1794.

POEMS FROM THE ROSSETTI MS.

II

Written *circa* 1800–1810

My Spectre around me night and day

i

My Spectre around me night and day
Like a wild beast guards my way;
My Emanation far within
Weeps incessantly for my sin.

My Spectre] Probably composed in October or November, 1800, soon after Blake's removal to Felpham, when he resumed the use of his old sketch-book as a notebook for poetry. The symbolism, which is identical with that of the revised version of *The Four Zoas*, Book VII, points also to the same date. Cp. also for very close parallelisms *Milton*, ff. 32 and *32 (quoted on p. 380 of this ed.).

This poem is another of those left in very rough draft by the author, and subjected to a great many changes and revisions, before the stanzas finally approved by him were numbered i–xiv. Later, however, around a sketch of Daphne in the middle of the page, he added four complementary stanzas: 'O'er my sins thou sit and moan', 'What transgressions I commit'— numbered respectively '1' and '2'—and an unnumbered stanza 'Poor, pale, pitiable form', followed by another which is now almost illegible. These stanzas, which like xiii and xiv are in pencil, were evidently intended for insertion in the poem, though Blake has not clearly indicated their precise position. The stanzas numbered '1' and '2' (in this ed. 'A', 'B') are undoubtedly part of the speech of the 'Emanation' or 'Jealous Female', and hence, it would seem, ought immediately to precede ix and x, which in the *MS. Book* stand at the head of the sheet, Blake's 1 and 2 perhaps being intended to signify that these stanzas take precedence of everything upon the same page.

Again, the unnumbered stanza beginning 'Poor, pale, pitiable form' (in this

My Spectre around me night and day

ii

'A fathomless and boundless deep, 5
There we wander, there we weep;
On the hungry craving wind
My Spectre follows thee behind.

iii

'He scents thy footsteps in the snow,
Wheresoever thou dost go, 10
Thro' the wintry hail and rain.
When wilt thou return again?

ed. 'C'), is no less clearly part of the speech of the original speaker, the Man in his 'divided' or fallen state, and hence, with the partially obliterated stanza which follows it, ought, it may be presumed, to precede stanza xi, from which point the poem proceeds straightforwardly to its conclusion. I have accordingly incorporated stanzas A–C in the text in the position where they should be read, preserving, however, Blake's numbering of the original stanzas, and enclosing the supplementary ones within square brackets.

i Followed in the *MS. Book* by the two cancelled stanzas:

Thy [1st rdg. *Her*] weeping thou [*she*] shall ne'er give o'er.
I sin against thee [*her*] more and more;
And never will from sin be free
Till she forgives and comes to me.

Thou hast parted from my side:
Once thou wast a virgin bride:
Never shalt thou a true love [*lover*] find:
My Spectre follows thee behind.

ii Originally written:

A deep winter [*night*] dark and cold,
Within my heart thou didst unfold;
A fathomless and boundless deep;
There we wander, there we weep.

This is followed by another deleted stanza:

When my love did first begin,
Thou didst call that love a sin:
Secret trembling, night and day,
Driving all my loves away.

Poems from the Rossetti MS.

iv

'Dost thou not in pride and scorn
Fill with tempests all my morn,
And with jealousies and fears
Fill my pleasant nights with tears?

v

'Seven of my sweet loves thy knife
Has bereavèd of their life.
Their marble tombs I built with tears,
And with cold and shuddering fears.

vi

'Seven more loves weep night and day
Round the tombs where my loves lay,
And seven more loves attend each night
Around my couch with torches bright.

vii

'And seven more loves in my bed
Crown with wine my mournful head,
Pitying and forgiving all
Thy transgressions great and small.

viii

'When wilt thou return and view
My loves, and them to life renew?
When wilt thou return and live?
When wilt thou pity as I forgive?'

a

['O'er my sins thou sit and moan:
Hast thou no sins of thy own?
O'er my sins thou sit and weep,
And lull thy own sins fast asleep.]

---

13 Dost] Didst *MS. 1st rdg. del.*   32 as I forgive] and forgive
MS. 1st rdg. del.   a With interchange of the first and second persons.
the original draft reading throughout 'I' for 'thou', and 'thy' for 'my'—in

My Spectre around me night and day

b

['What transgressions I commit
Are for thy transgressions fit.
They thy harlots, thou their slave;
And my bed becomes their grave.]   40

ix

'Never, never, I return:
Still for victory I burn.
Living, thee alone I'll have;
And when dead I'll be thy grave.

x

'Thro' the Heaven and Earth and Hell   45
Thou shalt never, never quell:
I will fly and thou pursue:
Night and morn the flight renew.'

c

['Poor, pale, pitiable form
That I follow in a storm;   50
Iron tears and groans of lead
Bind around my aching head.]

xi

'Till I turn from Female love
And root up the Infernal Grove,
I shall never worthy be   55
To step into Eternity.

---

other words these lines as at first conceived were spoken to and not by the Emanation. Compare the converse change in stanza xi.   c Followed in the MS. by the partially illegible but unerased stanza:

        And let [? us go] to the . . . . . [? day]
        With many pleasing wiles . . . . .
        [? The man] that does not love your [? wiles]
        Will never [? win back] your smiles.

51, 53 I] thou *MS. 1st rdg. del.*   52 root] dig *MS. 1st rdg. del.*

Poems from the Rossetti MS.

xii

'And, to end thy cruel mocks,
Annihilate thee on the rocks,
And another form create
To be subservient to my fate. 60

xiii

'Let us agree to give up love,
And root up the Infernal Grove;
Then shall we return and see
The worlds of happy Eternity.

xiv

'And throughout all Eternity 65
I forgive you, you forgive me.
As our dear Redeemer said:
"This the Wine, and this the Bread."'

When Klopstock England defied

When Klopstock England defied,
Uprose William Blake in his pride;
For old Nobodaddy aloft
 . . and belch'd and cough'd;
Then swore a great oath that made Heaven quake, 5
And call'd aloud to English Blake.
Blake was giving his body ease,
At Lambeth beneath the poplar trees.

---

57 And] And I *MS. 1st rdg. del.*

When Klopstock, &c.] Swinburne (*Critical Essay*, pp. 31-2) refers the origin of this Rabelaisian *jeu d'esprit* to the passages from Klopstock rendered into English by Hayley for Blake's benefit during the latter's stay at Felpham in 1803 (Hayley's *Diary*, Mar. 26, 29); but the reference to Lambeth, and the repetition of l. 4 in 'Lafayette', point rather to its having been written about 1793.

When Klopstock England defied

From his seat then started he
And turn'd him round three times three.
The moon at that sight blush'd scarlet red,
The stars threw down their cups and fled,
And all the devils that were in hell,
Answerèd with a ninefold yell.
Klopstock felt the intripled turn,
And all his bowels began to churn,
And his bowels turn'd round three times three,
And lock'd in his soul with a ninefold key; ...
Then again old Nobodaddy swore
He ne'er had seen such a thing before,
Since Noah was shut in the ark,
Since Eve first chose her hellfire spark,
Since 'twas the fashion to go naked,
Since the old Anything was created. ...

Mock on, mock on, Voltaire, Rousseau

Mock on, mock on, Voltaire, Rousseau;
Mock on, mock on; 'tis all in vain!
You throw the sand against the wind,
And the wind blows it back again.

And every sand becomes a gem
Reflected in the beams divine;
Blown back they blind the mocking eye,
But still in Israel's paths they shine.

The Atoms of Democritus
And Newton's Particles of Light
Are sands upon the Red Sea shore,
Where Israel's tents do shine so bright.

---

15 intripled] ninefold *MS. 1st rdg. del.*   16 churn] burn *MS. 1st rdg. del.*   17 And ... round] They turned around *MS. 1st rdg. del.*   18 Two partially illegible lines omitted here.   24 Six partially illegible lines omitted here.

Poems from the Rossetti MS.

I saw a Monk of Charlemaine

i

I saw a Monk of Charlemaine
Arise before my sight:
I talk'd to the Grey Monk where he stood
In beams of infernal light.

ii

Gibbon arose with a lash of steel, 5
And Voltaire with a wracking wheel:
The Schools, in clouds of learning roll'd,
Arose with War in iron and gold.

I saw a Monk] The first draft of this piece, written without title in the *Rossetti MS.* not later than April 1803, consisted of fourteen stanzas, which Blake later separated into two poems 'To the Deists' in *Jerusalem*, and 'The Grey Monk' of the *Pickering MS.*, indicating the beginning of the latter by a line drawn above stanza v. In the version engraved for *Jerusalem*, where the length is reduced to seven stanzas, Blake's first change was to mark xii, xiii, and xiv for insertion after iv. He then wrote the revised version of xii:

> When Satan first the black bow bent
> And the Moral Law from the Gospel rent
> He forg'd the Law into a sword
> And spill'd the blood of Mercy's Lord—

adding in the margin the new stanza:

> Titus! Constantine! Charlemaine!
> O Voltaire! Rousseau! Gibbon! vain
> Your Grecian mocks [*mocks and iron* del.] and Roman sword
> Against this image of his Lord—

which (omitting the original xiii) is linked to xiv by the catchword 'A tear is, &c.' The stanzas thus rejected Blake converted into a second poem, which he transcribed into the *Pickering MS.*, with the title 'The Grey Monk'. This begins with the original fifth stanza, the line 'I see, I see, the Mother said' being changed to 'I die, I die, the Mother said'. The remaining stanzas (vi–xi) are arranged in the order of the *MS. Book*, with the interpolation of iv between v and vi, and xiv between x and xi, these two stanzas being common to both versions.　　ii Of this stanza we have the rejected variants:

134

I saw a Monk of Charlemaine

iii

'Thou lazy Monk,' they said afar,
'In vain condemning glorious War,
And in thy cell thou shall ever dwell.
Rise, War, and bind him in his cell!'

iv

The blood red ran from the Grey Monk's side,
His hands and feet were wounded wide,
His body bent, his arms and knees
Like to the roots of ancient trees.

v

'I see, I see,' the Mother said,
'My children will die for lack of bread.
What more has the merciless tyrant said?'
The Monk sat down on her stony bed.

vi

His eye was dry, no tear could flow;
A hollow groan first spoke his woe.
He trembled and shudder'd upon the bed;
At length with a feeble cry he said:

vii

'When God commanded this hand to write
In the studious hours of deep midnight,
He told me that all I wrote should prove
The bane of all that on Earth I love.

Gibbon plied his lash of steel,
Voltaire turned his wracking wheel,
Charlemaine and his barons bold
Stood by, and mocked in iron and gold.

and

The wheel of Voltaire whirl'd on high,
Gibbon aloud his lash does ply,
Charlemaine and his clouds of war [*and his barons bold* 1st rdg. del.]
Muster around the Polar Star.

   9, 10 'Seditious Monk' said Charlemaine,
    'The glory of War thou condemn'st in vain,'

MS. 1st rdg. del.

135

Poems from the Rossetti MS.

viii

'My brother starv'd between two walls;
Thy children's cry my soul appals: 30
I mock'd at the wrack and griding chain;
My bent body mocks at their torturing pain.

ix

'Thy father drew his sword in the North;
With his thousands strong he is [marchèd] forth;
Thy brother has armèd himself in steel 35
To revenge the wrongs thy children feel.

x

'But vain the sword and vain the bow,
They never can work War's overthrow,
The hermit's prayer and the widow's tear
Alone can free the world from fear. 40

xi

'The hand of Vengeance sought the bed
To which the purple tyrant fled;
The iron hand crush'd the tyrant's head,
And became a tyrant in his stead.

xii

'Until the tyrant himself relent, 45
The tyrant who first the black bow bent,
Slaughter shall heap the bloody plain:
Resistance and War is the tyrant's gain.

---

34 marchèd] deleted in MS. but no word substituted.   44 And usurpèd the tyrant's throne and bed. *MS. 1st rdg. del.*   xii Rewritten later in the form adopted in *Jerusalem*.

I saw a Monk of Charlemaine

xiii

'But the tear of love—and forgiveness sweet,
And submission to death beneath his feet—
The tear shall melt the sword of steel,
And every wound it has made shall heal.

xiv

'For the tear is an intellectual thing,
And a sigh is the sword of an Angel King,
And the bitter groan of the martyr's woe
Is an arrow from the Almighty's bow.'

Morning

To find the Western path,
Right thro' the Gates of Wrath
I urge my way;
Sweet Mercy leads me on
With soft repentant moan:
I see the break of day.

The war of swords and spears,
Melted by dewy tears,
Exhales on high;
The Sun is freed from fears,
And with soft grateful tears
Ascends the sky.

---

xiii Omitted in both the *Jerusalem* and *Pickering MS.* versions. 55 of the martyr's woe] for another's woe *MS. 1st rdg. del.*

Morning] 4-6 Or (since the original is without punctuation) *quaere* read :

> Sweet Mercy leads me on ;
> With soft repentant moan
> I see the break of day.

It may also here be pointed out that the accuracy of Mr. W. A. White's reading 'Mercy' for 'Morning' of all previous editors is confirmed by the diagram on f. 54 of *Jerusalem*, where 'Reason', 'Desire', 'Wrath', 'Pity', are arranged as North, South, East, and West around 'This World'.

Poems from the Rossetti MS.

The Birds

He. Where thou dwellest, in what grove,
　　Tell me Fair One, tell me Love;
　　Where thou thy charming nest dost build,
　　O thou pride of every field!

She. Yonder stands a lonely tree,
　　There I live and mourn for thee;
　　Morning drinks my silent tear,
　　And evening winds my sorrow bear.

He. O thou summer's harmony,
　　I have liv'd and mourn'd for thee;
　　Each day I mourn along the wood,
　　And night hath heard my sorrows loud.

She. Dost thou truly long for me?
　　And am I thus sweet to thee?
　　Sorrow now is at an end,
　　O my Lover and my Friend!

He. Come, on wings of joy we'll fly
　　To where my bower hangs on high;
　　Come, and make thy calm retreat
　　Among green leaves and blossoms sweet.

You don't believe

You don't believe—I won't attempt to make ye:
You are asleep—I won't attempt to wake ye.
Sleep on! sleep on! while in your pleasant dreams
Of Reason you may drink of Life's clear streams.
Reason and Newton, they are quite two things;
For so the swallow and the sparrow sings.

1 You don't believe I would attempt to make ye. *MS. 1st rdg. del.*

You don't believe

Reason says 'Miracle': Newton says 'Doubt.'
Aye! that's the way to make all Nature out.
'Doubt, doubt, and don't believe without experiment':
That is the very thing that Jesus meant,   10
When He said 'Only believe! believe and try!
Try, try, and never mind the reason why!'

If it is true what the Prophets write

If it is true, what the Prophets write,
That the heathen gods are all stocks and stones,
Shall we, for the sake of being polite,
Feed them with the juice of our marrow-bones?

And if Bezaleel and Aholiab drew   5
What the finger of God pointed to their view,
Shall we suffer the Roman and Grecian rods
To compel us to worship them as gods?

They stole them from the temple of the Lord
And worshipp'd them that they might make inspirèd art abhorr'd;   10

The wood and stone were call'd the holy things,
And their sublime intent given to their kings.
All the atonements of Jehovah spurn'd,
And criminals to sacrifices turn'd.

I will tell you what Joseph of Arimathea

I will tell you what Joseph of Arimathea
Said to my Fairy: was not it very queer?
'Pliny and Trajan! What! are you here?
Come before Joseph of Arimathea.
Listen patient, and when Joseph has done   5
'Twill make a fool laugh, and a fairy fun.'

If it is true, &c.] **10** And worshipp'd them to make, &c., *MS. 1st rdg. del.*

139

Poems from the Rossetti MS.

Why was Cupid a boy

Why was Cupid a boy,
And why a boy was he?
He should have been a girl,
For aught that I can see.

For he shoots with his bow, 5
And the girl shoots with her eye,
And they both are merry and glad,
And laugh when we do cry.

And to make Cupid a boy
Was the Cupid girl's mocking plan; 10
For a boy can't interpret the thing
Till he is become a man.

And then he's so pierc'd with cares,
And wounded with arrowy smarts,
That the whole business of his life 15
Is to pick out the heads of the darts.

'Twas the Greeks' love of war
Turn'd Love into a boy,
And woman into a statue of stone—
And away fled every joy. 20

9-12 In the first draft:
        Then to make Cupid a boy
        Was surely a woman's plan,
        For a boy ne'er learns so much
        Till he is become a man.

Now Art has lost its mental charms

Now Art has lost its mental charms

> ' Now Art has lost its mental charms
> France shall subdue the world in arms.'
> So spoke an Angel at my birth;
> Then said ' Descend thou upon earth,
> Renew the Arts on Britain's shore,   5
> And France shall fall down and adore.
> With works of art their armies meet
> And War shall sink beneath thy feet.
> But if thy nation Arts refuse,
> And if they scorn the immortal Muse,   10
> France shall the arts of peace restore
> And save thee from the ungrateful shore.'

Spirit who lov'st Britannia's Isle
Round which the fiends of commerce smile—

[Cetera desunt]

Now Art, &c.] Cp. a passage from Blake's *Advertisement* in the *MS. Book*: ' Let us teach Buonaparte and whomsoever else it may concern that it is not Arts that follow and attend upon Empire, but Empire that attends upon and follows the Arts.' Also an annotation in his copy of Reynolds' *Discourses*, p. cxxv : ' The foundation of Empire is Art and Science. Remove them, or degrade them, and the Empire is no more. Empire follows Art, and not vice versa as Englishmen suppose.'   12 And save thy works from Britain's shore. *MS. 1st rdg. del.*

Poems from the Rossetti MS.

I rose up at the dawn of day

I rose up at the dawn of day—
'Get thee away! get thee away!
Pray'st thou for riches? Away! away!
This is the Throne of Mammon grey.'

Said I: This, sure, is very odd;
I took it to be the Throne of God.
For everything besides I have:
It is only for riches that I can crave.

I have mental joy, and mental health,
And mental friends, and mental wealth;
I've a wife I love, and that loves me;
I've all but riches bodily.

I am in God's presence night and day,
And He never turns His face away;
The accuser of sins by my side doth stand,
And he holds my money-bag in his hand.

For my worldly things God makes him pay,
And he'd pay for more if to him I would pray;
And so you may do the worst you can do;
Be assur'd, Mr. Devil, I won't pray to you.

I rose up, &c.] Written under and partly around an entry dated Aug. 1807. Cp. a note written upon a different page of the *MS. Book* in the earlier part of the same year: 'Tuesday Jany. 20, 1807, between two and seven in the evening Despair.'   13-20 These two stanzas were a later addition.

I rose up at the dawn of day

Then if for riches I must not pray,
God knows, I little of prayers need say;
So, as a church is known by its steeple,
If I pray it must be for other people.

He says, if I do not worship him for a God, 25
I shall eat coarser food, and go worse shod;
So, as I don't value such things as these,
You must do, Mr. Devil, just as God please.

Poems from the Rossetti MS.

The Caverns of the Grave I've seen

> The Caverns of the Grave I've seen,
> And these I show'd to England's Queen.
> But now the Caves of Hell I view,
> Who shall I dare to show them to?
> What mighty soul in Beauty's form
> Shall dauntless view the infernal storm?
> Egremont's Countess can control
> The flames of Hell that round me roll;
> If she refuse, I still go on
> Till the Heavens and Earth are gone,
> Still admir'd by noble minds,
> Follow'd by Envy on the winds,
> Re-engrav'd time after time,
> Ever in their youthful prime,
> My designs unchang'd remain.
> Time may rage, but rage in vain.
> For above Time's troubled fountains,
> On the great Atlantic Mountains,
> In my Golden House on high,
> There they shine eternally.

The Caverns, &c.] Apparently dedicatory verses to accompany Blake's large water-colour painting of 'The Last Judgement', executed for the Countess of Egremont, being an elaboration of the earlier design for Blair's *Grave*, dedicated to Queen Charlotte. See Blake's description of this picture in a letter to Ozias Humphrey, dated 18th Feb., 1808 (*Letters*, ed. Russell, p. 198). These lines are found on a page of the *MS. Book* containing part of Blake's interpretative account of the work, headed 'For the Year 1810: Addition to Blake's Catalogue of Pictures, &c.' 1 Caverns] Visions *MS. 1st rdg. del.* 3 But] And *MS. 1st rdg. del.* 6 dauntless] dare to *MS. 1st rdg. del.* 7 can] dare *MS. 1st rdg. del.* 8 flames] doors *MS. 1st rdg. del.* 11 noble] worthy *MS. 1st rdg. del.* 15 unchang'd] shall still *MS. 1st rdg. del.*

ADDENDUM TO THE LATER POEMS IN THE ROSSETTI MS.

To the Queen

    The Door of Death is made of gold,
    That mortal eyes cannot behold;
    But when the mortal eyes are clos'd,
    And cold and pale the limbs repos'd,
    The soul awakes; and, wond'ring, sees   5
    In her mild hand the golden Keys:
    The Grave is Heaven's Golden Gate,
    And rich and poor around it wait;
    O Shepherdess of England's fold,
    Behold this Gate of Pearl and Gold!   10

    To dedicate to England's Queen
    The visions that my soul has seen,
    And, by her kind permission, bring
    What I have borne on solemn wing,
    From the vast regions of the Grave,   15
    Before her throne my wings I wave;
    Bowing before my Sov'reign's feet,
    'The Grave produc'd these blossoms sweet
    In mild repose from earthly strife;
    The blossoms of Eternal Life!'   20

To the Queen] This poem, Blake's Dedication to his Illustrations of Blair's *Grave* (published 1808), where it is printed in ordinary typography, may not unfitly be placed here in view of its close connection with the preceding lines, although it does not form part of the *Rossetti MS*.

POEMS FROM THE ROSSETTI MS.

III

Written *circa* 1810

THE EVERLASTING GOSPEL

α

The Vision of Christ that thou dost see
Is my vision's greatest enemy.
Thine has a great hook nose like thine,
Mine has a snub nose like to mine.

We have no entire or fair copy of this poem, the text of which is pieced together from passages scattered throughout the *MS. Book*. As these were written for the most part on vacant spaces of pages already partially filled with the draft of his Catalogue 'for the year 1810', it is clear that 'The Everlasting Gospel' was composed not earlier (though probably not much later) than this date.

The poem consists of eight sections, here numbered α-θ, the sequence of which in most cases has been indicated by Blake himself. Of these, besides the Prologue α and the Epilogue θ, the sections β, γ and ζ appear to be complete. So too the section ε 'Was Jesus born of a Virgin pure', which though not written into the *MS. Book* itself, but on a folded scrap of paper now bound in at the end of the volume, has happily been preserved from loss. This passage has no place assigned to it by the author, but its natural position would seem to be immediately before ζ, where I print it in the present arrangement. Of the remaining sections δ and η we possess only the opening lines, presumably intended, according to Blake's usual practice, to serve merely as catchwords to passages copied in full elsewhere. Probably these, like ε, were written upon separate pieces of paper, loosely inserted in the *MS. Book*, and lost before D. G. Rossetti purchased the volume from Samuel Palmer.

Title] First written at the head of the revised version of γ.

The Everlasting Gospel

Thine is the Friend of all Mankind; 5
Mine speaks in parables to the blind.
Thine loves the same world that mine hates;
Thy heaven doors are my hell gates.
Socrates taught what Meletus
Loath'd as a nation's bitterest curse, 10
And Caiaphas was in his own mind
A benefactor to mankind.
Both read the Bible day and night,
But thou read'st black where I read white.

β

Was Jesus gentle, or did He
Give any marks of gentility?
When twelve years old He ran away,
And left His parents in dismay.
When after three days' sorrow found, 5
Loud as Sinai's trumpet-sound:
'No earthly parents I confess—
My Heavenly Father's business!
Ye understand not what I say,
And, angry, force Me to obey. 10
Obedience is a duty then,
And favour gains with God and men.
John from the wilderness loud cried;
Satan gloried in his pride.
'Come,' said Satan, 'come away, 15
I'll soon see if you'll obey!
John for disobedience bled,
But you can turn the stones to bread.

β] 7, 8. In γ (l. 10) and ε (l. 34) Blake changed the last line of this couplet to 'I am doing My Father's business'.

147

Poems from the Rossetti MS.

God's high king and God's high priest
Shall plant their glories in your breast,
If Caiaphas you will obey,
If Herod you with bloody prey
Feed with the sacrifice, and be
Obedient, fall down, worship me.'
Thunders and lightnings broke around,
And Jesus' voice in thunders' sound:
'Thus I seize the spiritual prey.
Ye smiters with disease, make way.
I come your King and God to seize,
Is God a smiter with disease?'
The God of this world rag'd in vain:
He bound old Satan in His chain,
And, bursting forth, His furious ire
Became a chariot of fire.
Throughout the land He took His course,
And trac'd diseases to their source.
He curs'd the Scribe and Pharisee,
Trampling down hypocrisy.
Where'er His chariot took its way,
There Gates of Death let in the Day,
Broke down from every chain and bar;
And Satan in His spiritual war
Dragg'd at His chariot-wheels: loud howl'd
The God of this world: louder roll'd
The chariot-wheels, and louder still
His voice was heard from Zion's Hill,
And in His hand the scourge shone bright;
He scourg'd the merchant Canaanite
From out the Temple of His Mind,
And in his body tight does bind
Satan and all his hellish crew;
And thus with wrath He did subdue
The serpent bulk of Nature's dross,
Till He had nail'd it to the Cross.

The Everlasting Gospel

He took on sin in the Virgin's womb 55
And put it off on the Cross and tomb
To be worshipp'd by the Church of Rome.

γ

Was Jesus humble? or did He
Give any proofs of humility?
Boast of high things with humble tone,
And give with charity a stone?
When but a child He ran away, 5
And left His parents in dismay.
When they had wander'd three days long
These were the words upon His tongue:
'No earthly parents I confess:
I am doing My Father's business.' 10
When the rich learnèd Pharisee
Came to consult Him secretly,
Upon his heart with iron pen
He wrote 'Ye must be born again.'
He was too proud to take a bribe; 15
He spoke with authority, not like a Scribe.
He says with most consummate art
'Follow Me, I am meek and lowly of heart,
As that is the only way to escape
The miser's net and the glutton's trap. 20
What can be done with such desperate fools
Who follow after the heathen schools?

---

55 womb] Followed in MS. by the cancelled line with which this section of the poem originally ended:

> But on the Cross he sealed its doom.

γ] On another page of the *MS. Book* we find Blake's first draft of this passage containing 38, or with marginal additions, 46 lines. The variant readings of this earlier version, which I refer to as γ', are given in the footnotes.   11-14 In γ' these two couplets were written in the reversed order.

Poems from the Rossetti MS.

I was standing by when Jesus died;
What I call'd humility, they call'd pride.
He who loves his enemies betrays his friends.   25
This surely is not what Jesus intends;
But the sneaking pride of heroic schools,
And the Scribes' and Pharisees' virtuous rules,
For He acts with honest, triumphant pride,
And this is the cause that Jesus died.   30
He did not die with Christian ease,
Asking pardon of His enemies:
If He had, Caiaphas would forgive;
Sneaking submission can always live.
He had only to say that God was the Devil,   35
And the Devil was God, like a Christian civil;
Mild Christian regrets to the Devil confess
For affronting him thrice in the wilderness;
He had soon been bloody Caesar's elf,
And at last he would have been Caesar himself,   40
Like Dr. Priestly and Bacon and Newton—
Poor spiritual knowledge is not worth a button!
For thus the Gospel Sir Isaac confutes:
'God can only be known by His attributes;
And as for the indwelling of the Holy Ghost,   45
Or of Christ and His Father, it's all a boast
And pride, and vanity of the imagination,
That disdains to follow this world's fashion.'
To teach doubt and experiment
Certainly was not what Christ meant.   50
What was He doing all that time,
From twelve years old to manly prime?

25 betrays] hates *MS. 1st rdg. del.*   26 surely is not] is surely not γ'.
Followed in γ' by the couplet:

> He must mean the mere love of civility
> And so He must mean concerning humility.

29 But He acts with triumphant, honest pride γ'.   30 cause that] reason γ'.
31–50 These lines are an addition.

150

The Everlasting Gospel

Was He then idle, or the less
About His Father's business?
Or was His wisdom held in scorn   55
Before His wrath began to burn
In miracles throughout the land,
That quite unnerv'd the Seraph band?
If He had been Antichrist, Creeping Jesus,
He'd have done anything to please us;   60
Gone sneaking into synagogues,
And not us'd the Elders and Priests like dogs;
But humble as a lamb or ass
Obey'd Himself to Caiaphas.
God wants not man to humble himself: 65
That is the trick of the Ancient Elf.
This is the race that Jesus ran:
Humble to God, haughty to man,
Cursing the Rulers before the people
Even to the Temple's highest steeple,   70
And when He humbled Himself to God
Then descended the cruel rod.
'If Thou humblest Thyself, Thou humblest Me.
Thou also dwell'st in Eternity.
Thou art a Man: God is no more: 75
Thy own Humanity learn to adore,
For that is My spirit of life.
Awake, arise to spiritual strife,
And Thy revenge abroad display
In terrors at the last Judgement Day.   80

---

59 Antichrist, Creeping Jesus] a creeping Jesus *MS. 1st rdg. del.* For this epithet compare a passage from a letter of Blake to Cumberland, dated April 12, 1827 (Russell's ed., p. 222).   61 into synagogues] into the synagogues γ'.   63 Not humble as a lamb or an ass γ'.   64 Obey'd] Obey γ'.
57-8   Humble toward God, haughty toward man
       This is the race that Jesus ran.   γ'.

71 And] But γ'.   73 Why dost thou humble thyself to me γ' *1st rdg. del.*
76 Thy own] Thine own γ'.

Poems from the Rossetti MS.

God's mercy and long suffering
Is but the sinner to judgement to bring.
Thou on the Cross for them shalt pray—
And take revenge at the Last Day.'
Jesus replied, and thunders hurl'd: 85
'I never will pray for the world.
Once I did so when I pray'd in the Garden;
I wish'd to take with Me a bodily pardon.'
Can that which was of woman born,
In the absence of the morn, 90
When the Soul fell into sleep,
And Archangels round it weep,
Shooting out against the light
Fibres of a deadly night,
Reasoning upon its own dark fiction, 95
In doubt which is self-contradiction?
Humility is only doubt,
And does the sun and moon blot out,
Rooting over with thorns and stems
The buried soul and all its gems. 100
This life's five windows of the soul
Distorts the Heavens from pole to pole.

---

82 Is] Are γ'.   84 Whom thou shalt torment at the Last Day γ' *1st rdg. del.*   85–8 These lines are an addition.   95, 96 Cp. *The Gates of Paradise*, 'The Keys of the Gates', ll. 13–15:

> Two-horn'd reasoning, cloven fiction,
> In doubt which is self-contradiction,
> A dark Hermaphrodite, we stood.

97, 98 Cp. 'Auguries of Innocence,' ll. 109–10 (*Pickering MS.*, p. 174):

> If the sun and moon should doubt.
> They'd immediately go out.

99 Cp. *Jerusalem*, f. 43, l. 8: 'If we are wrathful Albion will destroy Jerusalem with rooty groves.'   101, 102 Cp. the proem to *Europe*, ll. 1–6 (p. 303).

The Everlasting Gospel

And leads you to believe a lie
When you see with, not thro', the eye
That was born in a night, to perish in a night,   105
When the soul slept in the beams of light.

δ

This was spoken by my Spectre to Voltaire, Bacon, &c.

Did Jesus teach doubt? or did He
Give any lessons of philosophy,
Charge Visionaries with deceiving,
Or call men wise for not believing? . . .

ε

Was Jesus born of a Virgin pure
With narrow soul and looks demure?
If He intended to take on sin
The Mother should an harlot been,
Just such a one as Magdalen,   5
With seven devils in her pen.
Or were Jew virgins still more curs'd,
And more sucking devils nurs'd?
Or what was it which He took on
That He might bring salvation?   10
A body subject to be tempted,
From neither pain nor grief exempted;
Or such a body as might not feel
The passions that with sinners deal?

103-6 Cp. 'Auguries of Innocence', ll. 125-8 (*Pickering MS.*, p. 174):

> We are led to believe a lie
> When we see not thro' the eye,
> Which was born in a night, to perish in a night,
> When the soul slept in beams of light.

ε] 7, 8 Interlineated in MS.

Poems from the Rossetti MS.

Yes, but they say He never fell. 15
Ask Caiaphas; for he can tell.—
' He mock'd the Sabbath, and He mock'd
The Sabbath's God, and He unlock'd
The evil spirits from their shrines,
And turn'd fishermen to divines; 20
O'erturn'd the tent of secret sins,
And its golden cords and pins,
In the bloody shrine of war
Pour'd around from star to star,—
Halls of justice, hating vice, 25
Where the Devil combs his lice.
He turn'd the devils into swine
That He might tempt the Jews to dine;
Since which, a pig has got a look
That for a Jew may be mistook. 30
" Obey your parents."—What says He?
" Woman, what have I to do with thee?
No earthly parents I confess:
I am doing My Father's business."
He scorn'd Earth's parents, scorn'd Earth's God, 35
And mock'd the one and the other's rod;
His seventy Disciples sent
Against Religion and Government—
They by the sword of Justice fell,
And Him their cruel murderer tell. 40
He left His father's trade to roam,
A wand'ring vagrant without home;
And thus He others' labour stole,
That He might live above control.
The publicans and harlots He 45
Selected for His company,

17-48 No quot. marks in MS.   21-4 A marginal addition.   24
Pour'd] Not legibly written in MS, perhaps 'Pass'd'.   25. 26 A later
marginal addition.   35 earth's God] his God *MS. 1st rdg. del*

154

The Everlasting Gospel

And from the adulteress turn'd away
God's righteous law, that lost its prey.

ζ

Was Jesus chaste? or did He
Give any lessons of chastity?
The Morning blushèd fiery red:
Mary was found in adulterous bed;
Earth groan'd beneath, and Heaven above   5
Trembled at discovery of Love
Jesus was sitting in Moses' chair.
They brought the trembling woman there.
Moses commands she be ston'd to death.
What was the sound of Jesus' breath?   10
He laid His hand on Moses' law;
The ancient Heavens, in silent awe,
Writ with curses from pole to pole,
All away began to roll.
The Earth trembling and naked lay   15
In secret bed of mortal clay;
On Sinai felt the Hand Divine
Pulling back the bloody shrine;
And she heard the breath of God,
As she heard by Eden's flood: 20
'Good and Evil are no more!
Sinai's trumpets cease to roar!
Cease, finger of God, to write!
The Heavens are not clean in Thy sight.
Thou art good, and Thou alone;   25
Nor may the sinner cast one stone.
To be good only, is to be
A God or else a Pharisee.

ζ] 27, 28 A marginal addition.

Poems from the Rossetti MS.

Thou Angel of the Presence Divine,
That didst create this Body of Mine, 30
Wherefore hast thou writ these laws
And created Hell's dark jaws?
My Presence I will take from thee:
A cold leper thou shalt be.
Tho' thou wast so pure and bright 35
That Heaven was impure in thy sight,
Tho' thy oath turn'd Heaven pale,
Tho' thy covenant built Hell's jail,
Tho' thou didst all to chaos roll
With the Serpent for its soul, 40
Still the breath Divine does move,
And the breath Divine is Love.
Mary, fear not! Let me see
The seven devils that torment thee.
Hide not from My sight thy sin, 45
That forgiveness thou may'st win.
Has no man condemnèd thee?'
'No man, Lord.' 'Then what is he
Who shall accuse thee? Come ye forth,
Fallen fiends of heavenly birth, 50
That have forgot your ancient love,
And driven away my trembling Dove.
You shall bow before her feet;
You shall lick the dust for meat;
And tho' you cannot love, but hate, 55
Shall be beggars at Love's gate.
What was thy love? Let Me see it;
Was it love or dark deceit?'
'Love too long from me has fled;
'Twas dark deceit, to earn my bread; 60
'Twas covet, or 'twas custom, or
Some trifle not worth caring for;
That they may call a shame and sin
Love's temple that God dwelleth in,

The Everlasting Gospel

And hide in secret hidden shrine 65
The naked Human Form Divine,
And render that a lawless thing
On which the Soul expands its wing.
But this, O Lord, this was my sin,
When first I let these devils in, 70
In dark pretence to chastity
Blaspheming Love, blaspheming Thee,
Thence rose secret adulteries,
And thence did covet also rise.
My sin Thou hast forgiven me; 75
Canst Thou forgive my blasphemy?
Canst Thou return to this dark hell,
And in my burning bosom dwell?
And canst Thou die that I may live?
And canst Thou pity and forgive?' 80
Then roll'd the shadowy Man away
From the limbs of Jesus, to make them His prey,
An ever devouring appetite,
Glittering with festering venoms bright;
Crying 'Crucify this cause of distress, 85
Who don't keep the secrets of holiness!
The mental powers by diseases we bind;
But He heals the deaf, the dumb, and the blind.
Whom God has afflicted for secret ends,
He comforts and heals and calls them friends.' 90
But, when Jesus was crucified,
Then was perfected His galling pride.
In three nights He devour'd His prey,
And still He devours the body of clay;
For dust and clay is the Serpent's meat, 95
Which never was made for Man to eat.

65-8 An addition.   85-90 An addition.   93, 94 Cp. *Jerusalem*,
f. 89, l. 13:
    In three days He devour'd the rejected corse of death.
95, 96 A marginal addition.

Poems from the Rossetti MS.

η

Seeing this False Christ, in fury and passion
I made my voice heard all over the nation.
What are those . . .

θ

[*Epilogue*]

I am sure this Jesus will not do,
Either for Englishman or Jew.

η] The '&c.', which follows in the *MS.*, shows that the whole of the passage, of which these were the opening lines, must have been transcribed elsewhere. With l. 3 compare 'What are those Golden Builders doing', a line which occurs in *Jerusalem*, fol. 12, and again in fol. 27 of the same poem (pp. 387 and 391 of this edition).

THE PICKERING MANUSCRIPT

Circa 1801–1803

THE PICKERING MS.

The Smile

There is a smile of love,
And there is a smile of deceit,
And there is a smile of smiles
In which these two smiles meet.

And there is a frown of hate,					5
And there is a frown of disdain,
And there is a frown of frowns
Which you strive to forget in vain,

For it sticks in the heart's deep core
And it sticks in the deep backbone—			10
And no smile that ever was smil'd,
But only one smile alone,

That betwixt the cradle and grave
It only once smil'd can be;
And, when it once is smil'd,					15
There's an end to all misery.

The Golden Net

Three Virgins at the break of day:—
'Whither, young man, whither away?
Alas for woe! alas for woe!'
They cry, and tears for ever flow.

The Golden Net] In its present form this poem is a fair copy of a rough draft in the *Rossetti MS.*, without title.

1 2 In the opening couplet Blake returns to his first version in the *Ross. MS.*, there afterwards altered to:

> Beneath the whitethorn's lovely may
> Three Virgins at the break of day.

the initial line of which, perhaps inadvertently omitted, seems necessary to explain the reference to 'the branches' in l. 10. D. G. Rossetti, followed by most editors, begins with a triplet.   3 Alas ... woe] Alas for woe! alas for woe! alas for woe! *Ross. MS.*

The Pickering MS.

The one was cloth'd in flames of fire, 5
The other cloth'd in iron wire,
The other cloth'd in tears and sighs
Dazzling bright before my eyes.
They bore a Net of golden twine
To hang upon the branches fine. 10
Pitying I wept to see the woe
That Love and Beauty undergo,
To be consum'd in burning fires
And in ungratified desires,
And in tears cloth'd night and day 15
Melted all my soul away.
When they saw my tears, a smile
That did Heaven itself beguile,
Bore the Golden Net aloft,
As on downy pinions soft, 20
Over the Morning of my day.
Underneath the net I stray,
Now entreating Burning Fire
Now entreating Iron Wire,
Now entreating Tears and Sighs— 25
O! when will the morning rise?

The Mental Traveller

I travell'd thro' a land of men,
A land of men and women too;
And heard and saw such dreadful things
As cold earth-wanderers never knew.

6, 24 iron wire] sweet desire *Ross. MS.* 1*st rdg. del.*   7 tears and sighs
sighs and tears *Ross. MS.* 1*st rdg. del.*   11 Followed in the *Ross. MS.* b
the deleted passage:

>   Wings they had that soft enclose
>   Round their body when they chose,
>   They would let them down at will,
>   Or make translucent...

20 on] by *Ross. MS.*   21 Over] O'er *Ross. MS.*   23 Burning Fire] flamin
fire *Ross. MS.*   26 When, O when, will Morning rise *Ross. MS.* 1*st rdg. de*

162

The Mental Traveller

For there the Babe is born in joy
That was begotten in dire woe;
Just as we reap in joy the fruit
Which we in bitter tears did sow.

And if the Babe is born a boy
He's given to a Woman Old,
Who nails him down upon a rock,
Catches his shrieks in cups of gold.

She binds iron thorns around his head,
She pierces both his hands and feet,
She cuts his heart out at his side,
To make it feel both cold and heat.

Her fingers number every nerve,
Just as a miser counts his gold;
She lives upon his shrieks and cries,
And she grows young as he grows old.

Till he becomes a bleeding Youth,
And she becomes a Virgin bright;
Then he rends up his manacles,
And binds her down for his delight.

He plants himself in all her nerves,
Just as a husbandman his mould;
And she becomes his dwelling-place
And garden fruitful seventyfold.

An agèd Shadow, soon he fades,
Wandering round an earthly cot,
Full fillèd all with gems and gold
Which he by industry had got.

And these are the gems of the human soul,
The rubies and pearls of a love-sick eye,
The countless gold of the aching heart,
The martyr's groan and the lover's sigh.

33-36] Cp. *Gnomic Verses* xx (p. 197 of this ed.).

The Pickering MS.

They are his meat, they are his drink;
He feeds the beggar and the poor
And the wayfaring traveller:
For ever open is his door.

His grief is their eternal joy;
They make the roofs and walls to ring;
Till from the fire on the hearth
A little Female Babe does spring.

And she is all of solid fire
And gems and gold, that none his hand
Dares stretch to touch her baby form,
Or wrap her in his swaddling-band.

But she comes to the man she loves,
If young or old, or rich or poor;
They soon drive out the Agèd Host,
A beggar at another's door.

He wanders weeping far away,
Until some other take him in;
Oft blind and age-bent, sore distrest,
Until he can a Maiden win.

And to allay his freezing age,
The poor man takes her in his arms;
The cottage fades before his sight,
The garden and its lovely charms.

The guests are scatter'd thro' the land,
For the eye altering alters all;
The senses roll themselves in fear,
And the flat earth becomes a ball;

The stars, sun, moon, all shrink away
A desert vast without a bound,
And nothing left to eat or drink,
And a dark desert all around

The Mental Traveller

The honey of her infant lips,
The bread and wine of her sweet smile,
The wild game of her roving eye,
Does him to infancy beguile;

For as he eats and drinks he grows
Younger and younger every day;
And on the desert wild they both
Wander in terror and dismay.

Like the wild stag she flees away,
Her fear plants many a thicket wild;
While he pursues her night and day,
By various arts of love beguil'd;

By various arts of love and hate,
Till the wide desert planted o'er
With labyrinths of wayward love,
Where roam the lion, wolf, and boar.

Till he becomes a wayward Babe,
And she a weeping Woman Old.
Then many a lover wanders here;
The sun and stars are nearer roll'd;

The trees bring forth sweet ecstasy
To all who in the desert roam;
Till many a city there is built,
And many a pleasant shepherd's home.

But when they find the Frowning Babe,
Terror strikes thro' the region wide:
They cry 'The Babe! the Babe is born!
And flee away on every side.

For who dare touch the Frowning Form,
His arm is wither'd to its root;
Lions, boars, wolves, all howling flee,
And every tree does shed its fruit.

The Pickering MS.

And none can touch that Frowning Form,
Except it be a Woman Old;
She nails him down upon the rock,
And all is done as I have told.

The Land of Dreams

Awake, awake, my little boy!
Thou wast thy mother's only joy;
Why dost thou weep in thy gentle sleep?
Awake! thy father does thee keep.

'O, what land is the Land of Dreams?
What are its mountains, and what are its streams?
O father! I saw my mother there,
Among the lilies by waters fair.

'Among the lambs, clothèd in white,
She walk'd with her Thomas in sweet delight.
I wept for joy, like a dove I mourn;
O! when shall I again return?'

Dear child, I also by pleasant streams
Have wander'd all night in the Land of Dreams;
But tho' calm and warm the waters wide,
I could not get to the other side.

'Father, O father! what do we here
In this land of unbelief and fear?
The Land of Dreams is better far,
Above the light of the morning star.'

Mary

Sweet Mary, the first time she ever was there,
Came into the ball-room among the fair;
The young men and maidens around her throng,
And these are the words upon every tongue:

Mary

'An Angel is here from the heavenly climes,
Or again does return the golden times;
Her eyes outshine every brilliant ray,
She opens her lips—'tis the Month of May.'

Mary moves in soft beauty and conscious delight,
To augment with sweet smiles all the joys of the night,
Nor once blushes to own to the rest of the fair
That sweet Love and Beauty are worthy our care.

In the morning the villagers rose with delight,
And repeated with pleasure the joys of the night,
And Mary arose among friends to be free,
But no friend from henceforward thou, Mary, shalt see.

Some said she was proud, some call'd her a whore,
And some, when she passèd by, shut to the door;
A damp cold came o'er her, her blushes all fled;
Her lilies and roses are blighted and shed

'O, why was I born with a different face?
Why was I not born like this envious race?
Why did Heaven adorn me with bountiful hand,
And then set me down in an envious land?

'To be weak as a lamb and smooth as a dove,
And not to raise envy, is call'd Christian love;
But if you raise envy your merit's to blame
For planting such spite in the weak and the tame.

'I will humble my beauty, I will not dress fine,
I will keep from the ball, and my eyes shall not shine,
And if any girl's lover forsakes her for me
I'll refuse him my hand, and from envy be free.'

21, 22 Cp. the lines in Blake's letter to Butts, dated Aug. 16, 1803:

> O why was I born with a different face?
> Why was I not born like the rest of my race?

The Pickering MS.

She went out in morning attir'd plain and neat;
'Proud Mary's gone mad,' said the child in the street;
She went out in morning in plain neat attire,   35
And came home in evening bespatter'd with mire.

She trembled and wept, sitting on the bedside,
She forgot it was night, and she trembled and cried;
She forgot it was night, she forgot it was morn,
Her soft memory imprinted with faces of scorn;   40

With faces of scorn and with eyes of disdain,
Like foul fiends inhabiting Mary's mild brain;
She remembers no face like the Human Divine,
All faces have envy, sweet Mary, but thine;

And thine is a face of sweet love in despair,   45
And thine is a face of mild sorrow and care,
And thine is a face of wild terror and fear
That shall never be quiet till laid on its bier.

The Crystal Cabinet

The Maiden caught me in the wild,
Where I was dancing merrily;
She put me into her Cabinet,
And lock'd me up with a golden key.

This Cabinet is form'd of gold   5
And pearl and crystal shining bright,
And within it opens into a world
And a little lovely moony night.

Another England there I saw,
Another London with its Tower,   10
Another Thames and other hills,
And another pleasant Surrey bower

The Crystal Cabinet

Another Maiden like herself,
Translucent, lovely, shining clear,
Threefold each in the other clos'd— 15
O, what a pleasant trembling fear!

O, what a smile! a threefold smile
Fill'd me, that like a flame I burn'd;
I bent to kiss the lovely Maid,
And found a threefold kiss return'd. 20

I strove to seize the inmost form
With ardour fierce and hands of flame,
But burst the Crystal Cabinet,
And like a weeping Babe became—

A weeping Babe upon the wild, 25
And weeping Woman pale reclin'd,
And in the outward air again
I fill'd with woes the passing wind.

The Grey Monk

'I die, I die!' the Mother said,
'My children die for lack of bread.
What more has the merciless tyrant said?'
The Monk sat down on the stony bed.

The blood red ran from the Grey Monk's side, 5
His hands and feet were wounded wide,
His body bent, his arms and knees
Like to the roots of ancient trees.

The original draft of 'The Grey Monk' is found in the *Rossetti MS.*, where it forms part of the poem beginning 'I saw a Monk of Charlemaine'. This earlier version consisted of fourteen stanzas, which Blake afterwards separated into two poems—transcribing nine stanzas, arranged in a slightly different order and with some changes noted below, into the *Pickering MS.*, under the title 'The Grey Monk', and engraving five, with two others added later, as the untitled lines at the end of his 'Address to the Deists' (*Jerusalem*, f. 52). Stanzas ii and viii of this version are common to all three poems.
1 I die, I die] I see, I see *Ross. MS.*   2 die] will die *Ross. MS.*   4 the stony bed] her stony bed *Ross. MS.*

The Pickering MS.

His eye was dry; no tear could flow:
A hollow groan first spoke his woe.
He trembled and shudder'd upon the bed;
At length with a feeble cry he said:

'When God commanded this hand to write
In the studious hours of deep midnight,
He told me the writing I wrote should prove
The bane of all that on Earth I love.

'My brother starv'd between two walls,
His children's cry my soul appalls;
I mock'd at the wrack and griding chain,
My bent body mocks their torturing pain.

'Thy father drew his sword in the North,
With his thousands strong he marchèd forth,
Thy brother has arm'd himself in steel,
To avenge the wrongs thy children feel.

'But vain the sword and vain the bow,
They never can work War's overthrow.
The hermit's prayer and the widow's tear
Alone can free the world from fear.

'For a tear is an intellectual thing,
And a sigh is the sword of an Angel King,
And the bitter groan of the martyr's woe
Is an arrow from the Almighty's bow.

'The hand of Vengeance found the bed
To which the purple tyrant fled;
The iron hand crush'd the tyrant's head,
And became a tyrant in his stead.'

---

15 the writing] that all *Ross. MS.*   20 mocks their] mocks at their *Ross. MS.*   22 marchèd] is marched *Ross. MS.*   24 avenge] revenge *Ross. MS.*   29 a tear] the tear *Ross. MS.*   33 found] sought *Ross. MS.*

Auguries of Innocence

Auguries of Innocence

To see a World in a grain of sand,
And a Heaven in a wild flower,
Hold Infinity in the palm of your hand,
And Eternity in an hour.

A robin redbreast in a cage
Puts all Heaven in a rage.
A dove-house fill'd with doves and pigeons
Shudders Hell thro' all its regions.
A dog starv'd at his master's gate
Predicts the ruin of the State.
A horse misus'd upon the road
Calls to Heaven for human blood.
Each outcry of the hunted hare
A fibre from the brain does tear.
A skylark wounded in the wing,
A cherubim does cease to sing.
The game-cock clipt and arm'd for fight
Does the rising sun affright.
Every wolf's and lion's howl
Raises from Hell a Human soul.
The wild deer, wandering here and there,
Keeps the Human soul from care.
The lamb misus'd breeds public strife,
And yet forgives the butcher's knife.
The bat that flits at close of eve
Has left the brain that won't believe.
The owl that calls upon the night
Speaks the unbeliever's fright.

The title 'Auguries of Innocence' probably, as Mr. Yeats conjectures, refers only to the opening quatrain, although the MS. itself has no space or line separating it from the couplets which follow. These proverbs are here placed in the sequence in which they appear in the MS., where they were doubtless transcribed from scattered jottings elsewhere. I append an attempt, made in my earlier edition of Blake, to rearrange them in an order which will enable the poem to be read *'hole, instead of as a series of disconnected distiches.

The Pickering MS.

He who shall hurt the little wren
Shall never be belov'd by men.
He who the ox to wrath has mov'd
Shall never be by woman lov'd.
The wanton boy that kills the fly
Shall feel the spider's enmity.
He who torments the chafer's sprite
Weaves a bower in endless night.
The caterpillar on the leaf
Repeats to thee thy mother's grief.
Kill not the moth nor butterfly,
For the Last Judgement draweth nigh.
He who shall train the horse to war
Shall never pass the polar bar.
The beggar's dog and widow's cat,
Feed them, and thou wilt grow fat.
The gnat that sings his summer's song
Poison gets from Slander's tongue.
The poison of the snake and newt
Is the sweat of Envy's foot.
The poison of the honey-bee
Is the artist's jealousy.
The prince's robes and beggar's rags
Are toadstools on the miser's bags.
A truth that's told with bad intent
Beats all the lies you can invent.
It is right it should be so;
Man was made for joy and woe;
And when this we rightly know,
Thro' the world we safely go.
Joy and woe are woven fine,
A clothing for the soul divine;

37, 38 Cp. *The Gates of Paradise*, 'Keys of the Gates,' ll. 1, 2 :

> The caterpillar on the leaf
> Reminds thee of thy mother's grief.

Auguries of Innocence

Under every grief and pine
Runs a joy with silken twine.
The babe is more than swaddling-bands;
Throughout all these human lands
Tools were made, and born were hands, 65
Every farmer understands.
Every tear from every eye
Becomes a babe in Eternity;
This is caught by Females bright,
And return'd to its own delight. 70
The bleat, the bark, bellow, and roar
Are waves that beat on Heaven's shore.
The babe that weeps the rod beneath
Writes revenge in realms of death.
The beggar's rags, fluttering in air, 75
Does to rags the heavens tear.
The soldier, arm'd with sword and gun,
Palsied strikes the summer's sun.
The poor man's farthing is worth more
Than all the gold on Afric's shore. 80
One mite wrung from the labourer's hands
Shall buy and sell the miser's lands ·
Or, if protected from on high,
Does that whole nation sell and buy.
He who mocks the infant's faith 85
Shall be mock'd in Age and Death.
He who shall teach the child to doubt
The rotting grave shall ne'er get out.
He who respects the infant's faith
Triumphs over Hell and Death. 90
The child's toys and the old man's reasons
Are the fruits of the two seasons.
The questioner, who sits so sly,
Shall never know how to reply.

93 Cp. *Milton*, f. 43, ll. 12-17 (p. 381 of this ed.).

The Pickering MS.

He who replies to words of Doubt
Doth put the light of knowledge out.
The strongest poison ever known
Came from Caesar's laurel crown.
Nought can deform the human race
Like to the armour's iron brace.
When gold and gems adorn the plough
To peaceful arts shall Envy bow.
A riddle, or the cricket's cry,
Is to Doubt a fit reply.
The emmet's inch and eagle's mile
Make lame Philosophy to smile.
He who doubts from what he sees
Will ne'er believe, do what you please.
If the Sun and Moon should doubt,
They'd immediately go out.
To be in a passion you good may do,
But no good if a passion is in you.
The whore and gambler, by the state
Licensed, build that nation's fate.
The harlot's cry from street to street
Shall weave Old England's winding-sheet
The winner's shout, the loser's curse,
Dance before dead England's hearse.
Every night and every morn
Some to misery are born.
Every morn and every night
Some are born to sweet delight.
Some are born to sweet delight,
Some are born to endless night.
We are led to believe a lie
When we see not thro' the eye,
Which was born in a night, to perish in a night,
When the Soul slept in beams of light.

126 When we see with, not thro' the eye 1*st rdg. del.*   Cp. 'Everlasting Gospel' γ, ll. 103-106 (p. 153 of this ed.).

Auguries of Innocence

God appears, and God is Light,
To those poor souls who dwell in Night;
But does a Human Form display
To those who dwell in realms of Day.

[*Editor's arrangement*]

To see a World in a grain of sand,
And a Heaven in a wild flower,
Hold Infinity in the palm of your hand,
And Eternity in an hour.

A robin redbreast in a cage
Puts all Heaven in a rage.
A dove-house fill'd with doves and pigeons
Shudders Hell thro' all its regions.
A dog starv'd at his master's gate
Predicts the ruin of the State.
A horse misus'd upon the road
Calls to Heaven for human blood.
Each outcry of the hunted hare
A fibre from the brain does tear.
A skylark wounded in the wing,
A cherubim does cease to sing.
The game-cock clipt and arm'd for fight
Does the rising sun affright.
Every wolf's and lion's howl
Raises from Hell a Human soul.
The wild deer, wandering here and there,
Keeps the Human soul from care.
The lamb misus'd breeds public strife,
And yet forgives the butcher's knife.
He who shall hurt the little wren
Shall never be belov'd by men.
He who the ox to wrath has mov'd
Shall never be by woman lov'd.
The wanton boy that kills the fly
Shall feel the spider's enmity.
He who torments the chafer's sprite
Weaves a bower in endless night.
The caterpillar on the leaf
Repeats to thee thy mother's grief.
Kill not the moth nor butterfly,
For the Last Judgement draweth nigh.

The Pickering MS.

He who shall train the horse to war
Shall never pass the polar bar.
The beggar's dog and widow's cat,
Feed them, and thou wilt grow fat.

The bat that flits at close of eve
Has left the brain that won't believe.
The owl that calls upon the night
Speaks the unbeliever's fright.
The gnat that sings his summer's song
Poison gets from Slander's tongue.
The poison of the snake and newt
Is the sweat of Envy's foot.
The poison of the honey-bee
Is the artist's jealousy.
A truth that's told with bad intent
Beats all the lies you can invent.

Joy and woe are woven fine,
A clothing for the soul divine ;
Under every grief and pine
Runs a joy with silken twine.
It is right it should be so ;
Man was made for joy and woe ;
And when this we rightly know,
Thro' the world we safely go.

The babe is more than swaddling-bands ;
Throughout all these human lands
Tools were made, and born were hands,
Every farmer understands.
Every tear from every eye
Becomes a babe in Eternity ;
This is caught by Females bright,
And return'd to its own delight.
The bleat, the bark, bellow, and roar
Are waves that beat on Heaven's shore.
The babe that weeps the rod beneath
Writes revenge in realms of death.
He who mocks the infant's faith
Shall be mock'd in Age and Death.
He who shall teach the child to doubt
The rotting grave shall ne'er get out.
He who respects the infant's faith
Triumphs over Hell and Death.

Auguries of Innocence

The child's toys and the old man's reasons
Are the fruits of the two seasons.
The questioner, who sits so sly,
Shall never know how to reply.
He who replies to words of Doubt
Doth put the light of knowledge out.
A riddle, or the cricket's cry,
Is to Doubt a fit reply.
The emmet's inch and eagle's mile
Make lame Philosophy to smile.
He who doubts from what he sees
Will ne'er believe, do what you please.
If the sun and moon should doubt,
They'd immediately go out.

The prince's robes and beggar's rags
Are toadstools on the miser's bags.
The beggar's rags, fluttering in air,
Does to rags the heavens tear.
The poor man's farthing is worth more
Than all the gold on Afric's shore.
One mite wrung from the labourer's hands
Shall buy and sell the miser's lands ;
Or, if protected from on high,
Does that whole nation sell and buy.
The soldier, arm'd with sword and gun,
Palsied strikes the summer's sun.
The strongest poison ever known
Came from Caesar's laurel crown.
Nought can deform the human race
Like to the armour's iron brace.
When gold and gems adorn the plough
To peaceful arts shall Envy bow.
To be in a passion you good may do,
But no good if a passion is in you.
The whore and gambler, by the state
Licensed, build that nation's fate.
The harlot's cry from street to street
Shall weave Old England's winding-sheet.
The winner's shout, the loser's curse,
Dance before dead England's hearse.

Every night and every morn
Some to misery are born.

The Pickering MS.

Every morn and every night
Some are born to sweet delight.
Some are born to sweet delight,
Some are born to endless night.
We are led to believe a lie
When we see not thro' the eye,
Which was born in a night, to perish in a night,
When the Soul slept in beams of light.
God appears, and God is Light,
To those poor souls who dwell in Night;
But does a Human Form display
To those who dwell in realms of Day.

Long John Brown and Little Mary Bell

Little Mary Bell had a Fairy in a nut,
Long John Brown had the Devil in his gut;
Long John Brown lov'd little Mary Bell,
And the Fairy drew the Devil into the nutshell.

Her Fairy skipp'd out and her Fairy skipp'd in; 5
He laugh'd at the Devil, saying 'Love is a sin.'
The Devil he raged, and the Devil he was wroth,
And the Devil enter'd into the young man's broth.

He was soon in the gut of the loving young swain,
For John ate and drank to drive away love's pain; 10
But all he could do he grew thinner and thinner,
Tho' he ate and drank as much as ten men for his dinner.

Some said he had a wolf in his stomach day and night,
Some said he had the Devil, and they guess'd right;
The Fairy skipp'd about in his glory, joy and pride, 15
And he laugh'd at the Devil till poor John Brown died.

Then the Fairy skipp'd out of the old nutshell,
And woe and alack for pretty Mary Bell!
For the Devil crept in when the Fairy skipp'd out,
And there goes Miss Bell with her fusty old nut. 20

Title] At first 'John Brown and Mary Bell'.   1, 3 Little] Pretty 1st
rdg. del.   2, 3 Long] Young 1st rdg. del.

William Bond

William Bond

I wonder whether the girls are mad,
And I wonder whether they mean to kill,
And I wonder if William Bond will die,
For assuredly he is very ill.

He went to church in a May morning,
Attended by Fairies, one, two, and three;
But the Angels of Providence drove them away,
And he return'd home in misery.

He went not out to the field nor fold,
He went not out to the village nor town,
But he came home in a black, black cloud,
And took to his bed, and there lay down.

And an Angel of Providence at his feet,
And an Angel of Providence at his head,
And in the midst a black, black cloud,
And in the midst the sick man on his bed.

And on his right hand was Mary Green,
And on his left hand was his sister Jane,
And their tears fell thro' the black, black cloud
To drive away the sick man's pain.

'O William, if thou dost another love,
Dost another love better than poor Mary,
Go and take that other to be thy wife,
And Mary Green shall her servant be.'

'Yes, Mary, I do another love,
Another I love far better than thee,
And another I will have for my wife;
Then what have I to do with thee?

The Pickering MS.

' For thou art melancholy pale,
And on thy head is the cold moon's shine, 30
But she is ruddy and bright as day,
And the sunbeams dazzle from her eyne.'

Mary trembled and Mary chill'd,
And Mary fell down on the right-hand floor,
That William Bond and his sister Jane 35
Scarce could recover Mary more.

When Mary woke and found her laid
On the right hand of her William dear,
On the right hand of his loved bed,
And saw her William Bond so near, 40

The Fairies that fled from William Bond
Dancèd around her shining head;
They dancèd over the pillow white,
And the Angels of Providence left the bed.

I thought Love lived in the hot sunshine, 45
But O, he lives in the moony light!
I thought to find Love in the heat of day,
But sweet Love is the comforter of night.

Seek Love in the pity of others' woe,
In the gentle relief of another's care, 50
In the darkness of night and the winter's snow,
In the naked and outcast, seek Love there!

45-52 All editors place the last two stanzas in inverted commas, as though the speech were William Bond's. I treat it rather as that of the narrator of the story, who begins the poem in the first person.

POEMS

FROM

LETTERS

1800–1803

POEMS FROM LETTERS

To my dearest Friend, John Flaxman, these lines:

I bless thee, O Father of Heaven and Earth! that ever I saw
  Flaxman's face:
Angels stand round my spirit in Heaven; the blessèd of Heaven
  are my friends upon Earth
When Flaxman was taken to Italy, Fuseli was given to me for
  a season;
And now Flaxman hath given me Hayley, his friend, to be mine—
  such my lot upon Earth!
Now my lot in the Heavens is this: Milton lov'd me in childhood
  and show'd me his face;   5
Ezra came with Isaiah the Prophet, but Shakespeare in riper
  years gave me his hand;
Paracelsus and Behmen appear'd to me; terrors appear'd in the
  Heavens above;
The American War began; all its dark horrors pass'd before my
  face
Across the Atlantic to France; then the French Revolution
  commenc'd in thick clouds;
And my Angels have told me that, seeing such visions, I could
  not subsist on the Earth,   10
But by my conjunction with Flaxman, who knows to forgive
  nervous fear.

12 Sept., 1800.

For the setting of these poems see Mr. A. G. B. Russell's excellent edition of *The Letters of William Blake*, 1906, to which I owe the correct text of the first two pieces.

Poems from Letters

To my dear Friend, Mrs. Anna Flaxman

This song to the flower of Flaxman's joy,
To the blossom of hope for a sweet decoy;
Do all that you can, or all that you may,
To entice him to Felpham and far away.

Away to sweet Felpham, for Heaven is there; 5
The Ladder of Angels descends thro' the air;
On the turret its spiral does softly descend,
Thro' the village then winds, at my cot it does end.

You stand in the village and look up to Heaven;
The precious stones glitter on flights seventy-seven; 10
And my brother is there, and my friend and thine
Descend and ascend with the bread and the wine.

The bread of sweet thought and the wine of delight
Feed the village of Felpham by day and by night,
And at his own door the bless'd Hermit does stand, 15
Dispensing unceasing to all the wide land.

[To Thomas Butts]

To my friend Butts I write
My first vision of light,
On the yellow sands sitting.
The sun was emitting
His glorious beams 5
From Heaven's high streams.

To Anna Flaxman] In a letter dated 'H[ercules] B[uildings], Lambeth, 14 Sept., 1800,' the 'Hermit' being William Hayley, Blake's patron, who in letters to his friends loved to refer to himself as the 'Hermit of Eartham' or the 'Hermit of the Turret'. See also Blake's *Letters*, ed. Russell, *passim*.

To Thomas Butts] In a letter dated 'Felpham, Octr. 2^d, 1800', and addressed to 'Mr. Butts, Great Marlborough Street'. These verses are prefaced by the lines: 'Receive from me a return of verses such as Felpham produces by me, tho' not such as she produces by her Eldest Son; however, such as they are, I cannot resist the temptation to send them to you.'

To Thomas Butts

Over sea, over land,
My eyes did expand
Into regions of air,
Away from all care;   10
Into regions of fire,
Remote from desire;
The light of the morning
Heaven's mountains adorning:
In particles bright,   15
The jewels of light
Distinct shone and clear.
Amaz'd and in fear
I each particle gazèd,
Astonish'd, amazèd;   20
For each was a Man
Human-form'd.   Swift I ran,
For they beckon'd to me,
Remote by the sea,
Saying: 'Each grain of sand,   25
Every stone on the land,
Each rock and each hill,
Each fountain and rill,
Each herb and each tree,
Mountain, hill, earth, and sea,   30
Cloud, meteor, and star,
Are men seen afar.'
I stood in the streams
Of Heaven's bright beams,
And saw Felpham sweet   35
Beneath my bright feet,
In soft Female charms;
And in her fair arms
My Shadow I knew,
And my wife's Shadow too,   40
And my sister, and friend.
We like infants descend

Poems from Letters

In our Shadows on earth,
Like a weak mortal birth.
My eyes, more and more, 45
Like a sea without shore,
Continue expanding,
The Heavens commanding;
Till the jewels of light,
Heavenly men beaming bright, 50
Appear'd as One Man,
Who complacent began
My limbs to enfold
In His beams of bright gold;
Like dross purg'd away 55
All my mire and my clay.
Soft consum'd in delight,
In His bosom sun-bright
I remain'd. Soft He smil'd,
And I heard His voice mild, 60
Saying : 'This is My fold,
O thou ram horn'd with gold,
Who awakest from sleep
On the sides of the deep.
On the mountains around 65
The roarings resound
Of the lion and wolf,
The loud sea, and deep gulf.
These are guards of My fold,
O thou ram horn'd with gold! 70
And the voice faded mild :
I remain'd as a child ;
All I ever had known
Before me bright shone :
I saw you and your wife 75
By the fountains of life.
Such the vision to me
Appear'd on the sea.

To Mrs. Butts

To Mrs. Butts

    Wife of the friend of those I most revere,
Receive this tribute from a harp sincere;
Go on in virtuous seed-sowing on mould
Of human vegetation, and behold
Your harvest springing to eternal life,   5
Parent of youthful minds, and happy wife!

[To Thomas Butts]

    With Happiness stretch'd across the hills
In a cloud that dewy sweetness distils;
With a blue sky spread over with wings,
And a mild sun that mounts and sings;
With trees and fields full of fairy elves,   5
And little devils who fight for themselves—
Rememb'ring the verses that Hayley sung
When my heart knock'd against the root of my tongue—
With angels planted in hawthorn bowers,
And God Himself in the passing hours;   10
With silver angels across my way,
And golden demons that none can stay;
With my father hovering upon the wind,
And my brother Robert just behind,
And my brother John, the evil one,   15
In a black cloud making his moan,—
Tho' dead, they appear upon my path,

  To Mrs. Butts] These lines signed 'W. B.', which the author hopes Mrs. Butts 'will excuse', conclude the letter from which the preceding poem is taken.

  To Thomas Butts] In a letter dated 'Felpham, Novr. 22, 1802', in which Blake tells his correspondent that these lines 'were composed above a twelvemonth ago, while walking from Felpham to Lavant to meet my sister'.

Poems from Letters

Notwithstanding my terrible wrath;
They beg, they entreat, they drop their tears,
Fill'd full of hopes, fill'd full of fears— 20
With a thousand angels upon the wind,
Pouring disconsolate from behind
To drive them off, and before my way
A frowning thistle implores my stay.
What to others a trifle appears 25
Fills me full of smiles or tears;
For double the vision my eyes do see,
And a double vision is always with me.
With my inward eye, 'tis an Old Man grey,
With my outward, a Thistle across my way. 30
'If thou goest back.' the Thistle said,
'Thou art to endless woe betray'd;
For here does Theotormon lour,
And here is Enitharmon's bower;
And Los the Terrible thus hath sworn, 35
Because thou backward dost return,
Poverty, envy, old age, and fear,
Shall bring thy wife upon a bier;
And Butts shall give what Fuseli gave,
A dark black rock and a gloomy cave.' 40

I struck the Thistle with my foot,
And broke him up from his delving root.
'Must the duties of life each other cross?
Must every joy be dung and dross?
Must my dear Butts feel cold neglect 45
Because I give Hayley his due respect?
Must Flaxman look upon me as wild,
And all my friends be with doubts beguil'd?
Must my wife live in my sister's bane,
Or my sister survive on my love's pain? 50
The curses of Los, the terrible Shade,
And his dismal terrors make me afraid.'

To Thomas Butts

So I spoke, and struck in my wrath
The Old Man weltering upon my path.
Then Los appear'd in all his power:
In the sun he appear'd, descending before
My face in fierce flames; in my double sight
'Twas outward a sun, inward Los in his might.
' My hands are labour'd day and night,
And ease comes never in my sight.
My wife has no indulgence given
Except what comes to her from Heaven.
We eat little, we drink less,
This Earth breeds not our happiness.
Another sun feeds our life's streams,
We are not warmèd with thy beams;
Thou measurest not the time to me,
Nor yet the space that I do see;
My mind is not with thy light array'd,
Thy terrors shall not make me afraid.'

When I had my defiance given,
The sun stood trembling in heaven;
The moon, that glow'd remote below,
Became leprous and white as snow;
And every soul of men on the earth
Felt affliction, and sorrow, and sickness, and dearth.
Los flam'd in my path, and the sun was hot
With the bows of my mind and the arrows of thought.
My bowstring fierce with ardour breathes;
My arrows glow in their golden sheaves;
My brothers and father march before;
The heavens drop with human gore.

Now I a fourfold vision see,
And a fourfold vision is given to me;
'Tis fourfold in my supreme delight,
And threefold in soft Beulah's night,

Poems from Letters

And twofold always.—May God us keep
From single vision, and Newton's sleep!

[To Thomas Butts]

O! why was I born with a different face?
Why was I not born like the rest of my race?
When I look, each one starts; when I speak, I offend;
Then I'm silent and passive, and lose every friend.

Then my verse I dishonour, my pictures despise, 5
My person degrade, and my temper chastise;
And the pen is my terror, the pencil my shame;
All my talents I bury, and dead is my fame.

I am either too low, or too highly priz'd;
When elate I'm envied; when meek I'm despis'd. 10

To Thomas Butts] In a letter dated 'Felpham, August 16, 1803', in which Blake describes the circumstances which led to his trial for high treason. Prefaced by: 'Give me your advice in my perilous adventure: burn what I have peevishly written about my friend. I have been very much degraded and injuriously treated; but, if it all arise from my own fault, I ought to blame myself.'

1, 2] Cp. footnote to 'Mary', p. 167.

GNOMIC VERSES
EPIGRAMS
AND
SHORT SATIRICAL PIECES
Chiefly from
'THE ROSSETTI MANUSCRIPT'
(*circa* 1793–1810)

GNOMIC VERSES

I

Great things are done when men and mountains meet;
This is not done by jostling in the street.

To God
II

If you have form'd a circle to go into,
Go into it yourself, and see how you would do.

III

They said this mystery never shall cease:
The priest promotes war, and the soldier peace.

IV
An Answer to the Parson

Why of the sheep do you not learn peace?
Because I don't want you to shear my fleece.

V
Lacedaemonian Instruction

Come hither, my boy, tell me what thou seest there.
A fool tangled in a religious snare.

VI

Nail his neck to the cross: nail it with a nail.
Nail his neck to the cross: ye all have power over his tail.

Of the pieces in this section, all of which are taken from the *Rossetti MS.*, the greater number belong to the earlier entries and may be dated *circa* 1793. Another (no. XXII) would appear to have been written in 1806, while a few others—e.g. I, II, VI, XVIII, XIX, XXI, and XXIII—were probably composed between this date and 1810.

III 2 promotes] loves *MS. 1st rag. del.*

Gnomic Verses

VII

Love to faults is always blind;
Always is to joy inclin'd,
Lawless, wing'd and unconfin'd,
And breaks all chains from every mind.

Deceit to secrecy confin'd, 5
Lawful, cautious and refin'd;
To anything but interest blind,
And forges fetters for the mind.

VIII

There souls of men are bought and sold,
And milk-fed Infancy for gold;
And Youth to slaughter-houses led,
And Beauty, for a bit of bread.

VII These companion stanzas are written at the head of two opposite pages (106 and 107 reversed) of the *MS. Book*. I print them as one poem, their connexion being obvious, though not indicated by Blake himself. 3 Lawless, wing'd] Always wing'd *MS. 1st rdg.*, 'Always' being underlined, which was probably a hasty attempt at erasure.

5-8 First written:

> Deceit to secrecy inclin'd,
> Modest, prudish and confin'd,
> Never is to interest blind,
> And chains in fetters every mind.

VIII Written immediately below the first stanza of the preceding piece, and directly opposite to the first draft of stanza i of 'The Chimney Sweeper'. As the latter comes below the lines 'Deceit to secrecy confin'd', it is not unlikely that Blake here too wrote consecutive stanzas on blank spaces of opposite pages, and hence that this quatrain was originally intended to form part of 'The Chimney Sweeper'. See *Songs of Experience* (p. 104 of this ed.). 2 And cradled Infancy is sold *MS. 1st rdg. del.* 4 Beauty] Maidens *MS. 1st rdg. del.*

Gnomic Verses

IX

Soft Snow

I walkèd abroad on a snowy day:
I ask'd the soft Snow with me to play:
She play'd and she melted in all her prime;
And the Winter call'd it a dreadful crime.

X

Abstinence sows sand all over
The ruddy limbs and flaming hair,
But Desire gratified
Plants fruits of life and beauty there.

XI

Merlin's Prophecy

The harvest shall flourish in wintry weather
When two Virginities meet together:
The king and the priest must be tied in a tether
Before two Virgins can meet together.

XII

If you trap the moment before it's ripe,
The tears of repentance you'll certainly wipe;
But if once you let the ripe moment go,
You can never wipe off the tears of woe.

XIII

An Old Maid early ere I knew
Aught but the love that on me grew;
And now I'm cover'd o'er and o'er,
And wish that I had been a whore.

O! I cannot, cannot find
The undaunted courage of a virgin mind;
For early I in love was crost,
Before my flower of love was lost.

IX 4 Oh, that sweet love should be thought a crime! *MS. 1st rdg. del.*
Cp. the introductory lines to 'A Little Girl Lost' in the *Songs of Experience.*
XII 1 trap] catch *MS. 1st rdg. del.*   4 You can] You'll *MS. 1st rdg. del.*

Gnomic Verses

XIV

The sword sung on the barren heath,
The sickle in the fruitful field:
The sword he sung a song of death,
But could not make the sickle yield.

XV

O lapwing! thou fliest around the heath,
Nor seest the net that is spread beneath.
Why dost thou not fly among the corn fields?
They cannot spread nets where a harvest yields.

XVI

Terror in the house does roar;
But Pity stands before the door.

XVII

Several Questions Answered

1

[Eternity]

He who bends to himself a Joy
Doth the wingèd life destroy;
But he who kisses the Joy as it flies
Lives in Eternity's sunrise.

2

The look of love alarms,
Because it's fill'd with fire;
But the look of soft deceit
Shall win the lover's hire.

---

xvii These five short pieces, the rough drafts of which are found on three separate pages in the *MS. Book*, were afterwards transcribed by Blake in their present form and sequence under the general title 'Several Questions Answered'.   1–4 First written on another page with title 'Eternity'. 1 bends] binds *Max Plowman, conj.*   2 Doth] Does *MS. 1st draft*. 3 kisses] just kisses *MS. 1st draft, 1st rdg. del.*   4 Eternity's] an eternal *MS. 1st draft, 1st rdg. del.*   6 it's] 'tis *MS. 1st draft*.

Gnomic Verses

3

Soft deceit and idleness,
These are Beauty's sweetest dress.

4

[The Question answered]

What is it men in women do require?
The lineaments of gratified desire.
What is it women do in men require?
The lineaments of gratified desire.

5

An ancient Proverb

Remove away that black'ning church,
Remove away that marriage hearse,
Remove away that man of blood—
You'll quite remove the ancient curse.

XVIII

If I e'er grow to man's estate,
O! give to me a woman's fate.
May I govern all, both great and small,
Have the last word, and take the wall.

XIX

Since all the riches of this world
May be gifts from the Devil and earthly kings,
I should suspect that I worshipp'd the Devil
If I thank'd my God for worldly things.

9, 10 Blake at first began this couplet with the line afterwards deleted:
Which are beauty's sweetest dress?
11–14 Title only in first draft.   11, 13 in] of *MS. 1st draft, 1st rdg. del.*
17 man] place *MS. 1st draft, 1st rdg. del.*   18 You'll] 'Twill *MS. 1st draft, 1st rdg. del.*

Gnomic Verses

XX

Riches

> The countless gold of a merry heart,
> The rubies and pearls of a loving eye,
> The indolent never can bring to the mart,
> Nor the secret hoard up in his treasury.

XXI

> The Angel that presided o'er my birth
> Said 'Little creature, form'd of joy and mirth,
> Go, love without the help of anything on earth.'

XXII

> Grown old in love from seven till seven times seven,
> I oft have wish'd for Hell, for ease from Heaven.

XXIII

> Do what you will this life's a fiction,
> And is made up of contradiction.

ON ART AND ARTISTS

I

Advice of the Popes who succeeded the Age of Raphael

> Degrade first the Arts if you'd mankind degrade,
> Hire idiots to paint with cold light and hot shade,
> Give high price for the worst, leave the best in disgrace,
> And with labours of ignorance fill every place.

---

xx 3 indolent] idle man *MS. 1st rdg. del.*   4 secret] cunning *MS. 1st rdg. del.*

xxi 2 form'd . . . mirth] thou art form'd for mirth *MS. 1st rdg. del.*

xxiii Written elsewhere in the *MS. Book*:

> This corporeal life's a fiction
> And is made up of contradiction.

On Art and Artists] Of the Epigrams grouped together in this section, written *circa* 1808-9, nos. I, V, XV, XXII, XXIV, XXX, XXXI, and XXXII are taken from

On Art and Artists

II

On the great encouragement given by English nobility and gentry to Correggio, Rubens, Reynolds, Gainsborough, Catalani, Du Crow, and Dilbury Doodle

As the ignorant savage will sell his own wife
For a sword, or a cutlass, a dagger, or knife;
So the taught, savage Englishman, spends his whole fortune
On a smear, or a squall, to destroy picture or tune;
And I call upon Colonel Wardle   5
To give these rascals a dose of caudle!

III

I askèd my dear friend Orator Prig:
'What's the first part of oratory?' He said: 'A great wig.
'And what is the second?' Then, dancing a jig
And bowing profoundly, he said: 'A great wig.'
'And what is the third?' Then he snored like a pig,   5
And, puffing his cheeks out, replied: 'A great wig.'
So if a great painter with questions you push,
'What's the first part of painting?' he'll say: 'A paint-brush.'

Blake's marginal annotations to his copy of Vol. I of Sir Joshua Reynolds' *Works* (2nd edition, 1798), containing the first eight 'Discourses'. Others occasioned by the six later 'Discourses' were jotted down in the *MS. Book*, whence also the remainder of the Epigrams and satirical pieces on Art and artists have been excerpted.

For prose parallelisms to the Epigrams readers may consult Blake's *Descriptive Catalogue*, the 'Advertisement', and 'Catalogue for 1810' from the *Rossetti MS.*, as well as the marginalia to Reynolds mentioned above, or refer to my earlier edition of the *Poems* where the more important of these illustrative passages have been quoted.

II Title: Du Crow] Pierre Ducros. Cp. Blake's *Letters*, ed. Russell, p. 204.
2 For a button, a bauble [buckle *2nd rdg. del.*], a bead, or a knife *MS. 1st rdg. del.* 3 taught] wise *MS. 1st rdg. del.*; learned *MS. 2nd rdg. del.*
4 On] For *MS. 1st rdg. del.*   to destroy] that is not *MS. 1st rdg. del.*
5 For Colonel Wardle see Hunt's *Examiner*, 1809, *passim*.

III Blake has marked this piece 'to come in *Barry: a Poem*'.   6 And, puffing his cheeks out,] And thrust out his cheeks and *MS. 1st rdg. del.*

On Art and Artists

'And what is the second?' with most modest blush,
He'll smile like a cherub, and say: 'A paint-brush.' 10
'And what is the third?' he'll bow like a rush,
With a leer in his eye, he'll reply: 'A paint-brush.'
Perhaps this is all a painter can want:
But, look yonder—that house is the house of Rembrandt!

IV

'O dear Mother Outline! of wisdom most sage,
What's the first part of painting?' She said: 'Patronage.'
'And what is the second, to please and engage?'
She frowned like a fury, and said: 'Patronage.'
'And what is the third? She put off old age, 5
And smil'd like a siren, and said: 'Patronage.'

V

[On the Foundation of the Royal Academy]

When nations grow old, the Arts grow cold,
And Commerce settles on every tree;
And the poor and the old can live upon gold,
For all are born poor, aged sixty-three.

VI

These are the idiots' chiefest arts:
To blend and not define the parts
The swallow sings, in courts of kings,
That fools have their high finishings.

And this the princes' golden rule, 5
The laborious stumble of a fool.
To make out the parts is the wise man's aim,
But to loose them the fool makes his foolish game.

vi 3 The swallow sings] Let it be told *MS. 1st rdg. del.*

On Art and Artists

VII

The cripple every step drudges and labours,
And says: 'Come, learn to walk of me, good neighbours.'
Sir Joshua in astonishment cries out:
'See, what great labour! pain in modest doubt!

' He walks and stumbles as if he crep,
And how high labour'd is every step!'
Newton and Bacon cry 'Being badly nurst,
He is all experiments from last to first.'

VIII

You say their pictures well painted be,
And yet they are blockheads you all agree:
Thank God! I never was sent to school
To be flogg'd into following the style of a fool.
The errors of a wise man make your rule,
Rather than the perfections of a fool.

IX

When you look at a picture, you always can see
If a man of sense has painted he.
Then never flinch, but keep up a jaw
About freedom, and 'Jenny sink awa'.'
As when it smells of the lamp, we can
Say all was owing to the skilful man;
For the smell of water is but small:
So e'en let ignorance do it all.

VII 4 His pains are more than others, there's no doubt *MS. 1st rdg. ael.*
VIII 4 To learn to admire the works of a fool *MS. 1st rdg. del.*
IX 4 Jenny sink awa'] i. e. 'Je ne sais quoi'.   5 we] all *MS. 1st rdg. del.*

On Art and Artists

X

The Washerwoman's Song

I wash'd them out and wash'd them in,
And they told me it was a great sin.

XI

English Encouragement of Art: Cromek's opinions put into rhyme

If you mean to please everybody you will
Set to work both ignorance and skill.
For a great multitude are ignorant,
And skill to them seems raving and rant.
Like putting oil and water in a lamp,   5
'Twill make a great splutter with smoke and damp.
For there is no use as it seems to me
Of lighting a lamp, when you don't wish to see.

XII

When I see a Rubens, Rembrandt, Correggio,
I think of the crippled Harry and slobbering Joe;
And then I question thus: Are artists' rules
To be drawn from the works of two manifest fools?
Then God defend us from the Arts I say!   5
Send battle, murder, sudden death, O pray!
Rather than be such a blind human fool
I'd be an ass, a hog, a worm, a chair, a stool!

X Possibly a reference to Blake's manner of using water-colour; cp. the allusion to 'water' in the preceding epigram.

XI I print here the earlier and clearer version of this piece, Blake's subsequent changes being noted below.   2 'Menny wouver' both bunglishness and skill *MS. 2nd rdg.*   5 putting] displaying *MS. 2nd rdg.*   6 'Twill make a great splutter] 'Twill hold forth a huge splutter *MS. 2nd rdg.*   7 For there is no use] For it's all sheer loss *MS. 2nd rdg.*   8 Of displaying up a light when we want not to see *MS. 2nd rdg.*

XII 1 When I see a Rembrandt or Correggio *MS. 1st rdg. del.*   3 question thus] say to myself *MS. 1st rdg. del.*   6 O] we *MS. 1st rdg. del.*

On Art and Artists

XIII

Give pensions to the learned pig,
Or the hare playing on a tabor;
Anglus can never see perfection
But in the journeyman's labour.

XIV

[On Sir Joshua Reynolds' disappointment at his first impressions of Raphael]

Some look to see the sweet outlines,
And beauteous forms that Love does wear;
Some look to find out patches, paint,
Bracelets and stays and powder'd hair.

XV

Sir Joshua prais├d Rubens with a smile,
By calling his the ornamental style;
And yet his praise of Flaxman was the smartest,
When he called him the ornamental artist.
But sure such ornaments we well may spare 5
As crooked limbs and lousy heads of hair.

XVI

Sir Joshua praises Michael Angelo.
'Tis Christian mildness when knaves praise a foe;
But 'twould be madness, all the world would say,
Should Michael Angelo praise Sir Joshua—
Christ us'd the Pharisees in a rougher way. 5

---

xv 6 Like a filthy infectious head of hair *MS. 1st rdg. del.* **A crooked stick and a lousy head of hair** *MS. 2nd rdg. del.*

xvi 2 And counts it outrage thus to praise his foe *MS. 1st rdg. del.* 3 all the world would] that we all must *MS. 1st rdg. del.* 5 This line added later.

On Art and Artists

XVII

Can there be anything more mean,
More malice in disguise,
Than praise a man for doing what
That man does most despise?
Reynolds lectures exactly so
When he praises Michael Angelo.

XVIII

To the Royal Academy

A strange erratum in all the editions
Of Sir Joshua Reynolds' lectures
Should be corrected by the young gentlemen
And the Royal Academy's directors.

Instead of 'Michael Angelo,'
Read 'Rembrandt'; for it is fit
To make mere common honesty
In all that he has writ.

XIX

Florentine Ingratitude

Sir Joshua sent his own portrait to
The birthplace of Michael Angelo,
And in the hand of the simpering fool
He put a dirty paper scroll,
And on the paper, to be polite,
Did 'Sketches by Michael Angelo' write.
The Florentines said ''Tis a Dutch-English bore,
Michael Angelo's name writ on Rembrandt's door.'

---

xvii 3 what] that *MS. 1st rdg. del.*   4 That man] Which he *MS. 1st rdg. del.*   5 This Reynolds' lectures plainly shew *MS. 1st rdg. del.*

xviii 6–8   . . . . . and you will know
That Sir Joshua Reynolds now wished to speak
Of Michael Angelo.   *MS. 1st rdg. del.*

7 mere common] either sense or *MS. 1st rdg. del.*

On Art and Artists

The Florentines call it an English fetch,
For Michael Angelo never did sketch; 10
Every line of his has meaning,
And needs neither suckling nor weaning.
'Tis the trading English-Venetian cant
To speak Michael Angelo, and act Rembrandt:
It will set his Dutch friends all in a roar 15
To write 'Mich. Ang.' on Rembrandt's door;
But you must not bring in your hand a lie
If you mean that the Florentines should buy.
Giotto's circle or Apelles' line
Were not the work of sketchers drunk with wine; 20
Nor of the city clock's running . . . fashion;
Nor of Sir Isaac Newton's calculation.

XX

No real style of colouring ever appears,
But advertising in the newspapers.
Look there—you'll see Sir Joshua's colouring:
Look at his pictures—all has taken wing!

XXI

When Sir Joshua Reynolds died
All Nature was degraded;
The King dropp'd a tear into the Queen's ear,
And all his pictures faded.

XIX 18 Following this in the *MS. Book* are the lines:

> These verses were written by a very envious man,
> Who whatever likeness he may have to Michael Angelo
> Never can have any to Sir Jehoshuan.

19–22 These lines written later at foot of page. Another rdg. was:

> Nor of the city clock's idle facilities
> Which sprang from Sir Isaac Newton's great abilities.

XX 4 all has taken wing] 'tis quite another thing *MS.* 1*st rdg. del.*

On Art and Artists

A Pitiful Case XXII

The villain at the gallows tree,
When he is doom'd to die,
To assuage his misery
In virtue's praise does cry.

So Reynolds when he came to die,
To assuage his bitter woe,
Thus aloud did howl and cry:
'Michael Angelo! Michael Angelo!'

XXIII

[On Sir Joshua Reynolds]

O Reader, behold the Philosopher's grave!
He was born quite a Fool, but he died quite a Knave.

XXIV

I, Rubens, am a statesman and a saint.
Deceptions [both]—and so I'll learn to paint.

XXV

[On the school of Rubens]

Swelled limbs, with no outline that you can descry,
That stink in the nose of a stander-by;
But all the pulp-wash'd, painted, finish'd with labour,
Of an hundred journeymen's—how-d'ye do neighbour?

XXVI

To English Connoisseurs

You must agree that Rubens was a fool,
And yet you make him master of your School,

XXII 7 did howl and] was heard to *MS. 1st rdg. del.*
XXIV   Rubens had been a statesman or a saint;
         He mixed them both—and so he learn'd to paint.
                                    MS. 1st rdg. del.

On Art and Artists

And give more money for his slobberings
Than you will give for Raphael's finest things.
I understood Christ was a carpenter 5
And not a brewer's servant, my good Sir.

XXVII

A Pretty Epigram for the encouragement of those who have paid great sums in the Venetian and Flemish ooze

Nature and Art in this together suit:
What is most grand is always most minute.
Rubens thinks tables, chairs and stools are grand,
But Raphael thinks a head, a foot, a hand.

XXVIII

Raphael, sublime, majestic, graceful, wise—
His executive power must I despise?
Rubens, low, vulgar, stupid, ignorant—
His power of execution I must grant,
Learn the laborious stumble of a fool! 5
And from an idiot's action form my rule?—
Go, send your Children to the Slobbering School!

XXIX

On the Venetian Painter

He makes the lame to walk, we all agree,
But then he strives to blind all who can see

XXX

A pair of stays to mend the shape
Of crookèd humpy woman,
Put on, O Venus; now thou art
Quite a Venetian Roman.

XXVII Title] A Pretty Epigram for those who have given high prices for bad pictures *MS. 1st rdg. del.*

On Art and Artists

XXXI

Venetian! all thy colouring is no more
Than bolster'd plasters on a crooked whore.

XXXII

To Venetian Artists

That God is colouring Newton does show,
And the Devil is a black outline, all of us know.
Perhaps this little fable may make us merry:
A dog went over the water without a wherry;
A bone which he had stolen he had in his mouth; 5
He cared not whether the wind was north or south.
As he swam he saw the reflection of the bone.
'This is quite perfection—one generalizing tone!
Outline! There's no outline, there's no such thing:
All is chiaroscuro, poco-pen—it's all colouring!' 10
Snap, snap! He has lost shadow and substance too.
He had them both before. 'Now how do ye do?'
'A great deal better than I was before:
Those who taste colouring love it more and more.'

XXXIII

All pictures that's painted with sense and with thought
Are painted by madmen, as sure as a groat;
For the greater the fool is the pencil more blest,
As when they are drunk they always paint best.
They never can Raphael it, Fuseli it, nor Blake it; 5
If they can't see an outline, pray how can they make it?
When men will draw outlines begin you to jaw them;
Madmen see outlines and therefore they draw them.

XXXII 8 Here's two for one, what a brilliant tone *MS. 1st rdg. del.*
9, 10 A marginal addition.

On Art and Artists

XXXIV

Call that the public voice which is their error!
Like as a monkey, peeping in a mirror,
Admires all his colours brown and warm,
And never once perceives his ugly form.

ON FRIENDS AND FOES

I

I am no Homer's hero you all know;
I profess not generosity to a foe.
My generosity is to my friends,
That for their friendship I may make amends.
The generous to enemies promotes their ends, 5
And becomes the enemy and betrayer of his friends.

II

Anger and wrath my bosom rends:
I thought them the errors of friends.
But all my limbs with warmth glow:
I find them the errors of the foe.

III

If you play a game of chance, know, before you begin,
If you are benevolent you will never win.

The Epigrams arranged in this section, all taken from the *Rossetti MS.* and written *circa* 1807-10, refer to the unhappy period in Blake's history, when, embittered by the treatment of Cromek, and the ungenerous attitude of contemporaries towards his art, culminating in Hunt's attack in the *Examiner*, he conceived himself to be the victim of a conspiracy, and became wholly alienated from most of his old friends. Cp. Gilchrist's *Life*, 1 (chap. 26 and *passim*), Blake's *Letters*, ed. Russell, and his own references in the 'Advertisement' and the *Descriptive Catalogue*.

1 6 Cp. 'Everlasting Gospel', γ 25:

> He who loves his enemies betrays his friends.

On Friends and Foes

[Of Hayley's birth]   IV

    Of H——'s birth this was the happy lot:
    His mother on his father him begot.

[On Hayley]   V

    To forgive enemies H —— does pretend,
    Who never in his life forgave a friend,
    And when he could not act upon my wife
    Hired a villain to bereave my life.

To H[ayley]   VI

    Thy friendship oft has made my heart to ache:
    Do be my enemy—for friendship's sake.

VII
On H[ayle]y's Friendship

    When H——y finds out what you cannot do,
    That is the very thing he'll set you to;
    If you break not your neck, 'tis not his fault;
    But pecks of poison are not pecks of salt.

VIII
On H[ayley] the Pickthank

    I write the rascal thanks, till he and I
    With thanks and compliments are quite drawn dry.

---

v 4 This line, as well as any other, may serve as an illustration of Blake's habit of embodying old phrases, passages, or even entire stanzas in pieces written sometimes after an interval of years. Cp. with the above, composed *circa* 1809, the lines from 'Fair Elenor':

    He seeks thy love; who, coward in the night,
    Hirèd a villain to bereave my life,

probably one of the earliest poems included in the *Poetical Sketches* printed in 1783, and, according to the 'Advertisement', written at least six years earlier.

On Friends and Foes

IX

My title as a genius thus is prov'd:
Not prais'd by Hayley, nor by Flaxman lov'd.

To F[laxman]   X

You call me mad, 'tis folly to do so,
To seek to turn a madman to a foe.
If you think as you speak, you are an ass;
If you do not, you are but what you was.

To F[laxman]   XI

I mock thee not, though I by thee am mockèd;
Thou call'st me madman, but I call thee blockhead.

To Nancy F[laxman]   XII

How can I help thy husband's copying me?
Should that make difference 'twixt me and thee?

XIII

To F[laxman] and S[tothard]

I found them blind: I taught them how to see;
And now they know neither themselves nor me.
'Tis excellent to turn a thorn to a pin,
A fool to a bolt, a knave to a glass of gin.

---

x 4 but what] just what *MS. 1st rdg. del.*

XIII Title] The words 'and S.' are an addition.   1 them] him *MS. 1st rdg. del.*   2 they know ... themselves] he knows ... himself *MS. 1st rdg. del.* Blake introduces this couplet into his *Descriptive Catalogue* (1809).

On Friends and Foes

To S[tothar]d   XIV

> You all your youth observ'd the golden rule,
> Till you're at last become the golden fool:
> I sport with fortune, merry, blithe and gay,
> Like to the lion sporting with his prey.
> Take you the hide and horns which you may wear,   5
> Mine is the flesh—the bones may be your share.

Cromek speaks   XV

> I always take my judgement from a fool
> Because his judgement is so very cool;
> Not prejudiced by feelings great or small,
> Amiable state! he cannot feel at all.

On S[tothard]   XVI

> You say reserve and modesty he has,
> Whose heart is iron, his head wood, and his face brass.
> The fox, the owl, the beetle, and the bat
> By sweet reserve and modesty get fat.

[On Stothard]   XVII

> S——, in childhood, on the nursery floor,
> Was extreme old and most extremely poor:
> He has grown old, and rich, and what he will;
> He is extreme old, and extreme poor still.

XIV In its original form this epigram was written in the third person, 'he' for 'you', 'his' for 'your', 'he's' for 'you're' in l. 2, and 'He has' for 'Take you' in l. 5.

XV 2 Because I know he always judges cool *MS. 1st rdg. del.* 4 Amiable state!] Because we know *MS. 1st rdg. del.*

XVI 3, 4 Blake uses this couplet in his *Descriptive Catalogue*, with the change of 'owl' to 'mole' in l. 3.

On Friends and Foes

XVIII
Mr. Stothard to Mr. Cromek

> For Fortune's favours you your riches bring,
> But Fortune says she gave you no such thing
> Why should you be ungrateful to your friends,—
> Sneaking and backbiting, and odds and ends?

XIX
Mr. Cromek to Mr. Stothard

> Fortune favours the brave, old proverbs say;
> But not with money; that is not the way.
> Turn back! turn back! you travel all in vain;
> Turn through the iron gate down Sneaking Lane.

[On Cromek]   XX

> Cr—— loves artists as he loves his meat:
> He loves the Art; but 'tis the art to cheat.

[On Cromek]   XXI

> A petty sneaking knave I knew—
> O! Mr. Cr——, how do ye do?

[On P——]   XXII

> P—— lovèd me not as he lov'd his friends;
> For he lov'd them for gain, to serve his ends:
> He lovèd me, and for no gain at all,
> But to rejoice and triumph in my fall.

XXII 1 P——] Not, perhaps, as I formerly thought, Thomas Phillips, R.A., painter of the portrait of Blake engraved for Blair's *Grave*, but more probably Sir Richard Phillips, for whom Blake executed several engravings. (See Russell's *Engravings of William Blake*, and edition of Blake's *Letters*, *passim*.) With this thumb-nail sketch of Phillips the reader may be interested to compare the full-length portrait of 'The Publisher', drawn by George Borrow in his *Lavengro* (Vol. II, *passim*.)

On Friends and Foes

XXIII
[On William Haines]

The Sussex men are noted fools,
And weak is their brain pan—
I wonder if H—— the painter
Is not a Sussex man.

XXIV
[On Fuseli]

The only man that e'er I knew
Who did not make me almost spew
Was Fuseli: he was both Turk and Jew—
And so, dear Christian friends, how do you do?

XXV
[To Hunt]

'Madman' I have been call'd: 'Fool' they call thee.
I wonder which they envy—thee or me?

XXVI
To H[unt]

You think Fuseli is not a great painter. I'm glad.
This is one of the best compliments he ever had

XXVII
[On certain Mystics]

Cosway, Frazer, and Baldwin of Egypt's lake
Fear to associate with Blake.
This life is a warfare against evils;
They heal the sick: he casts out devils.

XXIII Written about 1809, the date of the publication of Hayley's *Life of Romney*, to which William Haines and Blake both contributed engravings.

XXIV 4 dear Christian friends] sweet Christians *MS. 1st rdg. del.*

XXV, XXVI Both these epigrams, which immediately follow each other in the *MS. Book*, are evidently addressed to Hunt, and were occasioned by the reference of the latter to Fuseli and Blake in the *Examiner*, no. 75, June 4, 1809. or the later attack in no. 90, Sept. 17, 1809 Cp. also no. XXVIII, ll. 15 sqq.

On Friends and Foes

Hayley, Flaxman, and Stothard are also in doubt 5
Lest their virtue should be put to the rout.
One grins, t'other spits, and in corners hides,
And all the virtuous have shown their backsides.

XXVIII

—And his legs carried it like a long fork,
Reached all the way from Chichester to York,
From York all across Scotland to the sea;
This was a man of men, as seems to me.
Not only in his mouth his own soul lay, 5
But my soul also would he bear away.
Like as a pedlar bears his weary pack,
He would bear my soul buckled to his back.
But once, alas! committing a mistake,
He bore the wretched soul of William Blake 10
That he might turn it into eggs of gold;
But neither back nor mouth those eggs could hold.
His under jaw dropp'd as those eggs he laid,
And all my eggs are addled and decay'd.
The Examiner, whose very name is Hunt, 15
Call'd Death a madman, trembling for the affront;

XXVIII This biographical fragment, of which the opening lines are lacking, was probably composed soon after Sept. 17, 1809, when the article on 'Mr. Blake's Exhibition' appeared in Leigh Hunt's *Examiner* (no. 90). The speaker 'Stewhard' is evidently Stothard, and the 'he' of the opening lines Cromek, elsewhere called 'Bob Screwmuch'. 'Death' is a nickname for Blake (possibly because of his association with Blair's *Grave*); 'Yorkshire Jack Hemp' for Flaxman; 'Felpham Billy' for Hayley; and 'Daddy, Jack Hemp's parson' for Dr. Malkin of the *Father's Memoirs*; while Chichester was the scene of Blake's trial for high treason at the instance of the 'Dragoon' (see Gilchrist I, chap. xix). 8, 14 I give here the original and clearer readings. Later Blake changed l. 8 to 'So Stewhard's soul he buckled to his back', and l. 14 to 'And Stewhard's eggs', &c., but failed to make corresponding changes of person in the rest of the poem. 16 trembling for the affront] Deadly the affront *MS. 1st rdg. del.*

On Friends and Foes

Like trembling hare sits on his weakly paper
On which he used to dance and sport and caper.
Yorkshire Jack Hemp and Quibble, blushing daw,
Clapp'd Death into the corner of their jaw,   20
And Felpham Billy rode out every morn,
Horseback with Death, over the fields of corn;
Who with iron hand cuff'd, in the afternoon,
The ears of Billy's Lawyer and Dragoon.
And Cur my lawyer, and Daddy, Jack Hemp's parson,   25
Both went to law with Death to keep our ears on.
For how to starve Death we had laid a plot
Against his price—but Death was in the pot.
He made them pay his price, alackaday!
He knew both Law and Gospel better than they.   30
O that I ne'er had seen that William Blake,
Or could from Death Assassinette wake!
We thought—Alas, that such a thought could be!—
That Blake would etch for him and draw for me.
For 'twas a kind of bargain Screwmuch made   35
That Blake's designs should be by us display'd,
Because he makes designs so very cheap.
Then Screwmuch at Blake's soul took a long leap.
'Twas not a mouse. 'Twas Death in a disguise.
And I, alas! live to weep out my eyes.   40
And Death sits laughing on their monuments
On which he's written 'Receivèd the contents.'
But I have writ—so sorrowful my thought is—
His epitaph; for my tears are aquafortis.
'Come, Artists, knock your head against this stone,   45
For sorrow that our friend Bob Screwmuch's gone.'
And now the Muses upon me smile and laugh
I'll also write my own dear epitaph,

19 Yorkshire] And Yorkshire *MS. 1st rdg. del.*
43, 44   But I have writ with tears, as aquafortis,
         This Epitaph—so sorrowful my thought is.   *MS. 1st rdg. del.*

On Friends and Foes

And I'll be buried near a dyke
That my friends may weep as much as they like: 50
'Here lies Stewhard the Friend of all [mankind;
He has not left one enemy behind.]'

XXIX

—For this is being a friend just in the nick,
Not when he's well, but waiting till he's sick;
He calls you to his help; be you not mov'd
Until, by being sick, his wants are prov'd.

You see him spend his soul in prophecy: 5
Do you believe it a confounded lie,
Till some bookseller, and the public fame,
Prove there is truth in his extravagant claim.

For 'tis atrocious in a friend you love
To tell you anything that he can't prove, 10
And 'tis most wicked in a Christian nation
For any man to pretend to inspiration.

XXX

Was I angry with Hayley who us'd me so ill,
Or can I be angry with Felpham's old mill?
Or angry with Flaxman, or Cromek, or Stothard,
Or poor Schiavonetti, whom they to death bother'd?
Or angry with Macklin, or Boydell, or Bowyer, 5
Because they did not say 'O what a beau ye are'?
At a friend's errors anger show,
Mirth at the errors of a foe.

---

51 In the MS. 'Here lies Stewhard the Friend of all, &c.' I complete the couplet from the 'Epitaph on John Trot' (p. 221).

XXIX Following a wholly erased stanza in the *MS.* 9 atrocious] most wicked *MS. 1st rdg. del.*

XXX 3 Or angry with Boydell or Bowyer or Bu[tts]] *MS. 1st rdg. del.*
5 Macklin, Boydell, Bowyer] Publishers for whom Blake engraved. Cp. a reference to the same trio in a letter to Hayley dated 11th December, 1805 (Blake's *Letters*, ed. Russell, p. 187).

On Friends and Foes

XXXI

Having given great offence by writing in prose,
I'll write in verse as soft as Bartoloze.
Some blush at what others can see no crime in;
But nobody sees any harm in riming.
Dryden, in rime, cries 'Milton only plann'd':   5
Every fool shook his bells throughout the land.
Tom Cooke cut Hogarth down with his clean graving:
Thousands of connoisseurs with joy ran raving.
Thus, Hayley on his toilette seeing the soap,
Cries, 'Homer is very much improv'd by Pope.'   10
Some say I've given great provision to my foes,
And that now I lead my false friends by the nose.
Flaxman and Stothard, smelling a sweet savour,
Cry 'Blakified drawing spoils painter and engraver';
While I, looking up to my umbrella,   15
Resolv'd to be a very contrary fellow,
Cry, looking quite from skumference to centre:
'No one can finish so high as the original Inventor.'
Thus poor Schiavonetti died of the Cromek—
A thing that's tied around the Examiner's neck!   20
This is my sweet apology to my friends,
That I may put them in mind of their latter ends.
If men will act like a maid smiling over a churn,
They ought not, when it comes to another's turn,

XXXI 1 Cp. Hunt's reference to Blake's 'Descriptive Catalogue', *Examiner*, no. 90, Sept. 17, 1809.   4 But nobody at all sees harm in riming *MS. 1st rdg. del.*   8 How many thousands of connoisseurs ran raving *MS. 1st rdg. del.*   9 Thus] *An addition.*   10 Cries] Says *MS. 1st rdg. del.*

11, 12   I've given great provision to my foes,
         But now I'll lead my false friends by the nose. *MS. 1st rdg. del.*,
'Some say' in l. 11, and 'that' in l. 12 being marginal additions.   17 Cry Tom Cooke proves from circumference to centre *MS. 1st rdg. del.*   19, 20 A reference to Cromek's 'Account of Mr. Schiavonetti' in the *Examiner*, July 1, 1810.

On Friends and Foes

To grow sour at what a friend may utter, 25
Knowing and feeling that we all have need of butter.
False friends, fie! fie! Our friendship you shan't sever;
In spite we will be greater friends than ever.

MISCELLANEOUS EPIGRAMS

I

His whole life is an epigram smart, smooth and neatly penn'd,
Plaited quite neat to catch applause, with a hang-noose at the end.

II

He has observ'd the golden rule,
Till he 's become the golden fool.

III

—And in melodious accents I
Will sit me down, and cry 'I! I!

xxxi 27 fie! fie!] O no! *MS. 1st rdg. del.* you shan't] ne'er shall *MS. 1st rdg. del.*   28 In spite] For now *MS. 1st rdg. del.*

Miscellaneous Epigrams] All these (written *circa* 1807-9) are taken from the *Rossetti MS.*, with the exception of no. xi, which is one of Blake's marginalia in his copy of Reynolds' *Discourses*.

I 1 The first word, which is very indistinctly written, may be either 'His' or 'Her'; all editors print the latter, but 'His' on the whole seems the more probable reading. The same words, it may be noted, are confused in the Song, 'Love and Harmony combine' (*Poetical Sketches*, p. 10 of this ed.).

II A variant of the first couplet of an epigram addressed to Stothard, see p. 212, no. xiv.

III Following the prose passage in Blake's 'Advertisement' in the *MS. Book*: 'I demand therefore of the amateurs of art the encouragement which is my due. If they continue to refuse, theirs is the loss, not mine, and theirs is the contempt of posterity. I have enough in the approbation of fellow labourers. This is my glory, and my exceeding great reward. I go on, and nothing can hinder my course.'

Miscellaneous Epigrams

IV

Some people admire the work of a fool,
For it's sure to keep your judgement cool;
It does not reproach you with want of wit;
It is not like a lawyer serving a writ.

V

He's a blockhead who wants a proof of what he can't perceive;
And he's a fool who tries to make such a blockhead believe.

VI

Great men and fools do often me inspire;
But the greater fool, the greater liar.

VII

Some men, created for destruction, come
Into the world, and make the world their home.
Be they as vile and base as e'er they can,
They'll still be callèd 'The World's Honest Man.'

An Epitaph VIII

Come knock your heads against this stone,
For sorrow that poor John Thompson's gone.

Another IX

I was buried near this dyke,
That my friends may weep as much as they like.

IV A variant and more general form of the epigram on Cromek, see p. 212, no. xv.

VII 3, 4 Friend Caiaphas is one, do what he can,
  He'll still be callèd 'The World's Honest Man.'
  MS. 2nd rdg. del.

VIII, IX, X Cp. the slightly different form of these three epitaphs in the lines beginning 'And his legs carried it like a long fork', p. 215, no. XXVIII.

Miscellaneous Epigrams

Another   X

    Here lies John Trot, the friend of all mankind:
    He has not left one enemy behind.
    Friends were quite hard to find, old authors say;
    But now they stand in everybody's way.

XI

When France got free, Europe, 'twixt fools and knaves,
Were savage first to France, and after—slaves.

XII

On the virginity of the Virgin Mary and Johanna Southcott

    Whate'er is done to her she cannot know,
    And if you'll ask her she will swear it so.
    Whether 'tis good or evil none's to blame:
    No one can take the pride, no one the shame.

XIII

Imitation of Pope: a compliment to the Ladies

    Wondrous the gods, more wondrous are the men,
    More wondrous, wondrous still, the cock and hen,
    More wondrous still the table, stool and chair;
    But ah! more wondrous still the charming fair.

XIV

When a man has married a wife, he finds out whether
Her knees and elbows are only glued together.

XV

To Chloe's breast young Cupid slyly stole,
But he crept in at Myra's pocket-hole.

    XII 2 swear it] tell you *MS. 1st rdg. del.*

TIRIEL

(MS. *circa* 1788-89)

TIRIEL

I

And agèd Tiriel stood before the gates of his beautiful palace
With Myratana, once the Queen of all the western plains;
But now his eyes were darkenèd, and his wife fading in death.
They stood before their once delightful palace; and thus the voice
Of agèd Tiriel arose, that his sons might hear in their gates:— 5

'Accursèd race of Tiriel! behold your father;
Come forth and look on her that bore you! Come, you accursed
    sons!
In my weak arms I here have borne your dying mother.
Come forth, sons of the Curse, come forth! see the death of
    Myratana!'

His sons ran from their gates, and saw their agèd parents stand;
And thus the eldest son of Tiriel rais'd his mighty voice:— 11

'Old man! unworthy to be call'd the father of Tiriel's race!
For every one of those thy wrinkles, each of those grey hairs
Are cruel as death, and as obdurate as the devouring pit!
Why should thy sons care for thy curses, thou accursèd man? 15
Were we not slaves till we rebell'd? Who cares for Tiriel's curse?
His blessing was a cruel curse; his curse may be a blessing.'

He ceas'd: the agèd man rais'd up his right hand to the heavens.
His left supported Myratana, shrinking in pangs of death:

---

1 Followed in the MS. by a del. half-line:
          But dark were his once piercing eyes . . .

Tiriel

The orbs of his large eyes he open'd, and thus his voice went forth:— 20

'Serpents, not sons, wreathing around the bones of Tiriel!
Ye worms of death, feasting upon your agèd parent's flesh!
Listen! and hear your mother's groans! No more accursèd sons
She bears; she groans not at the birth of Heuxos or Yuva.
These are the groans of death, ye serpents! these are the groans of death! 25
Nourish'd with milk, ye serpents, nourish'd with mother's tears and cares!
Look at my eyes, blind as the orbless skull among the stones!
Look at my bald head! Hark! listen, ye serpents, listen! ...
What, Myratana! What, my wife! O Soul! O Spirit! O Fire!
What, Myratana! art thou dead? Look here, ye serpents, look!
The serpents sprung from her own bowels have drain'd her dry as this. 31
Curse on your ruthless heads, for I will bury her even here!'

So saying, he began to dig a grave with his agèd hands;
But Heuxos call'd a son of Zazel to dig their mother a grave.

'Old Cruelty, desist! and let us dig a grave for thee. 35
Thou hast refus'd our charity, thou hast refus'd our food,
Thou hast refus'd our clothes, our beds, our houses for thy dwelling,
Choosing to wander like a son of Zazel in the rocks.
Why dost thou curse? Is not the curse now come upon your head? 39
Was it not you enslav'd the sons of Zazel? And they have curs'd,
And now you feel it. Dig a grave, and let us bury our mother.'

'There, take the body, cursèd sons! and may the heavens rain wrath
As thick as northern fogs, around your gates, to choke you up!
That you may lie as now your mother lies, like dogs cast out,
The stink of your dead carcases annoying man and beast, 45
Till your white bones are bleach'd with age for a memorial.

Tiriel

No! your remembrance shall perish; for, when your carcases
Lie stinking on the earth, the buriers shall arise from the East,
And not a bone of all the sons of Tiriel remain.
Bury your mother! but you cannot bury the curse of Tiriel.'   50

He ceas'd, and darkling o'er the mountains sought his pathless way.

II

He wander'd day and night: to him both day and night were dark.
The sun he felt, but the bright moon was now a useless globe:
O'er mountains and thro' vales of woe the blind and agèd man
Wander'd, till he that leadeth all led him to the vales of Har.   55

And Har and Heva, like two children, sat beneath the oak:
Mnetha, now agèd, waited on them, and brought them food and clothing;
But they were as the shadow of Har, and as the years forgotten.
Playing with flowers and running after birds they spent the day,
And in the night like infants slept, delighted with infant dreams.

Soon as the blind wanderer enter'd the pleasant gardens of Har,
They ran weeping, like frighted infants, for refuge in Mnetha's arms.   62
The blind man felt his way, and cried: 'Peace to these open doors!
Let no one fear, for poor blind Tiriel hurts none but himself.
Tell me, O friends, where am I now, and in what pleasant place?'

'This is the valley of Har,' said Mnetha, 'and this the tent of Har.   66
Who art thou, poor blind man, that takest the name of Tiriel on thee?
Tiriel is King of all the West. Who art thou? I am Mnetha;
And this is Har and Heva, trembling like infants by my side.'

Tiriel

'I know Tiriel is King of the West, and there he lives in joy. 70
No matter who I am, O Mnetha! If thou hast any food,
Give it me; for I cannot stay; my journey is far from hence.'

Then Har said: 'O my mother Mnetha, venture not so near him;
For he is the king of rotten wood, and of the bones of death; 74
He wanders without eyes, and passes thro' thick walls and doors.
Thou shalt not smite my mother Mnetha, O thou eyeless man!'

'A wanderer, I beg for food: you see I cannot weep:
I cast away my staff, the kind companion of my travel,
And I kneel down that you may see I am a harmless man.'

He kneelèd down. And Mnetha said: 'Come, Har and Heva, rise!
80
He is an innocent old man, and hungry with his travel.'

Then Har arose, and laid his hand upon old Tiriel's head.

'God bless thy poor bald pate! God bless thy hollow winking eyes!
God bless thy shrivell'd beard! God bless thy many-wrinkled forehead!
Thou hast no teeth, old man! and thus I kiss thy sleek bald head.
85
Heva, come kiss his bald head, for he will not hurt us, Heva.

Then Heva came, and took old Tiriel in her mother's arms.

'Bless thy poor eyes, old man, and bless the old father of Tiriel!
Thou art my Tiriel's old father; I know thee thro' thy wrinkles,
Because thou smellest like the fig-tree, thou smellest like ripe figs.

76 Followed by a del. line:
> O venerable, O most piteous, O most woeful day!

78 Followed by a del. line:
> But I can kneel down at your door. I am a harmless man.

Tiriel

How didst thou lose thy eyes, old Tiriel? Bless thy wrinkled face!' 91

Mnetha said: 'Come in, agèd wanderer! tell us of thy name.
Why shouldest thou conceal thyself from those of thine own flesh?'

'I am not of this region,' said Tiriel dissemblingly.
'I am an agèd wanderer, once father of a race 95
Far in the North; but they were wicked, and were all destroy'd,
And I their father sent an outcast. I have told you all.
Ask me no more, I pray, for grief hath seal'd my precious sight.'

'O Lord!' said Mnetha, 'how I tremble! Are there then more people,
More human creatures on this earth, beside the sons of Har?'

'No more,' said Tiriel, 'but I, remain on all this globe; 101
And I remain an outcast. Hast thou anything to drink?'

Then Mnetha gave him milk and fruits, and they sat down together.

III

They sat and ate, and Har and Heva smil'd on Tiriel.

'Thou art a very old old man, but I am older than thou. 105
How came thine hair to leave thy forehead? how came thy face so brown?
My hair is very long, my beard doth cover all my breast.

91 Followed by two del. lines:
    The agèd Tiriel could not speak, his heart was full of grief;
    He strove against his rising passions, but still he could not speak.
94 Followed by a del. line:
    Fearing to tell them who he was, because of the weakness of Har.

Tiriel

God bless thy piteous face! To count the wrinkles in thy face
Would puzzle Mnetha. Bless thy face! for thou art Tiriel.'

'Tiriel I never saw but once: I sat with him and ate;   110
He was as cheerful as a prince, and gave me entertainment;
But long I stay'd not at his palace, for I am forc'd to wander.'

'What! wilt thou leave us too?' said Heva: 'thou shalt not leave us too,
For we have many sports to show thee, and many songs to sing;
And after dinner we will walk into the cage of Har,   115
And thou shalt help us to catch birds, and gather them ripe cherries.
Then let thy name be Tiriel, and never leave us more.'

'If thou dost go,' said Har, 'I wish thine eyes may see thy folly.
My sons have left me; did thine leave thee? O, 'twas very cruel!'

'No! venerable man,' said Tiriel, 'ask me not such things,   120
For thou dost make my heart to bleed: my sons were not like thine,
But worse. O never ask me more, or I must flee away!

'Thou shalt not go,' said Heva, 'till thou hast seen our singing-birds,
And heard Har sing in the great cage, and slept upon our fleeces.
Go not! for thou art so like Tiriel that I love thine head,   125
Tho' it is wrinkled like the earth parch'd with the summer heat.'

Then Tiriel rose up from the seat, and said: 'God bless these tents!
My journey is o'er rocks and mountains, not in pleasant vales:
I must not sleep nor rest, because of madness and dismay.'

   109 Followed by two del. lines:
   Tiriel could scarce dissemble more, and his tongue could scarce refrain,
   But still he fear'd that Har and Heva would die of joy and grief.
   127 Followed by a del. line:
   God bless my benefactors, for I cannot tarry longer.
   129 Followed by a del. line:
   Then Mnetha led him to the door and gave to him his staff.

Tiriel

And Mnetha said: 'Thou must not go to wander dark, alone; 130
But dwell with us, and let us be to thee instead of eyes,
And I will bring thee food, old man, till death shall call thee hence.

Then Tiriel frown'd, and answer'd: 'Did I not command you, saying,
"Madness and deep dismay possess the heart of the blind man,
The wanderer who seeks the woods, leaning upon his staff?"' 135

Then Mnetha, trembling at his frowns, led him to the tent door,
And gave to him his staff, and bless'd him.   He went on his way.

But Har and Heva stood and watch'd him till he enter'd the wood;
And then they went and wept to Mnetha: but they soon forgot their tears.

IV

Over the weary hills the blind man took his lonely way; 140
To him the day and night alike was dark and desolate;

But far he had not gone when Ijim from his woods came down,
Met him at entrance of the forest, in a dark and lonely way.

'Who art thou, eyeless wretch, that thus obstruct'st the lion's path?
Ijim shall rend thy feeble joints, thou tempter of dark Ijim! 145
Thou hast the form of Tiriel, but I know thee well enough.
Stand from my path, foul fiend!   Is this the last of thy deceits,
To be a hypocrite, and stand in shape of a blind beggar?'

The blind man heard his brother's voice, and kneel'd down on his knee.

'O brother Ijim, if it is thy voice that speaks to me, 150
Smite not thy brother Tiriel, tho' weary of his life.
My sons have smitten me already; and, if thou smitest me,
The curse that rolls over their heads will rest itself on thine.
'Tis now seven years since in my palace I beheld thy face.'

154 Followed by a del. line:
> Seven years of sorrow; then the curse of Zazel . . .

Tiriel

'Come, thou dark fiend, I dare thy cunning! know that Ijim scorns
To smite thee in the form of helpless age and eyeless policy.
Rise up! for I discern thee, and I dare thy eloquent tongue.
Come! I will lead thee on thy way, and use thee as a scoff.'

'O brother Ijim, thou beholdest wretched Tiriel:
Kiss me, my brother, and then leave me to wander desolate!'

'No! artful fiend, but I will lead thee; dost thou want to go?
Reply not, lest I bind thee with the green flags of the brook.
Aye! now thou art discover'd, I will use thee like a slave.'

When Tiriel heard the words of Ijim, he sought not to reply:
He knew 'twas vain, for Ijim's words were as the voice of Fate.

And they went on together, over hills, thro' woody dales,
Blind to the pleasures of the sight, and deaf to warbling birds:
All day they walk'd, and all the night beneath the pleasant moon,
Westwardly journeying, till Tiriel grew weary with his travel.

'O Ijim, I am faint and weary, for my knees forbid
To bear me further: urge me not, lest I should die with travel.
A little rest I crave, a little water from a brook,
Or I shall soon discover that I am a mortal man,
And you will lose your once-lov'd Tiriel. Alas! how faint I am!'

'Impudent fiend!' said Ijim, 'hold thy glib and eloquent tongue!
Tiriel is a king, and thou the tempter of dark Ijim.
Drink of this running brook, and I will bear thee on my shoulders.'

He drank; and Ijim rais'd him up, and bore him on his shoulders:
All day he bore him; and, when evening drew her solemn curtain,
Enter'd the gates of Tiriel's palace, and stood and call'd aloud:—

'Heuxos, come forth! I here have brought the fiend that troubles Ijim.
Look! know'st thou aught of this grey beard, or of these blinded eyes?'

Tiriel

Heuxos and Lotho ran forth at the sound of Ijim's voice,
And saw their agèd father borne upon his mighty shoulders.
Their eloquent tongues were dumb, and sweat stood on their
    trembling limbs: 185
They knew 'twas vain to strive with Ijim. They bow'd and silent
    stood.

'What, Heuxos! call thy father, for I mean to sport to-night.
This is the hypocrite that sometimes roars a dreadful lion;
Then I have rent his limbs, and left him rotting in the forest
For birds to eat. But I have scarce departed from the place, 190
But like a tiger he would come: and so I rent him too.
Then like a river he would seek to drown me in his waves;
But soon I buffeted the torrent: anon like to a cloud
Fraught with the swords of lightning; but I brav'd the vengeance
    too.
Then he would creep like a bright serpent; till around my neck,
While I was sleeping, he would twine: I squeez'd his poisonous
    soul.   196
Then like a toad, or like a newt, would whisper in my ears;
Or like a rock stood in my way, or like a poisonous shrub.
At last I caught him in the form of Tiriel, blind and old, 199
And so I'll keep him! Fetch your father, fetch forth Myratana!'

They stood confounded, and thus Tiriel rais'd his silver voice:—

'Serpents, not sons, why do you stand? Fetch hither Tiriel!
Fetch hither Myratana! and delight yourselves with scoffs;
For poor blind Tiriel is return'd, and this much-injur'd head
Is ready for your bitter taunts. Come forth, sons of the
    Curse!'

Meantime the other sons of Tiriel ran around their father, 206
Confounded at the terrible strength of Ijim: they knew 'twas
    vain.
Both spear and shield were useless, and the coat of iron mail,

Tiriel

When Ijim stretch'd his mighty arm; the arrow from his limbs
Rebounded, and the piercing sword broke on his naked flesh. 210

'Then is it true, Heuxos, that thou hast turn'd thy agèd parent
To be the sport of wintry winds?' said Ijim, 'is this true?
It is a lie, and I am like the tree torn by the wind,
Thou eyeless fiend, and you dissemblers! Is this Tiriel's house?
It is as false as Matha, and as dark as vacant Orcus. 215
Escape, ye fiends! for Ijim will not lift his hand against ye.'

So saying, Ijim gloomy turn'd his back, and silent sought
The secret forests, and all night wander'd in desolate ways.

V

And agèd Tiriel stood and said: 'Where does the thunder sleep?
Where doth he hide his terrible head? And his swift and fiery
    daughters, 220
Where do they shroud their fiery wings, and the terrors of their
    hair?
Earth, thus I stamp thy bosom! Rouse the earthquake from his
    den,
To raise his dark and burning visage thro' the cleaving ground,
To thrust these towers with his shoulders! Let his fiery dogs
Rise from the centre, belching flames and roarings, dark smoke! 225
Where art thou, Pestilence, that bathest in fogs and standing lakes?

  210 Followed by the del. lines:

    Then Ijim said: 'Lotho, Clithyma, Makuth, fetch your father!
    Why do you stand confounded thus? Heuxos, why art thou silent?'

    'O noble Ijim, thou hast brought our father to our eyes,
    That we may tremble and repent before thy mighty knees.
    O! we are but the slaves of Fortune, and that most cruel man
    Desires our deaths, O Ijim! . . .
                       . . . if the eloquent voice of Tiriel
    Hath work'd our ruin, we submit nor strive against stern fate.'

    He spoke, kneel'd upon his knee. Then Ijim on the pavement
    Set agèd Tiriel in deep thought whether these things were so.

Tiriel

Rise up thy sluggish limbs, and let the loathsomest of poisons
Drop from thy garments as thou walkest, wrapp'd in yellow clouds!
Here take thy seat in this wide court; let it be strewn with dead;
And sit and smile upon these cursèd sons of Tiriel!   230
Thunder, and fire, and pestilence, hear you not Tiriel's curse?'
He ceas'd. The heavy clouds confus'd roll'd round the lofty towers,
Discharging their enormous voices at the father's curse.
The earth tremblèd; fires belchèd from the yawning clefts;
And when the shaking ceas'd, a fog possess'd the accursèd clime.

The cry was great in Tiriel's palace: his five daughters ran,   236
And caught him by the garments, weeping with cries of bitter woe.

'Aye, now you feel the curse, you cry! but may all ears be deaf
As Tiriel's, and all eyes as blind as Tiriel's to your woes!
May never stars shine on your roofs! may never sun nor moon   240
Visit you, but eternal fogs hover around your walls!
Hela, my youngest daughter, you shall lead me from this place;
And let the curse fall on the rest, and wrap them up together!'

He ceas'd: and Hela led her father from the noisome place.
In haste they fled; while all the sons and daughters of Tiriel,   245
Chain'd in thick darkness, utterèd cries of mourning all the night.
And in the morning, lo! an hundred men in ghastly death!
The four daughters, stretch'd on the marble pavement, silent all,
Fall'n by the pestilence!—the rest mop'd round in guilty fears;
And all the children in their beds were cut off in one night.   250
Thirty of Tiriel's sons remain'd, to wither in the palace,
Desolate, loathèd, dumb, astonish'd—waiting for black death.

VI

And Hela led her father thro' the silence of the night,
Astonish'd, silent, till the morning beams began to spring.

'Now, Hela, I can go with pleasure, and dwell with Har and Heva,
Now that the curse shall clean devour all those guilty sons.   256

Tiriel

This is the right and ready way; I know it by the sound
That our feet make.   Remember, Hela, I have savèd thee from death;
Then be obedient to thy father, for the curse is taken off thee.
I dwelt with Myratana five years in the desolate rock;   260
And all that time we waited for the fire to fall from heaven,
Or for the torrents of the sea to overwhelm you all.
But now my wife is dead, and all the time of grace is past:
You see the parent's curse.   Now lead me where I have commanded.'

'O leaguèd with evil spirits, thou accursèd man of sin!   265
True, I was born thy slave!   Who ask'd thee to save me from death?
'Twas for thyself, thou cruel man, because thou wantest eyes.'

'True, Hela, this is the desert of all those cruel ones.
Is Tiriel cruel?   Look! his daughter, and his youngest daughter,
Laughs at affection, glories in rebellion, scoffs at love.   270
I have not ate these two days.   Lead me to Har and Heva's tent,
Or I will wrap thee up in such a terrible father's curse
That thou shalt feel worms in thy marrow creeping thro' thy bones.
Yet thou shalt lead me!   Lead me, I command, to Har and Heva!'

'O cruel! O destroyer! O consumer! O avenger!   275
To Har and Heva I will lead thee: then would that they would curse!
Then would they curse as thou hast cursèd!   But they are not like thee!
O! they are holy and forgiving, fill'd with loving mercy,
Forgetting the offences of their most rebellious children,
Or else thou wouldest not have liv'd to curse thy helpless children.'

'Look on my eyes, Hela, and see, for thou hast eyes to see,   281
The tears swell from my stony fountains.   Wherefore do I weep?

Tiriel

Wherefore from my blind orbs art thou not seiz'd with poisonous stings?
Laugh, serpent, youngest venomous reptile of the flesh of Tiriel!
Laugh! for thy father Tiriel shall give thee cause to laugh,   285
Unless thou lead me to the tent of Har, child of the Curse!'

'Silence thy evil tongue, thou murderer of thy helpless children!
I lead thee to the tent of Har; not that I mind thy curse,
But that I feel they will curse thee, and hang upon thy bones
Fell shaking agonies, and in each wrinkle of that face   290
Plant worms of death to feast upon the tongue of terrible curses.'

'Hela, my daughter, listen! thou art the daughter of Tiriel.
Thy father calls. Thy father lifts his hand unto the heavens,
For thou hast laughèd at my tears, and curs'd thy agèd father.
Let snakes rise from thy bedded locks, and laugh among thy curls!'   295

He ceas'd. Her dark hair upright stood, while snakes infolded round
Her madding brows: her shrieks appall'd the soul of Tiriel.

'What have I done, Hela, my daughter? Fear'st thou now the curse,
Or wherefore dost thou cry? Ah, wretch, to curse thy agèd father!
Lead me to Har and Heva, and the curse of Tiriel   300
Shall fail. If thou refuse, howl in the desolate mountains!'

VII

She, howling, led him over mountains and thro' frighted vales,
Till to the caves of Zazel they approach'd at eventide.
Forth from their caves old Zazel and his sons ran, when they saw
Their tyrant prince blind, and his daughter howling and leading him.   305

Tiriel

They laugh'd and mockèd; some threw dirt and stones as they
    pass'd by;
But when Tiriel turn'd around and rais'd his awful voice,
Some fled away; but Zazel stood still, and thus begun:—

'Bald tyrant, wrinkled cunning, listen to Zazel's chains!
'Twas thou that chainèd thy brother Zazel! Where are now
    thine eyes?   310
Shout, beautiful daughter of Tiriel! thou singest a sweet song!
Where are you going? Come and eat some roots, and drink
    some water.
Thy crown is bald, old man; the sun will dry thy brains away,
And thou wilt be as foolish as thy foolish brother Zazel.'

The blind man heard, and smote his breast, and trembling
    passèd on.   315
They threw dirt after them, till to the covert of a wood
The howling maiden led her father, where wild beasts resort,
Hoping to end her woes; but from her cries the tigers fled.
All night they wander'd thro' the wood; and when the sun
    arose,
They enter'd on the mountains of Har: at noon the happy tents
Were frighted by the dismal cries of Hela on the mountains.   321

But Har and Heva slept fearless as babes on loving breasts.
Mnetha awoke: she ran and stood at the tent door, and saw
The agèd wanderer led towards the tents; she took her bow,
And chose her arrows, then advanc'd to meet the terrible pair.   325

VIII

And Mnetha hasted, and met them at the gate of the lower
    garden.
'Stand still, or from my bow receive a sharp and wingèd death!'

Tiriel

Then Tiriel stood, saying: 'What soft voice threatens such bitter things?
Lead me to Har and Heva; I am Tiriel, King of the West.'

And Mnetha led them to the tent of Har; and Har and Heva
Ran to the door. When Tiriel felt the ankles of agèd Har, 331
He said: 'O weak mistaken father of a lawless race,
Thy laws, O Har, and Tiriel's wisdom, end together in a curse.

Why is one law given to the lion and the patient ox?
And why men bound beneath the heavens in a reptile form, 335
A worm of sixty winters creeping on the dusky ground?
The child springs from the womb; the father ready stands to form
The infant head, while the mother idle plays with her dog on her couch:
The young bosom is cold for lack of mother's nourishment, and milk
Is cut off from the weeping mouth with difficulty and pain: 340
The little lids are lifted, and the little nostrils open'd:
The father forms a whip to rouse the sluggish senses to act,
And scourges off all youthful fancies from the new-born man.
Then walks the weak infant in sorrow, compell'd to number footsteps
Upon the sand. And when the drone has reach'd his crawling length, 345

333 Followed by a del. half-line:
        Thy God of Love, thy Heaven of Joy . . .

334 Followed by the del. lines:
Dost thou not see that men cannot be formèd all alike,
Some nostril'd wide, breathing out blood; some close shut up
In silent deceit, poisons inhaling from the morning rose,
With daggers hid beneath their lips and poison in their tongue;
Or eyed with little sparks of Hell, or with infernal brands,
Flinging flames of discontent and plagues of dark despair;
Or those whose mouths are graves, whose teeth the gates of eternal death.
Can wisdom be put in a silver rod, or love in a golden bowl?
Is the sun a king, warmed without wool? or does he cry with a voice
Of thunder? Does he look upon the sun, and laugh or stretch
His little hands unto the depths of the sea, to bring forth
The deadly cunning of the scaly tribe, and spread it to the morning?

Tiriel

Black berries appear that poison all round him.   Such was Tiriel,
Compell'd to pray repugnant, and to humble the immortal spirit;
Till I am subtil as a serpent in a paradise,
Consuming all, both flowers and fruits, insects and warbling birds.
And now my paradise is fall'n, and a drear sandy plain   350
Returns my thirsty hissings in a curse on thee, O Har,
Mistaken father of a lawless race!—My voice is past.'

He ceas'd, outstretch'd at Har and Heva's feet in awful death.

346 Followed by a del. line:
   Hypocrisy, the idiot's wisdom, and the wise man's folly.

THE
BOOK OF THEL

(Engraved 1789)

Thel's Motto.
>   Does the Eagle know what is in the pit;
>   Or wilt thou go ask the Mole?
>   Can Wisdom be put in a silver rod,
>   Or Love in a golden bowl?

I

The daughters of [the] Seraphim led round their sunny flocks—
All but the youngest: she in paleness sought the secret air,
To fade away like morning beauty from her mortal day:
Down by the river of Adona her soft voice is heard,
And thus her gentle lamentation falls like morning dew:—

'O life of this our spring! why fades the lotus of the water?
Why fade these children of the spring, born but to smile and fall?
Ah! Thel is like a wat'ry bow, and like a parting cloud;
Like a reflection in a glass; like shadows in the water;
Like dreams of infants, like a smile upon an infant's face;
Like the dove's voice; like transient day; like music in the air.
Ah! gentle may I lay me down, and gentle rest my head,
And gentle sleep the sleep of death, and gentle hear the voice
Of Him that walketh in the garden in the evening time.'

The Lily of the Valley, breathing in the humble grass,
Answered the lovely maid and said: 'I am a wat'ry weed,
And I am very small, and love to dwell in lowly vales;

The Book of Thel

So weak, the gilded butterfly scarce perches on my head.
Yet I am visited from heaven, and He that smiles on all
Walks in the valley, and each morn over me spreads His hand,
Saying, " Rejoice, thou humble grass, thou new-born lily-flower,
Thou gentle maid of silent valleys and of modest brooks ;
For thou shalt be clothèd in light, and fed with morning manna,
Till summer's heat melts thee beside the fountains and the springs,
To flourish in eternal vales." Then why should Thel complain?
Why should the mistress of the vales of Har utter a sigh?'

She ceas'd, and smil'd in tears, then sat down in her silver shrine.

Thel answer'd : ' O thou little Virgin of the peaceful valley,
Giving to those that cannot crave, the voiceless, the o'ertired ;
Thy breath doth nourish the innocent lamb, he smells thy milky garments,
He crops thy flowers while thou sittest smiling in his face,
Wiping his mild and meeking mouth from all contagious taints.
Thy wine doth purify the golden honey ; thy perfume,
Which thou dost scatter on every little blade of grass that springs,
Revives the milkèd cow, and tames the fire-breathing steed.
But Thel is like a faint cloud kindled at the rising sun :
I vanish from my pearly throne, and who shall find my place?'

' Queen of the vales,' the Lily answer'd, ' ask the tender Cloud,
And it shall tell thee why it glitters in the morning sky,
And why it scatters its bright beauty thro' the humid air.
Descend, O little Cloud, and hover before the eyes of Thel.'

The Cloud descended, and the Lily bowèd her modest head,
And went to mind her numerous charge among the verdant grass.

II

' O little Cloud,' the Virgin said, ' I charge thee tell to me
Why thou complainest not, when in one hour thou fade away :
Then we shall seek thee, but not find. Ah ! Thel is like to thee :
I pass away : yet I complain, and no one hears my voice.'

The Book of Thel

The Cloud then show'd his golden head and his bright form
    emerg'd,
Hovering and glittering on the air before the face of Thel.

'O Virgin, know'st thou not our steeds drink of the golden springs
Where Luvah doth renew his horses? Look'st thou on my youth, 55
And fearest thou, because I vanish and am seen no more,
Nothing remains? O Maid, I tell thee, when I pass away,
It is to tenfold life, to love, to peace, and raptures holy:
Unseen descending, weigh my light wings upon balmy flowers,
And court the fair-eyed dew, to take me to her shining tent: 60
The weeping virgin, trembling, kneels before the risen sun,
Till we arise link'd in a golden band and never part,
But walk united, bearing food to all our tender flowers.'

'Dost thou, O little Cloud? I fear that I am not like thee,
For I walk thro' the vales of Har, and smell the sweetest flowers,
But I feed not the little flowers; I hear the warbling birds, 66
But I feed not the warbling birds; they fly and seek their food:
But Thel delights in these no more, because I fade away;
And all shall say, "Without a use this shining woman liv'd,
Or did she only live to be at death the food of worms?"' 70

The Cloud reclin'd upon his airy throne, and answer'd thus:—

'Then if thou art the food of worms, O Virgin of the skies,
How great thy use, how great thy blessing! Everything that lives
Lives not alone nor for itself. Fear not, and I will call
The weak Worm from its lowly bed, and thou shalt hear its voice.
Come forth, Worm of the silent valley, to thy pensive Queen.' 76

The helpless Worm arose, and sat upon the Lily's leaf,
And the bright Cloud sail'd on, to find his partner in the vale.

III

Then Thel astonish'd view'd the Worm upon its dewy bed.

'Art thou a Worm? Image of weakness, art thou but a Worm?
I see thee like an infant wrappèd in the Lily's leaf. 81

The Book of Thel

Ah! weep not, little voice, thou canst not speak, but thou canst weep.
Is this a Worm? I see thee lay helpless and naked, weeping,
And none to answer, none to cherish thee with mother's smiles.'

The Clod of Clay heard the Worm's voice and rais'd her pitying head:
She bow'd over the weeping infant, and her life exhal'd
In milky fondness: then on Thel she fix'd her humble eyes.

'O Beauty of the vales of Har! we live not for ourselves.
Thou seest me, the meanest thing, and so I am indeed.
My bosom of itself is cold, and of itself is dark;
But He, that loves the lowly, pours His oil upon my head,
And kisses me, and binds His nuptial bands around my breast,
And says: "Thou mother of my children, I have lovèd thee,
And I have given thee a crown that none can take away."
But how this is, sweet Maid, I know not, and I cannot know;
I ponder, and I cannot ponder; yet I live and love.'

The Daughter of Beauty wip'd her pitying tears with her white veil,
And said: 'Alas! I knew not this, and therefore did I weep.
That God would love a worm I knew, and punish the evil foot
That wilful bruis'd its helpless form; but that He cherish'd it
With milk and oil I never knew, and therefore did I weep;
And I complain'd in the mild air, because I fade away,
And lay me down in thy cold bed, and leave my shining lot.'

'Queen of the vales,' the matron Clay answer'd, 'I heard thy sighs,
And all thy moans flew o'er my roof, but I have call'd them down.
Wilt thou, O Queen, enter my house? 'Tis given thee to enter
And to return: fear nothing, enter with thy virgin feet.'

IV

The eternal gates' terrific Porter lifted the northern bar:
Thel enter'd in and saw the secrets of the land unknown.
She saw the couches of the dead, and where the fibrous roots

The Book of Thel

Of every heart on earth infixes deep its restless twists:
A land of sorrows and of tears where never smile was seen.

She wander'd in the land of clouds thro' valleys dark, list'ning
Dolours and lamentations; waiting oft beside a dewy grave
She stood in silence, list'ning to the voices of the ground,   115
Till to her own grave-plot she came, and there she sat down,
And heard this voice of sorrow breathèd from the hollow pit.

'Why cannot the Ear be closèd to its own destruction?
Or the glist'ning Eye to the poison of a smile?
Why are Eyelids stor'd with arrows ready drawn,   120
Where a thousand fighting men in ambush lie,
Or an Eye of gifts and graces show'ring fruits and coinèd gold?
Why a Tongue impress'd with honey from every wind?
Why an Ear, a whirlpool fierce to draw creations in?
Why a Nostril wide inhaling terror, trembling, and affright?   125
Why a tender curb upon the youthful, burning boy?
Why a little curtain of flesh on the bed of our desire?'

The Virgin started from her seat, and with a shriek
Fled back unhinder'd till she came into the vales of Har.

THE END.

THE MARRIAGE OF HEAVEN & HELL

THE MARRIAGE
OF
HEAVEN AND HELL

(Engraved *circa* 1790)

The Argument

    Rintrah roars, and shakes his fires in the burden'd air;
Hungry clouds swag on the deep.

    Once meek, and in a perilous path,
The just man kept his course along
The vale of death.
Roses are planted where thorns grow,
And on the barren heath
Sing the honey bees.

    Then the perilous path was planted,
And a river and a spring
On every cliff and tomb,
And on the bleachèd bones
Red clay brought forth;

    Till the villain left the paths of ease,
To walk in perilous paths, and drive
The just man into barren climes.

    Now the sneaking serpent walks
In mild humility,
And the just man rages in the wilds
Where lions roam.

    Rintrah roars, and shakes his fires in the burden'd air,
Hungry clouds swag on the deep.

The Marriage

As a new heaven is begun, and it is now thirty-three years since its advent, the Eternal Hell revives. And lo! Swedenborg is the Angel sitting at the tomb: his writings are the linen clothes folded up. Now is the dominion of Edom, and the return of Adam into Paradise. See Isaiah xxxiv and xxxv chap.

Without Contraries is no progression. Attraction and Repulsion, Reason and Energy, Love and Hate, are necessary to Human existence.

From these contraries spring what the religious call Good and Evil. Good is the passive that obeys Reason. Evil is the active springing from Energy.

Good is Heaven. Evil is Hell.

The Voice of the Devil

All Bibles or sacred codes have been the causes of the following Errors:—

1. That Man has two real existing principles, viz. a Body and a Soul.
2. That Energy, call'd Evil, is alone from the Body; and that Reason, call'd Good, is alone from the Soul.
3. That God will torment Man in Eternity for following his Energies.

But the following Contraries to these are True:—

1. Man has no Body distinct from his Soul; for that call'd Body is a portion of Soul discern'd by the five Senses, the chief inlets of Soul in this age.
2. Energy is the only life, and is from the Body; and Reason is the bound or outward circumference of Energy.
3. Energy is Eternal Delight.

Those who restrain Desire, do so because theirs is weak enough to be restrained; and the restrainer or Reason usurps its place and governs the unwilling.

# of Heaven and Hell

And being restrained, it by degrees becomes passive, till it is only the shadow of Desire.

The history of this is written in *Paradise Lost*, and the Governor or Reason is call'd Messiah.

And the original Archangel, or possessor of the command of the Heavenly Host, is call'd the Devil or Satan, and his children are call'd Sin and Death.

But in the Book of Job, Milton's Messiah is called Satan.

For this history has been adopted by both parties.

It indeed appear'd to Reason as if Desire was cast out; but the Devil's account is, that the Messiah fell, and formed a Heaven of what he stole from the Abyss.

This is shown in the Gospel, where he prays to the Father to send the Comforter, or Desire, that Reason may have Ideas to build on; the Jehovah of the Bible being no other than he who dwells in flaming fire.

Know that after Christ's death, he became Jehovah.

But in Milton, the Father is Destiny, the Son a Ratio of the five senses, and the Holy-ghost Vacuum!

Note. The reason Milton wrote in fetters when he wrote of Angels and God, and at liberty when of Devils and Hell, is because he was a true Poet, and of the Devil's party without knowing it.

A Memorable Fancy

As I was walking among the fires of Hell, delighted with the enjoyments of Genius, which to Angels look like torment and insanity, I collected some of their Proverbs; thinking that as the sayings used in a nation mark its character, so the Proverbs of Hell show the nature of Infernal wisdom better than any description of buildings or garments.

When I came home, on the abyss of the five senses, where a flat-sided steep frowns over the present world, I saw a mighty Devil, folded in black clouds, hovering on the sides of the rock:

The Marriage

with corroding fires he wrote the following sentence now perceived by the minds of men, and read by them on earth:—

How do you know but ev'ry Bird that cuts the airy way,
Is an immense World of Delight, clos'd by your senses five?

Proverbs of Hell

In seed time learn, in harvest teach, in winter enjoy.
Drive your cart and your plough over the bones of the dead.
The road of excess leads to the palace of wisdom.
Prudence is a rich, ugly old maid courted by Incapacity.
He who desires but acts not, breeds pestilence.
The cut worm forgives the plough.
Dip him in the river who loves water.
A fool sees not the same tree that a wise man sees.
He whose face gives no light, shall never become a star.
Eternity is in love with the productions of time.
The busy bee has no time for sorrow.
The hours of folly are measur'd by the clock; but of wisdom, no clock can measure.
All wholesome food is caught without a net or a trap.
Bring out number, weight, and measure in a year of dearth.
No bird soars too high, if he soars with his own wings.
A dead body revenges not injuries.
The most sublime act is to set another before you.
If the fool would persist in his folly he would become wise.
Folly is the cloak of knavery.
Shame is Pride's cloak.
Prisons are built with stones of Law, brothels with bricks of Religion.
The pride of the peacock is the glory of God.
The lust of the goat is the bounty of God.
The wrath of the lion is the wisdom of God.
The nakedness of woman is the work of God.

of Heaven and Hell

Excess of sorrow laughs. Excess of joy weeps.

The roaring of lions, the howling of wolves, the raging of the stormy sea, and the destructive sword are portions of eternity too great for the eye of man.

The fox condemns the trap, not himself.

Joys impregnate. Sorrows bring forth.

Let man wear the fell of the lion, woman the fleece of the sheep.

The bird a nest, the spider a web, man friendship.

The selfish, smiling fool, and the sullen, frowning fool shall be both thought wise, that they may be a rod.

What is now proved was once only imagin'd.

The rat, the mouse, the fox, the rabbit watch the roots; the lion, the tiger, the horse, the elephant watch the fruits.

The cistern contains: the fountain overflows.

One thought fills immensity.

Always be ready to speak your mind, and a base man will avoid you.

Everything possible to be believ'd is an image of truth.

The eagle never lost so much time as when he submitted to learn of the crow.

The fox provides for himself; but God provides for the lion.

Think in the morning. Act in the noon. Eat in the evening. Sleep in the night.

He who has suffer'd you to impose on him, knows you.

As the plough follows words, so God rewards prayers.

The tigers of wrath are wiser than the horses of instruction.

Expect poison from the standing water.

You never know what is enough unless you know what is more than enough.

Listen to the fool's reproach! it is a kingly title!

The eyes of fire, the nostrils of air, the mouth of water, the beard of earth.

The weak in courage is strong in cunning.

The apple tree never asks the beech how he shall grow; nor the lion, the horse, how he shall take his prey.

The thankful receiver bears a plentiful harvest.

The Marriage

If others had not been foolish, we should be so.

The soul of sweet delight can never be defil'd.

When thou seest an eagle, thou seest a portion of Genius; lift up thy head!

As the caterpillar chooses the fairest leaves to lay her eggs on, so the priest lays his curse on the fairest joys.

To create a little flower is the labour of ages.

Damn braces. Bless relaxes.

The best wine is the oldest, the best water the newest.

Prayers plough not! Praises reap not!

Joys laugh not! Sorrows weep not!

The head Sublime, the heart Pathos, the genitals Beauty, the hands and feet Proportion.

As the air to a bird or the sea to a fish, so is contempt to the contemptible.

The crow wish'd everything was black, the owl that everything was white.

Exuberance is Beauty.

If the lion was advised by the fox, he would be cunning.

Improvement makes straight roads; but the crooked roads without improvement are roads of Genius.

Sooner murder an infant in its cradle than nurse unacted desires.

Where man is not, nature is barren.

Truth can never be told so as to be understood, and not be believ'd.

Enough! or Too much.

The ancient Poets animated all sensible objects with Gods or Geniuses, calling them by the names and adorning them with the properties of woods, rivers, mountains, lakes, cities, nations, and whatever their enlarged and numerous senses could perceive.

And particularly they studied the Genius of each city and country, placing it under its Mental Deity;

Till a System was formed, which some took advantage of, and

of Heaven and Hell

enslav'd the vulgar by attempting to realise or abstract the Mental Deities from their objects—thus began Priesthood;

Choosing forms of worship from poetic tales.

And at length they pronounc'd that the Gods had order'd such things.

Thus men forgot that All Deities reside in the Human breast.

A Memorable Fancy

The Prophets Isaiah and Ezekiel dined with me, and I asked them how they dared so roundly to assert that God spoke to them; and whether they did not think at the time that they would be misunderstood, and so be the cause of imposition.

Isaiah answer'd: 'I saw no God, nor heard any, in a finite organical perception; but my senses discover'd the infinite in everything, and as I was then persuaded, and remain confirm'd, that the voice of honest indignation is the voice of God, I cared not for consequences, but wrote.'

Then I asked: 'Does a firm persuasion that a thing is so, make it so?'

He replied: 'All Poets believe that it does, and in ages of imagination this firm persuasion removed mountains; but many are not capable of a firm persuasion of anything.'

Then Ezekiel said: 'The philosophy of the East taught the first principles of human perception. Some nations held one principle for the origin, and some another: we of Israel taught that the Poetic Genius (as you now call it) was the first principle and all the others merely derivative, which was the cause of our despising the Priests and Philosophers of other countries, and prophesying that all Gods would at last be proved to originate in ours and to be the tributaries of the Poetic Genius. It was this that our great poet, King David, desired so fervently and invokes so pathetically, saying by this he conquers enemies and governs kingdoms; and we so loved our God, that we cursed in his name all the Deities of surrounding nations, and asserted that they had rebelled. From these opinions the vulgar came to think that all nations would at last be subject to the Jews.'

'This,' said he, 'like all firm persuasions, is come to pass; for all nations believe the Jews' code and worship the Jews' god, and what greater subjection can be?'

I heard this with some wonder, and must confess my own conviction. After dinner I ask'd Isaiah to favour the world with his lost works; he said none of equal value was lost. Ezekiel said the same of his.

I also asked Isaiah what made him go naked and barefoot three years. He answer'd: 'The same that made our friend Diogenes, the Grecian.'

I then asked Ezekiel why he ate dung, and lay so long on his right and left side. He answer'd, 'The desire of raising other men into a perception of the infinite: this the North American tribes practise, and is he honest who resists his genius or conscience only for the sake of present ease or gratification?'

The ancient tradition that the world will be consumed in fire at the end of six thousand years is true, as I have heard from Hell.

For the cherub with his flaming sword is hereby commanded to leave his guard at tree of life; and when he does, the whole creation will be consumed and appear infinite and holy, whereas it now appears finite and corrupt.

This will come to pass by an improvement of sensual enjoyment.

But first the notion that man has a body distinct from his soul is to be expunged; this I shall do by printing in the infernal method, by corrosives, which in Hell are salutary and medicinal, melting apparent surfaces away, and displaying the infinite which was hid.

If the doors of perception were cleansed everything would appear to man as it is, infinite.

For man has closed himself up till he sees all things thro' narrow chinks of his cavern.

# of Heaven and Hell

A Memorable Fancy

I was in a Printing-house in Hell, and saw the method in which knowledge is transmitted from generation to generation.

In the first chamber was a Dragon-Man, clearing away the rubbish from a cave's mouth; within, a number of Dragons were hollowing the cave.

In the second chamber was a Viper folding round the rock and the cave, and others adorning it with gold, silver, and precious stones.

In the third chamber was an Eagle with wings and feathers of air: he caused the inside of the cave to be infinite. Around were numbers of Eagle-like men who built palaces in the immense cliffs.

In the fourth chamber were Lions of flaming fire, raging around and melting the metals into living fluids.

In the fifth chamber were Unnamed forms, which cast the metals into the expanse.

There they were received by Men who occupied the sixth chamber, and took the forms of books and were arranged in libraries.

The Giants who formed this world into its sensual existence, and now seem to live in it in chains, are in truth the causes of its life and the sources of all activity; but the chains are the cunning of weak and tame minds which have power to resist energy. According to the proverb, the weak in courage is strong in cunning.

Thus one portion of being is the Prolific, the other the Devouring. To the Devourer it seems as if the producer was in his chains; but it is not so, he only takes portions of existence and fancies that the whole.

But the Prolific would cease to be Prolific unless the Devourer, as a sea, received the excess of his delights.

Some will say: 'Is not God alone the Prolific? I answer: God only Acts and Is, in existing beings or Men.

The Marriage

These two classes of men are always upon earth, and they should be enemies: whoever tries to reconcile them seeks to destroy existence.

Religion is an endeavour to reconcile the two.

Note. Jesus Christ did not wish to unite, but to separate them, as in the Parable of sheep and goats! And He says: 'I came not to send Peace, but a Sword.'

Messiah or Satan or Tempter was formerly thought to be one of the Antediluvians who are our Energies.

A Memorable Fancy

An Angel came to me and said: 'O pitiable, foolish young man! O horrible! O dreadful state! Consider the hot, burning dungeon thou art preparing for thyself to all Eternity, to which thou art going in such career.'

I said: 'Perhaps you will be willing to show me my eternal lot, and we will contemplate together upon it, and see whether your lot or mine is most desirable.'

So he took me thro' a stable, and thro' a church, and down into the church vault, at the end of which was a mill. Thro' the mill we went, and came to a cave. Down the winding cavern we groped our tedious way, till a void boundless as a nether sky appear'd beneath us, and we held by the roots of trees, and hung over this immensity. But I said: 'If you please, we will commit ourselves to this void, and see whether Providence is here also. If you will not, I will.' But he answer'd: 'Do not presume, O young man, but as we here remain, behold thy lot which will soon appear when the darkness passes away.'

So I remain'd with him, sitting in the twisted root of an oak. He was suspended in a fungus, which hung with the head downward into the deep.

By degrees we beheld the infinite Abyss, fiery as the smoke of a burning city; beneath us, at an immense distance, was the sun, black but shining; round it were fiery tracks on which revolv'd

of Heaven and Hell

vast spiders, crawling after their prey, which flew, or rather swum, in the infinite deep, in the most terrific shapes of animals sprung from corruption; and the air was full of them, and seem'd composed of them—these are Devils, and are called Powers of the Air. I now asked my companion which was my eternal lot? He said: 'Between the black and white spiders.'

But now, from between the black and white spiders, a cloud and fire burst and rolled thro' the deep, blackening all beneath; so that the nether deep grew black as a sea, and rolled with a terrible noise. Beneath us was nothing now to be seen but a black tempest, till looking East between the clouds and the waves we saw a cataract of blood mixed with fire, and not many stones' throw from us appear'd and sunk again the scaly fold of a monstrous serpent. At last, to the East, distant about three degrees, appear'd a fiery crest above the waves. Slowly it reared like a ridge of golden rocks, till we discover'd two globes of crimson fire, from which the sea fled away in clouds of smoke; and now we saw it was the head of Leviathan. His forehead was divided into streaks of green and purple like those on a tiger's forehead. Soon we saw his mouth and red gills hang just above the raging foam, tinging the black deep with beams of blood, advancing toward us with all the fury of a Spiritual Existence.

My friend the Angel climb'd up from his station into the mill: I remain'd alone, and then this appearance was no more; but I found myself sitting on a pleasant bank beside a river, by moonlight, hearing a harper, who sung to the harp; and his theme was: 'The man who never alters his opinion is like standing water, and breeds reptiles of the mind.'

But I arose and sought for the mill, and there I found my Angel, who, surprised, asked me how I escaped.

I answer'd: 'All that we saw was owing to your metaphysics; for when you ran away, I found myself on a bank by moonlight hearing a harper. But now we have seen my eternal lot, shall I

The Marriage

show you yours?' He laugh'd at my proposal; but I, by force, suddenly caught him in my arms, and flew westerly thro' the night, till we were elevated above the earth's shadow; then I flung myself with him directly into the body of the sun. Here I clothed myself in white, and taking in my hand Swedenborg's volumes, sunk from the glorious clime, and passed all the planets till we came to Saturn. Here I stay'd to rest, and then leap'd into the void between Saturn and the fixed stars.

'Here,' said I, 'is your lot, in this space—if space it may be call'd.' Soon we saw the stable and the church, and I took him to the altar and open'd the Bible, and lo! it was a deep pit, into which I descended, driving the Angel before me. Soon we saw seven houses of brick. One we enter'd; in it were a number of monkeys, baboons, and all of that species, chain'd by the middle, grinning and snatching at one another, but withheld by the shortness of their chains. However, I saw that they sometimes grew numerous, and then the weak were caught by the strong, and with a grinning aspect, first coupled with, and then devour'd, by plucking off first one limb and then another, till the body was left a helpless trunk. This, after grinning and kissing it with seeming fondness, they devour'd too; and here and there I saw one savourily picking the flesh off of his own tail. As the stench terribly annoy'd us both, we went into the mill, and I in my hand brought the skeleton of a body, which in the mill was Aristotle's Analytics.

So the Angel said: 'Thy phantasy has imposed upon me, and thou oughtest to be ashamed.'

I answer'd: 'We impose on one another, and it is but lost time to converse with you whose works are only Analytics.'

I have always found that Angels have the vanity to speak of themselves as the Only Wise. This they do with a confident insolence sprouting from systematic reasoning.

of Heaven and Hell

Thus Swedenborg boasts that what he writes is new; tho' it is only the Contents or Index of already publish'd books.

A man carried a monkey about for a show, and because he was a little wiser than the monkey, grew vain, and conceiv'd himself as much wiser than seven men. It is so with Swedenborg: he shows the folly of churches, and exposes hypocrites, till he imagines that all are religious, and himself the single one on earth that ever broke a net.

Now hear a plain fact: Swedenborg has not written one new truth. Now hear another: he has written all the old falsehoods.

And now hear the reason. He conversed with Angels who are all religious, and conversed not with Devils who all hate religion, for he was incapable thro' his conceited notions.

Thus Swedenborg's writings are a recapitulation of all superficial opinions, and an analysis of the more sublime—but no further.

Have now another plain fact. Any man of mechanical talents may, from the writings of Paracelsus or Jacob Behmen, produce ten thousand volumes of equal value with Swedenborg's, and from those of Dante or Shakespear an infinite number.

But when he has done this, let him not say that he knows better than his master, for he only holds a candle in sunshine.

A Memorable Fancy

Once I saw a Devil in a flame of fire, who arose before an Angel that sat on a cloud, and the Devil utter'd these words:—

'The worship of God is: Honouring his gifts in other men, each according to his genius, and loving the greatest men best: those who envy or calumniate great men hate God; for there is no other God.'

The Angel hearing this became almost blue; but mastering himself he grew yellow, and at last white, pink, and smiling, and then replied:—

'Thou Idolater! is not God One? and is not he visible in Jesus Christ? and has not Jesus Christ given his sanction to the law of

The Marriage of Heaven and Hell

ten commandments? and are not all other men fools, sinners, and nothings?'

The Devil answer'd: 'Bray a fool in a mortar with wheat, yet shall not his folly be beaten out of him. If Jesus Christ is the greatest man, you ought to love Him in the greatest degree. Now hear how He has given His sanction to the law of ten commandments. Did He not mock at the sabbath, and so mock the sabbath's God; murder those who were murder'd because of Him; turn away the law from the woman taken in adultery; steal the labour of others to support Him; bear false witness when He omitted making a defence before Pilate; covet when He pray'd for His disciples, and when He bid them shake off the dust of their feet against such as refused to lodge them? I tell you, no virtue can exist without breaking these ten commandments. Jesus was all virtue, and acted from impulse, not from rules.'

When he had so spoken, I beheld the Angel, who stretched out his arms, embracing the flame of fire, and he was consumed, and arose as Elijah.

Note.—This Angel, who is now become a Devil, is my particular friend. We often read the Bible together in its infernal or diabolical sense, which the world shall have if they behave well.

I have also The Bible of Hell, which the world shall have whether they will or no.

One Law for the Lion and Ox is Oppression.

THE

FRENCH REVOLUTION.

A POEM,

IN SEVEN BOOKS.

BOOK THE FIRST.

LONDON:

PRINTED FOR J. JOHNSON, N° 72, ST PAUL'S CHURCH-YARD.

MDCCXCI.

[PRICE ONE SHILLING.]

ADVERTISEMENT

The remaining Books of this Poem are finished, and will be published in their Order.

THE
FRENCH REVOLUTION

BOOK THE FIRST

(Printed 1791)

The dead brood over Europe : the cloud and vision descends over cheerful France ;
O cloud well appointed ! Sick, sick, the Prince on his couch ! wreath'd in dim
And appalling mist ; his strong hand outstretch'd, from his shoulder down the bone,
Runs aching cold into the sceptre, too heavy for mortal grasp—no more
To be swayèd by visible hand, nor in cruelty bruise the mild flourishing mountains. 5

Sick the mountains ! and all their vineyards weep, in the eyes of the kingly mourner ;
Pale is the morning cloud in his visage. Rise, Necker ! the ancient dawn calls us
To awake from slumbers of five thousand years. I awake, but my soul is in dreams ;
From my window I see the old mountains of France, like agèd men, fading away.

Troubled, leaning on Necker, descends the King to his chamber of council ; shady mountains 10
In fear utter voices of thunder ; the woods of France embosom the sound ;

The French Revolution

Clouds of wisdom prophetic reply, and roll over the palace roof heavy.
Forty men, each conversing with woes in the infinite shadows of his soul,
Like our ancient fathers in regions of twilight, walk, gathering round the King:
Again the loud voice of France cries to the morning; the morning prophesies to its clouds. 15

For the Commons convene in the Hall of the Nation. France shakes! And the heavens of France
Perplex'd vibrate round each careful countenance! Darkness of old times around them
Utters loud despair, shadowing Paris; her grey towers groan, and the Bastille trembles.
In its terrible towers the Governor stood, in dark fogs list'ning the horror;
A thousand his soldiers, old veterans of France, breathing red clouds of power and dominion. 20
Sudden seiz'd with howlings, despair, and black night, he stalk'd like a lion from tower
To tower; his howlings were heard in the Louvre; from court to court restless he dragg'd
His strong limbs; from court to court curs'd the fierce torment unquell'd,
Howling and giving the dark command; in his soul stood the purple plague,
Tugging his iron manacles, and piercing thro' the seven towers dark and sickly, 25
Panting over the prisoners like a wolf gorg'd. And the den nam'd Horror held a man
Chain'd hand and foot; round his neck an iron band, bound to the impregnable wall;
In his soul was the serpent coil'd round in his heart, hid from the light, as in a cleft rock:
And the man was confin'd for a writing prophetic. In the tower nam'd Darkness was a man

The French Revolution

Pinion'd down to the stone floor, his strong bones scarce cover'd with sinews; the iron rings 30
Were forg'd smaller as the flesh decay'd: a mask of iron on his face hid the lineaments
Of ancient Kings, and the frown of the eternal lion was hid from the oppressèd earth.
In the tower namèd Bloody, a skeleton yellow remainèd in its chains on its couch
Of stone, once a man who refus'd to sign papers of abhorrence; the eternal worm
Crept in the skeleton. In the den nam'd Religion, a loathsome sick woman bound down 35
To a bed of straw; the seven diseases of earth, like birds of prey, stood on the couch
And fed on the body: she refus'd to be whore to the Minister, and with a knife smote him.
In the tower nam'd Order, an old man, whose white beard cover'd the stone floor like weeds
On margin of the sea, shrivell'd up by heat of day and cold of night; his den was short
And narrow as a grave dug for a child, with spiders' webs wove, and with slime 40
Of ancient horrors cover'd, for snakes and scorpions are his companions; harmless they breathe
His sorrowful breath: he, by conscience urg'd, in the city of Paris rais'd a pulpit,
And taught wonders to darken'd souls. In the den nam'd Destiny a strong man sat,
His feet and hands cut off, and his eyes blinded; round his middle a chain and a band
Fasten'd into the wall; fancy gave him to see an image of despair in his den, 45
Eternally rushing round, like a man on his hands and knees, day and night without rest:
He was friend to the favourite. In the seventh tower, nam'd the tower of God, was a man

The French Revolution

Mad, with chains loose, which he dragg'd up and down; fed with hopes year by year, he pinèd
For liberty.—Vain hopes! his reason decay'd, and the world of attraction in his bosom
Centred, and the rushing of chaos overwhelm'd his dark soul: he was confin'd 50
For a letter of advice to a King, and his ravings in winds are heard over Versailles.

But the dens shook and trembled: the prisoners look up and assay to shout; they listen,
Then laugh in the dismal den, then are silent; and a light walks round the dark towers.
For the Commons convene in the Hall of the Nation; like spirits of fire in the beautiful
Porches of the Sun, to plant beauty in the desert craving abyss, they gleam 55
On the anxious city: all children new-born first behold them, tears are fled,
And they nestle in earth-breathing bosoms. So the city of Paris, their wives and children,
Look up to the morning Senate and visions of sorrow leave pensive streets.

But heavy-brow'd jealousies lour o'er the Louvre; and terrors of ancient Kings
Descend from the gloom and wander thro' the palace, and weep round the King and his Nobles; 60
While loud thunders roll, troubling the dead. Kings are sick throughout all the earth!
The voice ceas'd: the Nation sat; and the triple forg'd fetters of times were unloos'd.
The voice ceas'd: the Nation sat; but ancient darkness and trembling wander thro' the palace.

As in day of havoc and routed battle, among thick snades of discontent,

The French Revolution

On the soul-skirting mountains of sorrow cold waving, the Nobles
    fold round the King;   65
Each stern visage lock'd up as with strong bands of iron, each
    strong limb bound down as with marble,
In flames of red wrath burning, bound in astonishment a quarter
    of an hour.

Then the King glow'd: his Nobles fold round, like the sun of old
    time quench'd in clouds;
In their darkness the King stood; his heart flam'd, and utter'd a
    with'ring heat, and these words burst forth:

'The nerves of five thousand years' ancestry tremble, shaking the
    heavens of France;   70
Throbs of anguish beat on brazen war foreheads; they descend
    and look into their graves.
I see thro' darkness, thro' clouds rolling round me, the spirits of
    ancient Kings
Shivering over their bleachèd bones; round them their counsellors
    look up from the dust,
Crying: "Hide from the living! Our bonds and our prisoners
    shout in the open field.
Hide in the nether earth! Hide in the bones! Sit obscurèd in
    the hollow scull!   75
Our flesh is corrupted, and we wear away. We are not numberèd
    among the living. Let us hide
In stones, among roots of trees. The prisoners have burst their
    dens.
Let us hide! let us hide in the dust! and plague and wrath and
    tempest shall cease."

He ceas'd, silent pond'ring; his brows folded heavy, his forehead
    was in affliction.
Like the central fire from the window he saw his vast armies
    spread over the hills,   80
Breathing red fires from man to man, and from horse to horse: then
    his bosom

The French Revolution

Expanded like starry heaven; he sat down: his Nobles took their ancient seats.

Then the ancientest Peer, Duke of Burgundy, rose from the Monarch's right hand, red as wines
From his mountains; an odour of war, like a ripe vineyard, rose from his garments,
And the chamber became as a clouded sky; o'er the Council he stretch'd his red limbs 85
Cloth'd in flames of crimson; as a ripe vineyard stretches over sheaves of corn,
The fierce Duke hung over the Council; around him crowd, weeping in his burning robe,
A bright cloud of infant souls: his words fall like purple autumn on the sheaves:

'Shall this marble-built heaven become a clay cottage, this earth an oak stool, and these mowers
From the Atlantic mountains mow down all this great starry harvest of six thousand years? 90
And shall Necker, the hind of Geneva, stretch out his crook'd sickle o'er fertile France,
Till our purple and crimson is faded to russet, and the kingdoms of earth bound in sheaves,
And the ancient forests of chivalry hewn, and the joys of the combat burnt for fuel;
Till the power and dominion is rent from the pole, sword and sceptre from sun and moon,
The law and gospel from fire and air, and eternal reason and science 95
From the deep and the solid, and man lay his faded head down on the rock
Of eternity, where the eternal lion and eagle remain to devour?
This to prevent, urg'd by cries in day, and prophetic dreams hovering in night,
To enrich the lean earth that craves, furrow'd with ploughs, whose seed is departing from her,

The French Revolution

Thy Nobles have gather'd thy starry hosts round this rebellious city, 100
To rouse up the ancient forests of Europe, with clarions of cloud-breathing war,
To hear the horse neigh to the drum and trumpet, and the trumpet and war shout reply.
Stretch the hand that beckons the eagles of heaven: they cry over Paris, and wait
Till Fayette point his finger to Versailles—the eagles of heaven must have their prey!'

He ceas'd, and burn'd silent: red clouds roll round Necker; a weeping is heard o'er the palace. 105
Like a dark cloud Necker paus'd, and like thunder on the just man's burial day he paus'd.
Silent sit the winds, silent the meadows; while the husbandman and woman of weakness
And bright children look after him into the grave, and water his clay with love,
Then turn towards pensive fields: so Necker paus'd, and his visage was cover'd with clouds.

The King lean'd on his mountains; then lifted his head and look'd on his armies, that shone 110
Thro' heaven, tinging morning with beams of blood; then turning to Burgundy, troubled:—
'Burgundy, thou wast born a lion! My soul is o'ergrown with distress
For the Nobles of France, and dark mists roll round me and blot the writing of God
Written in my bosom. Necker rise! leave the kingdom, thy life is surrounded with snares.
We have call'd an Assembly, but not to destroy; we have given gifts, not to the weak; 115
I hear rushing of muskets and bright'ning of swords; and visages, redd'ning with war,

The French Revolution

Frowning and looking up from brooding villages and every dark'ning city.

Ancient wonders frown over the kingdom, and cries of women and babes are heard,

And tempests of doubt roll around me, and fierce sorrows, because of the Nobles of France.

Depart! answer not! for the tempest must fall, as in years that are passèd away.' 120

Dropping a tear the old man his place left, and when he was gone out

He set his face toward Geneva to flee; and the women and children of the city

Kneel'd round him and kissèd his garments and wept: he stood a short space in the street,

Then fled; and the whole city knew he was fled to Geneva, and the Senate heard it.

But the Nobles burn'd wrathful at Necker's departure, and wreath'd their clouds and waters 125

In dismal volumes; as, risen from beneath, the Archbishop of Paris arose

In the rushing of scales, and hissing of flames, and rolling of sulphurous smoke:—

'Hearken, Monarch of France, to the terrors of heaven, and let thy soul drink of my counsel!

Sleeping at midnight in my golden tower, the repose of the labours of men

Wav'd its solemn cloud over my head. I awoke; a cold hand passèd over my limbs, and behold! 130

An agèd form, white as snow, hov'ring in mist, weeping in the uncertain light.

Dim the form almost faded, tears fell down the shady cheeks; at his feet many cloth'd

In white robes, strewn in air censers and harps. silent they lay prostrated;

The French Revolution

Beneath, in the awful void, myriads descending and weeping thro' dismal winds;
Endless the shady train shiv'ring descended, from the gloom where the agèd form wept. 135
At length, trembling, the vision sighing, in a low voice like the voice of the grasshopper, whisper'd:
"My groaning is heard in the abbeys, and God, so long worshipp'd, departs as a lamp
Without oil; for a curse is heard hoarse thro' the land, from a godless race
Descending to beasts; they look downward, and labour, and forget my holy law;
The sound of prayer fails from lips of flesh, and the holy hymn from thicken'd tongues; 140
For the bars of Chaos are burst; her millions prepare their fiery way
Thro' the orbèd abode of the holy dead, to root up and pull down and remove,
And Nobles and Clergy shall fail from before me, and my cloud and vision be no more;
The mitre become black, the crown vanish, and the sceptre and ivory staff
Of the ruler wither among bones of death; they shall consume from the thistly field, 145
And the sound of the bell, and voice of the sabbath, and singing of the holy choir
Is turn'd into songs of the harlot in day, and cries of the virgin in night.
They shall drop at the plough and faint at the harrow, unredeem'd, unconfess'd, unpardon'd;
The priest rot in his surplice by the lawless lover, the holy beside the accursèd,
The King, frowning in purple, beside the grey ploughman, and their worms embrace together." 150
The voice ceas'd: a groan shook my chamber. I slept, for the cloud of repose returnèd;

The French Revolution

But morning dawn'd heavy upon me. I rose to bring my Prince heaven-utter'd counsel.
Hear my counsel, O King! and send forth thy Generals; the command of Heaven is upon thee!
Then do thou command, O King! to shut up this Assembly in their final home;
Let thy soldiers possess this city of rebels, that threaten to bathe their feet 155
In the blood of Nobility, trampling the heart and the head; let the Bastille devour
These rebellious seditious; seal them up, O Anointed! in everlasting chains.'
He sat down: a damp cold pervaded the Nobles, and monsters of worlds unknown
Swam round them, watching to be deliverèd—when Aumont, whose chaos-born soul
Eternally wand'ring, a comet and swift-falling fire, pale enter'd the chamber. 160
Before the red Council he stood, like a man that returns from hollow graves:—

'Awe-surrounded, alone thro' the army, a fear and a with'ring blight blown by the north,
The Abbé de Sieyes from the Nation's Assembly, O Princes and Generals of France,
Unquestionèd, unhinderèd! Awe-struck are the soldiers; a dark shadowy man in the form
Of King Henry the Fourth walks before him in fires; the captains like men bound in chains 165
Stood still as he pass'd: he is come to the Louvre, O King, with a message to thee!
The strong soldiers tremble, the horses their manes bow, and the guards of thy palace are fled!'

Uprose awful in his majestic beams Bourbon's strong Duke; his proud sword, from his thigh

The French Revolution

Drawn, he threw on the earth: the Duke of Bretagne and the Earl of Bourgogne
Rose inflam'd, to and fro in the chamber, like thunder-clouds ready to burst. 170

'What damp all our fires, O spectre of Henry!' said Bourbon, 'and rend the flames
From the head of our King? Rise, Monarch of France! command me, and I will lead
This army of superstition at large, that the ardour of noble souls, quenchless,
May yet burn in France, nor our shoulders be plough'd with the furrows of poverty.'

Then Orleans, generous as mountains, arose and unfolded his robe, and put forth 175
His benevolent hand, looking on the Archbishop, who changèd as pale as lead,
Would have risen but could not: his voice issuèd harsh grating; instead of words harsh hissings
Shook the chamber; he ceas'd abash'd. Then Orleans spoke; all was silent.
He breath'd on them, and said: 'O Princes of fire, whose flames are for growth, not consuming,
Fear not dreams, fear not visions, nor be you dismay'd with sorrows which flee at the morning! 180
Can the fires of Nobility ever be quench'd, or the stars by a stormy night?
Is the body diseas'd when the members are healthful? can the man be bound in sorrow
Whose ev'ry function is fill'd with its fiery desire? can the soul, whose brain and heart
Cast their rivers in equal tides thro' the great Paradise, languish because the feet,
Hands, head, bosom, and parts of love follow their high breathing joy? 185

The French Revolution

And can Nobles be bound when the people are free, or God weep when his children are happy?
Have you never seen Fayette's forehead, or Mirabeau's eyes, or the shoulders of Target,
Or Bailly the strong foot of France, or Clermont the terrible voice, and your robes
Still retain their own crimson?—Mine never yet faded, for fire delights in its form!
But go, merciless man, enter into the infinite labyrinth of another's brain   190
Ere thou measure the circle that he shall run. Go, thou cold recluse, into the fires
Of another's high flaming rich bosom, and return unconsum'd, and write laws.
If thou canst not do this, doubt thy theories, learn to consider all men as thy equals,
Thy brethren, and not as thy foot or thy hand, unless thou first fearest to hurt them.'

The Monarch stood up; the strong Duke his sword to its golden scabbard return'd;   195
The Nobles sat round like clouds on the mountains, when the storm is passing away:—
'Let the Nation's Ambassador come among Nobles, like incense of the valley!'

Aumont went out and stood in the hollow porch, his ivory wand in his hand;
A cold orb of disdain revolv'd round him, and coverèd his soul with snows eternal.
Great Henry's soul shudderèd, a whirlwind and fire tore furious from his angry bosom;   200
He indignant departed on horses of heav'n. Then the Abbé de Sieyes rais'd his feet
On the steps of the Louvre; like a voice of God following a storm, the Abbé follow'd

The French Revolution

The pale fires of Aumont into the chamber; as a father that bows to his son,
Whose rich fields inheriting spread their old glory, so the voice of the people bowèd
Before the ancient seat of the kingdom and mountains to be renewèd.   205

' Hear, O heavens of France! the voice of the people, arising from valley and hill,
O'erclouded with power. Hear the voice of valleys, the voice of meek cities,
Mourning oppressèd on village and field, till the village and field is a waste.
For the husbandman weeps at blights of the fife, and blasting of trumpets consume
The souls of mild France; the pale mother nourishes her child to the deadly slaughter.   210
When the heavens were seal'd with a stone, and the terrible sun clos'd in an orb, and the moon
Rent from the nations, and each star appointed for watchers of night,
The millions of spirits immortal were bound in the ruins of sulphur heaven
To wander enslav'd; black, depress'd in dark ignorance, kept in awe with the whip
To worship terrors, bred from the blood of revenge and breath of desire   215
In bestial forms, or more terrible men; till the dawn of our peaceful morning,
Till dawn, till morning, till the breaking of clouds, and swelling of winds, and the universal voice;
Till man raise his darken'd limbs out of the caves of night. His eyes and his heart
Expand—Where is Space? where, O Sun, is thy dwelling? where thy tent, O faint slumb'rous Moon?
Then the valleys of France shall cry to the soldier: " Throw down thy sword and musket,   220

The French Revolution

And run and embrace the meek peasant." Her Nobles shall hear and shall weep, and put off
The red robe of terror, the crown of oppression, the shoes of contempt, and unbuckle
The girdle of war from the desolate earth. Then the Priest in his thund'rous cloud
Shall weep, bending to earth, embracing the valleys, and putting his hand to the plough,
Shall say: "No more I curse thee; but now I will bless thee: no more in deadly black   225
Devour thy labour; nor lift up a cloud in thy heavens, O laborious plough;
That the wild raging millions, that wander in forests, and howl in law-blasted wastes,
Strength madden'd with slavery, honesty bound in the dens of superstition,
May sing in the village, and shout in the harvest, and woo in pleasant gardens
Their once savage loves, now beaming with knowledge, with gentle awe adornèd;   230
And the saw, and the hammer, the chisel, the pencil, the pen, and the instruments
Of heavenly song sound in the wilds once forbidden, to teach the laborious ploughman
And shepherd, deliver'd from clouds of war, from pestilence, from night-fear, from murder,
From falling, from stifling, from hunger, from cold, from slander, discontent and sloth,
That walk in beasts and birds of night, driven back by the sandy desert,   235
Like pestilent fogs round cities of men; and the happy earth sing in its course,
The mild peaceable nations be openèd to heav'n, and men walk with their fathers in bliss."
Then hear the first voice of the morning: "Depart, O clouds of night, and no more

The French Revolution

Return; be withdrawn cloudy war, troops of warriors depart, nor around our peaceable city
Breathe fires; but ten miles from Paris let all be peace, nor a soldier be seen!"' 240

He ended: the wind of contention arose, and the clouds cast their shadows; the Princes
Like the mountains of France, whose agèd trees utter an awful voice, and their branches
Are shatter'd; till gradual a murmur is heard descending into the valley,
Like a voice in the vineyards of Burgundy when grapes are shaken on grass,
Like the low voice of the labouring man, instead of the shout of joy; 245
And the palace appear'd like a cloud driven abroad; blood ran down the ancient pillars.
Thro' the cloud a deep thunder, the Duke of Burgundy, delivers the King's command:—

'Seest thou yonder dark castle, that moated around, keeps this city of Paris in awe?
Go, command yonder tower, saying: "Bastille, depart! and take thy shadowy course;
Overstep the dark river, thou terrible tower, and get thee up into the country ten miles. 250
And thou black southern prison, move along the dusky road to Versailles; there
Frown on the gardens"—and, if it obey and depart, then the King will disband
This war-breathing army; but, if it refuse, let the Nation's Assembly thence learn
That this army of terrors, that prison of horrors, are the bands of the murmuring kingdom.'

Like the morning star arising above the black waves, when a shipwreck'd soul sighs for morning, 255

The French Revolution

Thro' the ranks, silent, walk'd the Ambassador back to the Nation's Assembly, and told
The unwelcome message. Silent they heard; then a thunder roll'd round loud and louder;
Like pillars of ancient halls and ruins of times remote, they sat.
Like a voice from the dim pillars Mirabeau rose; the thunders subsided away;
A rushing of wings around him was heard as he brighten'd, and cried out aloud: 260
'Where is the General of the Nation?' The walls re-echo'd: 'Where is the General of the Nation?'

Sudden as the bullet wrapp'd in his fire, when brazen cannons rage in the field,
Fayette sprung from his seat saying 'Ready!' Then bowing like clouds, man toward man, the Assembly
Like a Council of Ardours seated in clouds, bending over the cities of men,
And over the armies of strife, where their children are marshall'd together to battle, 265
They murmuring divide; while the wind sleeps beneath, and the numbers are counted in silence,
While they vote the removal of War, and the pestilence weighs his red wings in the sky.

So Fayette stood silent among the Assembly, and the votes were given, and the numbers numb'red;
And the vote was that Fayette should order the army to remove ten miles from Paris.

The agèd Sun rises appall'd from dark mountains, and gleams a dusky beam 270
On Fayette; but on the whole army a shadow, for a cloud on the eastern hills
Hover'd, and stretch'd across the city, and across the army, and across the Louvre.

The French Revolution

Like a flame of fire he stood before dark ranks, and before expecting captains:
On pestilent vapours around him flow frequent spectres of religious men, weeping
In winds; driven out of the abbeys, their naked souls shiver in keen open air; 275
Driven out by the fiery cloud of Voltaire, and thund'rous rocks of Rousseau,
They dash like foam against the ridges of the army, uttering a faint feeble cry.

Gleams of fire streak the heavens, and of sulphur the earth, from Fayette as he lifted his hand;
But silent he stood, till all the officers rush round him like waves
Round the shore of France, in day of the British flag, when heavy cannons 280
Affright the coasts, and the peasant looks over the sea and wipes a tear:
Over his head the soul of Voltaire shone fiery; and over the army Rousseau his white cloud
Unfolded, on souls of war, living terrors, silent list'ning toward Fayette.
His voice loud inspir'd by liberty, and by spirits of the dead, thus thunder'd:—

'The Nation's Assembly command that the Army remove ten miles from Paris; 285
Nor a soldier be seen in road or in field, till the Nation command return.'

Rushing along iron ranks glittering, the officers each to his station
Depart, and the stern captain strokes his proud steed, and in front of his solid ranks
Waits the sound of trumpet; captains of foot stand each by his cloudy drum:
Then the drum beats, and the steely ranks move, and trumpets rejoice in the sky. 290

The French Revolution

Dark cavalry, like clouds fraught with thunder, ascend on the hills, and bright infantry, rank
Behind rank, to the soul-shaking drum and shrill fife, along the roads glitter like fire.

The noise of trampling, the wind of trumpets, smote the Palace walls with a blast.
Pale and cold sat the King in midst of his Peers, and his noble heart sunk, and his pulses
Suspended their motion; a darkness crept over his eyelids, and chill cold sweat 295
Sat round his brows faded in faint death; his Peers pale like mountains of the dead,
Cover'd with dews of night, groaning, shaking forests and floods. The cold newt,
And snake, and damp toad on the kingly foot crawl, or croak on the awful knee,
Shedding their slime; in folds of the robe the crown'd adder builds and hisses
From stony brows: shaken the forests of France, sick the kings of the nations, 300
And the bottoms of the world were open'd, and the graves of archangels unseal'd:
The enormous dead lift up their pale fires and look over the rocky cliffs.

A faint heat from their fires reviv'd the cold Louvre; the frozen blood reflow'd.
Awful uprose the King; him the Peers follow'd; they saw the courts of the Palace
Forsaken, and Paris without a soldier, silent. For the noise was gone up 305
And follow'd the army; and the Senate in peace sat beneath morning's beam.

END OF THE FIRST BOOK.

A SONG
OF
LIBERTY

(Engraved *circa* 1792)

A SONG OF LIBERTY

1. The Eternal Female groan'd! It was heard over all the Earth.

2. Albion's coast is sick, silent.   The American meadows faint!

3. Shadows of Prophecy shiver along by the lakes and the rivers, and mutter across the ocean.   France, rend down thy dungeon!

4. Golden Spain, burst the barriers of old Rome!

5. Cast thy keys, O Rome! into the deep, down falling, even to eternity down falling,

6. And weep.

7. In her trembling hands she took the new-born terror, howling.

8. On those infinite mountains of light, now barr'd out by the Atlantic sea, the new-born fire stood before the starry king!

9. Flagg'd with grey-brow'd snows and thunderous visages, the jealous wings wav'd over the deep.

10. The speary hand burnèd aloft, unbuckled was the shield; forth went the hand of Jealousy among the flaming hair, and hurl'd the new-born wonder thro' the starry night.

11. The fire, the fire, is falling!

12. Look up! look up! O citizen of London, enlarge thy countenance!   O Jew, leave counting gold! return to thy oil and wine.   O African! black African! Go, wingèd thought, widen his forehead!

A Song of Liberty

13. The fiery limbs, the flaming hair, shot like the sinking sun into the western sea.

14. Wak'd from his eternal sleep, the hoary element, roaring, fled away.

15. Down rush'd, beating his wings in vain, the jealous King; his grey-brow'd counsellors, thunderous warriors, curl'd veterans, among helms, and shields, and chariots, horses, elephants, banners, castles, slings, and rocks,

16. Falling, rushing, ruining! buried in the ruins, on Urthona's dens;

17. All night beneath the ruins; then, their sullen flames faded, emerge round the gloomy King.

18. With thunder and fire, leading his starry hosts thro' the waste wilderness, he promulgates his ten commands, glancing his beamy eyelids over the deep in dark dismay,

19. Where the son of fire in his eastern cloud, while the morning plumes her golden breast,

20. Spurning the clouds written with curses, stamps the stony law to dust, loosing the eternal horses from the dens of night, crying: *Empire is no more! and now the lion and wolf shall cease.*

Chorus

Let the Priests of the Raven of dawn no longer, in deadly black, with hoarse note curse the sons of joy! Nor his accepted brethren—whom, tyrant, he calls free—lay the bound or build the roof! Nor pale Religion's lechery call that Virginity that wishes but acts not!

For everything that lives is Holy!

The Eye sees more than the Heart knows.
Printed by Will.ᵐ Blake: 1793.

VISIONS
OF
THE DAUGHTERS OF ALBION

(Engraved 1793)

The Argument

  I lovèd Theotormon,
  And I was not ashamèd;
  I trembled in my virgin fears,
  And I hid in Leutha's vale!

  I pluckèd Leutha's flower,   5
  And I rose up from the vale;
  But the terrible thunders tore
  My virgin mantle in twain.

Visions

Enslav'd, the Daughters of Albion weep; a trembling lamentation
Upon their mountains; in their valleys, sighs toward America.

For the soft soul of America, Oothoon, wander'd in woe
Along the vales of Leutha, seeking flowers to comfort her;
And thus she spoke to the bright Marigold of Leutha's vale:— 5

'Art thou a flower? art thou a nymph? I see thee now a flower,
Now a nymph! I dare not pluck thee from thy dewy bed!'

The Golden nymph replied: 'Pluck thou my flower, Oothoon the
  mild!

Visions of the Daughters of Albion

Another flower shall spring, because the soul of sweet delight
Can never pass away.' She ceas'd, and clos'd her golden shrine. 10

Then Oothoon pluck'd the flower, saying: 'I pluck thee from thy bed,
Sweet flower, and put thee here to glow between my breasts;
And thus I turn my face to where my whole soul seeks.'

Over the waves she went in wing'd exulting swift delight,
And over Theotormon's reign took her impetuous course. 15

Bromion rent her with his thunders; on his stormy bed
Lay the faint maid, and soon her woes appall'd his thunders hoarse.

Bromion spoke: 'Behold this harlot here on Bromion's bed,
And let the jealous dolphins sport around the lovely maid!
Thy soft American plains are mine, and mine thy north and south: 20
Stamp'd with my signet are the swarthy children of the sun;
They are obedient, they resist not, they obey the scourge;
Their daughters worship terrors and obey the violent.
Now thou may'st marry Bromion's harlot, and protect the child
Of Bromion's rage, that Oothoon shall put forth in nine moons' time.' 25

Then storms rent Theotormon's limbs: he roll'd his waves around,
And folded his black jealous waters round the adulterate pair.
Bound back to back in Bromion's caves, terror and meekness dwell:

At entrance Theotormon sits, wearing the threshold hard
With secret tears; beneath him sound like waves on a desert shore 30
The voice of slaves beneath the sun, and children bought with money,
That shiver in religious caves beneath the burning fires
Of lust, that belch incessant from the summits of the earth.

Oothoon weeps not; she cannot weep, her tears are lockèd up;
But she can howl incessant, writhing her soft snowy limbs, 35
And calling Theotormon's Eagles to prey upon her flesh.

Visions of the Daughters of Albion

'I call with holy voice ! Kings of the sounding air,
Rend away this defilèd bosom that I may reflect
The image of Theotormon on my pure transparent breast.'

The Eagles at her call descend and rend their bleeding prey : 40
Theotormon severely smiles ; her soul reflects the smile,
As the clear spring, muddied with feet of beasts, grows pure and
  smiles.

The Daughters of Albion hear her woes, and echo back her sighs.

' Why does my Theotormon sit weeping upon the threshold,
And Oothoon hovers by his side, persuading him in vain ? 45
I cry : Arise, O Theotormon ! for the village dog
Barks at the breaking day ; the nightingale has done lamenting ;
The lark does rustle in the ripe corn, and the eagle returns
From nightly prey, and lifts his golden beak to the pure east,
Shaking the dust from his immortal pinions to awake 50
The sun that sleeps too long. Arise, my Theotormon ! I am pure,
Because the night is gone that clos'd me in its deadly black.
They told me that the night and day were all that I could see ;
They told me that I had five senses to enclose me up ;
And they enclos'd my infinite brain into a narrow circle, 55
And sunk my heart into the Abyss, a red, round globe, hot burning,
Till all from life I was obliterated and erasèd.
Instead of morn arises a bright shadow, like an eye
In the eastern cloud ; instead of night a sickly charnel-house,
That Theotormon hears me not. To him the night and morn 60
Are both alike ; a night of sighs, a morning of fresh tears ;
And none but Bromion can hear my lamentations.

' With what sense is it that the chicken shuns the ravenous hawk ?
With what sense does the tame pigeon measure out the expanse ?
With what sense does the bee form cells ? Have not the mouse
  and frog 65
Eyes and ears and sense of touch ? Yet are their habitations
And their pursuits as different as their forms and as their joys.
Ask the wild ass why he refuses burdens, and the meek camel

Visions of the Daughters of Albion

Why he loves man. Is it because of eye, ear, mouth, or skin,
Or breathing nostrils? No! for these the wolf and tiger have. 70
Ask the blind worm the secrets of the grave, and why her spires
Love to curl round the bones of death; and ask the rav'nous snake
Where she gets poison, and the wing'd eagle why he loves the sun;
And then tell me the thoughts of man, that have been hid of old.

'Silent I hover all the night, and all day could be silent, 75
If Theotormon once would turn his lovèd eyes upon me.
How can I be defil'd when I reflect thy image pure?
Sweetest the fruit that the worm feeds on, and the soul prey'd on by woe,
The new-wash'd lamb ting'd with the village smoke, and the bright swan
By the red earth of our immortal river. I bathe my wings, 80
And I am white and pure to hover round Theotormon's breast.'

Then Theotormon broke his silence, and he answerèd:—

'Tell me what is the night or day to one o'erflow'd with woe?
Tell me what is a thought, and of what substance is it made?
Tell me what is a joy, and in what gardens do joys grow? 85
And in what rivers swim the sorrows? And upon what mountains
Wave shadows of discontent? And in what houses dwell the wretched,
Drunken with woe, forgotten, and shut up from cold despair?

'Tell me where dwell the thoughts, forgotten till thou call them forth? 89
Tell me where dwell the joys of old, and where the ancient loves,
And when will they renew again, and the night of oblivion past,
That I might traverse times and spaces far remote, and bring
Comforts into a present sorrow and a night of pain?
Where goest thou, O thought? to what remote land is thy flight?
If thou returnest to the present moment of affliction, 95
Wilt thou bring comforts on thy wings, and dews and honey and balm,
Or poison from the desert wilds, from the eyes of the envier?'

Visions of the Daughters of Albion

Then Bromion said, and shook the cavern with his lamentation :—

'Thou knowest that the ancient trees seen by thine eyes have fruit;
But knowest thou that trees and fruits flourish upon the earth   100
To gratify senses unknown—trees, beasts, and birds unknown;
Unknown, not unperceiv'd, spread in the infinite microscope,
In places yet unvisited by the voyager, and in worlds
Over another kind of seas, and in atmospheres unknown?
Ah! are there other wars, beside the wars of sword and fire?   105
And are there other sorrows beside the sorrows of poverty?
And are there other joys beside the joys of riches and ease?
And is there not one law for both the lion and the ox?
And is there not eternal fire, and eternal chains
To bind the phantoms of existence from eternal life?'   110

Then Oothoon waited silent all the day and all the night;
But when the morn arose, her lamentation renew'd :
The Daughters of Albion hear her woes, and echo back her sighs.

'O Urizen! Creator of men! mistaken Demon of heaven!
Thy joys are tears, thy labour vain to form men to thine image.
How can one joy absorb another? Are not different joys   116
Holy, eternal, infinite? and each joy is a Love.

'Does not the great mouth laugh at a gift, and the narrow eyelids mock
At the labour that is above payment? And wilt thou take the ape
For thy counsellor, or the dog for a schoolmaster to thy children?
Does he who contemns poverty, and he who turns with abhorrence
From usury feel the same passion, or are they movèd alike?
How can the giver of gifts experience the delights of the merchant?
How the industrious citizen the pains of the husbandman?
How different far the fat fed hireling with hollow drum,   125
Who buys whole corn-fields into wastes, and sings upon the heath!
How different their eye and ear! How different the world to them!
With what sense does the parson claim the labour of the farmer?
What are his nets and gins and traps ; and how does he surround him

Visions of the Daughters of Albion

With cold floods of abstraction, and with forests of solitude,   130
To build him castles and high spires, where kings and priests may dwell;
Till she who burns with youth, and knows no fixèd lot, is bound
In spells of law to one she loathes? And must she drag the chain
Of life in weary lust? Must chilling, murderous thoughts obscure
The clear heaven of her eternal spring; to bear the wintry rage
Of a harsh terror, driv'n to madness, bound to hold a rod   136
Over her shrinking shoulders all the day, and all the night
To turn the wheel of false desire, and longings that wake her womb
To the abhorrèd birth of cherubs in the human form,
That live a pestilence and die a meteor, and are no more;   140
Till the child dwell with one he hates, and do the deed he loathes,
And the impure scourge force his seed into its unripe birth,
Ere yet his eyelids can behold the arrows of the day?

'Does the whale worship at thy footsteps as the hungry dog;
Or does he scent the mountain prey because his nostrils wide   145
Draw in the ocean? Does his eye discern the flying cloud
As the raven's eye; or does he measure the expanse like the vulture?
Does the still spider view the cliffs where eagles hide their young;
Or does the fly rejoice because the harvest is brought in?
Does not the eagle scorn the earth, and despise the treasures beneath?   150
But the mole knoweth what is there, and the worm shall tell it thee.
Does not the worm erect a pillar in the mouldering churchyard
And a palace of eternity in the jaws of the hungry grave?
Over his porch these words are written: "Take thy bliss, O Man!
And sweet shall be thy taste, and sweet thy infant joys renew!"   155

'Infancy! fearless, lustful, happy, nestling for delight
In laps of pleasure: Innocence! honest, open, seeking
The vigorous joys of morning light, open to virgin bliss,
Who taught thee modesty, subtil modesty, child of night and sleep?

Visions of the Daughters of Albion

When thou awakest wilt thou dissemble all thy secret joys,   160
Or wert thou not awake when all this mystery was disclos'd?
Then com'st thou forth a modest virgin knowing to dissemble,
With nets found under thy night pillow, to catch virgin joy
And brand it with the name of whore, and sell it in the night
In silence, ev'n without a whisper, and in seeming sleep.   165
Religious dreams and holy vespers light thy smoky fires:
Once were thy fires lighted by the eyes of honest morn.
And does my Theotormon seek this hypocrite modesty,
This knowing, artful, secret, fearful, cautious, trembling hypocrite?
Then is Oothoon a whore indeed! and all the virgin joys   170
Of life are harlots; and Theotormon is a sick man's dream;
And Oothoon is the crafty slave of selfish holiness.

'But Oothoon is not so, a virgin fill'd with virgin fancies,
Open to joy and to delight wherever beauty appears:
If in the morning sun I find it, there my eyes are fix'd   175
In happy copulation; if in evening mild, wearièd with work,
Sit on a bank and draw the pleasures of this free-born joy.

'The moment of desire! the moment of desire! The virgin
That pines for man shall awaken her womb to enormous joys
In the secret shadows of her chamber: the youth shut up from   180
The lustful joy shall forget to generate, and create an amorous image
In the shadows of his curtains and in the folds of his silent pillow
Are not these the places of religion, the rewards of continence,
The self-enjoyings of self-denial? Why dost thou seek religion?
Is it because acts are not lovely that thou seekest solitude,   185
Where the horrible darkness is impressèd with reflections of desire?

'Father of Jealousy, be thou accursèd from the earth!
Why hast thou taught my Theotormon this accursèd thing,
Till beauty fades from off my shoulders, darken'd and cast out,
A solitary shadow wailing on the margin of nonentity?   190

'I cry: Love! Love! Love! happy happy Love! free as the mountain wind!

Visions of the Daughters of Albion

Can that be Love, that drinks another as a sponge drinks water,
That clouds with jealousy his nights, with weepings all the day,
To spin a web of age around him, grey and hoary, dark;
Till his eyes sicken at the fruit that hangs before his sight? 195
Such is self-love that envies all, a creeping skeleton,
With lamplike eyes watching around the frozen marriage bed!

'But silken nets and traps of adamant will Oothoon spread,
And catch for thee girls of mild silver, or of furious gold.
I'll lie beside thee on a bank, and view their wanton play 200
In lovely copulation, bliss on bliss, with Theotormon:
Red as the rosy morning, lustful as the first-born beam,
Oothoon shall view his dear delight; nor e'er with jealous cloud
Come in the heaven of generous love, nor selfish blightings bring.

'Does the sun walk, in glorious raiment, on the secret floor 205
Where the cold miser spreads his gold; or does the bright cloud drop
On his stone threshold? Does his eye behold the beam that brings
Expansion to the eye of pity; or will he bind himself
Beside the ox to thy hard furrow? Does not that mild beam blot
The bat, the owl, the glowing tiger, and the king of night? 210
The sea-fowl takes the wintry blast for a cov'ring to her limbs,
And the wild snake the pestilence to adorn him with gems and gold;
And trees, and birds, and beasts, and men behold their eternal joy.
Arise, you little glancing wings, and sing your infant joy!
Arise, and drink your bliss, for everything that lives is holy!' 215

Thus every morning wails Oothoon; but Theotormon sits
Upon the margin'd ocean conversing with shadows dire.

The Daughters of Albion hear her woes, and echo back her sighs.

THE END

AMERICA
a
PROPHECY

LAMBETH
Printed by William Blake, in the year 1793

AMERICA

A PROPHECY

(Engraved 1793)

Preludium

The shadowy Daughter of Urthona stood before red Orc,
When fourteen suns had faintly journey'd o'er his dark abode:
His food she brought in iron baskets, his drink in cups of iron.
Crown'd with a helmet and dark hair the nameless Female stood;
A quiver with its burning stores, a bow like that of night,   5
When pestilence is shot from heaven—no other arms she need!
Invulnerable tho' naked, save where clouds roll round her loins
Their awful folds in the dark air: silent she stood as night;
For never from her iron tongue could voice or sound arise,
But dumb till that dread day when Orc assay'd his fierce embrace.

'Dark Virgin,' said the hairy Youth, 'thy father stern, abhorr'd,   11
Rivets my tenfold chains, while still on high my spirit soars;
Sometimes an eagle screaming in the sky, sometimes a lion
Stalking upon the mountains, and sometimes a whale, I lash
The raging fathomless abyss; anon a serpent folding   15
Around the pillars of Urthona, and round thy dark limbs
On the Canadian wilds I fold; feeble my spirit folds;
For chain'd beneath I rend these caverns: when thou bringest food
I howl my joy, and my red eyes seek to behold thy face—
In vain! these clouds roll to and fro, and hide thee from my sight.

Silent as despairing love, and strong as jealousy,   21
The hairy shoulders rend the links; free are the wrists of fire;

America

Round the terrific loins he seiz'd the panting, struggling womb;
It joy'd: she put aside her clouds and smilèd her first-born smile,
As when a black cloud shows its lightnings to the silent deep.   25

Soon as she saw the Terrible Boy, then burst the virgin cry:—

'I know thee, I have found thee, and I will not let thee go:
Thou art the image of God who dwells in darkness of Africa,
And thou art fall'n to give me life in regions of dark death.
On my American plains I feel the struggling afflictions   30
Endur'd by roots that writhe their arms into the nether deep.
I see a Serpent in Canada who courts me to his love,
In Mexico an Eagle, and a Lion in Peru;
I see a Whale in the South Sea, drinking my soul away.
O what limb-rending pains I feel! thy fire and my frost   35
Mingle in howling pains, in furrows by thy lightnings rent.
This is Eternal Death, and this the torment long foretold!'

A Prophecy

The Guardian Prince of Albion burns in his nightly tent:
Sullen fires across the Atlantic glow to America's shore,
Piercing the souls of warlike men who rise in silent night.
Washington, Franklin, Paine, and Warren, Gates, Hancock, and Green
Meet on the coast glowing with blood from Albion's fiery Prince.

Washington spoke: 'Friends of America! look over the Atlantic sea;   6
A bended bow is lifted in Heaven, and a heavy iron chain
Descends, link by link, from Albion's cliffs across the sea, to bind
Brothers and sons of America; till our faces pale and yellow,
Heads depress'd, voices weak, eyes downcast, hands work-bruis'd,   10
Feet bleeding on the sultry sands, and the furrows of the whip
Descend to generations, that in future times forget.'

The strong voice ceas'd; for a terrible blast swept over the heaving sea:

America

The eastern cloud rent: on his cliffs stood Albion's wrathful
    Prince,
A dragon form, clashing his scales: at midnight he arose,   15
And flam'd red meteors round the land of Albion beneath;
His voice, his locks, his awful shoulders, and his glowing eyes
Appear to the Americans upon the cloudy night.

Solemn heave the Atlantic waves between the gloomy nations,
Swelling, belching from its deeps red clouds and raging fires.   20
Albion is sick! America faints! Enrag'd the Zenith grew.
As human blood shooting its veins all round the orbèd heaven,
Red rose the clouds from the Atlantic in vast wheels of blood,
And in the red clouds rose a Wonder o'er the Atlantic sea—
Intense! naked! a Human fire, fierce glowing, as the wedge   25
Of iron heated in the furnace; his terrible limbs were fire,
With myriads of cloudy terrors, banners dark, and towers
Surrounded: heat but not light went thro' the murky atmosphere.

The King of England looking westward trembles at the vision.

Albion's Angel stood beside the Stone of Night, and saw   30
The Terror like a comet, or more like the planet red,
That once enclos'd the terrible wandering comets in its sphere.
Then, Mars, thou wast our centre, and the planets three flew
    round
Thy crimson disk; so, ere the Sun was rent from thy red sphere,
The Spectre glow'd, his horrid length staining the temple long   35
With beams of blood; and thus a voice came forth, and shook the
    temple:—

'The morning comes, the night decays, the watchmen leave their
    stations;
The grave is burst, the spices shed, the linen wrappèd up;
The bones of death, the cov'ring clay, the sinews shrunk and dry'd
Reviving shake, inspiring move, breathing, awakening,   40
Spring like redeemèd captives, when their bonds and bars are burst
Let the slave grinding at the mill run out into the field,
Let him look up into the heavens and laugh in the bright air;

America

Let the enchainèd soul, shut up in darkness and in sighing,
Whose face has never seen a smile in thirty weary years,   45
Rise and look out; his chains are loose, his dungeon doors are open;
And let his wife and children return from the oppressor's scourge.
They look behind at every step, and believe it is a dream,
Singing: "The Sun has left his blackness, and has found a fresher morning,
And the fair Moon rejoices in the clear and cloudless night;   50
For Empire is no more, and now the Lion and Wolf shall cease."'

In thunders ends the voice.   Then Albion's Angel wrathful burnt
Beside the Stone of Night; and, like the Eternal Lion's howl
In famine and war, reply'd: 'Art thou not Orc, who serpent-form'd
Stands at the gate of Enitharmon to devour her children?   55
Blasphemous Demon, Antichrist, hater of Dignities,
Lover of wild rebellion, and transgressor of God's Law,
Why dost thou come to Angel's eyes in this terrific form?'

The Terror answer'd: 'I am Orc, wreath'd round the accursèd tree:
The times are ended; shadows pass, the morning 'gins to break;
The fiery joy, that Urizen perverted to ten commands,   61
What night he led the starry hosts thro' the wide wilderness,
That stony Law I stamp to dust; and scatter Religion abroad
To the four winds as a torn book, and none shall gather the leaves;
But they shall rot on desert sands, and consume in bottomless deeps,   65
To make the deserts blossom, and the deeps shrink to their fountains,
And to renew the fiery joy, and burst the stony roof;
That pale religious lechery, seeking Virginity,
May find it in a harlot, and in coarse-clad honesty
The undefil'd, tho' ravish'd in her cradle night and morn;   70
For everything that lives is holy, life delights in life;
Because the soul of sweet delight can never be defil'd.
Fires enwrap the earthly globe, yet Man is not consum'd;

America

Amidst the lustful fires he walks; his feet become like brass,
His knees and thighs like silver, and his breast and head like
    gold. 75

'Sound! sound! my loud war-trumpets, and alarm my Thirteen
    Angels!
Loud howls the Eternal Wolf! the Eternal Lion lashes his tail!
America is dark'ned; and my punishing Demons, terrifièd,
Crouch howling before their caverns deep, like skins dry'd in the
    wind. 79
They cannot smite the wheat, nor quench the fatness of the earth;
They cannot smite with sorrows, nor subdue the plough and spade;
They cannot wall the city, nor moat round the castle of princes;
They cannot bring the stubbèd oak to overgrow the hills;
For terrible men stand on the shores, and in their robes I see
Children take shelter from the lightnings: there stands Washington,
And Paine, and Warren, with their foreheads **rear'd** toward the
    East— 86
But clouds obscure my agèd sight. A vision from afar!
Sound! sound! my loud war-trumpets, and alarm my Thirteen
    Angels!
Ah, vision from afar! Ah, rebel form that rent the ancient
Heavens! Eternal Viper self-renew'd, rolling in clouds, 90
I see thee in thick clouds and darkness on America's shore,
Writhing in pangs of abhorrèd birth; red flames the crest rebellious
And eyes of death; the harlot womb, oft openèd in vain,
Heaves in enormous circles: now the times are return'd upon thee,
Devourer of thy parent, now thy unutterable torment renews. 95
Sound! sound! my loud war-trumpets, and alarm my Thirteen
    Angels!
Ah, terrible birth! a young one bursting! Where is the weeping
    mouth,
And where the mother's milk? Instead, those ever-hissing jaws
And parchèd lips drop with fresh gore: now roll thou in the clouds;
Thy mother lays her length outstretch'd upon the shore beneath.

America

Sound! sound! my loud war-trumpets, and alarm my Thirteen
    Angels!   101
Loud howls the Eternal Wolf! the Eternal Lion lashes his tail!'

Thus wept the Angel voice, and as he wept the terrible blasts
Of trumpets blew a loud alarm across the Atlantic deep.
No trumpets answer; no reply of clarions or of fifes: 105
Silent the Colonies remain and refuse the loud alarm.

On those vast shady hills between America and Albion's shore,
Now barr'd out by the Atlantic sea, call'd Atlantean hills,
Because from their bright summits you may pass to the Golden
    World,
An ancient palace, archetype of mighty Emperies,   110
Rears its immortal pinnacles, built in the forest of God
By Ariston, the King of Beauty, for his stolen bride.

Here on their magic seats the Thirteen Angels sat perturb'd,
For clouds from the Atlantic hover o'er the solemn roof.

Fiery the Angels rose, and as they rose deep thunder roll'd   115
Around their shores, indignant burning with the fires of Orc;
And Boston's Angel cried aloud as they flew thro' the dark night.

He cried: 'Why trembles honesty; and, like a murderer,
Why seeks he refuge from the frowns of his immortal station?
Must the generous tremble, and leave his joy to the idle, to the
    pestilence   120
That mock him? Who commanded this? What God? What Angel?
To keep the gen'rous from experience till the ungenerous
Are unrestrain'd performers of the energies of nature;
Till pity is become a trade, and generosity a science   124
That men get rich by; and the sandy desert is giv'n to the strong?
What God is he writes laws of peace, and clothes him in a tempest?
What pitying Angel lusts for tears, and fans himself with sighs?
What crawling villain preaches abstinence and wraps himself
In fat of lambs? No more I follow, no more obedience pay!'

America

So cried he, rending off his robe and throwing down his sceptre
In sight of Albion's Guardian; and all the Thirteen Angels
Rent off their robes to the hungry wind, and threw their golden
    sceptres
Down on the land of America; indignant they descended
Headlong from out their heav'nly heights, descending swift as fires
Over the land; naked and flaming are their lineaments seen
In the deep gloom; by Washington and Paine and Warren they
    stood;
And the flame folded, roaring fierce within the pitchy night,
Before the Demon red, who burnt towards America,
In black smoke, thunders, and loud winds, rejoicing in its terror,
Breaking in smoky wreaths from the wild deep, and gath'ring thick
In flames as of a furnace on the land from North to South,
What time the Thirteen Governors, that England sent, convene
In Bernard's house. The flames cover'd the land; they rouse;
    they cry;
Shaking their mental chains, they rush in fury to the sea
To quench their anguish; at the feet of Washington down fall'n
They grovel on the sand and writhing lie, while all
The British soldiers thro' the Thirteen States sent up a howl
Of anguish, threw their swords and muskets to the earth, and run
From their encampments and dark castles, seeking where to hide
From the grim flames, and from the visions of Orc, in sight
Of Albion's Angel; who, enrag'd, his secret clouds open'd
From North to South, and burnt outstretch'd on wings of wrath,
    cov'ring
The eastern sky, spreading his awful wings across the heavens.
Beneath him roll'd his num'rous hosts, all Albion's Angels camp'd
Darken'd the Atlantic mountains; and their trumpets shook the
    valleys,
Arm'd with diseases of the earth to cast upon the Abyss—
Their numbers forty millions, must'ring in the eastern sky.

In the flames stood and view'd the armies drawn out in the sky,
Washington, Franklin, Paine, and Warren, Allen, Gates, and Lee,

America

And heard the voice of Albion's Angel give the thunderous command; 160
His plagues, obedient to his voice, flew forth out of their clouds,
Falling upon America, as a storm to cut them off,
As a blight cuts the tender corn when it begins to appear.
Dark is the heaven above, and cold and hard the earth beneath:
And, as a plague-wind, fill'd with insects, cuts off man and beast,
And, as a sea o'erwhelms a land in the day of an earthquake, 166
Fury, rage, madness, in a wind swept through America;
And the red flames of Orc, that folded roaring, fierce, around
The angry shores; and the fierce rushing of th' inhabitants together!
The citizens of New York close their books and lock their chests;
The mariners of Boston drop their anchors and unlade; 171
The scribe of Pennsylvania casts his pen upon the earth;
The builder of Virginia throws his hammer down in fear.

Then had America been lost, o'erwhelm'd by the Atlantic,
And Earth had lost another portion of the Infinite; 175
But all rush together in the night in wrath and raging fire.
The red fires rag'd! The plagues recoil'd! Then roll'd they back with fury
On Albion's Angels: then the Pestilence began in streaks of red
Across the limbs of Albion's Guardian; the spotted plague smote Bristol's,
And the Leprosy London's Spirit, sickening all their bands: 180
The millions sent up a howl of anguish and threw off their hammer'd mail,
And cast their swords and spears to earth, and stood, a naked multitude:
Albion's Guardian writhèd in torment on the eastern sky,
Pale, quiv'ring toward the brain his glimmering eyes, teeth chattering,
Howling and shuddering, his legs quivering, convuls'd each muscle and sinew: 185
Sick'ning lay London's Guardian, and the ancient mitred York,
Their heads on snowy hills, their ensigns sick'ning in the sky.

America

The plagues creep on the burning winds, driven by flames of Orc,
And by the fierce Americans rushing together in the night,
Driven o'er the Guardians of Ireland, and Scotland and Wales.
They, spotted with plagues, forsook the frontiers; and their banners, sear'd 191
With fires of hell, deform their ancient Heavens with shame and woe.
Hid in his caves the Bard of Albion felt the enormous plagues,
And a cowl of flesh grew o'er his head, and scales on his back and ribs;
And, rough with black scales, all his Angels fright their ancient heavens. 195
The doors of marriage are open, and the Priests, in rustling scales,
Rush into reptile coverts, hiding from the fires of Orc,
That play around the golden roofs in wreaths of fierce desire,
Leaving the Females naked and glowing with the lusts of youth.

For the Female Spirits of the dead, pining in bonds of religion, 200
Run from their fetters; reddening, and in long-drawn arches sitting,
They feel the nerves of youth renew, and desires of ancient times
Over their pale limbs, as a vine when the tender grape appears.

Over the hills, the vales, the cities rage the red flames fierce: 204
The Heavens melted from North to South; and Urizen, who sat
Above all heavens, in thunders wrapp'd, emerg'd his leprous head
From out his holy shrine, his tears in deluge piteous
Falling into the deep sublime; flagg'd with grey-brow'd snows
And thunderous visages, his jealous wings wav'd over the deep;
Weeping in dismal howling woe, he dark descended, howling 210
Around the smitten bands, clothèd in tears and trembling, shudd'ring, cold.
His storèd snows he pourèd forth, and his icy magazine,
He open'd on the deep, and on the Atlantic sea, white, shiv'ring;
Leprous his limbs, all over white, and hoary was his visage;
Weeping in dismal howlings before the stern Americans, 215
Hiding the Demon red with clouds and cold mists from the earth;

America

Till Angels and weak men twelve years should govern o'er the strong;
And then their end should come, when France receiv'd the Demon's light.

Stiff shudderings shook the heav'nly thrones! France, Spain, and Italy
In terror view'd the bands of Albion, and the ancient Guardians,
Fainting upon the elements, smitten with their own plagues! 221
They slow advance to shut the five gates of their law-built Heaven,
Filled with blasting fancies and with mildews of despair,
With fierce disease and lust, unable to stem the fires of Orc.
But the five gates were consum'd, and their bolts and hinges melted; 225
And the fierce flames burnt round the heavens, and round the abodes of men.

FINIS

EUROPE
a
PROPHECY

LAMBETH
Printed by Will Blake 1794

EUROPE

A PROPHECY

(Engraved 1794)

'Five windows light the cavern'd Man: thro' one he breathes the
    air;
Thro' one hears music of the spheres; thro' one the Eternal Vine
Flourishes, that he may receive the grapes; thro' one can look
And see small portions of the Eternal World that ever groweth;
Thro' one himself pass out what time he please, but he will not;
For stolen joys are sweet, and bread eaten in secret pleasant.'   6

So sang a Fairy, mocking, as he sat on a streak'd tulip,
Thinking none saw him: when he ceas'd I started from the trees,
And caught him in my hat, as boys knock down a butterfly.
'How know you this,' said I, 'small Sir? where did you learn this
    song?'   10
Seeing himself in my possession, thus he answer'd me:
'My Master, I am yours! command me, for I must obey.'

'Then tell me, what is the Material World, and is it dead?'
He, laughing, answer'd: 'I will write a book on leaves of flowers,
If you will feed me on love-thoughts, and give me now and then
A cup of sparkling poetic fancies; so, when I am tipsy,   16
I'll sing to you to this soft lute, and show you all alive
The World, when every particle of dust breathes forth its joy.'

I took him home in my warm bosom: as we went along   19
Wild flowers I gatherèd; and he show'd me each Eternal Flower:
He laugh'd aloud to see them whimper because they were pluck'd.
They hover'd round me like a cloud of incense. When I came
Into my parlour and sat down, and took my pen to write,
My Fairy sat upon the table, and dictated EUROPE.

    These introductory lines, which Blake engraved as part of the poem, are
found, so far as I am aware, only in the copy of *Europe* in the possession of
the Linnell family, where it follows the frontispiece and title-page, and precedes the Preludium.

EUROPE: A PROPHECY

Preludium

The nameless Shadowy Female rose from out the breast of Orc,
Her snaky hair brandishing in the winds of Enitharmon;
And thus her voice arose:—

'O mother Enitharmon, wilt thou bring forth other sons,
To cause my name to vanish, that my place may not be found? 5
For I am faint with travel,
Like the dark cloud disburden'd in the day of dismal thunder.

'My roots are brandish'd in the heavens, my fruits in earth beneath
Surge, foam, and labour into life, first born and first consum'd!
Consumèd and consuming! 10
Then why shouldst thou, Accursèd Mother, bring me into life?

'I wrap my turban of thick clouds around my lab'ring head,
And fold the sheety waters as a mantle round my limbs;
Yet the red sun and moon
And all the overflowing stars rain down prolific pains. 15

'Unwilling I look up to heaven, unwilling count the stars:
Sitting in fathomless abyss of my immortal shrine
I seize their burning power,
And bring forth howling terrors, all-devouring fiery kings,

'Devouring and devourèd, roaming on dark and desolate mountains,
In forests of Eternal Death, shrieking in hollow trees. 21
Ah, mother Enitharmon!
Stamp not with solid form this vig'rous progeny of fires.

'I bring forth from my teeming bosom myriads of flames,
And thou dost stamp them with a signet; then they roam abroad,
And leave me void as death. 26
Ah! I am drown'd in shady woe and visionary joy.

Europe

'And who shall bind the Infinite with an eternal band
To compass it with swaddling bands? and who shall cherish it
With milk and honey? 30
I see it smile, and I roll inward, and my voice is past.'

        She ceas'd, and roll'd her shady clouds
        Into the secret place.

A Prophecy

The deep of winter came,
What time the Secret Child
Descended through the orient gates of the Eternal day:
War ceas'd, and all the troops like shadows fled to their abodes.

Then Enitharmon saw her sons and daughters rise around; 5
Like pearly clouds they meet together in the crystal house;
And Los, possessor of the Moon, joy'd in the peaceful night,
Thus speaking, while his num'rous sons shook their bright fiery
    wings:—

'Again the night is come,
That strong Urthona takes his rest; 10
And Urizen, unloos'd from chains,
Glows like a meteor in the distant North.
Stretch forth your hands and strike the elemental strings!
Awake the thunders of the deep!

'The shrill winds wake, 15
Till all the sons of Urizen look out and envy Los.
Seize all the spirits of life, and bind
Their warbling joys to our loud strings!
Bind all the nourishing sweets of earth
To give us bliss, that we may drink the sparkling wine of Los! 20
And let us laugh at war,
Despising toil and care,
Because the days and nights of joy in lucky hours renew.

Europe

Arise, O Orc, from thy deep den!
First-born of Enitharmon, rise!
And we will crown thy head with garlands of the ruddy vine;
For now thou art bound,
And I may see thee in the hour of bliss, my eldest-born.'

The horrent Demon rose, surrounded with red stars of fire,
Whirling about in furious circles round the Immortal Fiend.

Then Enitharmon down descended into his red light,
And thus her voice rose to her children: the distant heavens reply :—

'Now comes the night of Enitharmon's joy!
Who shall I call? Who shall I send,
That Woman, lovely Woman, may have dominion?
Arise, O Rintrah! thee I call, and Palamabron, thee!
Go! tell the Human race that Woman's love is Sin;
That an Eternal life awaits the worms of sixty winters,
In an allegorical abode, where existence hath never come.
Forbid all Joy; and, from her childhood, shall the little Female
Spread nets in every secret path.

'My weary eyelids draw towards the evening; my bliss is yet but new.

Arise! O Rintrah, eldest-born, second to none but Orc!
O lion Rintrah, raise thy fury from thy forests black!
Bring Palamabron, hornèd priest, skipping upon the mountains,
And silent Elynittria, the silver-bowèd queen.
Rintrah, where hast thou hid thy bride?
Weeps she in desert shades?
Alas! my Rintrah, bring the lovely jealous Ocalythron.

'Arise, my son! bring all thy brethren, O thou King of Fire!
Prince of the Sun! I see thee with thy innumerable race,
Thick as the summer stars;
But each, ramping, his golden mane shakes,
And thine eyes rejoice because of strength, O Rintrah, furious King!'

Europe

Enitharmon slept   55
Eighteen hundred years. Man was a dream,
The night of Nature and their harps unstrung !
She slept in middle of her nightly song
Eighteen hundred years, a Female dream.

Shadows of men in fleeting bands upon the winds   60
Divide the heavens of Europe ;
Till Albion's Angel, smitten with his own plagues, fled with his bands.
The cloud bears hard on Albion's shore,
Fill'd with immortal Demons of futurity :
In council gather the smitten Angels of Albion ;   65
The cloud bears hard upon the council-house, down rushing
On the heads of Albion's Angels.

One hour they lay buried beneath the ruins of that hall ;
But as the stars rise from the Salt Lake, they arise in pain,   69
In troubled mists, o'erclouded by the terrors of struggling times.

In thoughts perturb'd they rose from the bright ruins, silent following
The fiery King, who sought his ancient temple, serpent-form'd,
That stretches out its shady length along the Island white.
Round him roll'd his clouds of war ; silent the Angel went
Along the infinite shores of Thames to golden Verulam.   75
There stand the venerable porches, that high-towering rear
Their oak-surrounded pillars, form'd of massy stones, uncut
With tool, stones precious !—such eternal in the heavens,
Of colours twelve (few known on earth) give light in the opaque,
Plac'd in the order of the stars ; when the five senses whelm'd   80
In deluge o'er the earth-born man, then turn'd the fluxile eyes
Into two stationary orbs, concentrating all things :
The ever-varying spiral ascents to the Heavens of Heavens
Were bended downward, and the nostrils' golden gates shut,
Turn'd outward, barr'd, and petrify'd against the Infinite.   85

Thought chang'd the Infinite to a Serpent, that which pitieth
To a devouring flame ; and Man fled from its face and hid

Europe

In forests of night: then all the eternal forests were divided
Into earths, rolling in circles of Space, that like an ocean rush'd
And overwhelmèd all except this finite wall of flesh.   90
Then was the Serpent temple form'd, image of Infinite,
Shut up in finite revolutions, and Man became an Angel,
Heaven a mighty circle turning, God a tyrant crown'd.

Now arriv'd the ancient Guardian at the southern porch,
That planted thick with trees of blackest leaf, and in a vale   95
Obscure enclos'd the Stone of Night; oblique it stood, o'erhung
With purple flowers and berries red, image of that sweet South,
Once open to the heavens, and elevated on the human neck,
Now overgrown with hair, and cover'd with a stony roof.
Downward 'tis sunk beneath th' attractive North, that round the feet,   100
A raging whirlpool, draws the dizzy enquirer to his grave.

> Albion's Angel rose upon the Stone of Night.
> He saw Urizen on the Atlantic;
> And his brazen Book,
> That Kings and Priests had copièd on Earth,   105
> Expanded from North to South.

And the clouds and fires pale roll'd round in the night of Enitharmon,
Round Albion's cliffs and London's walls: still Enitharmon slept.
Rolling volumes of grey mist involve Churches, Palaces, Towers;
For Urizen unclasp'd his Book, feeding his soul with pity.   110
The youth of England, hid in gloom, curse the pain'd heavens, compell'd
Into the deadly night to see the form of Albion's Angel.
Their parents brought them forth, and Agèd Ignorance preaches, canting,
On a vast rock, perceiv'd by those senses that are clos'd from thought——
Bleak, dark, abrupt it stands, and overshadows London city.   115
'They saw his bony feet on the rock, the flesh consum'd in flames

Europe

They saw the Serpent temple lifted above, shadowing the Island
    white;
They heard the voice of Albion's Angel, howling in flames of
    Orc,
Seeking the trump of the Last Doom.

Above the rest the howl was heard from Westminster, louder and
    louder: 120
The Guardian of the secret codes forsook his ancient mansion,
Driven out by the flames of Orc; his furr'd robes and false locks
Adhered and grew one with his flesh and nerves, and veins shot
    thro' them.
With dismal torment sick, hanging upon the wind, he fled
Grovelling, along Great George Street, thro' the Park gate: all
    the soldiers   125
Fled from his sight: he dragg'd his torments to the wilderness.

Thus was the howl thro' Europe!
For Orc rejoic'd to hear the howling shadows;
But Palamabron shot his lightnings, trenching down his wide back;
And Rintrah hung with all his legions in the nether deep.   130

Enitharmon laugh'd in her sleep to see (O woman's triumph!)
Every house a den, every man bound: the shadows are fill'd
With spectres, and the windows wove over with curses of iron:
Over the doors 'Thou shalt not', and over the chimneys 'Fear
    is written:
With bands of iron round their necks fasten'd into the walls   135
The citizens, in leaden gyves the inhabitants of suburbs
Walk heavy; soft and bent are the bones of villagers.

Between the clouds of Urizen the flames of Orc roll heavy
Around the limbs of Albion's Guardian, his flesh consuming:
Howlings and hissings, shrieks and groans, and voices of despair
Arise around him in the cloudy heavens of Albion. Furious,   141
The red-limb'd Angel seiz'd in horror and torment
The trump of the Last Doom; but he could not blow the iron tube!
Thrice he assay'd presumptuous to awake the dead to Judgement.

Europe

A mighty Spirit leap'd from the land of Albion,   145
Nam'd Newton: he seiz'd the trump, and blow'd the enormous blast!
Yellow as leaves of autumn, the myriads of Angelic hosts
Fell thro' the wintry skies, seeking their graves,
Rattling their hollow bones in howling and lamentation.

Then Enitharmon woke, nor knew that she had slept;   150
And eighteen hundred years were fled
As if they had not been.
She call'd her sons and daughters
To the sports of night
Within her crystal house,   155
And thus her song proceeds:—

' Arise, Ethinthus! tho' the earth-worm call,
Let him call in vain,
Till the night of holy shadows
And human solitude is past!   160

' Ethinthus, Queen of Waters, how thou shinest in the sky!
My daughter, how do I rejoice! for thy children flock around,
Like the gay fishes on the wave, when the cold moon drinks the dew.
Ethinthus! thou art sweet as comforts to my fainting soul,
For now thy waters warble round the feet of Enitharmon.   165

' Manatha-Varcyon! I behold thee flaming in my halls.
Light of thy mother's soul! I see thy lovely eagles round;
Thy golden wings are my delight, and thy flames of soft delusion.

' Where is my luring bird of Eden? Leutha, silent love!
Leutha, the many-colour'd bow delights upon thy wings!   170
Soft soul of flowers, Leutha!
Sweet smiling Pestilence! I see thy blushing light;
Thy daughters, many changing,
Revolve like sweet perfumes ascending, O Leutha, Silken Queen!

' Where is the youthful Antamon, Prince of the Pearly Dew?   175
O Antamon! why wilt thou leave thy mother Enitharmon?

Europe

Alone I see thee, crystal form,
Floating upon the bosom'd air,
With lineaments of gratified desire.
My Antamon! the seven churches of Leutha seek thy love.   180

'I hear the soft Oothoon in Enitharmon's tents;
Why wilt thou give up woman's secrecy, my melancholy child?
Between two moments Bliss is ripe.
O Theotormon! robb'd of joy, I see thy salt tears flow
Down the steps of my crystal house.   185

'Sotha and Thiralatha! secret dwellers of dreamful caves,
Arise and please the horrent Fiend with your melodious songs;
Still all your thunders, golden-hoof'd, and bind your horses black.
Orc! smile upon my children,
Smile, son of my afflictions!   190
Arise, O Orc, and give our mountains joy of thy red light!'

She ceas'd; for all were forth at sport beneath the solemn moon,
Waking the stars of Urizen with their immortal songs;
That Nature felt thro' all her pores the enormous revelry,
Till Morning oped the eastern gate;   195
Then every one fled to his station, and Enitharmon wept.

But terrible Orc, when he beheld the morning in the East,
Shot from the heights of Enitharmon,
And in the vineyards of red France appear'd the light of his fury.

The Sun glow'd fiery red!   200
The furious Terrors flew around
On golden chariots, raging with red wheels, dropping with blood!
The Lions lash their wrathful tails!
The Tigers couch upon the prey and suck the ruddy tide;
And Enitharmon groans and cries in anguish and dismay   205

Then Los arose: his head he rear'd, in snaky thunders clad;
And with a cry that shook all Nature to the utmost pole,
Call'd all his sons to the strife of blood.

FINIS

THE
BOOK
OF
URIZEN

(Engraved 1794)

THE [FIRST] BOOK OF URIZEN

Preludium to the First Book of Urizen

    Of the primeval Priest's assum'd power,
When Eternals spurn'd back his Religion,
And gave him a place in the North,
Obscure, shadowy, void, solitary.

    Eternals! I hear your call gladly.   5
Dictate swift wingèd words, and fear not
To unfold your dark visions of torment.

The Book of Urizen

Chap. I

1. Lo, a Shadow of horror is risen
In Eternity! unknown, unprolific,
Self-clos'd, all-repelling. What Demon
Hath form'd this abominable Void,
This soul-shudd'ring Vacuum? Some said
It is Urizen. But unknown, abstracted,
Brooding, secret, the dark Power hid.

2. Times on times he divided, and measur'd
Space by space in his ninefold darkness,
Unseen, unknown; changes appear'd
Like desolate mountains, rifted furious
By the black winds of perturbation.

3. For he strove in battles dire,
In unseen conflictions with Shapes,
Bred from his forsaken wilderness,
Of beast, bird, fish, serpent, and element,
Combustion, blast, vapour, and cloud.

4. Dark, revolving in silent activity,
Unseen in tormenting passions,
An Activity unknown and horrible,
A self-contemplating Shadow,
In enormous labours occupièd.

5. But Eternals beheld his vast forests;
Ages on ages he lay, clos'd, unknown,
Brooding, shut in the deep; all avoid
The petrific, abominable Chaos.

6. His cold horrors, silent, dark Urizen
Prepar'd; his ten thousands of thunders,
Rang'd in gloom'd array, stretch out across
The dread world; and the rolling of wheels,
As of swelling seas, sound in his clouds,

The Book of Urizen

In his hills of stor'd snows, in his mountains
Of hail and ice; voices of terror
Are heard, like thunders of autumn,
When the cloud blazes over the harvests. 35

Chap. II

1. Earth was not, nor globes of attraction;
The will of the Immortal expanded
Or contracted his all-flexible senses;
Death was not, but Eternal life sprung.

2. The sound of a trumpet the heavens 40
Awoke, and vast clouds of blood roll'd
Round the dim rocks of Urizen, so nam'd
That solitary one in Immensity.

3. Shrill the trumpet! and myriads of Eternity
Muster around the bleak deserts, 45
Now fill'd with clouds, darkness, and waters,
That roll'd perplex'd, lab'ring; and utter'd
Words articulate, bursting in thunders,
That roll'd on the tops of his mountains:—

4. 'From the depths of dark solitude, from 50
The Eternal abode in my Holiness,
Hidden, set apart, in my stern counsels,
Reserv'd for the days of futurity,
I have sought for a joy without pain,
For a solid without fluctuation. 55
Why will you die, O Eternals?
Why live in unquenchable burnings?

5. 'First I fought with the fire, consum'd
Inwards into a deep world within,
A Void immense, wild, dark and deep, 60
Where nothing was—Nature's wide womb,

The Book of Urizen

And self-balanc'd, stretch'd o'er the void,
I alone, even I! the winds merciless
Bound; but condensing in torrents
They fall and fall; strong I repell'd
The vast waves, and arose on the waters
A wide World of solid obstruction.

6. 'Here alone I, in books form'd of metals,
Have written the secrets of Wisdom,
The secrets of dark Contemplation,
By fightings and conflicts dire
With terrible monsters sin-bred,
Which the bosoms of all inhabit—
Seven deadly Sins of the Soul.

7. 'Lo! I unfold my darkness, and on
This rock place, with strong hand, the Bock
Of Eternal brass, written in my solitude:

8. 'Laws of peace, of love, of unity,
Of pity, compassion, forgiveness;
Let each choose one habitation,
His ancient infinite mansion,
One command, one joy, one desire,
One curse, one weight, one measure,
One King, one God, one Law.'

Chap. III

1. The voice ended: they saw his pale visage
Emerge from the darkness, his hand
On the rock of Eternity unclasping
The Book of brass.   Rage seiz'd the strong—

2. Rage, fury, intense indignation,
In cataracts of fire, blood, and gall,
In whirlwinds of sulphurous smoke,
And enormous forms of energy,

The Book of Urizen

In living creations appear'd,
In the flames of eternal fury.

3. Sund'ring, dark'ning, thund'ring,   95
Rent away with a terrible crash,
Eternity roll'd wide apart,
Wide asunder rolling;
Mountainous, all around
Departing, departing, departing,   100
Leaving ruinous fragments of life,
Hanging, frowning cliffs, and, all between,
An Ocean of voidness unfathomable.

4. The roaring fires ran o'er the heav'ns
In whirlwinds and cataracts of blood,   105
And o'er the dark deserts of Urizen
Fires pour thro' the void, on all sides,
On Urizen's self-begotten armies.

5. But no light from the fires! all was darkness
In the flames of Eternal fury.   110

6. In fierce anguish and quenchless flames
To the deserts and rocks he ran raging,
To hide; but he could not. Combining,
He dug mountains and hills in vast strength,
He pilèd them in incessant labour,   115
In howlings and pangs and fierce madness,
Long periods in burning fires labouring;
Till hoary, and age-broke, and agèd,
In despair and the shadows of death.

7. And a roof vast, petrific, around   120
On all sides he fram'd, like a womb,
Where thousands of rivers, in veins
Of blood, pour down the mountains to cool
The eternal fires, beating without
From Eternals; and like a black Globe,   125

The Book of Urizen

View'd by sons of Eternity, standing
On the shore of the infinite ocean,
Like a human heart, struggling and beating,
The vast world of Urizen appear'd.

8. And Los, round the dark globe of Urizen,
Kept watch for Eternals to confine
The obscure separation alone;
For Eternity stood wide apart,
As the stars are apart from the earth.

9. Los wept, howling around the dark Demon,
And cursing his lot; for in anguish
Urizen was rent from his side,
And a fathomless Void for his feet,
And intense fires for his dwelling.

10. But Urizen, laid in a stony sleep,
Unorganiz'd, rent from Eternity.

11. The Eternals said: 'What is this? Death?
Urizen is a clod of clay!'

12. Los howl'd in a dismal stupor,
Groaning, gnashing, groaning,
Till the wrenching apart was heaied.

13. But the wrenching of Urizen heal'd not.
Cold, featureless, flesh or clay,
Rifted with direful changes,
He lay in a dreamless night,

14. Till Los rous'd his fires, affrighted
At the formless, unmeasurable Death.

Chap. IV

1. Los, smitten with astonishment,
Frighten'd at the hurtling bones

The Book of Urizen

2. And at the surging, sulphureous,
Perturbèd, immortal, mad raging

3. In whirlwinds, and pitch, and nitre
Round the furious limbs of Los.

4. And Los formèd nets and gins,
And threw the nets round about.

5. He watch'd in shudd'ring fear
The dark changes, and bound every change
With rivets of iron and brass.

6. And these were the changes of Urizen :—

Chap. IV [A]

1. Ages on ages roll'd over him ;
In stony sleep ages roll'd over him,
Like a dark waste stretching, changeable,
By earthquakes riv'n, belching sullen fires :
On ages roll'd ages in ghastly
Sick torment ; around him in whirlwinds
Of darkness the Eternal Prophet howl'd,
Beating still on his rivets of iron,
Pouring solder of iron ; dividing
The horrible night into watches.

2. And Urizen (so his eternal name)
His prolific delight obscur'd more and more,
In dark secrecy hiding in surging
Sulphureous fluid his phantasies.
The Eternal Prophet heav'd the dark bellows,
And turn'd restless the tongs, and the hammer
Incessant beat, forging chains new and new,
Numb'ring with links hours, days, and years.

3. The Eternal mind, bounded, began to roll
Eddies of wrath, ceaseless, round and round,
And the sulphureous foam, surging thick,

The Book of Urizen

Settled, a lake, bright and shining clear,
White as the snow on the mountains cold.

4. Forgetfulness, dumbness, necessity,
In chains of the mind lockèd up,
Like fetters of ice shrinking together,   190
Disorganiz'd, rent from Eternity,
Los beat on his fetters of iron;
And heated his furnaces, and pour'd
Iron solder and solder of brass.

5. Restless turn'd the Immortal, enchain'd,   195
Heaving dolorous, anguish'd, unbearable;
Till a roof, shaggy, wild, enclos'd
In an orb his fountain of thought.

6. In a horrible, dreamful slumber,
Like the linkèd infernal chain,   200
A vast Spine writh'd in torment
Upon the winds, shooting pain'd
Ribs, like a bending cavern;
And bones of solidness froze
Over all his nerves of joy—   205
And a first Age passèd over,
And a state of dismal woe.

7. From the caverns of his jointed Spine
Down sunk with fright a red
Round Globe, hot, burning, deep,   210
Deep down into the Abyss;
Panting, conglobing, trembling,
Shooting out ten thousand branches
Around his solid bones—
And a second Age passèd over,   215
And a state of dismal woe.

8. In harrowing fear rolling round,
His nervous Brain shot branches

The Book of Urizen

Round the branches of his Heart,
On high, into two little orbs,
And fixèd in two little caves,
Hiding carefully from the wind,
His Eyes beheld the deep—
And a third Age passèd over,
And a state of dismal woe.

9. The pangs of hope began.
In heavy pain, striving, struggling,
Two Ears, in close volutions,
From beneath his orbs of vision
Shot spiring out, and petrified
As they grew—And a fourth Age passèd,
And a state of dismal woe.

10. In ghastly torment sick,
Hanging upon the wind,
Two Nostrils bent down to the deep—
And a fifth Age passèd over,
And a state of dismal woe.

11. In ghastly torment sick,
Within his ribs bloated round
A craving, hungry Cavern;
Thence arose his channell'd Throat,
And, like a red flame, a Tongue
Of thirst and of hunger appear'd—
And a sixth Age passèd over,
And a state of dismal woe.

12. Enragèd and stifled with torment,
He threw his right Arm to the North,
His left Arm to the South,
Snooting out in anguish deep,
And his Feet stamp'd the nether Abyss
In trembling and howling and dismay—

The Book of Urizen

And a [seventh] Age passèd over,
And a state of dismal woe.

Chap. V

1. In terrors Los shrunk from his task:
His great hammer fell from his hand;
His fires beheld, and sickening
Hid their strong limbs in smoke;
For with noises, ruinous, loud,
With hurtlings and clashings and groans,
The Immortal endur'd his chains,
Tho' bound in a deadly sleep.

2. All the myriads of Eternity,
All the wisdom and joy of life
Roll like a sea around him;
Except what his little orbs
Of sight by degrees unfold.

3. And now his Eternal life,
Like a dream, was obliterated.

4. Shudd'ring, the Eternal Prophet smote
With a stroke from his North to South region.
The bellows and hammer are silent now;
A nerveless silence his prophetic voice
Seiz'd; a cold Solitude and dark Void
The Eternal Prophet and Urizen clos'd.

5. Ages on ages roll'd over them,
Cut off from life and light, frozen
Into horrible forms of deformity.
Los suffer'd his fires to decay;

---

252 seventh] second *in the engraved original, but corrected to* seventh *in The Four Zoas*, Night IV, ll. 208-45; *where the whole of this passage from stanza 3 to the end of the chapter is rewritten in a slightly altered form.*

The Book of Urizen

Then he look'd back with anxious desire,
But the Space, undivided by existence,
Struck horror into his soul.

6. Los wept, obscur'd with mourning,
His bosom earthquak'd with sighs;
He saw Urizen, deadly, black,
In his chains bound; and Pity began,

7. In anguish dividing and dividing—
For Pity divides the soul—
In pangs, Eternity on Eternity,
Life in cataracts pour'd down his cliffs.
The Void shrunk the lymph into Nerves,
Wand'ring wide on the bosom of night,
And left a round globe of blood
Trembling upon the Void.
Thus the Eternal Prophet was divided
Before the death image of Urizen;
For in changeable clouds and darkness,
In a winterly night beneath,
The Abyss of Los stretch'd immense;
And now seen, now obscur'd, to the eyes
Of Eternals the visions remote
Of the dark separation appear'd:
As glasses discover Worlds
In the endless Abyss of space,
So the expanding eyes of Immortals
Beheld the dark visions of Los,
And the globe of life-blood trembling.

8. The globe of life-blood trembled,
Branching out into roots,
Fibrous, writhing upon the winds,
Fibres of blood, milk, and tears,
In pangs, Eternity on Eternity.
At length in tears and cries embodied,

The Book of Urizen

A Female form, trembling and pale,
Waves before his deathy face.

9. All Eternity shudder'd at sight   315
Of the first Female, now separate,
Pale as a cloud of snow,
Waving before the face of Los.

10. Wonder, awe, fear, astonishment
Petrify the Eternal myriads   320
At the first Female form now separate.
They call'd her Pity, and fled.

11. 'Spread a Tent with strong curtains around them!
Let cords and stakes bind in the Void,
That Eternals may no more behold them.'   325

12. They began to weave curtains of darkness,
They erected large pillars round the Void,
With golden hooks fasten'd in the pillars;
With infinite labour the Eternals
A woof wove, and callèd it Science.   330

Chap. VI

1. But Los saw the Female, and pitièd;
He embrac'd her; she wept, she refus'd;
In perverse and cruel delight
She fled from his arms, yet he follow'd.

2. Eternity shudder'd when they saw   335
Man begetting his likeness
On his own Divided Image!

3. A time passèd over: the Eternals
Began to erect the tent,
When Enitharmon, sick,   340
Felt a Worm within her womb.

The Book of Urizen

4. Yet helpless it lay, like a Worm
In the trembling womb,
To be moulded into existence.

5. All day the Worm lay on her bosom;
All night within her womb
The Worm lay till it grew to a Serpent,
With dolorous hissings and poisons
Round Enitharmon's loins folding.

6. Coil'd within Enitharmon's womb
The Serpent grew, casting its scales;
With sharp pangs the hissings began
To change to a grating cry—
Many sorrows and dismal throes,
Many forms of fish, bird, and beast
Brought forth an Infant form
Where was a Worm before.

7. The Eternals their tent finishèd,
Alarm'd with these gloomy visions,
When Enitharmon, groaning,
Produc'd a Man-Child to the light.

8. A shriek ran thro' Eternity,
And a paralytic stroke,
At the birth of the Human Shadow.

9. Delving earth in his resistless way,
Howling, the Child with fierce flames
Issu'd from Enitharmon.

10. The Eternals closèd the tent;
They beat down the stakes, the cords
Stretch'd for a work of Eternity—
No more Los beheld Eternity!

11. In his hands he seiz'd the Infant,
He bathèd him in springs of sorrow,
He gave him to Enitharmon.

The Book of Urizen

Chap. VII

1. They namèd the child Orc; he grew, 375
Fed with milk of Enitharmon.

2. Los awoke her.   O sorrow and pain!
A tight'ning girdle grew
Around his bosom.   In sobbings
He burst the girdle in twain; 380
But still another girdle
Oppress'd his bosom.   In sobbings
Again he burst it.   Again
Another girdle succeeds.
The girdle was form'd by day; 385
By night was burst in twain.

3. These falling down on the Rock
Into an iron Chain,
In each other link by link lock'd.

4. They took Orc to the top of a mountain. 390
O how Enitharmon wept!
They chain'd his young limbs to the Rock
With the Chain of Jealousy,
Beneath Urizen's deathful Shadow.

5. The Dead heard the voice of the Child, 395
And began to awake from sleep;
All things heard the voice of the Child,
And began to awake to life.

6. And Urizen, craving with hunger,
Stung with the odours of Nature, 400
Explor'd his dens around.

7. He form'd a line and a plummet
To divide the Abyss beneath;
He form'd a dividing rule;

The Book of Urizen

8. He formèd scales to weigh,
He formèd massy weights;
He formèd a brazen quadrant;
He formèd golden compasses,
And began to explore the Abyss;
And he planted a garden of fruits.

9. But Los encircled Enitharmon
With fires of Prophecy
From the sight of Urizen and Orc.

10. And she bore an enormous race.

Chap. VIII

1. Urizen explor'd his dens,
Mountain, moor, and wilderness,
With a globe of fire lighting his journey—
A fearful journey, annoy'd
By cruel enormities, forms
Of life on his forsaken mountains.

2. And his World teem'd vast enormities,
Fright'ning, faithless, fawning,
Portions of life, similitudes
Of a foot, or a hand, or a head,
Or a heart, or an eye; they swam mischievous,
Dread terrors, delighting in blood!

3. Most Urizen sicken'd to see
His eternal creations appear,
Sons and daughters of sorrow, on mountains,
Weeping, wailing. First Thiriel appear'd,
Astonish'd at his own existence,
Like a man from a cloud born; and Utha,
From the waters emerging, laments;
Grodna rent the deep earth, howling,
Amaz'd; his heavens immense crack

The Book of Urizen

Like the ground parch'd with heat; then Fuzon
Flam'd out, first begotten, last born;
All his Eternal sons in like manner;
His daughters, from green herbs and cattle,
From monsters and worms of the pit. 440

4. He in darkness clos'd view'd all his race,
And his soul sicken'd! He curs'd
Both sons and daughters; for he saw
That no flesh nor spirit could keep
His iron laws one moment. 445

5. For he saw that Life liv'd upon Death:
The Ox in the slaughter-house moans;
The Dog at the wintry door;
And he wept, and he callèd it Pity,
And his tears flowèd down on the winds. 450

6. Cold he wander'd on high, over their Cities,
In weeping and pain and woe;
And wherever he wander'd, in sorrows
Upon the agèd Heavens,
A cold Shadow follow'd behind him 455
Like a spider's web, moist, cold, and dim,
Drawing out from his sorrowing soul,
The dungeon-like heaven dividing,
Wherever the footsteps of Urizen
Walkèd over the cities in sorrow; 460

7. Till a Web, dark and cold, throughout all
The tormented element stretch'd
From the sorrows of Urizen's soul.
And the Web is a Female in embryo;
None could break the Web, no wings of fire, 465

8. So twisted the cords, and so knotted
The meshes, twisted like to the human brain.

9. And all call'd it the Net of Religion.

The Book of Urizen

Chap. IX

1. Then the Inhabitants of those Cities
Felt their Nerves change into Marrow,
And hardening Bones began
In swift diseases and torments,
In throbbings and shootings and grindings,
Thro' all the coasts; till weaken'd
The Senses inward rush'd, shrinking
Beneath the dark Net of infection;

2. Till the shrunken eyes, clouded over,
Discern'd not the woven Hypocrisy;
But the streaky slime in their heavens,
Brought together by narrowing perceptions,
Appear'd transparent air; for their eyes
Grew small like the eyes of a man,
And, in reptile forms shrinking together,
Of seven feet stature they remain'd.

3. Six days they shrunk up from existence,
And on the seventh day they rested,
And they bless'd the seventh day, in sick hope,
And forgot their Eternal life.

4. And their Thirty Cities divided
In form of a Human Heart.
No more could they rise at will
In the infinite Void, but bound down
To earth by their narrowing perceptions,
They livèd a period of years;
Then left a noisome body
To the jaws of devouring darkness.

5. And their children wept, and built
Tombs in the desolate places,
And form'd Laws of Prudence, and call'd them
The Eternal Laws of God.

The Book of Urizen

6. And the Thirty Cities remain'd,
Surrounded by salt floods, now call'd
Africa : its name was then Egypt.

7. The remaining sons of Urizen
Beheld their brethren shrink together
Beneath the Net of Urizen.
Persuasion was in vain ;
For the ears of the inhabitants
Were wither'd and deafen'd and cold,
And their eyes could not discern
Their brethren of other cities.

8. So Fuzon call'd all together
The remaining children of Urizen,
And they left the pendulous earth.
They callèd it Egypt, and left it.

9. And the salt Ocean rollèd englob'd.

THE END OF THE FIRST BOOK OF URIZEN

THE SONG of LOS

Lambeth Printed by W Blake 1795

THE
SONG OF LOS

(Engraved 1795)

Africa

I will sing you a song of Los, the Eternal Prophet:
He sung it to four harps, at the tables of Eternity,
In heart-formèd Africa.
Urizen faded! Ariston shudder'd!
And thus the Song began:—

Adam stood in the garden of Eden,
And Noah on the mountains of Ararat;
They saw Urizen give his Laws to the Nations
By the hands of the children of Los.

Adam shudder'd! Noah faded! Black grew the sunny African
When Rintrah gave Abstract Philosophy to Brahma in the East.
(Night spoke to the Cloud:
'Lo! these Human-form'd spirits, in smiling hypocrisy, war
Against one another; so let them war on, slaves to the eternal
    elements.')
Noah shrunk beneath the waters,
Abram fled in fires from Chaldaea;
Moses beheld upon Mount Sinai forms of dark delusion.

To Trismegistus, Palamabron gave an abstract Law;
To Pythagoras, Socrates, and Plato.

Times rollèd on o'er all the sons of Har: time after time

The Song of Los

Orc on Mount Atlas howl'd, chain'd down with the Chain of
    Jealousy;
Then Oothoon hover'd over Judah and Jerusalem,
And Jesus heard her voice—a Man of Sorrows!—He receiv'd
A Gospel from wretched Theotormon.

The human race began to wither; for the healthy built   25
Secluded places, fearing the joys of Love,
And the diseasèd only propagated.
So Antamon call'd up Leutha from her valleys of delight,
And to Mahomet a loose Bible gave;
But in the North, to Odin, Sotha gave a Code of War,   30
Because of Diralada, thinking to reclaim his joy.

These were the Churches, Hospitals, Castles, Palaces,
Like nets and gins and traps, to catch the joys of Eternity,
        And all the rest a desert;
Till, like a dream, Eternity was obliterated and erasèd,   35

Since that dread day when Har and Heva fled,
Because their brethren and sisters liv'd in War and Lust;
And, as they fled, they shrunk
Into two narrow doleful forms,
Creeping in reptile flesh upon   40
The bosom of the ground;
And all the vast of Nature shrunk
Before their shrunken eyes.

Thus the terrible race of Los and Enitharmon gave
Laws and Religions to the sons of Har, binding them more   45
And more to Earth, closing and restraining;
Till a Philosophy of Five Senses was complete:
Urizen wept, and gave it into the hands of Newton and Locke.

Clouds roll heavy upon the Alps round Rousseau and Voltaire,
And on the mountains of Lebanon round the deceasèd Gods   50
Of Asia, and on the deserts of Africa round the Fallen Angels.
The Guardian Prince of Albion burns in his nightly tent.

The Song of Los

Asia

> The Kings of Asia heard
> The howl rise up from Europe,
> And each ran out from his Web,
> From his ancient woven Den;
> For the darkness of Asia was startled
> At the thick-flaming, thought-creating fires of Orc.
>
> And the Kings of Asia stood
> And crièd in bitterness of soul :—
>
> 'Shall not the King call for Famine from the heath,
> Nor the Priest for Pestilence from the fen,
> To restrain, to dismay, to thin
> The inhabitants of mountain and plain,
> In the day of full-feeding prosperity
> And the night of delicious songs?
>
> Shall not the Counsellor throw his curb
> Of Poverty on the laborious,
> To fix the price of labour,
> To invent allegoric riches?
>
> And the privy admonishers of men
> Call for Fires in the City,
> For heaps of smoking ruins,
> In the night of prosperity and wantonness,
>
> To turn man from his path,
> To restrain the child from the womb,
> To cut off the bread from the city;
> That the remnant may learn to obey,
>
> That the pride of the heart may fail,
> That the lust of the eyes may be quench'd,
> That the delicate ear in its infancy
> May be dull'd, and the nostrils clos'd up,
> To teach Mortal Worms the path
> That leads from the gates of the Grave?'

The Song of Los

Urizen heard them cry,
And his shudd'ring, waving wings
Went enormous above the red flames, 35
Drawing clouds of despair thro' the Heavens
Of Europe as he went.
And his Books of brass, iron, and gold
Melted over the land as he flew,
Heavy-waving, howling, weeping. 40

And he stood over Judaea,
And stay'd in his ancient place,
And stretch'd his clouds over Jerusalem;

For Adam, a mouldering skeleton,
Lay bleach'd on the garden of Eden; 45
And Noah, as white as snow,
On the mountains of Ararat.

Then the thunders of Urizen bellow'd aloud
From his woven darkness above.

Orc, raging in European darkness, 50
Arose like a pillar of fire above the Alps,
Like a serpent of fiery flame!
      The sullen Earth
      Shrunk!

Forth from the dead dust, rattling bones to bones 55
Join. Shaking, convuls'd, the shiv'ring Clay breathes,
And all Flesh naked stands: Fathers and Friends,
Mothers and Infants, Kings and Warriors.

The Grave shrieks with delight, and shakes
Her hollow womb, and clasps the solid stem: 60
Her bosom swells with wild desire;
And milk and blood and glandous wine
In rivers rush, and shout and dance,
On mountain, dale, and plain.

      THE SONG OF LOS IS ENDED
         Urizen Wept.

THE BOOK of LOS

LAMBETH
Printed by W Blake 1795

THE
BOOK OF LOS

(Engraved 1795)

Chap. I

1. Eno, agèd Mother,
Who the chariot of Leutha guides,
Since the day of thunders in old time,

2. Sitting beneath the eternal Oak,
Trembled and shook the steadfast Earth,
And thus her speech broke forth:—

3. 'O Times remote!
When Love and Joy were adoration,
And none impure were deem'd,
Not eyeless Covet,
Nor thin-lipp'd Envy,
Nor bristled Wrath,
Nor Curlèd Wantonness;

4. 'But Covet was pourèd full,
Envy fed with fat of lambs,
Wrath with lion's gore,
Wantonness lull'd to sleep
With the virgin's lute,
Or sated with her love;

5. 'Till Covet broke his locks and bars,
And slept with open doors;
Envy sung at the rich man's feast;
Wrath was follow'd up and down

The Book of Los

By a little ewe lamb;
And Wantonness on his own true love
Begot a giant race.

6. Raging furious, the flames of desire
Ran thro' heaven and earth, living flames,
Intelligent, organiz'd, arm'd
With destruction and plagues. In the midst
The Eternal Prophet, bound in a chain,
Compell'd to watch Urizen's shadow,

7. Rag'd with curses and sparkles of fury:
Round the flames roll, as Los hurls his chains,
Mounting up from his fury, condens'd.
Rolling round and round, mounting on high
Into Vacuum, into nonentity,
Where nothing was; dash'd wide apart,
His feet stamp the eternal fierce-raging
Rivers of wide flame; they roll round
And round on all sides, making their way
Into darkness and shadowy obscurity.

8. Wide apart stood the fires: Los remain'd
In the Void between fire and fire:
In trembling and horror they beheld him;
They stood wide apart, driv'n by his hands
And his feet, which the nether Abyss
Stamp'd in fury and hot indignation.

9. But no light from the fires! all was
Darkness round Los: heat was not; for bound up
Into fiery spheres from his fury,
The gigantic flames trembled and hid.

10. Coldness, darkness, obstruction, a Solid
Without fluctuation, hard as adamant,
Black as marble of Egypt, impenetrable,
Bound in the fierce raging Immortal;
And the separated fires, froze in

The Book of Los

A vast Solid, without fluctuation,
Bound in his expanding clear senses.

Chap. II

1 The Immortal stood frozen amidst
The vast Rock of Eternity, times
And times, a night of vast durance,
Impatient, stifled, stiffen'd, hard'ned;

2. Till impatience no longer could bear
The hard bondage: rent, rent, the vast Solid,
With a crash from Immense to Immense,

3. Crack'd across into numberless fragments
The Prophetic wrath, struggling for vent,
Hurls apart, stamping furious to dust,
And crumbling with bursting sobs, heaves
The black marble on high into fragments.

4. Hurl'd apart on all sides as a falling
Rock, the innumerable fragments away
Fell asunder; and horrible Vacuum
Beneath him, and on all sides round,

5. 'Falling! falling! Los fell and fell,
Sunk precipitant, heavy, down! down!
Times on times, night on night, day on day—
Truth has bounds, Error none—falling, falling,
Years on years, and ages on ages;
Still he fell thro' the Void, still a Void
Found for falling, day and night without end:
For tho' day or night was not, their spaces
Were measur'd by his incessant whirls
In the horrid Vacuity bottomless.

6. The Immortal revolving, indignant,
First in wrath threw his limbs, like the babe

337

The Book of Los

New-born into our world: wrath subsided,
And contemplative thoughts first arose;
Then aloft his head rear'd in the Abyss,
And his downward-borne fall chang'd oblique.

7. Many ages of groans! till there grew
Branchy forms, organizing the Human
Into finite inflexible organs;

8. Till in process from falling he bore
Sidelong on the purple air, wafting
The weak breeze in efforts o'erwearièd:

9. Incessant the falling Mind labour'd
Organizing itself, till the Vacuum
Became Element, pliant to rise,
Or to fall, or to swim, or to fly,
With ease searching the dire Vacuity.

Chap. III

1. The Lungs heave incessant, dull, and heavy;
For as yet were all other parts formless,
Shiv'ring, clinging around like a cloud,
Dim and glutinous as the white Polypus,
Driv'n by waves and englob'd on the tide.

2. And the unformèd part crav'd repose;
Sleep began; the Lungs heave on the wave:
Weary, overweigh'd, sinking beneath
In a stifling black fluid, he woke.

3. He arose on the waters; but soon
Heavy falling, his organs like roots
Shooting out from the seed, shot beneath,
And a vast World of Waters around him
In furious torrents began.

The Book of Los

4. Then he sunk, and around his spent Lungs
Began intricate pipes that drew in
The spawn of the waters, outbranching
An immense Fibrous Form, stretching out
Thro' the bottoms of Immensity: raging.

5. He rose on the floods; then he smote
The wild deep with his terrible wrath,
Separating the heavy and thin.

6. Down the heavy sunk, cleaving around
To the fragments of Solid: uprose
The thin, flowing round the fierce fires
That glow'd furious in the Expanse.

Chap. IV

1. Then Light first began: from the fires,
Beams, conducted by fluid so pure,
Flow'd around the Immense.   Los beheld
Forthwith, writhing upon the dark Void,
The Backbone of Urizen appear,
Hurtling upon the wind,
Like a serpent, like an iron chain,
Whirling about in the Deep.

2. Upfolding his Fibres together
To a Form of impregnable strength,
Los, astonish'd and terrifièd, built
Furnaces; he formed an Anvil,
A Hammer of adamant: then began
The binding of Urizen day and night.

3. Circling round the dark Demon with howlings,
Dismay, and sharp blightings, the Prophet
Of Eternity beat on his iron links.

4. And first from those Infinite fires,
The light that flow'd down on the winds

The Book of Los

He seiz'd, beating incessant, condensing
The subtil particles in an Orb.

5. Roaring indignant, the bright sparks
Endur'd the vast Hammer; but unwearièd
Los beat on the Anvil, till glorious
An immense Orb of fire he fram'd.

6. Oft he quench'd it beneath in the Deeps;
Then survey'd the all-bright mass.   Again
Seizing fires from the terrific Orbs,
He heated the round Globe, then beat;
While, roaring, his Furnaces endur'd
The chain'd Orb in their infinite wombs.

7. Nine ages completed their circles,
When Los heated the glowing mass, casting
It down into the Deeps: the Deeps fled
Away in redounding smoke: the Sun
Stood self-balanc'd.   And Los smil'd with joy:
He the vast Spine of Urizen seiz'd,
And bound down to the glowing Illusion.

8. But no light! for the Deep fled away
On all sides, and left an unform'd
Dark Vacuity: here Urizen lay
In fierce torments on his glowing bed;

9. Till his Brain in a rock, and his Heart
In a fleshy slough, formèd four rivers,
Obscuring the immense Orb of fire,
Flowing down into night; till a Form
Was completed, a Human Illusion,
In darkness and deep clouds involv'd.

THE END OF THE BOOK OF LOS

THE BOOK of AHANIA

LAMBETH
Printed by W Blake 1795

THE
BOOK OF AHANIA

(Engraved 1795)

Chap. I

1. Fuzon, on a chariot iron-wing'd,
On spikèd flames rose; his hot visage
Flam'd furious; sparkles his hair and beard
Shot down his wide bosom and shoulders.
On clouds of smoke rages his chariot,
And his right hand burns red in its cloud,
Moulding into a vast Globe his wrath,
As the thunder-stone is moulded,
Son of Urizen's silent burnings.

2. 'Shall we worship this Demon of smoke,'
Said Fuzon, 'this abstract Nonentity,
This cloudy God seated on waters,
Now seen, now obscur'd, King of Sorrow?'

3. So he spoke in a fiery flame,
On Urizen frowning indignant,
The Globe of wrath shaking on high.
Roaring with fury, he threw
The howling Globe; burning it flew,
Length'ning into a hungry beam. Swiftly,

4. Oppos'd to the exulting flam'd beam,
The broad Disk of Urizen upheav'd
Across the Void many a mile.

5. It was forg'd in mills where the winter
Beats incessant: ten winters the disk,
Unremitting, endur'd the cold hammer.

The Book of Ahania

6. But the strong arm that sent it remember'd
The sounding beam: laughing, it tore through
That beaten mass, keeping its direction,
The cold loins of Urizen dividing.

7. Dire shriek'd his invisible Lust! 30
Deep groan'd Urizen; stretching his awful hand,
Ahania (so name his parted Soul)
He seiz'd on his mountains of Jealousy.
He groan'd, anguish'd, and callèd her Sin,
Kissing her and weeping over her; 35
Then hid her in darkness, in silence,
Jealous, tho' she was invisible.

8. She fell down, a faint Shadow, wand'ring
In Chaos, and circling dark Urizen,
As the moon, anguish'd, circles the earth, 40
Hopeless! abhorr'd! a death-shadow,
Unseen, unbodièd, unknown,
The mother of Pestilence!

9. But the fiery beam of Fuzon
Was a pillar of fire to Egypt, 45
Five hundred years wand'ring on earth,
Till Los seiz'd it, and beat in a mass
With the body of the sun.

Chap. II

1. But the forehead of Urizen gathering,
And his eyes pale with anguish, his lips 50
Blue and changing, in tears and bitter
Contrition he prepar'd his Bow,

2. Form'd of Ribs, that in his dark solitude,
When obscur'd in his forests, fell monsters

342

The Book of Ahania

Arose.   For his dire Contemplations 55
Rush'd down like floods from his mountains,
In torrents of mud settling thick,
With eggs of unnatural production:
Forthwith hatching, some howl'd on his hills,
Some in vales, some aloft flew in air. 60

3. Of these, an enormous dread Serpent,
Scalèd and poisonous, hornèd,
Approach'd Urizen, even to his knees,
As he sat on his dark-rooted Oak.

4. With his horns he push'd furious: 65
Great the conflict and great the jealousy
In cold poisons; but Urizen smote him!

5. First he poison'd the rocks with his blood,
Then polish'd his ribs, and his sinews
Drièd, laid them apart till winter; 70
Then a Bow black prepar'd: on this Bow
A poisonèd Rock plac'd in silence.
He utter'd these words to the Bow:—

6. 'O Bow of the clouds of Secrecy!
O nerve of that lust-form'd monster! 75
Send this Rock swift, invisible, thro'
The black clouds on the bosom of Fuzon.'

7. So saying, in torment of his wounds
He bent the enormous ribs slowly—
A circle of darkness!—then fixèd 80
The sinew in its rest; then the Rock,
Poisonous source, plac'd with art, lifting difficult
Its weighty bulk.   Silent the Rock lay,

8. While Fuzon, his tigers unloosing,
Thought Urizen slain by his wrath. 85
'I am God!' said he, 'eldest of things.'

The Book of Ahania

9. Sudden sings the Rock; swift and invisible
On Fuzon flew, enter'd his bosom;
His beautiful visage, his tresses,
That gave light to the mornings of heaven, 90
Were smitten with darkness, deform'd,
And outstretch'd on the edge of the forest.

10. But the Rock fell upon the Earth,
Mount Sinai, in Arabia.

Chap. III

1. The Globe shook, and Urizen, seated 95
On black clouds, his sore wound anointed;
The ointment flow'd down on the Void
Mix'd with blood—here the snake gets her poison!

2. With difficulty and great pain Urizen
Lifted on high the dead corse: 100
On his shoulders he bore it to where
A Tree hung over the Immensity.

3. For when Urizen shrunk away
From Eternals, he sat on a Rock,
Barren—a Rock which himself, 105
From redounding fancies, had petrifièd.
Many tears fell on the Rock,
Many sparks of vegetation.
Soon shot the painèd root
Of Mystery under his heel: 110
It grew a thick tree: he wrote
In silence his Book of Iron;
Till the horrid plant bending its boughs,
Grew to roots when it felt the earth,
And again sprung to many a tree. 115

The Book of Ahania

4. Amaz'd started Urizen when
He beheld himself compassèd round
And high-roofèd over with trees.
He arose, but the stems stood so thick,
He with difficulty and great pain   120
Brought his Books—all but the Book
Of Iron—from the dismal shade.

5. The Tree still grows over the Void,
Enrooting itself all around,
An endless labyrinth of woe!   125

6. The corse of his first begotten
On the accursèd Tree of Mystery,
On the topmost stem of this Tree
Urizen nail'd Fuzon's corse.

Chap. IV

1. Forth flew the arrows of Pestilence   130
Round the pale living Corse on the Tree.

2. For in Urizen's slumbers of abstraction,
In the infinite ages of Eternity,
When his Nerves of Joy melted and flow'd,
A white Lake on the dark blue air,   135
In perturb'd pain and dismal torment,
Now stretching out, now swift conglobing,

3. Effluvia vapour'd above
In noxious clouds; these hover'd thick
Over the disorganiz'd Immortal,   140
Till petrific pain scurf'd o'er the Lakes,
As the bones of Man, solid and dark.

4. The clouds of Disease hover'd wide
Around the Immortal in torment,

The Book of Ahania

Perching around the hurtling bones—
Disease on disease, shape on shape,
Wingèd, screaming in blood and torment!

5. The Eternal Prophet beat on his Anvils,
Enrag'd in the desolate darkness;
He forg'd Nets of iron around,
And Los threw them around the bones.

6. The Shapes, screaming, flutter'd vain:
Some combin'd into muscles and glands,
Some organs for craving and lust;
Most remain'd on the tormented Void-
Urizen's army of horrors!

7. Round the pale living Corse on the Tree,
Forty years, flew the arrows of Pestilence.

8. Wailing and terror and woe
Ran thro' all his dismal world;
Forty years all his sons and daughters
Felt their skulls harden; then Asia
Arose in the pendulous deep.

9. They reptilize upon the Earth.

10. Fuzon groan'd on the Tree.

Chap. V

1. The lamenting voice of Ahania,
Weeping upon the Void!
And round the Tree of Fuzon,
Distant in solitary night,
Her voice was heard, but no form
Had she; but her tears from clouds
Eternal fell round the Tree.

2. And the voice cried: 'Ah, Urizen! Love!

The Book of Ahania

Flower of morning! I weep on the verge
Of Nonentity—how wide the Abyss
Between Ahania and thee!

3. 'I lie on the verge of the deep;
I see thy dark clouds ascend;
I see thy black forests and floods,
A horrible waste to my eyes!

4. 'Weeping I walk over rocks,
Over dens, and thro' valleys of death.
Why didst thou despise Ahania,
To cast me from thy bright presence
Into the World of Loneness?

5. 'I cannot touch his hand,
Nor weep on his knees, nor hear
His voice and bow, nor see his eyes
And joy; nor hear his footsteps, and
My heart leap at the lovely sound!
I cannot kiss the place
Whereon his bright feet have trod;
But I wander on the rocks
With hard necessity.

6. 'Where is my golden palace?
Where my ivory bed?
Where the joy of my morning hour?
Where the Sons of Eternity singing,

7. 'To awake bright Urizen, my King,
To arise to the mountain sport,
To the bliss of eternal valleys;

8. 'To awake my King in the morn,
To embrace Ahania's joy
On the breath of his open bosom,
From my soft cloud of dew to fall
In showers of life on his harvests?

The Book of Ahania

9. 'When he gave my happy soul
To the Sons of Eternal Joy;
When he took the Daughters of Life
Into my chambers of love; 210

10. 'When I found Babes of bliss on my beds,
And bosoms of milk in my chambers,
Fill'd with eternal seed—
O! eternal births sung round Ahania,
In interchange sweet of their joys! 215

11. 'Swell'd with ripeness and fat with fatness,
Bursting on winds, my odours,
My ripe figs and rich pomegranates,
In infant joy at thy feet,
O Urizen! sported and sang. 220

12. 'Then thou with thy lap full of seed,
With thy hand full of generous fire,
Walkèd forth from the clouds of morning;
On the virgins of springing joy,
On the Human soul to cast 225
The seed of eternal Science.

13. 'The sweat pourèd down thy temples,
To Ahania return'd in evening;
The moisture awoke to birth
My mother's joys, sleeping in bliss. 230

14. 'But now alone! over rocks, mountains,
Cast out from thy lovely bosom!
Cruel Jealousy, selfish Fear,
Self-destroying! how can delight
Renew in these chains of darkness, 235
Where bones of beasts are strown
On the bleak and snowy mountains,
Where bones from the birth are burièd
Before they see the light?'

FINIS

VALA

OR

The Death and

Judgement

of the

Ancient Man

a DREAM
of Nine Nights
by William Blake 1797

SELECTIONS FROM
THE FOUR ZOAS
SOMETIMES CALLED
'*VALA*'
(MS. *circa* 1797–1804)

[Introduction to Night the First]

The song of the Agèd Mother, which shook the heavens with wrath,
Hearing the march of long-resounding, strong, heroic Verse,
Marshall'd in order for the day of Intellectual Battle.

Four Mighty Ones are in every Man : a perfect Unity
Cannot exist but from the Universal Brotherhood of Eden,   5
The Universal Man, to Whom be glory evermore. Amen.
What are the Natures of those Living Creatures the Heavenly Father only
Knoweth : no Individual knoweth, nor can know in all Eternity.

Four Zoas, Night I, ll. 1-8

1-3 *Originally beginning with* :
               This is the Song of Eno . . . Vala
Blake altered this to :
  1 The Song of the Agèd Mother, which shook the heavens with wrath,
  2 And thus beginneth the Book of Vala, which whosoever reads
  3 If with his Intellect he comprehend . . .
  6 The heavens shall quake ; the Earth shall move and thunder, and the mountains
  7 With all their woods : the streams and valleys wail'd in dismal fear.
  4 To hear the sound of long resounding strong heroic verse,
  5 Marshall'd in order for the day of Intellectual Battle—
indicating the sequence of lines by the prefixed numerals. Later he deleted ll. 2, 3, 6, 7, *changed* To hear the sound *in l.* 4 *to* Hearing the march, *and again numbered the remaining lines in the order given in my text.*

Selections from 'The Four Zoas'

[The Wanderer]

Enion brooded o'er the rocks: the rough rocks groaning vegetate—
Such power was given to the solitary Wanderer—
The barkèd Oak, the long-limb'd Beech, the Chestnut-tree, the Pine,
The Pear-tree mild, the frowning Walnut, the sharp Crab, and
    Apple sweet;   4
The rough bark opens, twittering peep forth little beaks and wings,
The Nightingale, the Goldfinch, Robin, Lark, Linnet and Thrush;
The Goat leap'd from the craggy cliff, the Sheep awoke from the
    mould;
Upon its green stalk rose the Corn, waving innumerable,
Enfolding the bright infants from the desolating winds.

Four Zoas, Night I, from a deleted passage following l. 121.

[A Vision of Eternity]

Eternity appear'd above them as One Man, enfolded
In Luvah's robes of blood, and bearing all his afflictions:
As the sun shines down on the misty earth, such was the Vision.
But purple Night, and crimson Morning, and golden Day, descending
Thro' the clear changing atmosphere, display'd green fields among
The varying clouds, like Paradises stretch'd in the expanse,   6
With towns, and villages, and temples, tents, sheep-folds and
    pastures,
Where dwell the children of the Elemental worlds in harmony.

Ibid., Night II, ll. 107-12.

[The Song sung at the Feast of Los and Enitharmon]

The Mountain callèd out to the Mountain: 'Awake, O Brother
    Mountain!
Let us refuse the Plough and Spade, the heavy Roller and spikèd
Harrow; burn all these corn-fields; throw down all these fences!

  A Vision of Eternity] Cp. the lines in a letter to Butts, dated Felpham,
Oct. 2, 1800 (pp. 184-6 of this ed.).
  The Song] 1 The Mountain callèd out to the Mountain *changed afterwards
to the more symbolic* Ephraim callèd out to Zion.

Selections from 'The Four Zoas'

Fatten'd on human blood, and drunk with wine of life is better far
Than all these labours of the harvest and the vintage. See the river, 5
Red with the blood of Men, swells lustful round my rocky knees:
My clouds are not the clouds of verdant fields and groves of fruit,
But Clouds of Human Souls: my nostrils drink the Lives of Men.

'The Villages lament, they faint, outstretch'd upon the plain:
Wailing runs round the Valleys from the mill and from the barn:
But most the polish'd Palaces, dark, silent, bow with dread, 11
Hiding their books and pictures underneath the dens of Earth.

'The Cities send to one another saying: "My sons are mad
With wine of cruelty! Let us plait a scourge, O Sister City!
Children are nourish'd for the slaughter. Once the child was fed
With milk; but wherefore now are children fed with blood?"' 16

Four Zoas, Night II, ll. 128-43.

[The Song of Enitharmon over Los]

I seize the sphery harp, strike the strings!

At the first sound the golden Sun arises from the deep,
And shakes his awful hair;
The Echo wakes the moon to unbind her silver locks:
The golden Sun bears on my song, 5
And nine bright Spheres of harmony rise round the fiery king.

The joy of Woman is the death of her most best-belovèd,
Who dies for love of her
In torments of fierce jealousy and pangs of adoration:
The Lovers' night bears on my song, 10
And the nine Spheres rejoice beneath my powerful control.

They sing unceasing to the notes of my immortal hand.
The solemn, silent Moon
Reverberates the living harmony upon my limbs;
The birds and beasts rejoice and play,
And every one seeks for his mate to prove his inmost joy 15

1 harp] harps *MS. 1st rdg.*

351

Selections from 'The Four Zoas'

Furious and terrible they sport and rend the nether Deep;
The Deep lifts up his rugged head,
And, lost in infinite humming wings, vanishes with a cry.
The fading cry is ever dying: 20
The living voice is ever living in its inmost joy.

Arise, you little glancing wings and sing your infant joy!
Arise and drink your bliss!
For everything that lives is holy; for the Source of Life
Descends to be a Weeping Babe; 25
For the Earthworm renews the moisture of the sandy plain.

Now my left hand I stretch to Earth beneath,
And strike the terrible string.
I wake sweet joy in dens of sorrow, and I plant a smile
In forests of affliction, 30
And wake the bubbling springs of life in regions of dark death.

O, I am weary! Lay thine hand upon me, or I faint.
I faint beneath these beams of thine;
For thou hast touchèd my five Senses, and they answer'd thee.
Now I am nothing, and I sink, 35
And on the bed of silence sleep, till thou awakest me.

Four Zoas, Night II, ll. 551-86.

[The Wail of Enion]

I am made to sow the thistle for wheat, the nettle for a nourishing dainty:
I have planted a false oath in the earth; it has brought forth a Poison Tree:
I have chosen the serpent for a counsellor, and the dog
For a schoolmaster to my children:
I have blotted out from light and living the dove and nightingale,
And I have causèd the earthworm to beg from door to door: 6
I have taught the thief a secret path into the house of the just:
I have taught pale Artifice to spread his nets upon the morning

Wail of Enion] 3-4 Cp. *Visions of the Daughters of Albion*, ll. 119-20 (p. 289 of this ed.).

Selections from 'The Four Zoas'

My heavens are brass, my earth is iron, my moon a clod of clay,
My sun a pestilence burning at noon, and a vapour of death in
    night.   10

What is the price of Experience? Do men buy it for a song,
Or Wisdom for a dance in the street? No! it is bought with the
    price
Of all that a man hath—his house, his wife, his children.
Wisdom is sold in the desolate market where none come to buy,
And in the wither'd field where the farmer ploughs for bread in
    vain.   15

It is an easy thing to triumph in the summer's sun,
And in the vintage, and to sing on the waggon loaded with corn:
It is an easy thing to talk of patience to the afflicted,
To speak the laws of prudence to the houseless wanderer,
To listen to the hungry raven's cry in wintry season,   20
When the red blood is fill'd with wine and with the marrow of
    lambs:

It is an easy thing to laugh at wrathful elements;
To hear the dog howl at the wintry door, the ox in the slaughter-
    house moan;
To see a God on every wind and a blessing on every blast;
To hear sounds of Love in the thunderstorm that destroys our
    enemy's house;   25
To rejoice in the blight that covers his field, and the sickness that
    cuts off his children,
While our olive and vine sing and laugh round our door, and our
    children bring fruits and flowers.

Then the groan and the dolour are quite forgotten, and the slave
    grinding at the mill,
And the captive in chains, and the poor in the prison, and the
    soldier in the field
When the shatter'd bone hath laid him groaning among the
    happier dead: 30

Selections from 'The Four Zoas'

It is an easy thing to rejoice in the tents of prosperity—
Thus would I sing and thus rejoice; but it is not so with me.

Four Zoas, Night II, ll. 595-626.

[Winter]

Still the faint harps and silver voices calm the weary couch;
But from the caves of deepest Night, ascending in clouds of mist,
The Winter spread his wide black wings across from pole to pole;
Grim Frost beneath and terrible Snow, link'd in a marriage chain,
Began a dismal dance. The Winds around on pointed rocks   5
Settled like bats innumerable, ready to fly abroad.

Ibid, Night V, ll. 30-5.

[The Woes of Urizen in the Dens of Urthona]

Ah! how shall Urizen the King submit to this dark mansion?
Ah! how is this? Once on the heights I stretch'd my throne sublime.
The mountains of Urizen, once of silver, where the sons of wisdom dwelt,
And on whose tops the virgins sang, are rocks of Desolation.

My fountains, once the haunt of swans, now breed the scaly tortoise,   5
The houses of my harpers are become a haunt of crows,
The gardens of Wisdom are become a field of horrid graves,
And on the bones I drop my tears, and water them in vain.

Once how I walkèd from my Palace in gardens of delight!
The sons of wisdom stood around, the harpers follow'd with harps,   10
Nine virgins, cloth'd in light, compos'd the song to their immortal voices,
And at my banquets of new wine my head was crown'd with joy.

Then in my ivory pavilions I slumber'd in the noon,
And walkèd in the silent night among sweet-smelling flowers,

354

Selections from 'The Four Zoas'

Till on my silver bed I slept, and sweet dreams round me
 hover'd; 15
But now my land is darken'd and my wise men are departed.

My songs are turnèd to cries of lamentation
Heard on my mountains, and deep sighs under my palace roofs;
Because the steeds of Urizen, once swifter than the light,
Were kept back from my Lord and from his chariot of mercies.

O! did I keep the horses of the Day in silver pastures! 21
O! I refus'd the Lord of Day the horses of his Prince!
O! did I close my treasuries with roofs of solid stone,
And darken all my palace walls with envyings and hate!

O fool! to think that I could hide from his all-piercing eyes 25
The gold and silver and costly stones, his holy workmanship.
O fool! could I forget the light that fillèd my bright spheres
Was a reflection of his face who call'd me from the deep!

I well remember, for I heard the mild and holy voice
Saying: 'O Light, spring up and shine,' and I sprang up from the
 deep. 30
He gave to me a silver sceptre, and crown'd me with a golden
 crown,
And said: 'Go forth and guide my Son who wanders on the
 ocean.'

I went not forth: I hid myself in black clouds of my wrath:
I call'd the stars around my feet in the night of councils dark;
The stars threw down their spears, and fled naked away. 35
We fell: I seiz'd thee, dark Urthona, in my left hand, falling,

I seiz'd thee, beauteous Luvah; thou art faded like a flower,
And like a lily thy wife Vala, wither'd by winds.

17 to] into *MS. 1st rdg. del.*   32 And said] Saying *MS. 1st rdg. del.*
38 thy wife] is thy wife *MS. 1st rdg.*

Selections from 'The Four Zoas'

When thou didst bear the golden cup at the immortal tables,
Thy children smote their fiery wings, crown'd with the gold of
    Heaven.	40

Thy pure feet stept on the steps divine, too pure for other feet,
And thy fair locks shadow'd thine eyes from the divine effulgence.
Then thou didst keep with strong Urthona the living gates of
    Heaven;
But now thou art bow'd down with him, even to the gates of Hell.

Because thou gavest Urizen the wine of the Almighty	45
For steeds of Light, that they might run in thy golden chariot of
    pride,
I gave to thee the steeds. I pour'd the stolen wine,
And, drunken with the immortal draught, fell from my throne
    sublime.

I will arise, explore these dens, and find that deep pulsation
That shakes my caverns with strong shudders. Perhaps this is
    the Night	50
Of Prophecy, and Luvah hath burst his way from Enitharmon.
When Thought is clos'd in Caves, then Love shall show its root in
    deepest Hell.

Four Zoas, Night V, ll. 190-241.

[Los in his Wrath]

Los rear'd his mighty stature: on Earth stood his feet; above
The Moon his furious forehead, circled with black bursting thunders;
His naked limbs glitt'ring upon the dark blue sky, his knees
Bathèd in bloody clouds; his loins in fires of War, where spears
And swords rage, where the Eagles cry and Vultures laugh, saying:

'Now comes the night of carnage, now the flesh of Kings and
    Princes	6
Pamper'd in palaces for our food, the blood of Captains nurtur'd

Selections from 'The Four Zoas'

With lust and murder for our drink. The drunken Raven shall
   wander
All night among the slain, and mock the wounded that groan in
   the field.'

Four Zoas, Night VII, First Version, ll. 38-46.

[The War-Song of Orc]

Loud sounds the war-song round red Orc in his fury,
And round the nameless Shadowy Female in her howling terror,
When all the Elemental Gods join'd in the wondrous song:—
'Sound the war-trumpet terrific, souls clad in attractive steel!
Sound the shrill fife, Serpents of War! I hear the northern drum
Awake! I hear the flappings of the folding banners!   6
The Dragons of the North put on their armour;
Upon the eastern sea direct they take their course;
The glitt'ring of their horses' trappings stains the vault of night.

'Stop we the rising of the glorious King! spur, spur your clouds 10
Of death! O northern drum, awake! O hand of iron, sound
The northern drum! Now give the charge! bravely obscur'd
With darts of wintry hail! Again the black bow draw;
Again the elemental strings to your right breasts draw;
And let the thund'ring drum speed on the arrows black!'   15

Ibid., Night VII, First Version, ll. 142-56.

[Vala's Going Forth]

And she went forth and saw the forms of Life and of Delight
Walking on mountains, or flying in the open expanse of heaven.
She heard sweet voices in the winds, and in the voices of birds
That rose from waters; for the waters were as the voice of Luvah,
Not seen to her like waters, or like this dark world of death;   5
Tho' all those fair perfections, which men know only by name,
In beautiful substantial forms appear'd, and servèd her

10 clouds] steeds *MS. 1st rdg. del.*

Selections from 'The Four Zoas'

As food or drink or ornament, or in delightful works
To build her bowers. For the elements brought forth abundantly
The living Soul in glorious forms; and every one came forth, 10
Walking before her Shadowy face and bowing at her feet.
But, in vain, delights were pourèd forth on the howling Melancholy!
For her delight the Horse his proud neck bow'd, and his white mane;
And the strong Lion deign'd in his mouth to wear the golden bit;
While the far-beaming Peacock waited on the fragrant wind 15
To bring her fruits of sweet delight from trees of richest wonders;
And the strong-pinion'd Eagle bore the fire of Heaven in the night-season.

Four Zoas, Night VII, First Version, ll. 267-83.

[Urizen's Words of Wisdom]

And Urizen read in his Book of Brass in sounding tones:—
'Listen, O Daughters, to my voice! listen to the words of wisdom!
Compel the Poor to live upon a crust of bread by soft mild arts:
So shall [you] govern over all. Let Moral Duty tune your tongue,
But be your hearts harder than the nether millstone; 5
To bring the Shadow of Enitharmon beneath our wondrous Tree,
That Los may evaporate like smoke, and be no more.
Draw down Enitharmon to the Spectre of Urthona,
And let him have dominion over Los, the terrible Shade.
Smile when they frown, frown when they smile; and when a man looks pale 10
With labour and abstinence, say he looks healthy and happy;
And when his children sicken, let them die: there are enough
Born, even too many, and our earth will soon be overrun
Without these arts. If you would make the Poor live with temper,
With pomp give every crust of bread you give; with gracious cunning 15
Magnify small gifts; reduce the man to want a gift, and then give with pomp.

4-9 These lines are additions. In l. 4 'you' is miswritten 'be' in the MS.

358

Selections from 'The Four Zoas'

Say he smiles, if you hear him sigh; if pale, say he is ruddy.
Preach temperance: say he is overgorg'd, and drowns his wit
In strong drink, tho' you know that bread and water are all
He can afford. Flatter his wife, pity his children, till we can   20
Reduce all to our will, as spaniels are taught with art.'

Four Zoas, Night VII, Revised Version, ll. 109-29.

[The Shade of Enitharmon]

Her Shadow went forth and return'd. Now she was pale as snow,
When the mountains and hills are cover'd over, and the paths of men shut up;
But, when her Spirit return'd, as ruddy as a morning when
The ripe fruit blushes into joy in Heaven's eternal halls.

Ibid., Night VII, Revised Version, ll. 173-76.

[The Serpent Orc]

He saw Orc, a Serpent form, augmenting times on times
In the fierce battle; and he saw the Lamb of God, and the world of Los
Surrounded by his dark machines; for Orc augmented swift
In fury, a Serpent wondrous, among the constellations of Urizen.
A crest of fire rose on his forehead, red as the carbuncle;   5
Beneath, down to his eyelids, scales of pearl; then gold and silver,
Immingled with the ruby, overspread his visage; down
His furious neck, writhing contortive in dire budding pains,
The scaly armour shot out. Stubborn, down his back and bosom,
The emerald, onyx, sapphire, jasper, beryl, amethyst,   10
Strove in terrific emulation which should gain a place
Upon the mighty fiend—the fruit of the Mysterious Tree
Kneaded in Uvith's kneading-trough.

Ibid., Night VIII, ll. 53-70.

359

Selections from 'The Four Zoas'

[The Last Judgement]

                          Terrifièd at Non-Existence—
For such they deem'd the death of the body—Los his vegetable hands
Outstretch'd ; his right hand, branching out in fibrous strength,
Seiz'd the Sun ; his left hand, like dark roots, cover'd the Moon,
And tore them down, cracking the heavens across from immense
    to immense.   5
Then fell the fires of Eternity, with loud and shrill
Sound of loud Trumpet, thundering along from heaven to heaven,
A mighty sound articulate : 'Awake ! ye Dead, and come
To Judgement from the four winds ! awake, and come away !' 9
Folding like scrolls of the enormous volume of Heaven and Earth,
With thunderous noise and dreadful shakings, rocking to and fro,
The Heavens are shaken, and the Earth removèd from its place ;
The foundations of the eternal hills discover'd.
The thrones of Kings are shaken, they have lost their robes and crowns ;
The Poor smite their oppressors, they awake up to the harvest ; 15
The naked warriors rush together down to the seashore,
Trembling before the multitudes of slaves now set at liberty :
They are become like wintry flocks, like forests stripp'd of leaves.
The Oppressèd pursue like the wind ; there is no room for escape. . . .
The Books of Urizen unroll with dreadful noise ! The folding Serpent   20
Of Orc began to consume in fierce raving fire ; his fierce flames
Issu'd on all sides, gathering strength in animating volumes,
Roaring abroad on all the winds, raging intense, reddening
Into resistless pillars of fire, rolling round and round, gathering
Strength from the earths consum'd, and heavens, and all hidden abysses, 25
Where'er the Eagle has explor'd, or Lion or Tiger trod,

    In the MS. ll. 15, 17, 19, introducing a new feature—the retaliation of the oppressed—are additions.

Selections from 'The Four Zoas'

Or where the comets of the night, or stars of day
Have shot their arrows or long-beamèd spears in wrath and fury.

And all the while the Trumpet sounds.
From the clotted gore, and from the hollow den 30
Start forth the trembling millions into flames of mental fire,
Bathing their limbs in the bright visions of Eternity.

Then, like the doves from pillars of smoke, the trembling families
Of women and children throughout every nation under heaven
Cling round the men in bands of twenties and of fifties, pale 35
As snow that falls round a leafless tree upon the green.
Their oppressors are fall'n; they have stricken them; they awake
   to life.
Yet, pale, the Just man stands erect, and looking up to Heav'n.
Trembling and strucken by the universal stroke, the trees unroot;
The rocks groan horrible and run about; the mountains and 40
Their rivers cry with a dismal cry; the cattle gather together,
Lowing they kneel before the heavens; the wild beasts of the forests
Tremble. The Lion, shuddering, asks the Leopard: 'Feelest thou
The dread I feel, unknown before? My voice refuses to roar,
And in weak moans I speak to thee. This night, 45
Before the morning's dawn, the Eagle call'd the Vulture,
The Raven call'd the Hawk. I heard them from my forests,
Saying: "Let us go up far, for soon I smell upon the wind
A terror coming from the South." The Eagle and Hawk fled
   away
At dawn, and ere the sun arose, the Raven and Vulture follow'd.
Let us flee also to the North.' They fled. The Sons of Men 51
Saw them depart in dismal droves. The trumpets sounded loud,
And all the Sons of Eternity descended into Beulah.

Four Zoas, Night IX, ll. 5-23, 33-66

27 day] eternal day *MS. 1st rdg.* asterial day *MS. 2nd rdg.*
29 And all the while the trumpet sounds: 'Awake ye dead and come
  To Judgement': from the clotted gore and from the hollow den
                                                           MS. 1st rdg.
38 Yet] Then *MS. 1st rdg. del.* 47 forests] forests black *MS. 1st rdg.*

Selections from 'The Four Zoas'

[The Lament of Albion]

O weakness and O weariness! O war within my members!
My sons, exilèd from my breast, pass to and fro before me.
My birds are silent in my hills; flocks die beneath my branches;
My tents are fallen; my trumpets and the sweet sounds of my
    harp
Is silent on my clouded hills that belch forth storms and fires; 5
My milk of cows, and honey of bees, and fruit of golden harvest
Are gather'd in the scorching heat and in the driving rain.
My robe is turnèd to confusion, and my bright gold to stone.
Where once I sat, I weary walk in misery and pain;
For from within my wither'd breast, grown narrow with my woes,
The corn is turn'd to thistles, and the apples into poison;   11
The birds of song to murderous crows, my joys to bitter groans;
The voices of children in my tents to cries of helpless infants.
And all exilèd from the face of light and shine of morning,
In this dark World, a narrow house! I wander up and down: 15
I hear Mystery howling in these flames of Consummation.
When shall the Man of future times become as in days of old?
O weary life! why sit I here and give up all my powers

  2-15 A slightly altered form of this passage was afterwards engraved for *Jerusalem*, f. 19, ll. 1-16, with the general change of the first to third person, and a few other variant readings noted below.

  2 My sons, exilèd] His children exil'd *Jerusalem*.
  4 sounds] sound *Jerusalem*.
  5 Is] Are *Jerusalem*.
  7 Are] Is *Jerusalem*.
  8 Omitted in *Jerusalem*.
  9 Here follows in *Jerusalem* the additional line:
        His Giant beauty and perfection fall'n into dust.
 10 For] Till *Jerusalem*.   wither'd] narrow *MS. 1st rdg. del.*
 14 all exilèd] self-exilèd *Jerusalem*.
 15 this] the *Jerusalem*.
 16-24 Wtg. in *Jerusalem* where the passage concludes thus:
        Seeking for rest and finding none, and hidden far within,
        His Eon weeping in the cold and desolated Earth.

Selections from 'The Four Zoas'

To indolence, to the night of death, when indolence and mourning
Sit hovering over my dark threshold? Tho' I arise, look out   20
And scorn the war within my members, yet my heart is weak
And my head faint.—Yet will I look again into the morning!
Whence is this sound of rage of men drinking each other's blood,
Drunk with the smoking gore, and red, but not with nourishing wine.

Four Zoas, Night IX, ll. 98-121.

[Accuser and Accused]

They see him whom they have pierc'd; they wail because of him;
They magnify themselves no more against Jerusalem, nor
Against her little ones. The Innocent, accusèd before the judges,
Shines with immortal glory: trembling, the Judge springs from his throne,   4
Hiding his face in the dust beneath the prisoner's feet, and saying:
'Brother of Jesus, what have I done? Entreat thy Lord for me!
Perhaps I may be forgiven.'

Ibid., Night IX, ll. 264-70.

[The Tillage of Urizen]

Then seiz'd the sons of Urizen the plough: they polish'd it
From rust of ages: all its ornament of gold and silver and ivory
Re-shone across the field immense, where all the nations
Darken'd like mould in the divided fallows, where the weed
Triumphs in its own destruction. They took down the harness   5
From the blue walls of Heaven, starry, jingling, ornamented
With beautiful art, the study of Angels, the workmanship of Demons,
When Heaven and Hell in emulation strove in sports of glory.
The noise of rural work resounded thro' the heavens of heavens:
The horse[s] neigh from the battle, the wild bulls from the sultry waste,   10
The tigers from the forests, and the lions from the sandy deserts.

Selections from 'The Four Zoas'

They sing; they seize the instruments of harmony; they throw away
The spear, the bow, the gun, the mortar; they level the fortifications;
They beat the iron engines of destruction into wedges;
They give them to Urthona's sons. Ringing, the hammers sound
In dens of death, to forge the spade, the mattock, and the axe, 16
The heavy roller to break the clods, to pass over the nations.

Four Zoas, Night IX, ll. 290-306.

[Song of the Sinless Soul]

'Come forth, O Vala! from the grass and from the silent dew;
Rise from the dews of death, for the Eternal Man is risen!'

She rises among flowers and looks toward the eastern clearness;
She walks, yea runs—her feet are wing'd—on the tops of the bending grass;
Her garments rejoice in the vocal wind, and her hair glistens with dew. 5

She answer'd thus: 'Whose voice is this in the voice of the nourishing air,
In the spirit of the morning, awaking the Soul from its grassy bed?
Where dost thou dwell? for it is thee I seek, and but for thee
I must have slept eternally, nor have felt the dew of thy morning.
Look how the opening dawn advances with vocal harmony! 10
Look how the beams foreshow the rising of some glorious power!
The Sun is thine; he goeth forth in his majestic brightness.
O thou creating voice that callest! and who shall answer thee?

'Where dost thou flee, O Fair One! where dost thou seek thy happy place?
To yonder brightness? There I haste, for sure I came from thence; 15
Or I must have slept eternally, nor have felt the dew of morning.'

Selections from 'The Four Zoas'

'Eternally thou must have slept, nor have felt the morning dew,
But for yon nourishing Sun : 'tis that by which thou art arisen.
The birds adore the Sun ; the beasts rise up and play in his beams,
And every flower and every leaf rejoices in his light. 20
Then, O thou Fair One, sit thee down, for thou art as the grass,
Thou risest in the dew of morning, and at night art folded up.'

'Alas ! am I but as a flower ? Then will I sit me down ;
Then will I weep ; then I'll complain, and sigh for immortality,
And chide my maker, thee O Sun, that raisedst me to fall.' 25

So saying she sat down and wept beneath the apple-trees.

'O ! be thou blotted out, thou Sun, that raisedst me to trouble,
That gavest me a heart to crave, and raisedst me, thy phantom,
To feel thy heart, and see thy light, and wander here alone,
Hopeless, if I am like the grass, and so shall pass away.' 30

'Rise, sluggish Soul ! Why sitt'st thou here ? why dost thou sit
 and weep ?
Yon Sun shall wax old and decay, but thou shalt ever flourish.
The fruit shall ripen and fall down, and the flowers consume away,
But thou shalt still survive. Arise ! O dry thy dewy tears !'

'Ha ! shall I still survive ? Whence came that sweet and com-
 forting voice, 35
And whence that voice of sorrow ? O Sun ! thou art nothing now
 to me :
Go on thy course rejoicing, and let us both rejoice together !
I walk among His flocks and hear the bleating of His lambs.
O ! that I could behold His face and follow His pure feet ! 39
I walk by the footsteps of His flocks. Come hither, tender flocks !
Can you converse with a pure Soul that seeketh for her Maker ?
You answer not : then am I set your mistress in this garden.
I'll watch you and attend your footsteps. You are not like the birds
That sing and fly in the bright air ; but you do lick my feet,
And let me touch your woolly backs : follow me as I sing ; 45
For in my bosom a new Song arises to my Lord :

Selections from 'The Four Zoas'

'Rise up, O Sun! most glorious minister and light of day!
Flow on, ye gentle airs, and bear the voice of my rejoicing!
Wave freshly, clear waters, flowing around the tender grass;
And thou, sweet-smelling ground, put forth thy life in fruit and flowers! 50
Follow me, O my flocks, and hear me sing my rapturous song!
I will cause my voice to be heard on the clouds that glitter in the sun.
I will call, and who shall answer me? I shall sing; who shall reply?
For, from my pleasant hills, behold the living, living springs,
Running among my green pastures, delighting among my trees! 55
I am not here alone: my flocks, you are my brethren;
And you birds, that sing and adorn the sky, you are my sisters.
I sing, and you reply to my song; I rejoice, and you are glad.
Follow me, O my flocks! we will now descend into the valley.
O, how delicious are the grapes, flourishing in the sun! 60
How clear the spring of the rock, running among the golden sand!
How cool the breezes of the valley! And the arms of the branching trees
Cover us from the sun: come and let us sit in the shade.
My Luvah here hath plac'd me in a sweet and pleasant land,
And given me fruits and pleasant waters, and warm hills and cool valleys. 65
Here will I build myself a house, and here I'll call on His name;
Here I'll return, when I am weary, and take my pleasant rest.'

Four Zoas, Night IX, ll. 386-452.

[Vala in Lower Paradise]

So saying, she arose and walkèd round her beautiful house;
And then from her white door she look'd to see her bleating lambs,
But her flocks were gone up from beneath the trees into the hills.

'I see the hand that leadeth me doth also lead my flocks.'
She went up to her flocks, and turnèd oft to see her shining house.

Selections from 'The Four Zoas'

She stopp'd to drink of the clear spring, and eat the grapes and
    apples; 6
She bore the fruits in her lap; she gather'd flowers for her bosom.
She callèd to her flocks, saying: 'Follow me, O my flocks!'

They follow'd her to the silent valley beneath the spreading trees,
And on the river's margin she ungirded her golden girdle; 10
She stood in the river and view'd herself within the wat'ry glass,
And her bright hair was wet with the waters. She rose up from
    the river,
And as she rose her eyes were open'd to the world of waters;
She saw Tharmas sitting upon the rocks beside the wavy sea.

Four Zoas, Night IX, ll. 469-82.

SELECTIONS FROM

MILTON

(Engraved 1804-1809)

Preface

The stolen and perverted writings of Homer and Ovid, of Plato and Cicero, which all men ought to contemn, are set up by artifice against the Sublime of the Bible; but when the New Age is at leisure to pronounce, all will be set right, and those grand works of the more ancient, and consciously and professedly Inspired men will hold their proper rank, and the Daughters of Memory shall become the Daughters of Inspiration. Shakspeare and Milton were both curb'd by the general malady and infection from the silly Greek and Latin slaves of the sword.

Rouse up, O Young Men of the New Age! Set your foreheads against the ignorant hirelings! For we have hirelings in the Camp, the Court, and the University, who would, if they could, for ever depress mental, and prolong corporeal war. Painters! on you I call. Sculptors! Architects! suffer not the fashionable fools to depress your powers by the prices they pretend to give for contemptible works, or the expensive advertising boasts that they make of such works: believe Christ and His Apostles that there is a class of men whose whole delight is in destroying. We do not want either Greek or Roman models if we are but just and true to our own Imaginations, those Worlds of Eternity in which we shall live for ever, in Jesus our Lord.

Selections from 'Milton'

And did those feet in ancient time
  Walk upon England's mountains green?
And was the holy Lamb of God
  On England's pleasant pastures seen?

And did the Countenance Divine 5
  Shine forth upon our clouded hills?
And was Jerusalem builded here
  Among these dark Satanic Mills?

Bring me my bow of burning gold!
  Bring me my arrows of desire! 10
Bring me my spear! O clouds, unfold!
  Bring me my chariot of fire!

I will not cease from mental fight,
  Nor shall my sword sleep in my hand,
Till we have built Jerusalem 15
  In England's green and pleasant land.

Would to God that all the Lord's people were Prophets. Numbers xi. 29.

Milton, f. 2.

[The Invocation]

Daughters of Beulah! Muses who inspire the Poet's Song,
Record the journey of immortal Milton thro' your realms
Of terror and mild moony lustre, in soft Sexual delusions
Of varièd beauty, to delight the wanderer, and repose
His burning thirst and freezing hunger! Come into my hand, 5
By your mild power descending down the nerves of my right arm
From out the portals of my Brain, where by your ministry
The Eternal Great Humanity Divine planted His Paradise,
And in it caus'd the Spectres of the Dead to take sweet form
In likeness of Himself. Tell also of the False Tongue, vegetated
Beneath your land of Shadows, of its sacrifices and 11
Its offerings; even till Jesus, the image of the Invisible God,

Selections from 'Milton'

Became its prey; a curse, an offering, and an atonement
For Death Eternal, in the Heavens of Albion, and before the Gates
Of Jerusalem his Emanation, in the Heavens beneath Beulah!

Milton, f. 3, ll. 1-15.

[The Mills of Satan]

And the Mills of Satan were separated into a moony Space
Among the rocks of Albion's Temples, and Satan's Druid Sons
Offer the Human Victims throughout all the Earth; and Albion's
Dread Tomb, immortal on his Rock, overshadow'd the whole Earth,
Where Satan, making to himself Laws from his own identity,
Compell'd others to serve him in moral gratitude and submission,
Being call'd God, setting himself above all that is callèd God.
And all the Spectres of the Dead, calling themselves Sons of God,
In his Synagogues worship Satan under the Unutterable Name.

Ibid., f. 9, ll. 6-14.

[The Sin of Leutha]

The Sin was begun in Eternity, and will not rest to Eternity,
Till two Eternities meet together. Ah! lost! lost! lost for ever!

Ibid., f. 11, ll 10-11.

[Milton's Journey to Eternal Death]

Then Milton rose up from the Heavens of Albion ardorous:
The whole Assembly wept prophetic, seeing in Milton's face
And in his lineaments divine the shades of Death and Ulro;
He took off the robe of the Promise, and ungirded himself from the oath of God.

And Milton said: 'I go to Eternal Death! The Nations still
Follow after the detestable Gods of Priam, in pomp
Of warlike Selfhood, contradicting and blaspheming

Selections from 'Milton'

When will the Resurrection come to deliver the sleeping body
From corruptibility? O when, Lord Jesus! wilt Thou come?
Tarry no longer, for my soul lies at the gates of death. 10
I will arise and look forth for the morning of the grave;
I will go down to the sepulchre to see if morning breaks;
I will go down to self-annihilation and Eternal Death;
Lest the Last Judgement come and find me unannihilate,
And I be seiz'd and giv'n into the hands of my own Selfhood. 15
The Lamb of God is seen thro' mists and shadows, hov'ring
Over the sepulchres, in clouds of Jehovah and winds of Elohim,
A disk of blood, distant; and Heav'ns and Earths roll dark between.
What do I here before the Judgement without my Emanation,
With the Daughters of Memory, and not with the Daughters of
    Inspiration? 20
I, in my Selfhood, am that Satan! I am that Evil One!
He is my Spectre! In my obedience to loose him from my Hells,
To claim the Hells, my Furnaces, I go to Eternal Death.'

And Milton said: 'I go to Eternal Death!' Eternity shudder'd;
For he took the outside course, among the graves of the dead, 25
A mournful Shade. Eternity shudder'd at the image of Eternal
    Death.

Then on the verge of Beulah he beheld his own Shadow,
A mournful form, double, hermaphroditic, male and female
In one wonderful body, and he enter'd into it
In direful pain; for the dread Shadow, twenty-seven-fold, 30
Reach'd to the depths of direst Hell, and thence to Albion's land,
Which is this Earth of Vegetation on which now I write.

Milton, f. 12, ll. 10-41.

[The Nature of Infinity]

The nature of Infinity is this: That every thing has its
Own Vortex; and when once a traveller thro' Eternity
Has pass'd that Vortex, he perceives it roll backward behind

Selections from 'Milton'

His path, into a Globe itself enfolding, like a sun,
Or like a moon, or like a universe of starry majesty, 5
While he keeps onwards in his wondrous journey on the Earth,
Or like a human form, a friend with whom he liv'd benevolent.
As the eye of man views both the East and West, encompassing
Its vortex, and the North and South with all their starry host,
Also the rising sun and setting moon he views, surrounding 10
His corn-fields and his valleys of five hundred acres square.
Thus is the Earth one infinite plane, and not as apparent
To the weak traveller confin'd beneath the moony shade.
Thus is the Heaven a Vortex pass'd already, and the Earth
A Vortex not yet pass'd by the traveller thro' Eternity. 15

Milton, f. 14, ll. 21-35.

[The Sea of Time and Space]

First Milton saw Albion upon the Rock of Ages,
Deadly pale, outstretch'd, and snowy cold, storm-cover'd—
A Giant form of perfect beauty, outstretch'd on the Rock
In solemn death: the Sea of Time and Space thunder'd aloud
Against the Rock, which was enwrappèd with the weeds of Death. 5
Hovering over the cold bosom in its vortex, Milton bent down
To the bosom of Death: what was underneath soon seem'd above,
A cloudy heaven mingled with stormy seas in loudest ruin;
But as a wintry globe descends precipitant, thro' Beulah bursting,
With thunders loud and terrible, so Milton's Shadow fell 10
Precipitant, loud thund'ring, into the Sea of Time and Space.

Ibid., f. 14, ll. 36-46.

[The Mundane Shell]

The Mundane Shell is a vast Concave Earth, an immense
Harden'd Shadow of all things upon our Vegetated Earth,
Enlarg'd into Dimension and deform'd into indefinite Space,
In Twenty-seven Heavens and all their Hells, with Chaos
And Ancient Night and Purgatory. It is a cavernous Earth 5

Selections from 'Milton'

Of labyrinthine intricacy, twenty-seven folds of Opaqueness,
And finishes where the lark mounts.

Milton, f. 16, ll. 21-7.

[A River in Eden]

There is in Eden a sweet River of milk and liquid pearl
Nam'd Ololon, on whose mild banks dwelt those who Milton drove
Down into Ulro; and they wept in long-resounding song
For seven days of Eternity, and the River's living banks,
The mountains wail'd, and every plant that grew, in solemn sighs,
    lamented.   5

Ibid., f. 19, ll. 15-19.

[Los]

I am that Shadowy Prophet, who, six thousand years ago,
Fell from my station in the Eternal bosom. Six thousand years
Are finish'd. I return! Both Time and Space obey my will.
I in six thousand years walk up and down; for not one moment
Of Time is lost, nor one event of Space unpermanent;   5
But all remain; every fabric of six thousand years
Remains permanent: tho' on the Earth, where Satan
Fell and was cut off, all things vanish and are seen no more,
They vanish not from me and mine; we guard them first and last.
The Generations of Men run on in the tide of Time,   10
But leave their destin'd lineaments permanent for ever and ever.

Ibid., f. 20, ll. 15-25.

[Swedenborg]

O Swedenborg! strongest of men, the Samson shorn by the
    Churches;
Showing the Transgressors in Hell, the proud Warriors in Heaven,
Heaven as a Punisher, and Hell as One under Punishment;
With Laws from Plato and his Greeks to renew the Trojan Gods
In Albion, and to deny the value of the Saviour's blood.   5

Ibid., f. 20, ll. 50-4.

Selections from 'Milton'

[Whitefield and Wesley]

He sent his two Servants, Whitefield and Wesley: were they Prophets,
Or were they Idiots or Madmen?—Show us Miracles!
Can you have greater Miracles than these? Men who devote
Their life's whole comfort to entire scorn and injury and death?
Awake! thou sleeper on the Rock of Eternity, Albion, awake!
The trumpet of Judgement hath twice sounded: all Nations are awake,
But thou art still heavy and dull. Awake, Albion, awake!

Milton, f. 20, l. 61—f. 22, l. 5.

[The Forge of Los]

In Bowlahoola Los's Anvils stand and his Furnaces rage;
Thundering the Hammers beat, and the Bellows blow loud,
Living, self-moving, mourning, lamenting, and howling incessantly.
Bowlahoola thro' all its porches feels, tho' too fast founded,
Its pillars and porticoes to tremble at the force
Of mortal or immortal arm; and softly lilling flutes,
Accordant with the horrid labours, make sweet melody.
The Bellows are the Animal Lungs, the Hammers the Animal Heart,
The Furnaces the Stomach for digestion; terrible their fury!
Thousands and thousands labour, thousands play on instruments,
Stringèd or fluted, to ameliorate the sorrows of slavery.
Loud sport the dancers in the Dance of Death, rejoicing in carnage.
The hard dentant Hammers are lull'd by the flutes' lula lula,
The bellowing Furnaces' blare by the long-sounding clarion,
The double drum drowns howls and groans, the shrill fife shrieks and cries,
The crooked horn mellows the hoarse raving serpent—terrible but harmonious.

Ibid., f. 23, ll. 51-66.

Selections from 'Milton'

[The Wine-Press of Los]

But the Wine-press of Los is eastward of Golgonooza, before the Seat
Of Satan: Luvah laid the foundation, and Urizen finish'd it in howling woe.
How red the Sons and Daughters of Luvah! here they tread the grapes,
Laughing and shouting, drunk with odours; many fall, o'erwearièd;
Drown'd in the wine is many a youth and maiden: those around 5
Lay them on skins of tigers and of the spotted leopard and the wild ass,
Till they revive, or bury them in cool grots, making lamentation.

This Wine-press is call'd War on Earth: it is the Printing-Press
Of Los; and here he lays his words in order above the mortal brain,
As cogs are form'd in a wheel to turn the cogs of the adverse wheel. 10

Timbrels and violins sport round the Wine-presses; the little Seed,
The sportive Root, the Earth-worm, the Gold-beetle, the wise Emmet
Dance round the Wine-presses of Luvah; the Centipede is there,
The Ground-spider with many eyes, the Mole clothèd in velvet,
The ambitious Spider in his sullen web, the lucky Golden-spinner,
The Earwig arm'd, the tender Maggot, emblem of immortality, 16
The Flea, Louse, Bug, the Tape-worm; all the Armies of Disease,
Visible or invisible to the slothful, Vegetating Man;
The slow Slug, the Grasshopper, that sings and laughs and drinks—
Winter comes: he folds his slender bones without a murmur. 20

The cruel Scorpion is there, the Gnat, Wasp, Hornet, and the Honey-bee,

Selections from 'Milton'

The Toad and venomous Newt, the Serpent cloth'd in gems and gold:
They throw off their gorgeous raiment: they rejoice with loud jubilee,
Around the Wine-presses of Luvah, naked and drunk with wine.

There is the Nettle that stings with soft down, and there   25
The indignant Thistle, whose bitterness is bred in his milk,
Who feeds on contempt of his neighbour; there all the idle Weeds,
That creep around the obscure places, show their various limbs
Naked in all their beauty, dancing round the Wine-presses.

But in the Wine-presses the Human grapes sing not nor dance! 30
They howl and writhe in shoals of torment, in fierce flames consuming,
In chains of iron and in dungeons, circled with ceaseless fires,
In pits and dens and shades of death, in shapes of torment and woe—
The plates, and screws, and racks, and saws, and cords, and fires and cisterns,
The cruel joys of Luvah's Daughters, lacerating with knives   35
And whips their Victims, and the deadly sport of Luvah's Sons.

They dance around the dying, and they drink the howl and groan;
They catch the shrieks in cups of gold, they hand them to one another:
These are the sports of love, and these the sweet delights of amorous play,
Tears of the grape, the death-sweat of the cluster, the last sigh 40
Of the mild youth who listens to the luring songs of Luvah.

Milton, f. 24, ll. 1-41.

This passage was engraved with a few re-arrangements and verbal changes from the earlier version in the MS. of the *Four Zoas* (Night IX, ll. 746-69).

Selections from 'Milton'

[The Building of Time]

But others of the Sons of Los build Moments and Minutes and Hours,
And Days and Months and Years, and Ages and Periods: wondrous buildings!
And every Moment has a Couch of gold for soft repose—
A Moment equals a pulsation of the artery—
And between every two Moments stands a Daughter of Beulah,
To feed the Sleepers on their Couches with maternal care.
And every Minute has an azure Tent with silken Veils;
And every Hour has a bright golden Gate carvèd with skill;
And every Day and Night has Walls of brass and Gates of adamant,
Shining like precious stones, and ornamented with appropriate signs:
And every Month a silver-pavèd Terrace, builded high;
And every Year invulnerable Barriers with high Towers;
And every Age is moated deep with Bridges of silver and gold;
And every Seven Ages is encircled with a Flaming Fire.
Now Seven Ages is amounting to Two Hundred Years:
Each has its Guard, each Moment, Minute, Hour, Day, Month and Year;
All are the work of Fairy hands of the Four Elements:
The Guard are Angels of Providence on duty evermore.
Every Time less than a pulsation of the artery
Is equal in its period and value to Six Thousand Years;
For in this Period the Poet's Work is done; and all the great
Events of Time start forth and are conceiv'd in such a Period,
Within a Moment, a Pulsation of the Artery.

Milton, f. 27, l. 44—f. 28, l. 2.

[The Heavens and the Earth]

The Sky is an immortal Tent built by the Sons of Los;
And every Space that a Man views around his dwelling-place,

Selections from 'Milton'

Standing on his own roof, or in his garden on a mount
Of twenty-five cubits in height, such Space is his Universe:
And on its verge the Sun rises and sets, the Clouds bow
To meet the flat Earth and the Sea in such an order'd Space.
The Starry Heavens reach no further, but here bend and set
On all sides, and the two Poles turn on their valves of gold;
And if he move his dwelling-place, his Heavens also move
Where'er he goes, and all his neighbourhood bewail his loss.
Such are the Spaces callèd Earth, and such its dimension.
As to that false appearance which appears to the reasoner,
As of a Globe rolling thro' Voidness, it is a delusion of Ulro.

Milton, f. 28, ll. 4-16.

[The Birds and the Flowers]

Thou hearest the Nightingale begin the Song of Spring:
The Lark, sitting upon his earthy bed, just as the morn
Appears, listens silent; then, springing from the waving corn-field, loud
He leads the Choir of Day—trill! trill! trill! trill!
Mounting upon the wings of light into the great Expanse,
Re-echoing against the lovely blue and shining heavenly Shell;
His little throat labours with inspiration; every feather
On throat and breast and wings vibrates with the effluence Divine
All Nature listens silent to him, and the awful Sun
Stands still upon the mountain looking on this little Bird
With eyes of soft humility and wonder, love and awe.
Then loud from their green covert all the Birds begin their song:
The Thrush, the Linnet and the Goldfinch, Robin and the Wren
Awake the Sun from his sweet revery upon the mountain:
The Nightingale again assays his song, and thro' the day
And thro' the night warbles luxuriant; every Bird of song
Attending his loud harmony with admiration and love.
This is a Vision of the lamentation of Beulah over Ololon.

Thou perceivest the Flowers put forth their precious Odours;
And none can tell how from so small a centre comes such sweet,

Selections from 'Milton'

Forgetting that within that centre Eternity expands 21
Its ever-during doors, that Og and Anak fiercely guard.
First, ere the morning breaks, joy opens in the flowery bosoms,
Joy even to tears, which the Sun rising dries: first the Wild Thyme
And Meadow-sweet, downy and soft, waving among the reeds, 25
Light springing on the air, lead the sweet dance; they wake
The Honeysuckle sleeping on the oak; the flaunting beauty
Revels along upon the wind; the White-thorn, lovely May,
Opens her many lovely eyes; listening the Rose still sleeps—
None dare to wake her; soon she bursts her crimson-curtain'd bed
And comes forth in the majesty of beauty. Every Flower, 31
The Pink, the Jessamine, the Wallflower, the Carnation,
The Jonquil, the mild Lily opes her heavens; every Tree
And Flower and Herb soon fill the air with an innumerable dance,
Yet all in order sweet and lovely. Men are sick with love! 35
Such is a Vision of the lamentation of Beulah over Ololon.

Milton, f. 31, ll. 28-63.

[Love and Jealousy]

And the Divine Voice was heard in the Songs of Beulah, saying:
'When I first married you, I gave you all my whole soul;
I thought that you would love my loves and joy in my delights,
Seeking for pleasures in my pleasures, O Daughter of Babylon!
Then thou wast lovely, mild, and gentle; now thou art terrible 5
In Jealousy and unlovely in my sight, because thou hast cruelly
Cut off my loves in fury, till I have no Love left for thee.
Thy Love depends on him thou lovest, and on his dear loves
Depend thy pleasures, which thou hast cut off by Jealousy:
Therefore I show my Jealousy, and set before you Death. 10
Behold Milton, descended to redeem the Female Shade
From Death Eternal! such your lot to be continually redeem'd
By Death and misery of those you love, and by Annihilation.
When the Sixfold Female perceives that Milton annihilates
Himself, that seeing all his loves by her cut off, he leaves 15
Her also, entirely abstracting himself from Female loves,

Selections from 'Milton'

She shall relent in fear of death; she shall begin to give
Her maidens to her husband, delighting in his delight.
And then, and then alone, begins the happy Female joy,
As it is done in Beulah; and thou, O Virgin Babylon! Mother of
    Whoredoms,   20
Shalt bring Jerusalem in thine arms in the night watches; and
No longer turning her a wandering Harlot in the streets,
Shalt give her into the arms of God, your Lord and Husband.'
Such are the Songs of Beulah, in the Lamentations of Ololon.

Milton, f. 32, ll. 1-24.

[Reason and Imagination]

The Negation is the Spectre, the Reasoning Power in Man:
This is a false Body, an Incrustation over my Immortal
Spirit, a Selfhood which must be put off and annihilated alway.
To cleanse the Face of my Spirit by self-examination,
To bathe in the waters of Life, to wash off the Not Human,   5
I come in Self-annihilation and the grandeur of Inspiration;
To cast off Rational Demonstration by Faith in the Saviour,
To cast off the rotten rags of Memory by Inspiration,
To cast off Bacon, Locke, and Newton from Albion's covering,
To take off his filthy garments and clothe him with Imagination;
To cast aside from Poetry all that is not Inspiration,   11
That it no longer shall dare to mock with the aspersion of
    Madness
Cast on the Inspirèd by the tame high finisher of paltry Blots
Indefinite or paltry Rhymes, or paltry Harmonies,
Who creeps into State Government like a caterpillar to destroy; 15
To cast off the idiot Questioner, who is always questioning,
But never capable of answering; who sits with a sly grin
Silent plotting when to question, like a thief in a cave;
Who publishes Doubt and calls it Knowledge: whose Science is
    Despair,
Whose pretence to knowledge is Envy, whose whole Science is 20
To destroy the wisdom of ages, to gratify ravenous Envy

Selections from 'Milton'

That rages round him like a Wolf, day and night, without rest.
He smiles with condescension; he talks of Benevolence and Virtue,
And those who act with Benevolence and Virtue they murder time on time.
These are the destroyers of Jerusalem! these are the murderers 25
Of Jesus! who deny the Faith and mock at Eternal Life,
Who pretend to Poetry that they may destroy Imagination
By imitation of Nature's Images drawn from Remembrance.
These are the Sexual Garments, the Abomination of Desolation,
Hiding the Human Lineaments, as with an Ark and Curtains 30
Which Jesus rent, and now shall wholly purge away with Fire,
Till Generation is swallow'd up in Regeneration.

Milton, f. 42, l. 34 — f. 43, l. 28.

[The Song of the Shadowy Female]

My Garments shall be woven of sighs and heart-broken lamentations:
The misery of unhappy Families shall be drawn out into its border,
Wrought with the needle, with dire sufferings, poverty, pain, and woe,
Along the rocky Island and thence throughout the whole Earth.
There shall be the sick Father and his starving Family; there 5
The Prisoner in the stone Dungeon, and the Slave at the Mill.
I will have writings written all over it in Human words,
That every Infant that is born upon the Earth shall read
And get by rote, as a hard task of a life of sixty years.
I will have Kings inwoven upon it, and Counsellors and Mighty Men: 10
The Famine shall clasp it together with buckles and clasps,
And the Pestilence shall be its fringe, and the War its girdle;
To divide into Rahab and Tirzah, that Milton may come to our tents.

Selections from 'Milton'

For I will put on the Human Form, and take the Image of God,
Even Pity and Humanity; but my clothing shall be Cruelty. 15
And I will put on Holiness as a breastplate and as a helmet,
And all my ornaments shall be of the gold of broken hearts,
And the precious stones of anxiety and care, and desperation and death,
And repentance for sin, and sorrow, and punishment and fear;
To defend me from thy terrors, O Orc! my only belovèd! 20

Milton, f. 17*, ll. 6-25.

Jerusalem
The Emanation of The Giant Albion

1804
Printed by W. Blake S.th Molton S.^t

SELECTIONS FROM
JERUSALEM

(Engraved 1804–? 1820)

SHEEP   TO THE PUBLIC   *GOATS*

After my three years' slumber on the banks of the Ocean, I again display my Giant forms to the Public. My former Giants and Fairies having receiv'd the highest reward possible, the . . . and . . . of those with whom to be connected is to be . . ., I cannot doubt that this more consolidated and extended Work will be as kindly received. The Enthusiasm of the following Poem, the Author hopes . . . I also hope the Reader will be with me wholly One in Jesus our Lord, Who is the God . . . and Lord . . . to Whom the Ancients look'd, and saw His day afar off, with trembling and amazement.

The Spirit of Jesus is continual Forgiveness of Sin: he who waits to be righteous before he enters into the Saviour's Kingdom, the Divine Body, will never enter there. I am perhaps the most sinful of men: I pretend not to holiness; yet I pretend to love, to see, to converse with daily, as man with man, and the more to have an interest in the Friend of Sinners. Therefore . . . Reader . . . what you do not approve, and . . me for this energetic exertion of my talent.

    Reader ! . . . of books . . . of Heaven,
    And of that God from whom . . .
    Who in mysterious Sinai's awful cave
    To Man the wondrous art of writing gave;
    Again He speaks in thunder and in fire,   5
    Thunder of Thought and flames of fierce Desire.
    Even from the depths of Hell His voice I hear
    Within the unfathom'd caverns of my Ear.
    Therefore I print: nor vain my types shall be.   9
    Heaven, Earth, and Hell, henceforth shall live in harmony.

Selections from 'Jerusalem'

*Of the Measure in which
the following Poem is written.*

We who dwell on Earth can do nothing of ourselves; everything is conducted by Spirits, no less than Digestion or Sleep . . .

. . . .

When this Verse was first dictated to me, I consider'd a monotonous cadence like that used by Milton and Shakspeare, and all writers of English Blank Verse, derived from the modern bondage of Riming, to be a necessary and indispensable part of Verse. But I soon found that in the mouth of a true Orator such monotony was not only awkward, but as much a bondage as rime itself. I therefore have produced a variety in every line, both of cadences and number of syllables. Every word and every letter is studied and put into its fit place; the terrific numbers are reserved for the terrific parts, the mild and gentle for the mild and gentle parts, and the prosaic for inferior parts; all are necessary to each other. Poetry fetter'd fetters the Human Race. Nations are destroy'd or flourish, in proportion as their Poetry, Painting, and Music are destroy'd or flourish. The Primeval State of Man was Wisdom, Art, and Science.

Jerusalem, f. 3.

[Introduction]

This theme calls me in sleep night after night, and ev'ry morn
Awakes me at sunrise; then I see the Saviour over me
Spreading His beams of love, and dictating the words of this mild
    song:
'Awake! Awake! O sleeper of the Land of Shadows, wake! expand!
I am in you, and you in Me, mutual in Love Divine,
Fibres of love from man to man thro' Albion's pleasant land.'

Ibid., f. 4, ll. 3-8.

Introd.] *The opening lines of Chap. I, which is headed:*
    'Of the Sleep of Ulro, and of the passage through
    Eternal Death, and of the awaking to Eternal Life'

Selections from 'Jerusalem'

[The Reasoning Power]

And this is the manner of the Sons of Albion in their strength:
They take the Two Contraries which are call'd Qualities, with which
Every Substance is clothèd; they name them Good and Evil.
From them they make an Abstract, which is a Negation
Not only of the Substance from which it is derivèd,   5
A murderer of its own Body, but also a murderer
Of every Divine Member. It is the Reasoning Power,
An Abstract objecting power, that negatives everything.
This is the Spectre of Man, the Holy Reasoning Power,
And in its Holiness is closèd the Abomination of Desolation! 10
Jerusalem, f. 10, ll. 7-16.

[The Words of Los]

I must Create a System, or be enslav'd by another Man's;
I will not Reason and Compare: my business is to Create.
Ibid., f. 10, ll. 20-1.

[The Builders of Golgonooza]

What are those Golden Builders doing? Where was the burying-place
Of soft Ethinthus? near Tyburn's fatal Tree? Is that
Mild Zion's hill's most ancient promontory, near mournful
Ever-weeping Paddington? Is that Calvary and Golgotha
Becoming a building of Pity and Compassion? Lo!   5
The stones are Pity, and the bricks well-wrought Affections
Enamell'd with Love and Kindness; and the tiles engraven gold,
Labour of merciful hands; the beams and rafters are Forgiveness,
The mortar and cement of the work tears of Honesty, the nails
And the screws and iron braces are well-wrought Blandishments
And well-contrivèd words, firm fixing, never forgotten,   11
Always comforting the remembrance; the floors Humility,
The ceilings Devotion, the hearths Thanksgiving.
Prepare the furniture, O Lambeth, in thy pitying looms!
The curtains, woven tears and sighs, wrought into lovely forms 15

Selections from 'Jerusalem'

For Comfort; there the secret furniture of Jerusalem's chamber
Is wrought. Lambeth! the Bride, the Lamb's Wife loveth thee;
Thou art one with her, and knowest not of Self in thy supreme joy.
Go on, Builders in hope! tho' Jerusalem wanders far away
Without the Gate of Los, among the dark Satanic wheels.   20

Jerusalem, f. 12, ll. 25-44.

[A Vision of Albion]

I see the Fourfold Man; the Humanity in deadly sleep,
And its fallen Emanation, the Spectre and its cruel Shadow.
I see the Past, Present, and Future existing all at once
Before me. O Divine Spirit! sustain me on thy wings,
That I may awake Albion from his long and cold repose;   5
For Bacon and Newton, sheath'd in dismal steel, their terrors hang
Like iron scourges over Albion. Reasonings like vast Serpents
Enfold around my limbs, bruising my minute articulations.

I turn my eyes to the Schools and Universities of Europe,
And there behold the Loom of Locke, whose Woof rages dire,   10
Wash'd by the Water-wheels of Newton: black the cloth
In heavy wreaths folds over every Nation: cruel Works
Of many Wheels I view, wheel without wheel, with cogs tyrannic,
Moving by compulsion each other; not as those in Eden, which,
Wheel within wheel, in freedom revolve, in harmony and peace.   15

Ibid., f. 15, ll. 6-20.

[Punishment and Forgiveness]

Why should Punishment weave the veil with Iron Wheels of War,
When Forgiveness might it weave with Wings of Cherubim?

Ibid., f. 22, ll. 34-5.

[The Lament of Albion]

O what is Life and what is Man? O what is Death? Wherefore
Are you, my Children, natives in the Grave to where I go?
Or are you born to feed the hungry ravenings of Destruction,
To be the sport of Accident. to waste in Wrath and Love a weary

Selections from 'Jerusalem'

Life, in brooding cares and anxious labours, that prove but chaff?
O Jerusalem! Jerusalem! I have forsaken thy courts, 6
Thy pillars of ivory and gold, thy curtains of silk and fine
Linen, thy pavements of precious stones, thy walls of pearl
And gold, thy gates of Thanksgiving, thy windows of Praise,
Thy clouds of Blessing, thy Cherubims of Tender Mercy, 10
Stretching their Wings sublime over the Little Ones of Albion.
O Human Imagination! O Divine Body, I have crucifièd!
I have turnèd my back upon thee into the Wastes of Moral Law:
There Babylon is builded in the Waste, founded in Human desolation.
O Babylon! thy Watchman stands over thee in the night; 15
Thy severe Judge all the day long proves thee, O Babylon,
With provings of Destruction, with giving thee thy heart's desire.
But Albion is cast forth to the Potter, his Children to the Builders
To build Babylon, because they have forsaken Jerusalem.
The walls of Babylon are Souls of Men; her gates the Groans 20
Of Nations; her towers are the Miseries of once happy Families;
Her streets are pavèd with Destruction; her houses built with Death;
Her Palaces with Hell and the Grave; her Synagogues with Torments
Of ever-hardening Despair, squar'd and polish'd with cruel skill.

Jerusalem, f. 24, ll. 12-35.

[Jerusalem]

    Such Visions have appear'd to me,
    As I my order'd course have run:
    Jerusalem is nam'd Liberty
    Among the Sons of Albion.

Ibid., f. 26.

To the Jews

Jerusalem, the Emanation of the Giant Albion! Can it be? Is it a truth that the learned have explored? Was Britain the primitive seat of the Patriarchal Religion? If it is true, my title

Selections from 'Jerusalem'

page is also true, that Jerusalem was, and is, the Emanation of the Giant Albion. It is true, and cannot be controverted. Ye are united, O ye inhabitants of Earth, in One Religion—the Religion of Jesus, the most ancient, the Eternal, and the Everlasting Gospel. The Wicked will turn it to Wickedness, the Righteous to Righteousness. Amen! Huzza! Selah!

'All things begin and end in Albion's ancient Druid rocky shore.'

Your Ancestors derived their origin from Abraham, Heber, Shem, and Noah, who were Druids, as the Druid Temples (which are the patriarchal pillars and oak groves) over the whole Earth witness to this day.

You have a tradition that Man anciently contain'd in his mighty limbs all things in Heaven and Earth: this you received from the Druids.

'But now the starry Heavens are fled from the mighty limbs of Albion.'

Albion was the Parent of the Druids, and, in his Chaotic State of Sleep, Satan and Adam and the whole World was created by the Elohim.

> The fields from Islington to Marybone,
>   To Primrose Hill and Saint John's Wood,
> Were builded over with pillars of gold;
>   And there Jerusalem's pillars stood.
>
> Her Little Ones ran on the fields,   5
>   The Lamb of God among them seen,
> And fair Jerusalem, His Bride,
>   Among the little meadows green.
>
> Pancras and Kentish Town repose
>   Among her golden pillars high,   10
> Among her golden arches which
>   Shine upon the starry sky.

Selections from 'Jerusalem'

The Jew's-harp House and the Green Man,
    The Ponds where boys to bathe delight,
The fields of cows by William's farm,
    Shine in Jerusalem's pleasant sight.

She walks upon our meadows green;
    The Lamb of God walks by her side;
And every English child is seen,
    Children of Jesus and His Bride;

Forgiving trespasses and sins,
    Lest Babylon, with cruel Og,
With Moral and Self-righteous Law,
    Should crucify in Satan's Synagogue.

What are those Golden Builders doing
    Near mournful ever-weeping Paddington,
Standing above that mighty ruin,
    Where Satan the first victory won;

Where Albion slept beneath the fatal Tree,
    And the Druid's golden knife
Rioted in human gore,
    In offerings of Human Life?

They groan'd aloud on London Stone,
    They groan'd aloud on Tyburn's Brook:
Albion gave his deadly groan,
    And all the Atlantic mountains shook.

Albion's Spectre, from his loins,
    Tore forth in all the pomp of War;
Satan his name; in flames of fire
    He stretch'd his Druid pillars far.

Jerusalem fell from Lambeth's vale,
    Down thro' Poplar and Old Bow,
Thro' Malden, and across the sea,
    In war and howling, death and woe.

Selections from 'Jerusalem'

The Rhine was red with human blood;
    The Danube roll'd a purple tide;
On the Euphrates Satan stood,
    And over Asia stretch'd his pride.

He wither'd up sweet Zion's hill
    From every nation of the Earth;
He wither'd up Jerusalem's Gates,
    And in a dark land gave her birth.

He wither'd up the Human Form
    By laws of sacrifice for Sin,
Till it became a Mortal Worm,
    But O! translucent all within.

The Divine Vision still was seen,
    Still was the Human Form Divine;
Weeping, in weak and mortal clay,
    O Jesus! still the Form was Thine!

And Thine the Human Face; and Thine
    The Human Hands, and Feet, and Breath,
Entering thro' the Gates of Birth,
    And passing thro' the Gates of Death.

And O Thou Lamb of God! whom I
    Slew in my dark self-righteous pride,
Art Thou return'd to Albion's land,
    And is Jerusalem Thy Bride?

Come to my arms, and nevermore
    Depart; but dwell for ever here;
Create my spirit to Thy love;
    Subdue my Spectre to Thy fear.

Spectre of Albion! warlike Fiend!
    In clouds of blood and ruin roll'd,
I here reclaim thee as my own,
    My Selfhood—Satan arm'd in gold!

Selections from 'Jerusalem'

Is this thy soft Family-love,
  Thy cruel patriarchal pride;
Planting thy Family alone,
  Destroying all the World beside? 80

A man's worst Enemies are those
  Of his own House and Family;
And he who makes his Law a curse,
  By his own Law shall surely die!

In my Exchanges every land 85
  Shall walk; and mine in every land,
Mutual shall build Jerusalem,
  Both heart in heart and hand in hand.

If Humility is Christianity, you, O Jews! are the true Christians. If your tradition that Man contained in his limbs all animals is true, and they were separated from him by cruel sacrifices, and when compulsory cruel sacrifices had brought Humanity into a Feminine Tabernacle in the loins of Abraham and David, the Lamb of God, the Saviour, became apparent on Earth as the Prophets had foretold! The return of Israel is a return to mental sacrifice and war. Take up the Cross, O Israel! and follow Jesus.

Jerusalem, f. 27

[A Female Will]

What may Man be? who can tell? But what may Woman be,
To have power over Man from Cradle to corruptible Grave?
There is a Throne in every Man: it is the Throne of God.
This, Woman has claim'd as her own; and Man is no more:
Albion is the Tabernacle of Vala and her Temple, 5
And not the Tabernacle and Temple of the Most High.
O Albion! why wilt thou create a Female Will,
To hide the most evident God in a hidden covert, even
In the shadows of a Woman and a secluded Holy Place,
That we may pry after him as after a stolen treasure, 10
Hidden among the Dead and murèd up from the paths of Life?

Ibid., f. 34, ll. 25-35.

Selections from 'Jerusalem'

[The Universal Family]

Our Wars are wars of life, and wounds of love,
With intellectual spears, and long wingèd arrows of thought.
Mutual in one another's love and wrath all renewing,
We live as One Man: for, contracting our Infinite senses,
We behold multitude; or, expanding, we behold as One,   5
As One Man all the Universal Family; and that One Man
We call Jesus the Christ. And He in us, and we in Him,
Live in perfect harmony in Eden, the land of Life,
Giving, receiving, and forgiving each other's trespasses.
He is the Good Shepherd, He is the Lord and Master;   10
He is the Shepherd of Albion, He is all in all,
In Eden, in the garden of God, and in heavenly Jerusalem.
If we have offended, forgive us! take not vengeance against us!

Jerusalem, f. 38, ll. 14-26.

[Man's Spectre]

      Each Man is in his Spectre's power
      Until the arrival of that hour,
      When his Humanity awake,
      And cast his Spectre into the Lake.

Ibid., f. 41 (lines engraved in reverse on scroll).

[Pretences]

A pretence of Art to destroy Art; a pretence of Liberty
To destroy Liberty; a pretence of Religion to destroy Religion.

Ibid., f. 43, ll. 35-6.

Man's Spectre] *In the original draft on p. 12 of the Rossetti MS. this quatrain was at first written:*

      This world is in the Spectre's power
      Until the arrival of that hour,
      Until Humanity awake,
      And cast his own Spectre in the Lake—

followed by the unfinished stanza:

      And there to Eternity aspire
      The Selfhood in a flame of fire;
      Till then the Lamb of God . .

Selections from 'Jerusalem'

[Fourfold and Twofold Vision]

The Visions of Eternity, by reason of narrowèd perceptions,
Are become weak Visions of Time and Space, fix'd into furrows of Death; .
Till deep dissimulation is the only defence an honest man has left.

Jerusalem, f. 49, ll. 21-23.

[The Remembrance of Sin]

Come, O thou Lamb of God, and take away the remembrance of Sin!
To sin, and to hide the Sin in sweet deceit, is lovely:
To sin in the open face of day is cruel and pitiless; but
To record the Sin for a reproach, to let the Sun go down
In a remembrance of the Sin, is a woe and a horror,   5
A brooder of an Evil Day, and a Sun rising in blood.
Come then, O Lamb of God, and take away the remembrance of Sin!

Ibid., f. 50, ll. 24-30.

Rahab is an Eternal State.   TO THE DEISTS   *The Spiritual States of the Soul are all Eternal. Distinguish between the Man and his present State.*

He never can be a friend to the Human Race who is the preacher of Natural Morality or Natural Religion; he is a flatterer who means to betray, to perpetuate tyrant Pride and the Laws of that Babylon which, he foresees, shall shortly be destroyed with the Spiritual and not the Natural Sword. He is in the State named Rahab; which State must be put off before he can be the Friend of Man.

You, O Deists! profess yourselves the enemies of Christianity, and you are so: you are also the enemies of the Human Race and of Universal Nature. Man is born a Spectre, or Satan, and is altogether an Evil, and requires a new Selfhood continually, and must continually be changed into his direct Contrary. But

Selections from 'Jerusalem'

your Greek Philosophy, which is a remnant of Druidism, teaches that Man is righteous in his Vegetated Spectre—an opinion of fatal and accursed consequence to Man, as the Ancients saw plainly by Revelation, to the entire abrogation of Experimental Theory; and many believed what they saw, and prophesied of Jesus.

Man must and will have some religion; if he has not the religion of Jesus, he will have the religion of Satan, and will erect the synagogue of Satan, calling the Prince of this World 'God', and destroying all who do not worship Satan under the name of God. Will any one say: 'Where are those who worship Satan under the name of God?' Where are they? Listen! Every religion that preaches Vengeance for Sin is the religion of the Enemy and Avenger, and not of the Forgiver of Sin, and their God is Satan, named by the Divine Name. Your Religion, O Deists! Deism is the worship of the God of this World by the means of what you call Natural Religion and Natural Philosophy, and of Natural Morality or Self-Righteousness, the selfish virtues of the Natural Heart. This was the religion of the Pharisees who murdered Jesus. Deism is the same, and ends in the same.

Voltaire, Rousseau, Gibbon, Hume charge the spiritually Religious with hypocrisy; but how a Monk, or a Methodist either, can be a hypocrite, I cannot conceive. We are Men of like passions with others, and pretend not to be holier than others; therefore, when a Religious Man falls into sin, he ought not to be call'd a hypocrite: this title is more properly to be given to a player who falls into sin, whose profession is virtue and morality, and the making men self-righteous. Foote, in calling Whitefield hypocrite, was himself one; for Whitefield pretended not to be holier than others, but confessed his sins before all the world. Voltaire! Rousseau! you cannot escape my charge that you are Pharisees and hypocrites; for you are constantly talking of the virtues of the human heart, and particularly of your own; that you may accuse others, and especially the Religious, whose errors you, by this display of pretended virtue, chiefly design to expose. Rousseau thought Men good by nature: he found them evil, and found no friend. Friendship cannot exist without Forgiveness of

Selections from 'Jerusalem'

Sins continually. The book written by Rousseau, call'd his Confessions, is an apology and cloak for his sin, and not a confession.

But you also charge the poor Monks and Religious with being the causes of war, while you acquit and flatter the Alexanders and Cæsars, the Louises and Fredericks, who alone are its causes and its actors. But the Religion of Jesus, Forgiveness of Sin, can never be the cause of a war, nor of a single martyrdom.

Those who martyr others, or who cause war, are Deists, but never can be Forgivers of Sin. The glory of Christianity is to conquer by Forgiveness. All the destruction, therefore, in Christian Europe has arisen from Deism, which is Natural Religion.

> I saw a Monk of Charlemaine
> Arise before my sight:
> I talk'd with the Grey Monk as we stood
> In beams of infernal light.
>
> Gibbon arose with a lash of steel, 5
> And Voltaire with a racking wheel;
> The Schools, in clouds of learning roll'd,
> Arose with War in iron and gold.
>
> 'Thou lazy Monk!' they sound afar,
> 'In vain condemning glorious War; 10
> And in your cell you shall ever dwell:
> Rise, War, and bind him in his cell!'
>
> The blood red ran from the Grey Monk's side,
> His hands and feet were wounded wide,
> His body bent, his arms and knees 15
> Like to the roots of ancient trees.
>
> When Satan first the black bow bent
> And the Moral Law from the Gospel rent,
> He forg'd the Law into a sword,
> And spill'd the blood of Mercy's Lord. 20

1 Cp. the notes to 'I saw a Monk of Charlemaine' (*Rossetti MS.*, p. 134) and 'The Grey Monk' (*Pickering MS.*, p. 169).

Selections from 'Jerusalem'

Titus! Constantine! Charlemaine!
O Voltaire! Rousseau! Gibbon! Vain
Your Grecian mocks and Roman sword
Against this image of his Lord;

For a Tear is an Intellectual thing; 25
And a Sigh is the sword of an angel king;
And the bitter groan of a Martyr's woe
Is an arrow from the Almighty's bow.

Jerusalem, f. 52.

[Albion's Spectre]

But the Spectre, like a hoar-frost and a mildew, rose over Albion,
Saying: 'I am God, O Sons of Men! I am your Rational Power!
Am I not Bacon and Newton and Locke, who teach Humility to Man,
Who teach Doubt and Experiment? and my two wings, Voltaire, Rousseau?
Where is that Friend of Sinners, that Rebel against my Laws, 5
Who teaches Belief to the Nations and an unknown Eternal Life?
Come hither into the desert and turn these stones to bread!
Vain, foolish Man! wilt thou believe without Experiment,
And build a World of Phantasy upon my great Abyss,
A World of Shapes in craving lust and devouring appetite?' 10

Ibid., f. 54, ll. 15-24.

[The Holiness of Minute Particulars]

And many conversèd on these things as they labour'd at the furrow,
Saying: 'It is better to prevent misery than to release from misery;
It is better to prevent error than to forgive the criminal.
Labour well the Minute Particulars: attend to the Little Ones,
And those who are in misery cannot remain so long, 5
If we do but our duty: labour well the teeming Earth. . . .

Selections from 'Jerusalem'

He who would do good to another must do it in Minute Particulars.
General Good is the plea of the scoundrel, hypocrite, and flatterer;
For Art and Science cannot exist but in minutely organized
  Particulars, 9
And not in generalizing Demonstrations of the Rational Power:
The Infinite alone resides in Definite and Determinate Identity.
Establishment of Truth depends on destruction of Falsehood
  continually,
On Circumcision, not on Virginity, O Reasoners of Albion!

Jerusalem, f. 55, ll. 48-53, 60-6.

[A Vision of Joseph and Mary]

Behold! in the Visions of Elohim Jehovah, behold Joseph and
  Mary!
And be comforted, O Jerusalem! in the Visions of Jehovah Elohim.

She lookèd and saw Joseph the Carpenter in Nazareth, and Mary,
His espousèd Wife. And Mary said: 'If thou put me away
  from thee
Dost thou not murder me?' Joseph spoke in anger and fury:
  'Should I 5
Marry a harlot and an adulteress?' Mary answer'd: 'Art thou
  more pure
Than thy Maker, Who forgiveth Sins and calls again her that is
  lost?
Tho' she hates, He calls her again in love. I love my dear Joseph,
But he driveth me away from his presence; yet I hear the voice
  of God
In the voice of my husband: tho' he is angry for a moment he
  will not 10
Utterly cast me away: if I were pure, never could I taste the
  sweets
Of the Forgiveness of Sins; if I were holy, I never could behold
  the tears
Of love, of him who loves me in the midst of his anger in furnace
  of fire.

Selections from 'Jerusalem'

'Ah, my Mary,' said Joseph, weeping over and embracing her closely in
His arms, 'doth He forgive Jerusalem and not exact Purity from her who is
Polluted? I heard His voice in my sleep and His Angel in my dream,
Saying: "Doth Jehovah forgive a Debt only on condition that it shall
Be payèd? Doth He forgive Pollution only on conditions of Purity?
That Debt is not forgiven! That Pollution is not forgiven!
Such is the Forgiveness of the Gods, the Moral Virtues of the
Heathen, whose tender Mercies are Cruelty. But Jehovah's Salvation
Is without Money and without Price, in the Continual Forgiveness of Sins,
In the Perpetual Mutual Sacrifice in Great Eternity. For behold!
There is none that liveth and sinneth not! And this is the Covenant
Of Jehovah: 'If you forgive one another, so shall Jehovah forgive you;
That He Himself may dwell among you.' Fear not then to take
To thee Mary, thy Wife, for she is with Child by the Holy Ghost."'

Then Mary burst forth into a song! she flowèd like a river of
Many streams in the arms of Joseph, and gave forth her tears of joy
Like many waters, and emanating into gardens and palaces upon
Euphrates, and to forests and floods and animals, wild and tame, from
Gihon to Hiddekel, and to corn-fields and villages, and inhabitants
Upon Pison and Arnon and Jordan. And I heard the voice among
The Reapers, saying: 'Am I Jerusalem, the lost Adulteress? or am I
Babylon come up to Jerusalem?' And another voice answer'd, saying:

Selections from 'Jerusalem'

'Does the voice of my Lord call me again? am I pure thro' his Mercy
And Pity? Am I become lovely as a Virgin in his sight, who am
Indeed a Harlot drunken with the Sacrifice of Idols? Does He
Call her pure, as he did in the days of her Infancy, when she
Was cast out to the loathing of her person? The Chaldean took
Me from my cradle; the Amalekite stole me away upon his camels   41
Before I had ever beheld with love the face of Jehovah, or known
That there was a God of Mercy. O Mercy! O Divine Humanity!
O Forgiveness and Pity and Compassion! If I were pure I should never
Have known Thee: if I were unpolluted I should never have   45
Glorified Thy Holiness, or rejoicèd in thy great Salvation.'
Mary leanèd her side against Jerusalem: Jerusalem receivèd
The Infant into her hands in the Visions of Jehovah. Times passèd on.
Jerusalem fainted over the Cross and Sepulchre. She heard the voice:—
'Wilt thou make Rome thy Patriarch Druid, and the Kings of Europe his   50
Horsemen? Man in the Resurrection changes his Sexual Garments at will:
Every Harlot was once a Virgin, every Criminal an infant Love.'

Jerusalem, f. 61, ll. 1-52.

[Tirzah]

'O thou poor Human Form!' said she. 'O thou poor child of woe!
Why wilt thou wander away from Tirzah, why me compel to bind thee?
If thou dost go away from me, I shall consume upon these Rocks.
These fibres of thine eyes, that usèd to beam in distant heavens
Away from me, I have bound down with a hot iron: 5

Selections from 'Jerusalem'

These nostrils, that expanded with delight in morning skies,
I have bent downward with lead, melted in my roaring furnaces
Of affliction, of love, of sweet despair, of torment unendurable.
My soul is seven furnaces; incessant roars the bellows
Upon my terribly flaming heart; the molten metal runs
In channels thro' my fiery limbs—O love! O pity! O fear!
O pain! O the pangs, the bitter pangs of love forsaken!'

Jerusalem, f. 67, ll. 44-55.

[The Warrior and the Daughter of Albion]

Look! the beautiful Daughter of Albion sits naked upon the Stone,
Her panting Victim beside her; her heart is drunk with blood,
Tho' her brain is not drunk with wine; she goes forth from Albion
In pride of beauty, in cruelty of holiness, in the brightness
Of her tabernacle, and her ark and secret place. The beautiful Daughter
Of Albion delights the eyes of the Kings; their hearts and the
Hearts of their Warriors glow hot before Thor and Friga. O Moloch!
O Chemosh! O Bacchus! O Venus! O Double God of Generation!
The Heavens are cut like a mantle around from the Cliffs of Albion,
Across Europe, across Africa, in howlings and deadly War.
A sheet and veil and curtain of blood is let down from Heaven
Across the hills of Ephraim, and down Mount Olivet to
The Valley of the Jebusite . .
O beautiful Daughter of Albion, cruelty is thy delight!
O Virgin of terrible eyes, who dwellest by Valleys of springs
Beneath the Mountains of Lebanon, in the City of Rehob in Hamath,
Taught to touch the harp, to dance in the circle of Warriors

Selections from 'Jerusalem'

Before the Kings of Canaan, to cut the flesh from the Victim,
To roast the flesh in fire, to examine the Infant's limbs
In cruelties of holiness, to refuse the joys of love, to bring   20
The Spies from Egypt to raise jealousy in the bosoms of the twelve
Kings of Canaan; then to let the Spies depart to Meribah Kadesh,
To the place of the Amalekite.   I am drunk with unsatiated love;
I must rush again to War, for the Virgin has frown'd and refus'd.
Sometimes I curse, and sometimes bless thy fascinating beauty.   25
Once Man was occupièd in intellectual pleasures and energies;
But now my Soul is harrow'd with grief and fear, and love and desire,
And now I hate, and now I love, and Intellect is no more:
There is no time for anything but the torments of love and desire:
The Feminine and Masculine Shadows, soft, mild, and ever varying   30
In beauty, are Shadows now no more, but Rocks in Horeb.

Jerusalem, f. 68, ll. 11-23, 53-70.

[Men and States]

As the Pilgrim passes while the Country permanent remains,
So Men pass on, but States remain permanent for ever.

Ibid., f. 73, ll. 42-3.

To the Christians

Devils are False Religions.
Saul! Saul! why persecutest thou me?

> I give you the end of a golden string;
>   Only wind it into a ball,
> It will lead you in at Heaven's gate,
>   Built in Jerusalem's wall.

We are told to abstain from fleshly desires that we may lose no time from the Work of the Lord. Every moment lost is a moment that cannot be redeemed: every pleasure that intermingles

Selections from 'Jerusalem'

with the duty of our station is a folly unredeemable, and is planted like the seed of a wild flower among our wheat. All the tortures of repentance are tortures of self-reproach on account of our leaving the Divine Harvest to the Enemy, the struggles of entanglement with incoherent roots. I know of no other Christianity and of no other Gospel than the liberty both of body and mind to exercise the Divine Arts of Imagination—Imagination, the real and Eternal World of which this Vegetable Universe is but a faint shadow, and in which we shall live in our Eternal or Imaginative Bodies, when these Vegetable Mortal Bodies are no more. The Apostles knew of no other Gospel. What were all their spiritual gifts? What is the Divine Spirit? Is the Holy Ghost any other than an Intellectual Fountain? What is the harvest of the Gospel and its labours? What is that talent which it is a curse to hide? What are the treasures of Heaven which we are to lay up for ourselves? Are they any other than mental studies and performances? What are all the gifts of the Gospel? Are they not all mental gifts? Is God a Spirit who must be worshipped in spirit and in truth? And are not the gifts of the Spirit everything to Man? O ye Religious, discountenance every one among you who shall pretend to despise Art and Science! I call upon you in the name of Jesus! What is the life of Man but Art and Science? Is it meat and drink? Is not the Body more than raiment? What is Mortality but the things relating to the Body, which dies? What is Immortality but the things relating to the Spirit, which lives eternally? What is the Joy of Heaven but improvement in the things of the Spirit? What are the Pains of Hell but Ignorance, Bodily Lust, Idleness, and devastation of the things of the Spirit? Answer this to yourselves, and expel from among you those who pretend to despise the labours of Art and Science, which alone are the labours of the Gospel. Is not this plain and manifest to the thought? Can you think at all, and not pronounce heartily: that to labour in knowledge is to build up Jerusalem; and to despise knowledge is to despise Jerusalem and her Builders. And remember: He who despises and mocks a mental gift in another, calling it pride and selfishness and sin,

Selections from 'Jerusalem'

mocks Jesus, the giver of every mental gift, which always appear to the ignorance-loving hypocrite as sins; but that which is a sin in the sight of cruel Man, is not so in the sight of our kind God. Let every Christian, as much as in him lies, engage himself openly and publicly, before all the World, in some mental pursuit for the Building up of Jerusalem.

> I stood among my valleys of the south,
> And saw a flame of fire, even as a Wheel
> Of fire surrounding all the heavens: it went
> From west to east against the current of
> Creation, and devour'd all things in its loud
> Fury and thundering course round Heaven and Earth
> By it the Sun was roll'd into an orb;
> By it the Moon faded into a globe,
> Travelling thro' the night; for from its dire
> And restless fury Man himself shrunk up
> Into a little root a fathom long.
> And I askèd a Watcher and a Holy One
> Its name. He answer'd: 'It is the Wheel of Religion.'
> I wept and said: 'Is this the law of Jesus,
> This terrible devouring sword turning every way?'
> He answer'd: 'Jesus died because He strove
> Against the current of this Wheel: its name
> Is Caiaphas, the dark Preacher of Death,
> Of sin, of sorrow, and of punishment,
> Opposing Nature. It is Natural Religion.
> But Jesus is the bright Preacher of Life,
> Creating Nature from this fiery Law
> By self-denial and Forgiveness of Sin.
> Go, therefore, cast out devils in Christ's name,
> Heal thou the sick of spiritual disease,
> Pity the evil; for thou art not sent
> To smite with terror and with punishments
> Those that are sick, like to the Pharisees,
> Crucifying, and encompassing sea and land,

Selections from 'Jerusalem'

For proselytes to tyranny and wrath. 30
But to the Publicans and Harlots go:
Teach them true happiness, but let no curse
Go forth out of thy mouth to blight their peace.
For Hell is open'd to Heaven; thine eyes beheld
The dungeons burst, and the prisoners set free.' 35

England! awake! awake! awake!
   Jerusalem thy sister calls!
Why wilt thou sleep the sleep of death,
   And close her from thy ancient walls?

Thy hills and valleys felt her feet 40
   Gently upon their bosoms move:
Thy gates beheld sweet Zion's ways;
   Then was a time of joy and love.

And now the time returns again:
   Our souls exult, and London's towers 45
Receive the Lamb of God to dwell
   In England's green and pleasant bowers.

Jerusalem, f. 77.

[A Vision of Jerusalem]

I see thy Form, O lovely, mild Jerusalem! Wing'd with Six Wings
In the opacous Bosom of the Sleeper, lovely, threefold
In Head and Heart and Reins, three Universes of love and beauty.
Thy forehead bright, Holiness to the Lord! with gates of pearl
Reflects Eternity beneath thy azure wings of feathery down, 5
Ribb'd, delicate, and cloth'd with feather'd gold and azure and purple,
From thy white shoulders shadowing purity in holiness;
Thence, feather'd with soft crimson of the ruby, bright as fire,
Spreading into the azure wings which, like a canopy,
Bends over thy immortal Head in which Eternity dwells. 10

Selections from 'Jerusalem'

Albion! belovèd Land, I see thy mountains and thy hills
And valleys, and thy pleasant Cities, Holiness to the Lord.
I see the Spectres of thy Dead, O Emanation of Albion!

Thy Bosom white, translucent, cover'd with immortal gems,
A sublime ornament not obscuring the outlines of beauty,   15
Terrible to behold, for thy extreme beauty and perfection:
Twelvefold here all the Tribes of Israel I behold
Upon the Holy Land: I see the River of Life and Tree of Life.
I see the New Jerusalem descending out of Heaven
Between thy Wings of gold and silver, feather'd immortal,   20
Clear as the rainbow, as the cloud of the Sun's tabernacle.

Thy Reins cover'd with Wings translucent, sometimes covering
And sometimes spread abroad, reveal the flames of holiness
Which like a robe covers, and like a Veil of Seraphim
In flaming fire unceasing burns from Eternity to Eternity.   25
Twelvefold I there behold Israel in her Tents;
A Pillar of a Cloud by day, a Pillar of Fire by night
Guides them; there I behold Moab and Ammon and Amalek;
There Bells of silver round thy knees, living, articulate
Comforting sounds of love and harmony; and on thy feet   30
Sandals of gold and pearl; and Egypt and Assyria before me,
The Isles of Javan, Philistia, Tyre, and Lebanon.

Jerusalem, f. 86, ll. 1-32.

[The Worship of God]

It is easier to forgive an Enemy than to forgive a Friend.
The man who permits you to injure him deserves your vengeance;
He also will receive it. Go, Spectre! obey my most secret desire,
Which thou knowest without my speaking. Go to these Fiends
   of Righteousness,
Tell them to obey their Humanities, and not pretend Holiness,   **5**
When they are murderers. As far as my Hammer and Anvil
   permit,
Go tell them that the Worship of God is honouring His gifts

Selections from 'Jerusalem'

In other men, and loving the greatest men best, each according
To his Genius, which is the Holy Ghost in Man: there is no other
God than that God who is the intellectual fountain of Humanity.
He who envies or calumniates, which is murder and cruelty, 11
Murders the Holy One. Go tell them this, and overthrow their cup,
Their bread, their altar-table, their incense, and their oath,
Their marriage and their baptism, their burial and consecration.
I have tried to make friends by corporeal gifts, but have only 15
Made enemies; I never made friends but by spiritual gifts,
By severe contentions of friendship, and the burning fire of thought.
He who would see the Divinity must see Him in His Children,
One first in friendship and love, then a Divine Family, and in the midst
Jesus will appear. So he who wishes to see a Vision, a perfect Whole, 20
Must see it in its Minute Particulars, organized; and not as thou,
O Fiend of Righteousness, pretendest! thine is a disorganized
And snowy cloud, brooder of tempests and destructive War.
You smile with pomp and rigour, you talk of benevolence and virtue;
I act with benevolence and virtue, and get murder'd time after time; 25
You accumulate Particulars, and murder by analysing, that you
May take the aggregate, and you call the aggregate Moral Law;
And you call that swell'd and bloated Form a Minute Particular.
But General Forms have their vitality in Particulars; and every
Particular is a Man, a Divine Member of the Divine Jesus. 30

Jerusalem, f. 91, ll. 1-30.

[The Cry of Los]

I care not whether a man is Good or Evil; all that I care
Is whether he is a Wise man or a Fool. Go! put off Holiness,
And put on Intellect; or my thund'rous hammer shall drive thee
To wrath, which thou condemnest, till thou obey my voice.

Ibid., f. 91, ll. 54-7.

Selections from 'Jerusalem'

[Albion upon the Rock]

Albion cold lays on his Rock; storms and snows beat round him,
Beneath the Furnaces and the Starry Wheels and the Immortal Tomb;
Howling winds cover him; roaring seas dash furious against him;
In the deep darkness broad lightnings glare, long thunders roll.

The weeds of Death enwrap his hands and feet, blown incessant,
And wash'd incessant by the for-ever restless sea-waves, foaming abroad 6
Upon the white Rock. England, a Female Shadow, as deadly damps
Of the Mines of Cornwall and Derbyshire, lays upon his bosom heavy, [round
Movèd by the wind in volumes of thick cloud returning, folding
His loins and bosom, unremovable by swelling storms and loud rending 10
Of enragèd thunders. Around them the Starry Wheels of their Giant Sons
Revolve, and over them the Furnaces of Los and the Immortal Tomb, around,
Erin sitting in the Tomb, to watch them unceasing night and day:
And the Body of Albion was closèd apart from all Nations.

Over them the famish'd Eagle screams on bony wings, and around
Them howls the Wolf of famine; deep heaves the Ocean, black, thundering 16
Around the wormy Garments of Albion, then pausing in deathlike silence.

Time was Finishèd!

Jerusalem, f. 94. ll. 1-18.

[The Wrath of God]

The Breath Divine went forth over the morning hills. Albion rose
In anger, the wrath of God, breaking bright, flaming on all sides around

Selections from 'Jerusalem'

His awful limbs: into the Heavens he walkèd, clothèd in flames,
Loud thund'ring, with broad flashes of flaming lightning and pillars
Of fire, speaking the Words of Eternity in Human Forms, in direful
Revolutions of Action and Passion, thro' the Four Elements on all sides 6
Surrounding his awful Members. Thou seest the Sun in heavy clouds
Struggling to rise above the Mountains; in his burning hand
He takes his Bow, then chooses out his arrows of flaming gold;
Murmuring, the Bowstring breathes with ardour; clouds roll round the 10
Horns of the wide Bow; loud sounding winds sport on the mountain brows,
Compelling Urizen to his Furrow, and Tharmas to his Sheepfold,
And Luvah to his Loom.

Jerusalem, f. 95, ll. 5-17.

[The Divine Image]

Jesus said: 'Wouldest thou love one who never died
For thee, or ever die for one who had not died for thee?
And if God dieth not for Man, and giveth not Himself
Eternally for Man, Man could not exist; for Man is Love,
As God is Love: every kindness to another is a little Death 5
In the Divine Image; nor can Man exist but by Brotherhood.'

Ibid., f. 96, ll. 23-8.

[The End of the Song of Jerusalem]

All Human Forms identifièd, even Tree, Metal, Earth, and Stone; all
Human Forms identifièd, living, going forth and returning wearied
Into the Planetary lives of Years, Months, Days and Hours; reposing,
And then awaking into His bosom in the Life of Immortality.
And I heard the Name of their Emanations: they are namèd Jerusalem. 5

Ibid., f. 99, ll. 1-5.

VERSES

FROM

FOR THE SEXES
THE GATES OF PARADISE

Circa 1810

VERSES

FROM

'THE GATES OF PARADISE'

[Prologue]

  Mutual Forgiveness of each vice,
  Such are the Gates of Paradise,
  Against the Accuser's chief desire,
  Who walk'd among the stones of fire.
  Jehovah's Finger wrote the Law;   5
  Then wept; then rose in zeal and awe,
  And the dead corpse, from Sinai's heat,
  Buried beneath His Mercy-seat.
  O Christians! Christians! tell me why
  You rear it on your altars high?   10

In its original form (as published in 1793) *The Gates of Paradise* was a simple picture-book 'For Children', consisting of a frontispiece, title-page, and sixteen engraved plates of emblematic designs, the original pencil sketches for which are found in the *Rossetti MS*. Later (*circa* 1810) Blake converted this little book into one of his Prophetic Writings by changing the words 'For Children' of the title to 'For the Sexes', retouching the plates and legends, and adding a Prologue, Epilogue, and descriptive couplets entitled 'The Keys of the Gates', which embody in a digested form his maturer system of symbolism. At a still later date Blake again reworked upon the plates, and made a few further alterations in the text.

The version here given is taken from this second issue of the *Gates* 'For the Sexes', the variant readings of the earlier issue, and short descriptions of the plates themselves (without which the verses would be scarcely intelligible), being supplied in the footnotes.

Prologue 5 Finger] Fingers *For the Sexes, 1st issue.*
    7, 8   And in the midst of Sinai's heat
          Hid it beneath His Mercy Seat. *For the Sexes, 1st issue.*

Verses from 'The Gates of Paradise'

The Keys

> The Caterpillar on the leaf
> Reminds thee of thy Mother's grief.

of the Gates

>   1. My Eternal Man set in repose,
>   The Female from his darkness rose;
>   And she found me beneath a Tree,
>   A Mandrake, and in her Veil hid me.
>   Serpent Reasonings us entice
>   Of good and evil, virtue and vice,
>   2. Doubt self-jealous, Watery folly;
>   3. Struggling thro' Earth's melancholy;
>   4. Naked in Air, in shame and fear;
>   5. Blind in Fire, with shield and spear;
>   Two-horn'd Reasoning, cloven fiction,
>   In doubt, which is self-contradiction,

Frontispiece. A caterpillar on an oak leaf. On a second leaf a human chrysalis like a babe in swaddling clothes. *Legend*: What is Man? *with the lines*:

> The sun's light, when he unfolds it,
> Depends on the organ that beholds it.

1. A woman under a weeping willow, holding a babe in her left arm, pulls a mandrake out of the ground by its hair. *Legend*: I found him beneath a tree.

2. An old man, resting his hands on his knees, sits upon a rock beneath a leafless tree in a deluge of rain. The encroaching flood rises to his feet. *Legend*: Water, *with the line*: Thou waterest him with tears.

3. Crouching figure of a man emerging from a crevice in a rock. *Legend*: Earth, *with the line*: He struggles into life.

4. A man, nude, seated upon a white cloud, clasps his forehead with both hands and gazes steadfastly before him. Behind him the sky studded with stars. *Legend*: Air, *with the line*: On cloudy doubts and reasoning cares.

5. A fiend, blind, standing in flames, armed with spear and shield. *Legend*: Fire, *with the line*: That end in endless strife—*this and the three preceding lines forming a quatrain.*

Verses from 'The Gates of Paradise'

    A dark Hermaphrodite we stood—
    Rational truth, root of evil and good.
    Round me flew the Flaming Sword;   15
    Round her snowy Whirlwinds roar'd,
    Freezing her Veil, the Mundane Shell.
6. I rent the Veil where the Dead dwell:
    When weary Man enters his Cave,
    He meets his Saviour in the grave.   20
    Some find a Female Garment there,
    And some a Male, woven with care;
    Lest the Sexual Garments sweet
    Should grow a devouring Winding-sheet.
7. One dies! Alas! the Living and Dead!   25
    One is slain! and One is fled!
8. In Vain-glory hatcht and nurst,
    By double Spectres, self-accurst.
    My Son! my Son! thou treatest me
    But as I have instructed thee.   30
9. On the shadows of the Moon,
    Climbing thro' Night's highest noon;
10. In Time's Ocean falling, drown'd;

---

5. In l. 4 'we' is a revised rdg. of 'I' in the earlier issue.

6. A cherub issuing from an egg. *Legend*: At length for hatching ripe he breaks the shell.

7. A boy in garden, hat in hand, chases flying fairy. A second fairy lies crushed at his feet. *Legend*: Alas! [the original inscription written in centre of page with the addition of the words on either side and below] What are these? ... the Female Martyr! Is she also the Divine Image?

8. An old man, seated, with a sword in right hand, leans sorrowfully on his elbow, averting his head from the figure of a joyfully departing youth, who threatens him with a dart. *Legend*: My son! my son!

9. A man standing on edge of world prepares to mount a ladder reared against the crescent moon. Two lovers watch him. *Legend*: I want! I want!

10. A man drowning in sea, with one arm upthrust, and head just disappearing beneath the waves. *Legend*: Help! Help!

Verses from 'The Gates of Paradise'

11. In Agèd Ignorance profound,
     Holy and cold, I clipp'd the wings
     Of all sublunary things,
12. And in depths of my dungeons
     Closed the Father and the Sons.
13. But when once I did descry
     The Immortal Man that cannot die,
14. Thro' evening shades I haste away
     To close the labours of my day.
15. The Door of Death I open found,
     And the Worm weaving in the ground:
16. Thou'rt my Mother, from the womb;
     Wife, Sister, Daughter, to the tomb;
     Weaving to dreams the Sexual strife,
     And weeping over the Web of Life.

---

11. An old man wearing spectacles, seated under a tree, clips the wings of a boy who struggles to escape. Before him the setting sun. *Legend*: Aged Ignorance, *with the line*: Perceptive Organs closed, their Objects close.

12. An old man (Count Ugolino) with his two sons and two grandsons in dungeon cell. *Legend*: Does thy God, O Priest, take such vengeance as this?

13. A husband, wife, and two children, beside a bed on which lies a corpse, watch the ascending spirit of an old man who points upward. *Legend*: Fear and Hope are—Vision.

14. A man with a staff in his hand strides along a country lane. *Legend*: The traveller hasteth in the evening.

15. An old man, leaning on a crutch, passes through the gateway of a tomb. *Legend*: Death's door.

16. A woman in white cerements, seated on the ground in a burial crypt. A huge worm crawls around her feet. *Legend*: I have said to the worm: Thou art my mother and my sister.

Verses from 'The Gates of Paradise'

[Epilogue]

To the Accuser who is
The God of this World

Truly, my Satan, thou art but a dunce,
And dost not know the garment from the man;
Every harlot was a virgin once,
Nor canst thou ever change Kate into Nan.

Tho' thou art worship'd by the names divine 5
Of Jesus and Jehovah, thou art still
The Son of Morn in weary Night's decline.
The lost traveller's dream under the hill.

THE GHOST
OF
ABEL

(Engraved 1822)

THE GHOST OF ABEL

A REVELATION IN THE VISIONS OF JEHOVAH
SEEN BY WILLIAM BLAKE

To Lord Byron in the Wilderness :

      What doest thou here, Elijah ?
Can a Poet doubt the Visions of Jehovah ? Nature has no Outline,
But Imagination has. Nature has no Tune, but Imagination has.
Nature has no Supernatural, and dissolves: Imagination is
 Eternity.

SCENE—*A rocky Country.* EVE, *fainted, over the dead body of*
 ABEL, *which lays near a Grave.* ADAM *kneels by her.*
 JEHOVAH *stands above.*

Jehovah. Adam !
Adam.   I will not hear Thee more, Thou Spiritual Voice
Is this Death ?
Jehovah.   Adam !
Adam.   It is in vain : I will not hear Thee
Henceforth. Is this Thy Promise, that the Woman's seed
Should bruise the Serpent's head ? Is this the Serpent ? Ah !
Seven times, O Eve ! thou hast fainted over the Dead. Ah ! Ah !

       EVE *revives.*

Eve. Is this the Promise of Jehovah ? O ! it is all a vain delusion,
This Death, and this Life, and this Jehovah !   10
Jehovah.   Woman, lift thine eyes !

   A Voice is heard coming on.

Voice. O Earth, cover not thou my blood ! cover not thou my
 blood !

The Ghost of Abel

Enter the Ghost *of* ABEL.

Eve. Thou visionary Phantasm, thou art not the real Abel.
Abel. Among the Elohim, a Human Victim I wander: I am their House,
Prince of the Air, and our dimensions compass Zenith and Nadir.
Vain is Thy Covenant, O Jehovah! I am the Accuser and Avenger
Of Blood. O Earth! cover not thou the blood of Abel.
Jehovah. What Vengence dost thou require?
Abel. Life for Life! Life for Life!
Jehovah. He who shall take Cain's life must also die, O Abel!
And who is he? Adam, wilt thou, or Eve, thou do this?
Adam. It is all a vain delusion of the all-creative Imagination.
Eve, come away, and let us not believe these vain delusions.
Abel is dead, and Cain slew him. We shall also die a death,
And then—what then? be, as poor Abel, a Thought; or as
This? O! what shall I call Thee, Form Divine, Father of Mercies,
That appearest to my Spiritual Vision? Eve, seest thou also?
Eve. I see Him plainly with my Mind's Eye. I see also Abel living,
Tho' terribly afflicted, as we also are; yet Jehovah sees him
Alive and not dead. Were it not better to believe Vision
With all our might and strength, tho' we are fallen and lost?
Adam. Eve, thou hast spoken truly: let us kneel before His feet.

They kneel before JEHOVAH.

Abel. Are these the sacrifices of Eternity, O Jehovah—a broken spirit
And a contrite heart? O! I cannot forgive: the Accuser hath
Enter'd into me as into his house, and I loathe Thy Tabernacles.
As Thou hast said, so is it come to pass. My desire is unto Cain,
And he doth rule over me; therefore my soul in fumes of blood
Cries for Vengeance, Sacrifice on Sacrifice, Blood on Blood!

The Ghost of Abel

Jehovah. Lo! I have given you a Lamb for an Atonement, instead
Of the Transgressor, or no Flesh or Spirit could ever live. 40
Abel. Compellèd I cry, O Earth! cover not the blood of Abel.

ABEL *sinks down into the Grave, from which arises* SATAN, *armed in glittering scales, with a Crown and a Spear.*

Satan. I will have Human blood, and not the blood of bulls or goats,
And no Atonement, O Jehovah! The Elohim live on Sacrifice
Of Men: hence I am God of Men! Thou human, O Jehovah! 44
By the rock and oak of the Druid, creeping mistletoe, and thorn,
Cain's city built with human blood, not blood of bulls and goats,
Thou shalt Thyself be sacrificed to Me, thy God! on Calvary.
Jehovah. Such is My Will—(*Thunders*)—that thou thyself go to Eternal Death
In Self-Annihilation, even till Satan, self-subdu'd, put off Satan
Into the Bottomless Abyss, whose torment arises for ever and ever. 50

On each side a Chorus of Angels, entering, sing the following:—

The Elohim of the Heathen swore Vengeance for Sin! Then Thou stood'st
Forth, O Elohim Jehovah! in the midst of the darkness of the Oath, all clothèd
In Thy Covenant of the Forgiveness of Sins. Death, O Holy! Is this Brotherhood?
The Elohim saw their Oath Eternal Fire: they rollèd apart, trembling, over the
Mercy-seat, each in his station fixt in the firmament by Peace, Brotherhood, and Love. 55

The Curtain falls.

APPENDIX
TO
THE PROPHETIC BOOKS

THERE IS NO NATURAL RELIGION[1]
[Part the First]

THE ARGUMENT

Man has no notion of moral fitness but from Education. Naturally, he is only a Natural Organ, subject to Sense.

I

Man cannot naturally perceive but through his Natural or Bodily Organs

II

Man, by his Reasoning Power, can only compare and judge of what he has already perceiv'd.

III

From a Perception of only three Senses, or three Elements, none could deduce a fourth or fifth.

IV

None could have other than Natural or Organic Thoughts if he had none but Organic Perceptions.

V

Man's Desires are limited by his Perceptions; none can desire what he has not perceiv'd.

VI

The Desires and Perceptions of Man, untaught by anything but Organs of Sense, must be limited to Objects of Sense.

---

[1] This and the following tractate dealing with the same subject would appear to be the first examples of Blake's use of Illuminated Printing, 1788. On the order and arrangement of the plates here followed see my Bibliographical Introduction to the present work.

Appendix to the Prophetic Books

CONCLUSION

If it were not for the Poetic or Prophetic Character, the Philosophic and Experimental would soon be at the Ratio of all things; and stand still, unable to do other than repeat the same dull round over again.

[Part the Second]

I

Man's Perceptions are not bounded by Organs of Perception; he perceives more than Sense (tho' ever so acute) can discover.

II

Reason, or the Ratio of all we have already known, is not the same that it shall be when we know more.

III

[*Deest*]

IV

The Bounded is loathed by its possessor. The same dull round, even of a Universe, would soon become a Mill with complicated wheels.

V

If the Many become the same as the Few, when possess'd, 'More! More!' is the cry of a mistaken soul: less than All cannot satisfy Man.

VI

If any could desire what he is incapable of possessing, Despair must be his Eternal lot.

VII

The Desire of Man being Infinite, the possession is Infinite, and himself Infinite.

APPLICATION

He who sees the Infinite in all things sees God. He who sees the Ratio only, sees himself only.

THEREFORE

God becomes as we are, that we may be as He is.

All Religions are One

ALL RELIGIONS ARE ONE
The Voice of one crying in the Wilderness
THE ARGUMENT

As the true method of Knowledge is Experiment, the true faculty of knowing must be the faculty which experiences. This faculty I treat of:

Principle 1

That the Poetic Genius is the True Man, and that the Body or Outward Form of Man is derived from the Poetic Genius. Likewise that the Forms of all things are derived from their Genius, which by the Ancients was call'd an Angel and Spirit and Demon.

Principle 2

As all men are alike in Outward Form; so, and with the same infinite variety, all are alike in the Poetic Genius.

Principle 3

No man can think, write, or speak from his heart, but he must intend Truth. Thus all sects of Philosophy are from the Poetic Genius, adapted to the weaknesses of every individual.

Principle 4

As none by travelling over known lands can find out the unknown; so, from already acquired knowledge, Man could not acquire more; therefore an universal Poetic Genius exists.

Principle 5

The Religions of all Nations are derived from each Nation's different reception of the Poetic Genius, which is everywhere call'd the Spirit of Prophecy.

Principle 6

The Jewish and Christian Testaments are an original derivation from the Poetic Genius. This is necessary from the confined nature of bodily sensation.

Principle 7

As all men are alike, tho' infinitely various; so all Religions: and as all similars have one source the True Man is the source, he being the Poetic Genius.

Appendix to the Prophetic Books

[FROM BLAKE'S ENGRAVING OF THE LAOCOON]

To left of plate.

Spiritual War: Israel deliver'd from Egypt is Art deliver'd from Nature and Imitation.

A Poet, a Painter, a Musician, an Architect; the man or woman who is not one of these is not a Christian.

You must leave fathers and mothers and houses and lands if they stand in the way of Art.

The Eternal Body of Man is the Imagination; that is God Himself, the Divine Body, ישע Jesus; we are His Members.

It manifests itself in His Works of Art: In Eternity all is Vision!

The true Christian Charity not dependent on Money, the life's blood of poor families; that is on Caesar or Empire, or Natural Religion.

Money! which is the great Satan or Reason, the root of Good and Evil, in the Accusation of Sin.

Prayer is the study of Art.

Praise is the practice of Art.

Fasting, etc. all relate to Art.

The outward Ceremony is Antichrist.

These aphorisms are written around an engraving of the Laocoon, bearing the imprint, 'Drawn and Engraved by William Blake' (*circa* 1817). At the base of the group is the title, ' יה and his two sons Satan and Adam as they were copied from the Cherubim of Solomon's Temple by three Rhodians, and applied to Natural Fact, or History of Ilium.' Above the figure of Laocoon is the inscription 'The Angel of the Divine Presence מלאך יהוה', and to the left of his head 'OΦ18X☉', the two serpents being labelled respectively 'Good' and 'Evil'. Beneath the left hand of Laocoon, clenching the neck of the serpent, is the inscription 'לילית'.

These symbolic sayings fill the whole ground of the plate; and as they are written from all four sides, and squeezed into every vacant corner, the intended order, if any, is largely conjectural.

From Blake's Laocoon

Encircling the three figures.

Good and Evil are Riches and Poverty, a Tree of Misery propagating Generation and Death.

The Gods of Priam are the Cherubim of Moses and Solomon, the Hosts of Heaven.

Without unceasing Practice nothing can be done: Practice is Art. If you leave off you are lost.

Hebrew Art is called Sin, by the Deist Science.

All that we see is Vision; from Generated Organs, gone as soon as come; permanent in the Imagination; consider'd as nothing by the Natural Man.

Satan's wife, the Goddess Nature, is War and Misery, and Heroism a Miser.

At head of plate.

Where any view of Money exists, Art cannot be carried on, but War only; by pretences to the two Impossibilities, Chastity and Abstinence, Gods of the Heathen. (Read Matthew x. 9, 10).

He repented that He had made Adam (of the Female, the Adamah); and it grieved Him at His heart.

Art can never exist without Naked Beauty displayed.

The Gods of Greece and Egypt were Mathematical Diagrams. (See Plato's Works.)

What can be created can be destroyed.

Adam is only the Natural Man, and not the Soul or Imagination.

Divine Union deriding and denying Immediate Communion with God. The Spoilers say: 'Where are His Works that He did in the Wilderness?' Lo! what are these? Whence came they? These are not the Works of Egypt, nor Babylon, whose Gods are the Powers of this World, Goddess Nature; who first spoil and then destroy Imaginative Art, for their Glory is War and Dominion.

Empire against Art. (See Virgil's *Æneid.* Lib. VI, v. 848.)

Appendix to the Prophetic Books

To right of plate.

Jesus and His Apostles and Disciples were all Artists. Their Works were destroy'd by the Seven Angels of the Seven Churches in Asia, Antichrist, Science.

The Old and New Testaments are the great code of Art.

The whole business of Man is the Arts, and all things, common. No secrecy in Art.

Art is the Tree of Life.

God is Jesus.

Science is the Tree of Death.

For every pleasure Money is useless.

There are States in which all Visionary Men are accounted Mad Men: such are Greece and Rome, such is Empire or Tax. (See Luke ii. 1.)

The unproductive Man is not a Christian, much less the Destroyer.

What we call antique gems are the gems of Aaron's breast-plate.

Is not every Vice possible to Man described in the Bible openly?

All is not Sin that Satan calls so—all the Loves and Graces of Eternity.

Christianity is Art and not Money. Money is its Curse.

At foot of plate.

If Morality was Christianity, Socrates was the Saviour.

Art degraded, Imagination denied, War governed the Nations.

ON HOMER'S POETRY [1]

Every poem must necessarily be a perfect Unity, but why Homer's is peculiarly so I cannot tell: he has told the story of Bellerophon, and omitted the Judgement of Paris, which is not only a part but a principal part of Homer's subject.

---

[1] This and the following piece are engraved on a single plate, in Blake's Illuminated Printing, *circa* 1817.

On Homer's Poetry

But when a work has Unity, it is as much in a part as in the whole. The Torso is as much a Unity as the Laocoon.

As Unity is the cloak of Folly, so Goodness is the cloak of Knavery. Those who will have Unity exclusively in Homer come out with a Moral like a sting in the tail. Aristotle says Characters are either good or bad; now Goodness or Badness has nothing to do with Character. An apple tree, a pear tree, a horse, a lion are Characters; but a good apple tree or a bad is an apple tree still: a horse is not more a lion for being a bad horse; that is its Character: its Goodness or Badness is another consideration.

It is the same with the Moral of a whole poem as with the Moral Goodness of its parts. Unity and Morality are secondary considerations, and belong to Philosophy and not to Poetry, to Exception and not to Rule, to Accident and not to Substance. The Ancients called it eating of the Tree of Good and Evil.

The Classics! it is the Classics, and not Goths nor Monks, that desolate Europe with wars.

ON VIRGIL

Sacred Truth has pronounced that Greece and Rome, as Babylon and Egypt, so far from being parents of Arts and Sciences as they pretend, were destroyers of all Art. Homer, Virgil and Ovid confirm this opinion, and make us reverence the Word of God, the only light of antiquity that remains unperverted by War. Virgil in the *Æneid*, Book vi, line 848, says 'Let others study Art: Rome has somewhat better to do, namely War and Dominion'.

Rome and Greece swept Art into their maw and destroyed it; a warlike State never can produce Art. It will rob and plunder and accumulate into one place, and translate and copy and buy and sell and criticize, but not make. Grecian is Mathematic Form: Gothic is Living Form. Mathematic Form is eternal in the Reasoning Memory: Living Form is Eternal Existence.

FROM BLAKE'S *DESCRIPTIVE CATALOGUE*

(1809)

Sir Geffrey Chaucer and the Nine and twenty Pilgrims on their journey to Canterbury.[1]

The time chosen is early morning, before sunrise, when the jolly company are just quitting the Tabarde Inn. The Knight and Squire with the Squire's Yeoman lead the Procession; next follow the youthful Abbess, her Nun, and three Priests; her greyhounds attend her:

> 'Of small hounds had she that she fed
> With roast flesh, milk, and wastel bread.'

Next follow the Friar and Monk; then the Tapiser, the Pardoner, and the Sompnour and Manciple. After these 'Our Host', who occupies the centre of the cavalcade, directs them to the Knight as the person who would be likely to commence their task of each telling a tale in their order. After the Host follow the Shipman, the Haberdasher, the Dyer, the Franklin, the Physician, the Ploughman, the Lawyer, the Poor Parson, the Merchant, the Wife of Bath, the Miller, the Cook, the Oxford Scholar, Chaucer himself; and the Reeve comes as Chaucer has described:

> 'And ever he rode hinderest of the rout.'

[1] Blake's account of his tempera painting of the Canterbury Pilgrims, with a criticism of the rival work of Stothard (*Descriptive Catalogue*, No. III, pp. 7-34). The 'fresco', painted in 1808, and exhibited in the summer of 1809, was published as an engraving in October of the following year. This text, illustrated by the artist's reduction of part of the original plate (reproduced in Russell's *Engravings*, p. 92), was three years later separately reprinted as a small duodecimo volume entitled *The Prologue and Characters of Chaucer's Pilgrims, selected from his Canterbury Tales*. I have made no attempt to alter Blake's version of the passages quoted from Chaucer, which are reprinted in the somewhat debased form in which they occur in the *Catalogue*. They show that Blake could not have met with Tyrwhitt's great metrical restoration of 1775, and that by him, as by Waller, Chaucer must have been read with 'the glory of his numbers lost'.

From Blake's Descriptive Catalogue

These last are issuing from the gateway of the Inn; the Cook and the Wife of Bath are both taking their morning's draught of comfort. Spectators stand at the gateway of the Inn, and are composed of an old Man, a Woman, and Children.

The Landscape is an eastward view of the country, from the Tabarde Inn in Southwark, as it may be supposed to have appeared in Chaucer's time, interspersed with cottages and villages. The first beams of the Sun are seen above the horizon; some buildings and spires indicate the situation of the Great City. The Inn is a Gothic building, which Thynne in his Glossary says was the lodging of the Abbot of Hyde, by Winchester. On the Inn is inscribed its title, and a proper advantage is taken of this circumstance to describe the subject of the Picture. The words written over the gateway of the Inn are as follow: 'The Tabarde Inn, by Henry Baillie, the lodgynge-house for Pilgrims who journey to Saint Thomas's Shrine at Canterbury.'

The characters of Chaucer's Pilgrims are the characters which compose all ages and nations. As one age falls, another rises, different to mortal sight, but to immortals only the same; for we see the same characters repeated again and again, in animals, vegetables, minerals, and in men. Nothing new occurs in identical existence; Accident ever varies, Substance can never suffer change nor decay.

Of Chaucer's characters, as described in his Canterbury Tales, some of the names or titles are altered by time, but the characters themselves for ever remain unaltered; and consequently they are the physiognomies or lineaments of universal human life, beyond which Nature never steps. Names alter, things never alter. I have known multitudes of those who would have been monks in the age of monkery, who in this deistical age are deists. As Newton numbered the stars, and as Linnæus numbered the plants, so Chaucer numbered the classes of men.

The Painter has consequently varied the heads and forms of his personages into all Nature's varieties; the horses he has also varied to accord to their riders; the costume is correct according to authentic monuments.

From Blake's Descriptive Catalogue

The Knight and Squire with the Squire's Yeoman lead the Procession, as Chaucer has also placed them first in his Prologue The Knight is a true Hero, a good, great and wise man; his whole-length portrait on horseback, as written by Chaucer, cannot be surpassed. He has spent his life in the field, has ever been a conqueror, and is that species of character which in every age stands as the guardian of man against the oppressor. His son is like him, with the germ of perhaps greater perfection still, as he blends literature and the arts with his warlike studies. Their dress and their horses are of the first rate, without ostentation, and with all the true grandeur that unaffected simplicity when in high rank always displays. The Squire's Yeoman is also a great character, a man perfectly knowing in his profession:

'And in his hand he bare a mighty bow.

Chaucer describes here a mighty man, one who in war is the worthy attendant on noble heroes.

The Prioress follows these with her female Chaplain:

'Another Nonne also with her had she,
That was her Chaplaine, and Priests three.

This Lady is described also as of the first rank, rich and honoured. She has certain peculiarities and little delicate affectations, not unbecoming in her, being accompanied with what is truly grand and really polite; her person and face Chaucer has described with minuteness; it is very elegant, and was the beauty of our ancestors till after Elizabeth's time, when voluptuousness and folly began to be accounted beautiful.

Her companion and her three Priests were no doubt all perfectly delineated in those parts of Chaucer's work which are now lost; we ought to suppose them suitable attendants on rank and fashion.

The Monk follows these with the Friar. The Painter has also grouped with these the Pardoner and the Sompnour and the Manciple, and has here also introduced one of the rich citizens of London—characters likely to ride in company, all being above the common rank in life, or attendants on those who were so.

From Blake's Descriptive Catalogue

For the Monk is described by Chaucer, as a man of the first rank in society, noble, rich, and expensively attended; he is a leader of the age, with certain humorous accompaniments in his character, that do not degrade, but render him an object of dignified mirth, but also with other accompaniments not so respectable.

The Friar is a character of a mixed kind:

> 'A friar there was, a wanton and a merry;'

but in his office he is said to be a 'full solemn man'; eloquent, amorous, witty and satirical; young, handsome and rich; he is a complete rogue, with constitutional gaiety enough to make him a master of all the pleasures of the world:

> 'His neck was white as the flour de lis,
> Thereto strong he was as a champioun.'

It is necessary here to speak of Chaucer's own character, that I may set certain mistaken critics right in their conception of the humour and fun that occur on the journey. Chaucer is himself the great poetical observer of men, who in every age is born to record and eternize its acts. This he does as a master, as a father and superior, who looks down on their little follies from the Emperor to the Miller, sometimes with severity, oftener with joke and sport.

Accordingly Chaucer has made his Monk a great tragedian, one who studied poetical art. So much so that the generous Knight is, in the compassionate dictates of his soul, compelled to cry out:

> 'Ho,' quoth the Knyght, 'good Sir, no more of this;
> That ye have said is right ynough, I wis,
> And mokell more; for little heaviness
> Is right enough for much folk, as I guesse.
> I say, for me, it is a great disease,
> Whereas men have been in wealth and ease,
> To heare of their sudden fall, alas!
> And the contrary is joy and solas.'

From Blake's Descriptive Catalogue

The Monk's definition of tragedy in the proem to his tale is worth repeating:

> 'Tragedie is to tell a certain story,
> As old books us maken memory,
> Of hem that stood in great prosperity,
> And be fallen out of high degree,
> Into miserie, and ended wretchedly.'

Though a man of luxury, pride and pleasure, he is a master of art and learning, though affecting to despise it. Those who can think that the proud huntsman and noble housekeeper, Chaucer's Monk, is intended for a buffoon or burlesque character, know little of Chaucer.

For the Host who follows this group, and holds the centre of the cavalcade, is a first-rate character, and his jokes are no trifles; they are always, though uttered with audacity, and equally free with the Lord and the Peasant—they are always substantially and weightily expressive of knowledge and experience; Henry Baillie, the keeper of the greatest Inn of the greatest City, for such was the Tabarde Inn in Southwark near London, our Host, was also a leader of the age.

By way of illustration I instance Shakespeare's Witches in *Macbeth*. Those who dress them for the stage, consider them as wretched old women, and not, as Shakespeare intended, the Goddesses of Destiny; this shows how Chaucer has been misunderstood in his sublime work. Shakespeare's Fairies also are the rulers of the vegetable world, and so are Chaucer's; let them be so considered, and then the poet will be understood, and not else.

But I have omitted to speak of a very prominent character, the Pardoner, the Age's Knave, who always commands and domineers over the high and low vulgar. This man is sent in every age for a rod and scourge, and for a blight, for a trial of men, to divide the classes of men; he is in the most holy sanctuary, and he is suffered by Providence for wise ends, and has also his great use, and his grand leading destiny.

His companion the Sompnour is also a Devil of the first mag-

From Blake's Descriptive Catalogue

nitude, grand, terrific, rich, and honoured in the rank of which he holds the destiny. The uses to society are perhaps equal of the Devil and of the Angel; their sublimity who can dispute?

> 'In daunger had he at his own gise,
> The young girls of his diocese,
> And he knew well their counsel, &c.'

The principal figure in the next group is the Good Parson; an Apostle, a real Messenger of Heaven, sent in every age for its light and its warmth. This man is beloved and venerated by all, and neglected by all: he serves all, and is served by none. He is, according to Christ's definition, the greatest of his age: yet he is a Poor Parson of a town. Read Chaucer's description of the Good Parson, and bow the head and the knee to Him, Who in every age sends us such a burning and a shining light. Search, O ye rich and powerful, for these men and obey their counsel; then shall the golden age return. But alas! you will not easily distinguish him from the Friar or the Pardoner; they also are 'full solemn men', and their counsel you will continue to follow.

I have placed by his side the Sergeant-at-Lawe, who appears delighted to ride in his company, and between him and his brother the Ploughman; as I wish men of law would always ride with them, and take their counsel, especially in all difficult points. Chaucer's Lawyer is a character of great venerableness, a Judge and a real master of the jurisprudence of his age.

The Doctor of Physic is in this group; and the Franklin, the voluptuous country gentleman, contrasted with the Physician, and, on his other hand, with two Citizens of London. Chaucer's characters live age after age. Every age is a Canterbury Pilgrimage; we all pass on, each sustaining one of these characters; nor can a child be born who is not one or other of these characters of Chaucer. The Doctor of Physic is described as the first of his profession, perfect, learned, completely Master and Doctor in his art. Thus the reader will observe that Chaucer makes every one of his characters perfect in his kind; every one is an Antique Statue, the image of a class and not of an imperfect individual.

From Blake's Descriptive Catalogue

This group also would furnish substantial matter, on which volumes might be written. The Franklin is one who keeps open table, who is the genius of eating and drinking, the Bacchus; as the Doctor of Physic is the Æsculapius, the Host is the Silenus, the Squire is the Apollo, the Miller is the Hercules, &c. Chaucer's characters are a description of the eternal Principles that exist in all ages. The Franklin is voluptuousness itself, most nobly portrayed:

> 'It snewed in his house of meat and drink.'

The Ploughman is simplicity itself, with wisdom and strength for its stamina. Chaucer has divided the ancient character of Hercules between his Miller and his Ploughman. Benevolence is the Ploughman's great characteristic; he is thin with excessive labour, and not with old age as some have supposed:

> 'He would thresh, and thereto dike and delve,
> For Christe's sake, for every poore wight,
> Withouten hire, if it lay in his might.'

Visions of these eternal principles or characters of human life appear to poets in all ages; the Grecian gods were the ancient Cherubim of Phœnicia; but the Greeks, and since them the Moderns, have neglected to subdue the gods of Priam. These gods are visions of the eternal attributes, or divine names, which, when erected into gods, become destructive to humanity. They ought to be the servants, and not the masters of man or of society. They ought to be made to sacrifice to man, and not man compelled to sacrifice to them; for, when separated from man or humanity, who is Jesus the Saviour, the Vine of Eternity? They are thieves and rebels, they are destroyers.

The Ploughman of Chaucer is Hercules in his supreme Eternal State, divested of his Spectrous Shadow, which is the Miller, a terrible fellow, such as exists in all times and places for the trial of men, to astonish every neighbourhood with brutal strength and courage, to get rich and powerful, to curb the pride of Man.

From Blake's Descriptive Catalogue

The Reeve and the Manciple are two characters of the most consummate worldly wisdom. The Shipman, or Sailor, is a similar genius of Ulyssean art, but with the highest courage superadded.

The Citizens and their Cook are each leaders of a class. Chaucer has been somehow made to number four citizens, which would make his whole company, himself included, thirty-one. But he says there was but nine-and-twenty in his company:

'Full nine and twenty in a company.'

The Webbe, or Weaver, and the Tapiser, or Tapestry Weaver, appear to me to be the same person; but this is only an opinion, for 'full nine and twenty' may signify one more or less. But I daresay that Chaucer wrote 'A Webbe Dyer', that is a Cloth Dyer:

'A Webbe Dyer and a Tapiser.'

The Merchant cannot be one of the Three Citizens, as his dress is different, and his character is more marked, whereas Chaucer says of his rich citizens:

'All were yclothed in o liverie.'

The characters of Women Chaucer has divided into two classes, the Lady Prioress and the Wife of Bath. Are not these leaders of the ages of men? The Lady Prioress in some ages predominates; and in some the Wife of Bath, in whose character Chaucer has been equally minute and exact; because she is also a scourge and a blight. I shall say no more of her, nor expose what Chaucer has left hidden; let the young reader study what he has said of her: it is useful as a scarecrow. There are of such characters born too many for the peace of the world.

I come at length to the Clerk of Oxenford. This character varies from that of Chaucer, as the contemplative philosopher varies from the poetical genius. There are always these two classes of learned sages, the poetical and the philosophical. The Painter has put them side by side, as if the youthful clerk had put himself under the tuition of the mature poet. Let the Philosopher always be the servant and scholar of Inspiration, and all will be happy.

From Blake's Descriptive Catalogue

Such are the characters that compose this Picture, which was painted in self-defence against the insolent and envious imputation of unfitness for finished and scientific art, and this imputation most artfully and industriously endeavoured to be propagated among the public by ignorant hirelings. The Painter courts comparison with his competitors, who, having received fourteen hundred guineas and more from the profits of his designs in that well-known work, Designs for Blair's Grave, have left him to shift for himself; while others, more obedient to an employer's opinions and directions, are employed at a great expense to produce works in succession to his by which they acquired public patronage. This has hitherto been his lot—to get patronage for others and then to be left and neglected, and his work, which gained that patronage, cried down as eccentricity and madness—as unfinished and neglected by the artist's violent temper: he is sure the works now exhibited will give the lie to such aspersions.

Those who say that men are led by interest are knaves. A knavish character will often say: 'Of what interest is it to me to do so-and-so?' I answer: 'Of none at all, but the contrary, as you well know. It is of malice and envy that you have done this; hence I am aware of you, because I know that you act not from interest but from malice, even to your own destruction.' It is therefore become a duty which Mr. B. owes to the Public, who have always recognised him and patronized him, however hidden by artifices, that he should not suffer such things to be done, or be hindered from the public Exhibition of his finished productions by any calumnies in future.

The character and expression in this picture could never have been produced with Rubens' light and shadow, or with Rembrandt's, or anything Venetian or Flemish. The Venetian and Flemish practice is broken lines, broken masses, and broken colours. Mr. B.'s practice is unbroken lines, unbroken masses, and unbroken colours. Their art is to lose form; his art is to find form, and to keep it. His arts are opposite to theirs in all things.

As there is a class of men whose whole delight is in the destruction of men, so there is a class of artists whose whole art and science is

From Blake's Descriptive Catalogue

fabricated for the purpose of destroying Art. Who these are is soon known: 'by their works ye shall know them.' All who endeavour to raise up a style against Raphael, Mich. Angelo and the Antique; those who separate Painting from Drawing, who look if a picture is well drawn, and, if it is, immediately cry out that it cannot be well coloured—those are the men.

But to show the stupidity of this class of men, nothing need be done but to examine my rival's prospectus.

The two first characters in Chaucer, the Knight and the Squire, he has put among his rabble; and indeed his prospectus calls the Squire 'the fop of Chaucer's age'. Now hear Chaucer:

> 'Of his Stature, he was of even length,
> And wonderly deliver, and of great strength;
> And he had be sometime in Chivauchy,
> In Flanders, in Artois, and in Picardy,
> And borne him well, as of so litele space.'

Was this a fop?

> 'Well could he sit a horse, and faire ride,
> He could songs make, and eke well indite,
> Just, and eke dance, pourtray, and well write.'

Was this a fop?

> 'Curteis he was, and meek, and serviceable,
> And kerft before his fader at the table.'

Was this a fop?

It is the same with all his characters; he has done all by chance, or perhaps his fortune, money, money. According to his prospectus he has three Monks: these he cannot find in Chaucer, who has only one Monk, and that no vulgar character, as he has endeavoured to make him. When men cannot read, they should not pretend to paint. To be sure Chaucer is a little difficult to him who has only blundered over novels and catchpenny trifles of booksellers; yet a little pains ought to be taken, even by the ignorant and weak. He has put the Reeve, a vulgar fellow,

From Blake's Descriptive Catalogue

between his Knight and Squire, as if he was resolved to go contrary in everything to Chaucer, who says of the Reeve:

'And ever he rode hinderest of the rout.'

In this manner he has jumbled his dumb dollies together, and is praised by his equals for it; for both himself and his friend are equally masters of Chaucer's language. They both think that the Wife of Bath is a young beautiful blooming damsel; and H—— says that she is the 'Fair Wife of Bath', and that 'the Spring appears in her cheeks'. Now hear what Chaucer has made her say of herself, who is no modest one:

> 'But Lord! when it remembereth me
> Upon my youth and on my jollity,
> It tickleth me about the heart root.
> Unto this day it doth my heart boot
> That I have had my world as in my time;
> But age, alas, that all will envenime,
> Hath me bireft, my beauty and my pith
> Let go; farewell! the devil go therewith!
> The flower is gone; there is no more to tell:
> The bran, as best I can, I now mote sell;
> And yet, to be right merry, will I fond
> Now forth to tell of my fourth husbond.'

She has had four husbands, a fit subject for this painter; yet the painter ought to be very much offended with his friend H——, who has called his 'a common scene', 'and very ordinary forms'; which is the truest part of all, for it is so, and very wretchedly so indeed. What merit can there be in a picture of which such words are spoken with truth?

But the prospectus says that the Painter has represented Chaucer himself as a knave who thrusts himself among honest people to make game of, and laugh at them; though I must do justice to the Painter, and say that he has made him look more like a fool than a knave. But it appears in all the writings of Chaucer, and particularly in his Canterbury Tales, that he was very

From Blake's Descriptive Catalogue

devout, and paid respect to true enthusiastic superstition. He has laughed at his knaves and fools, as I do now; but he has respected his true Pilgrims, who are a majority of his company, and are not thrown together in the random manner that Mr. S—— has done. Chaucer has nowhere called the Ploughman old, worn out with 'age and labour', as the prospectus has represented him, and says that the picture has done so too. He is worn down with labour, but not with age. How spots of brown and yellow, smeared about at random, can be either young or old I cannot see. It may be an old man; it may be a young one; it may be anything that a prospectus pleases. But I know that where there are no lineaments there can be no character. And what connoisseurs call touch, I know by experience must be the destruction of all character and expression, as it is of every lineament.

The scene of Mr. S——'s picture is by Dulwich Hills, which was not the way to Canterbury; but perhaps the Painter thought he would give them a ride round about, because they were a burlesque set of scarecrows, not worth any man's respect or care.

But the Painter's thoughts being always upon gold, he has introduced a character that Chaucer has not—namely, a Goldsmith, for so the prospectus tells us. Why he has introduced a Goldsmith, and what is the wit of it, the prospectus does not explain. But it takes care to mention the reserve and modesty of the Painter. This makes a good epigram enough:

> 'The fox, the owl, the spider, and the mole,
> By sweet reserve and modesty get fat.'

But the prospectus tells us that the Painter has introduced a 'Sea Captain'; Chaucer has a Shipman, a sailor, a trading master of a vessel, called by courtesy Captain, as every master of a boat is; but this does not make him a Sea Captain. Chaucer has purposely omitted such a personage, as it only exists in certain periods: it is the soldier by sea. He who would be a soldier in inland nations is a sea-captain in commercial nations.

All is misconceived, and its mis-execution is equal to its misconception. I have no objection to Rubens and Rembrandt

From Blake's Descriptive Catalogue

being employed, or even to their living in a palace; but it shall not be at the expense of Raphael and Michael Angelo living in a cottage, and in contempt and derision. I have been scorned long enough by these fellows, who owe to me all that they have: it shall be so no longer.

> I found them blind, I taught them how to see;
> And now they know me not, nor yet themselves.

INDEX OF FIRST LINES

	PAGE
A Fairy leapt upon my knee	127
A flower was offer'd to me	97
A little black thing among the snow	104
A pair of stays to mend the shape	207
A petty sneaking knave I knew	213
A pretence of Art to destroy Art; a pretence of Liberty	394
A strange erratum in all the editions	204
Abstinence sows sand all over	195
Ah! how shall Urizen the King submit to this dark mansion?	354
Ah, Sunflower! weary of time	97
Albion cold lays on his Rock; storms and snows beat round him	409
All Human Forms identifièd, even Tree, Metal, Earth, and Stone; all	410
All pictures that's painted with sense and with thought	208
All the night in woe	90
An Old Maid early ere I knew	195
And agèd Tiriel stood before the gates of his beautiful palace	225
And did those feet in ancient time	370
And his legs carried it like a long fork	215
And in melodious accents I	219
And many conversèd on these things as they labour'd at the furrow	398
And she went forth and saw the forms of Life and of Delight	357
And the Divine Voice was heard in the Songs of Beulah, saying	380
And the Mills of Satan were separated into a moony Space	371
And this is the manner of the Sons of Albion in their strength	387
And Urizen read in his Book of Brass in sounding tones	358
Anger and wrath my bosom rends	209
Are not the joys of morning sweeter	120
As I walk'd forth one May morning	59
As I wander'd the forest	121
As the ignorant savage will sell his own wife	199
As the Pilgrim passes while the Country permanent remains	403
Awake, awake, my little boy!	166

Index of First Lines

	PAGE
Behold! in the Visions of Elohim Jehovah, behold Joseph and Mary!	399
But others of the Sons of Los build Moments and Minutes and Hours	378
But the Spectre, like a hoar-frost and a mildew, rose over Albion	398
But the Wine-press of Los is eastward of Golgonooza, before the Seat	376
Call that the public voice which is their error!	209
Can I see another's woe	78
Can there be anything more mean	204
Children of the future age	103
Come forth, O Vala! from the grass and from the silent dew	364
Come hither, my boy, tell me what thou seest there	193
Come hither, my Sparrows	122
Come, kings, and listen to my song	15
Come knock your heads against this stone	220
Come, O thou Lamb of God, and take away the remembrance of Sin!	395
Cosway, Frazer, and Baldwin of Egypt's lake	214
Cr —— loves artists as he loves his meat	213
Cruelty has a human heart	106
Daughters of Beulah! Muses who inspire the Poet's Song	370
Dear mother, dear mother, the Church is cold	92
Degrade first the Arts if you'd mankind degrade	198
Did Jesus teach doubt? or did He	153
Do what you will this life's a fiction	198
Does the Eagle know what is in the pit	241
Each Man is in his Spectre's power	394
Earth rais'd up her head	82
England! awake! awake! awake!	406
Enion brooded o'er the rocks: the rough rocks groaning vegetate	350
Eno, agèd Mother	335
Enslav'd, the Daughters of Albion weep; a trembling lamentation	285
Eternity appear'd above them as One Man enfolded	350
Father! father! where are you going?	79
First Milton saw Albion upon the Rock of Ages	373
Five windows light the cavern'd Man: thro' one he breathes the air	303
For Fortune's favours you your riches bring	213
For this is being a friend just in the nick	217
Fortune favours the brave, old proverbs say	213
Fresh from the dewy hill, the merry year	13
Fuzon, on a chariot iron-wing'd	341

446

Index of First Lines

	PAGE
Give pensions to the learned pig	203
Golden Apollo, that thro' heaven wide	18
Great men and fools do often me inspire	220
Great things are done when men and mountains meet	193
Grown old in love from seven till seven times seven	198
Hail Matrimony, made of Love!	59
Having given great offence by writing in prose	218
He has observ'd the golden rule	219
He makes the lame to walk, we all agree	207
He's a blockhead who wants a proof of what he can't perceive	220
He saw Orc, a Serpent form, augmenting times on times	359
He sent his two Servants, Whitefield and Wesley: were they Prophets	375
He who bends to himself a Joy	196
Hear the voice of the Bard!	81
Hear then the pride and knowledge of a sailor!	57
Her shadow went forth and return'd. Now she was pale as snow	359
Here lies John Trot, the friend of all mankind	221
His whole life is an epigram smart, smooth and neatly penn'd	219
Honour and Genius is all I ask	55
How can I help thy husband's copying me?	211
How sweet I roam'd from field to field	8
How sweet is the Shepherd's sweet lot!	67
I always take my judgement from a fool	212
I am made to sow the thistle for wheat, the nettle for a nourishing dainty	352
I am no Homer's hero you all know	209
I am sure this Jesus will not do	158
I am that Shadowy Prophet, who, six thousand years ago	374
I askèd a thief to steal me a peach	111
I askèd my dear friend Orator Prig	199
I bless thee, O Father of Heaven and Earth! that ever I saw Flaxman's face	183
I care not whether a man is Good or Evil; all that I care	408
'I die, I die!' the Mother said	169
I dreamt a dream! what can it mean?	94
I fear'd the fury of my wind	114
I found them blind: I taught them how to see	211
I give you the end of a golden string	403
I have no name	68
I heard an Angel singing	111
I laid me down upon a bank	110

447

Index of First Lines

	PAGE
I love the jocund dance	10
I love to rise in a summer morn	100
I lovèd Theotormon	285
I mock thee not, though I by thee am mockèd	211
I must Create a System, or be enslav'd by another Man's	387
I rose up at the dawn of day	142
I, Rubens, am a statesman and a saint	206
I saw a Chapel all of gold	110
I saw a Monk of Charlemaine (*Rossetti MS.*)	134
I saw a Monk of Charlemaine (*Jerusalem*)	397
I see the Fourfold Man; the Humanity in deadly sleep	388
I see thy Form, O lovely, mild Jerusalem! Wing'd with Six Wings	406
I seize the sphery harp, strike the strings!	351
I stood among my valleys of the south	405
I travell'd thro' a land of men	162
I walked abroad on a snowy day	195
I wander thro' each charter'd street	102
I was angry with my friend	94
I was buried near this dyke	220
I wash'd them out and wash'd them in	202
I went to the Garden of Love	98
I will sing you a song of Los, the Eternal Prophet	331
I will tell you what Joseph of Arimathea	139
I wonder whether the girls are mad	179
I write the rascal thanks, till he and I	210
If I e'er grow to man's estate	197
If it is true, what the Prophets write	139
If you have form'd a circle to go into	193
If you mean to please everybody you will	202
If you play a game of chance, know, before you begin	209
If you trap the moment before it's ripe	195
In Bowlahoola Los's Anvils stand and his Furnaces rage	375
In futurity	88
Is this a holy thing to see	93
It is easier to forgive an Enemy than to forgive a Friend	407
Jesus said: 'Wouldest thou love one who never died	410
Leave, O leave me to my sorrows	62
Let the brothels of Paris be openèd	123
Little Fly	84
Little Lamb, who made thee?	67
Little Mary Bell had a Fairy in a nut	178
Little Phoebus came strutting in	55

Index of First Lines

	PAGE
Lo, a Shadow of horror is risen	314
Lo! the Bat with leathern wing	58
Look! the beautiful Daughter of Albion sits naked upon the Stone	402
Los rear'd his mighty stature: on Earth stood his feet; above	356
Loud sounds the war-song round red Orc in his fury	357
Love and harmony combine	10
Love seeketh not itself to please	92
Love to faults is always blind	194
'Madman' I have been call'd: 'Fool' they call thee	214
Memory, hither come	11
Merry, merry sparrow!	73
Mock on, mock on, Voltaire, Rousseau	133
Mutual Forgiveness of each vice	413
My Garments shall be woven of sighs and heart-broken lamentations	382
My mother bore me in the southern wild	68
My mother groan'd, my father wept (*Songs of Experience*)	100
My mother groan'd, my father wept (*Rossetti MS.*)	115
My silks and fine array	9
My Spectre around me night and day	128
My title as a genius thus is prov'd	211
Nail his neck to the cross: nail it with a nail	193
Nature and Art in this together suit	207
Never seek to tell thy love	109
No real style of colouring ever appears	205
Nought loves another as itself	99
Now Art has lost its mental charms	141
O Autumn, laden with fruit, and stainèd	4
O dear Mother Outline! of wisdom most sage	200
O for a voice like thunder, and a tongue	42
O holy virgin! clad in purest white	6
O, I say, you Joe	62
O lapwing! thou fliest around the heath	196
O Reader, behold the Philosopher's grave!	206
O Rose, thou art sick!	95
O sons of Trojan Brutus, cloth'd in war	40
O Swedenborg! strongest of men, the Samson shorn by the Churches	374
'O thou poor Human Form!' said she. 'O thou poor child of woe!'	401
O thou who passest thro' our valleys in	3
O thou with dewy locks, who lookest down	3
O weakness and O weariness! O war within my members!	362
O what is Life and what is Man? O what is Death? Wherefore	388
O! why was I born with a different face?	190

BLAKE 449 Q

Index of First Lines

	PAGE
O Winter! bar thine adamantine doors	5
Of H —— 's birth this was the happy lot	210
Of the primeval Priest's assum'd power	313
Once a dream did weave a shade	77
Our Wars are wars of life, and wounds of love	394
P—— lovèd me not as he lov'd his friends	213
Phoebe drest like beauty's queen	57
Piping down the valleys wild	65
Pity would be no more	105
Prepare, prepare the iron helm of war	44
Raphael, sublime, majestic, graceful, wise	207
Reader! ... of books ... of heaven	385
Remove away that black'ning church	197
Rintrah roars, and shakes his fires in the burden'd air	247
S ——, in childhood, on the nursery floor	212
Seeing this False Christ, in fury and passion	158
Silent, silent Night	114
Since all the riches of this world	197
Sir Joshua praisèd Rubens with a smile	203
Sir Joshua praises Michael Angelo	203
Sir Joshua sent his own portrait to	204
Sleep! sleep! beauty bright	113
So saying, she arose and walkèd round her beautiful house	366
Soft deceit and idleness	197
Some look to see the sweet outlines	203
Some men, created for destruction, come	220
Some people admire the work of a fool	220
Sound the flute!	70
Still the faint harps and silver voices calm the weary couch	354
Such Visions have appear'd to me	389
Sweet dreams, form a shade	71
Sweet Mary, the first time she ever was there	166
Swelled limbs, with no outline that you can descry	206
Terrifièd at Non-Existence	360
Terror in the house does roar	196
That God is colouring Newton does show	208
The Angel that presided o'er my birth	198
The bell struck one, and shook the silent tower	6
The Breath Divine went forth over the morning hills. Albion rose	409
The Caterpillar on the leaf	414
The Caverns of the Grave I've seen	144
The countless gold of a merry heart	198

Index of First Lines

	PAGE
The cripple every step drudges and labours	201
The daughters of [the] Seraphim led round their sunny flocks	241
The dead brood over Europe: the cloud and vision descends over cheerful France	263
The deep of winter came	305
The Door of Death is made of gold	145
The fields from Islington to Marybone	390
The Good are attracted by men's perceptions	123
The Guardian Prince of Albion burns in his nightly tent	294
The harvest shall flourish in wintry weather	195
The Kings of Asia heard	333
The little boy lost in the lonely fen	79
The look of love alarms	196
The Maiden caught me in the wild	168
The modest Rose puts forth a thorn	98
The Mountain callèd out to the Mountain: 'Awake, O Brother Mountain!	350
The Mundane Shell is a vast Concave Earth, an immense	373
The nameless Shadowy Female rose from out the breast of Orc	304
The nature of Infinity is this: That every thing has its	372
The Negation is the Spectre, the Reasoning Power in Man	381
The only man that e'er I knew	214
The shadowy Daughter of Urthona stood before red Orc	293
The Sin was begun in Eternity, and will not rest to Eternity	371
The Sky is an immortal Tent built by the Sons of Los	378
The song of the Agèd Mother, which shook the heavens with wrath	349
The sun arises in the East	121
The sun descending in the west	75
The Sun does arise	66
The Sussex men are noted fools	214
The sword sung on the barren heath	196
The villain at the gallows tree	206
The Vision of Christ that thou dost see	146
The Visions of Eternity, by reason of narrowèd perceptions	395
The wild winds weep	12
Then Milton rose up from the Heavens of Albion ardorous	371
Then seiz'd the sons of Urizen the plough: they polish'd it	363
There is a smile of love	161
There is in Eden a sweet River of milk and liquid pearl	374
There's Doctor Clash	63
There souls of men are bought and sold	194
These are the idiots' chiefest arts	200
They said this mystery never shall cease	193

Index of First Lines

	PAGE
They see him whom they have pierc'd ; they wail because of him	363
This city and this country has brought forth many mayors	61
This song to the flower of Flaxman's joy	184
This theme calls me in sleep night after night, and ev'ry morn	386
Thou fair-hair'd angel of the evening	5
Thou hast a lap full of seed	118
Thou hearest the Nightingale begin the Song of Spring	379
Three Virgins at the break of day	161
Thy friendship oft has made my heart to ache	210
Tiger ! Tiger ! burning bright	85
To a lovely Myrtle bound	119
To be or not to be	60
To Chloe's breast young Cupid slyly stole	221
To find the Western path	137
To forgive enemies H—— does pretend	210
To Mercy, Pity, Peace, and Love	75
To my friend Butts I write	184
To see a World in a grain of sand	171
Truly, my Satan, thou art but a dunce	417
'Twas on a Holy Thursday, their innocent faces clean	72
Venetian ! all thy colouring is no more	208
Want Matches ?	58
Was I angry with Hayley who us'd me so ill	217
Was Jesus born of a Virgin pure	153
Was Jesus chaste ? or did He	155
Was Jesus gentle, or did He	147
Was Jesus humble ? or did He	149
Welcome, stranger, to this place	52
What are those Golden Builders doing ? Where was the burying-place	387
What is it men in women do require ?	197
What may Man be ? who can tell ? But what may Woman be	393
Whate'er is born of mortal birth	95
Whate'er is done to her she cannot know	221
When a man has married a wife, he finds out whether	221
When early morn walks forth in sober grey	13
When France got free, Europe, 'twixt fools and knaves	221
When H——y finds out what you cannot do	210
When I see a Rubens, Rembrandt, Correggio	202
When Klopstock England defied	132
When my mother died I was very young	74
When nations grow old, the Arts grow cold	200
When Old Corruption first begun	56

Index of First Lines

	PAGE
When silver snow decks Susan's clothes	20
When silver snow decks Sylvio's clothes	52
When Sir Joshua Reynolds died	205
When the green woods laugh with the voice of joy	69
When the voices of children are heard on the green (*Songs of Innocence*)	72
When the voices of children are heard on the green (*Songs of Experience*)	83
When you look at a picture, you always can see	201
Where thou dwellest, in what grove	138
Whether on Ida's shady brow	14
Why art thou silent and invisible	120
Why of the sheep do you not learn peace?	193
Why should I be bound to thee	118
Why should I care for the men of Thames	117
Why should Punishment weave the veil with Iron Wheels of War	388
Why was Cupid a boy	140
Wife of the friend of those I most revere	187
With Happiness stretch'd across the hills	187
Wondrous the gods, more wondrous are the men	221
You all your youth observ'd the golden rule	212
You call me mad, 'tis folly to do so	211
You don't believe—I won't attempt to make ye	138
You must agree that Rubens was a fool	206
You say reserve and modesty he has	212
You say their pictures well painted be	201
You think Fuseli is not a great painter. I'm glad	214
Youth of delight, come hither	96

THE END.

SET IN
GREAT BRITAIN
AT THE
UNIVERSITY PRESS
OXFORD
AND PRINTED BY
MERRITT AND HATCHER LTD.
LONDON AND HIGH WYCOMBE